Advanced Healthcare Systems

Scrivener Publishing
100 Cummings Center, Suite 541J
Beverly, MA 01915-6106

Artificial Intelligence and Soft Computing for Industrial Transformation

Series Editor: Dr. S. Balamurugan (sbnbala@gmail.com)

Scope: Artificial Intelligence and Soft Computing Techniques play an impeccable role in industrial transformation. The topics to be covered in this book series include Artificial Intelligence, Machine Learning, Deep Learning, Neural Networks, Fuzzy Logic, Genetic Algorithms, Particle Swarm Optimization, Evolutionary Algorithms, Nature Inspired Algorithms, Simulated Annealing, Metaheuristics, Cuckoo Search, Firefly Optimization, Bio-inspired Algorithms, Ant Colony Optimization, Heuristic Search Techniques, Reinforcement Learning, Inductive Learning, Statistical Learning, Supervised and Unsupervised Learning, Association Learning and Clustering, Reasoning, Support Vector Machine, Differential Evolution Algorithms, Expert Systems, Neuro Fuzzy Hybrid Systems, Genetic Neuro Hybrid Systems, Genetic Fuzzy Hybrid Systems and other Hybridized Soft Computing Techniques and their applications for Industrial Transformation. The book series is aimed to provide comprehensive handbooks and reference books for the benefit of scientists, research scholars, students and industry professional working towards next generation industrial transformation.

Publishers at Scrivener
Martin Scrivener (martin@scrivenerpublishing.com)
Phillip Carmical (pcarmical@scrivenerpublishing.com)

Advanced Healthcare Systems

Empowering Physicians with IoT-Enabled Technologies

Edited by

**Rohit Tanwar, S. Balamurugan,
R. K. Saini, Vishal Bharti
and Premkumar Chithaluru**

Scrivener
Publishing

WILEY

This edition first published 2022 by John Wiley & Sons, Inc., 111 River Street, Hoboken, NJ 07030, USA and Scrivener Publishing LLC, 100 Cummings Center, Suite 541J, Beverly, MA 01915, USA
© 2022 Scrivener Publishing LLC
For more information about Scrivener publications please visit www.scrivenerpublishing.com.

Wiley Global Headquarters
111 River Street, Hoboken, NJ 07030, USA

For details of our global editorial offices, customer services, and more information about Wiley products visit us at www.wiley.com.

Library of Congress Cataloging-in-Publication Data

ISBN 978-1-119-76886-9

Cover image: Pixabay.Com
Cover design by Russell Richardson

Contents

Preface

The applications and challenges of machine learning and artificial intelligence in the internet of things for healthcare applications are comprehensively covered in this book. Rapid developments in hardware, software and communication technologies have facilitated the emergence of internet-connected sensory devices that provide observations and data measurements from the physical world. The technology of internet-connected devices, referred to as the internet of things (IoT), continues to extend the current internet by providing connectivity and interactions between the physical and cyber worlds. The IoT is undoubtedly transforming the healthcare industry by redefining the space of devices and interaction of people in delivering healthcare solutions, resulting in applications that benefit patients, families, physicians, hospitals and insurance companies. The use of remote monitoring in the healthcare sector possible with IoT-enabled devices has the potential to keep patients safe and healthy, and empowers doctors to provide superlative care, thereby increasing patients' engagement and satisfaction as a result of their interactions with doctors becoming easier and more efficient. Furthermore, remote monitoring of patients' health helps reduce the length of hospital stays and prevents readmissions, in addition to having a major impact on reducing healthcare costs significantly and improving treatment outcomes.

In addition to increasing volume, the IoT generates big data characterized by its velocity in terms of time and location dependency, with a variety of multiple modalities and varying data quality. Intelligent processing and analysis of this big data are the keys to developing smart IoT applications, thereby making space for machine learning (ML) applications. Due to its computational tools that can substitute for human intelligence in the performance of certain tasks, artificial intelligence (AI) makes it possible for machines to learn from experience, adjust to new inputs and perform human-like tasks. Since IoT platforms provide an interface to gather the data from various devices, they can easily be deployed into AI/ML systems. The value of AI in this context is its ability to quickly mesh insights from data and automatically identify patterns and detect anomalies in the data that smart sensors and devices generate — information such as temperature, pressure, humidity, air quality, vibration and sound — that can be really helpful.

Our intent in publishing this book was to comprehensively discuss all of the applications and challenges of using ML and AI in the IoT for healthcare applications that will benefit research scholars working in this domain. Therefore, the 17 chapters of the book briefly discussed below present IoT concepts, frameworks and ideas on biomedical data analytics and information retrieval from the different biomedical domains. The editorial advisory board and expert reviewers have ensured the high caliber of the chapters through careful refereeing of the submitted papers. For the purpose of coherence, we have organized the chapters with respect to similarity of topics addressed, ranging from issues pertaining to the IoT for biomedical engineering and health informatics to computational intelligence for medical image processing and biomedical natural language processing.

- In Chapter 1, "Internet of Medical Things – State of the Art," Dr. Kishor Joshi and Dr. Ruchi Mehrotra present the latest technological advancements in the on-body segment of consumer health wearables. Since the traditional approach in healthcare is a more personalized touch-based system, it is not replaceable for diagnosis. Older, chronically ill patients need remote monitoring and medial management services that ensure that nurses or local healthcare assistants connect to doctors in urban or super-specialty fields for better services. This chapter indicates there is already a steep rise in internet of medical things (IoMT) products, but there is still huge potential for growth in the IoMT industry.
- In Chapter 2, "Issues and Challenges Related to Privacy and Security in Healthcare Using IoT, Fog and Cloud Computing" Hritu Raj, Mohit Kumar, Prashant Kumar, Amritpal Singh and Om Prakash Verma describe the complete architecture along with various challenges and security risks of the next generation healthcare industry with healthcare IoT sensor and fog computing. Furthermore, some methodologies used in various research papers are presented that address security and privacy-related issues in the IoT, Fog and Cloud computing environment.
- In Chapter 3, "Study of Thyroid Disease Diagnosis Using Machine Learning Technique," Shanu Verma, Dr. Rashmi Popli and Dr. Harish Kumar discuss Graves' disease, the

most common cause of hypothyroidism that is associated with eye disease. Thyroid cancer, which infects the gland at the base of the neck, has been increasing over the past few years. Endocrinologists believe that this is because the use of new technology, i.e., machine learning, has allowed the detection of thyroid cancer that may not have been detected in the past. According to the Cancer Registry, thyroid cancer is the second more common cancer among women, occurring 3 times more often in women than in men. This chapter studies thyroid disease using a machine learning algorithm.

- In Chapter 4, "A Review of Various Security and Privacy Innovations for IoT Applications in Healthcare," Mr. Abhishek Raghuvanshi, Dr. Umesh Kumar Singh and Mr. Chirag Joshi focus on the analysis of numerous security and privacy technologies in healthcare, intelligent communities and smart homes available for IoT applications. According to the findings of an industrial internet survey by the World Economic Forum, roughly two-thirds of respondents said the main issue was interoperability and protection. Most IoT apps are web applications and all of them still have denial-of-service and man-in-the-middle attacks as major threats to the security of their healthcare, smart city, smart home and other IoT applications.

- In Chapter 5, "Methods of Lung Segmentation Based on CT Images," Amit Verma and Thipendra P. Singh focus on the use of CT scan images for analysis of lung airways, lung parenchyma, and breathing mechanisms. For better diagnosis of any lung problems, the automatic, nearly accurate analysis of CT images is better than the manual method of doctors analyzing CT scans. In this chapter, automatic and semi-automatic methods of segmentation of lung CT images are discussed.

- In Chapter 6, "Handling Unbalanced Data in Clinical Images," Amit Verma focuses on various data-level and algorithm-level-based approaches developed to balance imbalanced data for improving the accuracy of the trained model. In this chapter, the concept and problem of imbalanced data is discussed and various approaches for balancing the data are also highlighted, in which one of the state-of-the-art methods called bagging is discussed in detail.

- In Chapter 7, "IoT-Based Health Monitoring System for Speech Impaired People Using Assistive Wearable Accelerometer," Dr. Madhumathy P., Ishita Banerjee and Digvijay Pandey describe IoT-based wireless communication systems with network devices connected to each other that communicate through open source internet access and establish connection between apps and devices for communication between the person being supervised and the medical supervisor. This system can also keep track of real-time records and emergency alerts. To handle the storage and analysis of data-related issues, IoT analytics is implemented.
- In Chapter 8, "Smart IoT Devices for the Elderly and People with Disabilities," K. N. D. Saile and Kolisetti Navatha focus on the huge changes brought about by the IoT-powered revolution in health management devices for the elderly and disabled like sensors, wearable devices, audio and video assistance, etc. All these are possible with the help of the IoT. In this chapter, we discuss the technology trends in devices made during the IoT era.
- In Chapter 9, "IoT-Based Health Monitoring and Tracking System for Soldiers," Dr. Madhumathy P., Kavitha N and Digvijay Pandey discuss smart sensors used in the medical treatment of soldiers. By tracking a soldier's location on the battlefield with a smart sensor attached to their body, more accurate body status information can be provided to medical units in order to offer more immediate care. These systems are designed to be implemented for complete mobility with a personal server, which in turn would give a message to the server base station through wireless mode. Soldiers are able to be identified at the earliest based on their unique IP address.
- In Chapter 10, "Cloud-IoT Secured Prediction System for Processing and Analysis of Healthcare Data Using Machine Learning Techniques," Dr. G. K. Kamalam, and Ms. S. Anitha discuss a cloud-IoT secured prediction system designed to improve healthcare performance by reducing the execution time of a patient's request, optimizing the desired selection of the massive amount of patient's facts and imparting a records retrieval process for those applications. Analysis of the experimental results show that the presented method performs better than existing benchmark systems

for considering parameters like disease prediction accuracy, sensitivity, specificity, F-measure, and computational time.

- In Chapter 11, "Cloud-IoT-Driven Healthcare: Review, Architecture, Security Implications and Open Research Issues," Junaid Latief Shah, Heena Farooq Bhat and Asif Iqbal Khan discuss security loopholes inherent in IoT architecture and the Cloud platform. The chapter also elaborates on various security countermeasures that have been proposed in the literature, highlighting their strengths and limitations. Also, a discussion on possible defense measures has been provided. The chapter culminates in underlining some burning research problems and security issues that need to be addressed for seamless healthcare services.

- In Chapter 12, "A Novel Usage of Artificial Intelligence and Internet of Things in Remote-Based Healthcare Applications," Dr. V. Arulkumar, D. Mansoor Hussain, S. Sridhar, and Dr. P. Vivekananda present the information necessary to reap the benefits of research capacity solutions through AI techniques. Healthcare services are among the applications enabled by the IoT. Advanced sensors may be used to monitor the health of permanent patients or may be inserted into the bodies of patients that can analyze, combine and prioritize the information gathered. Working with algorithms helps doctors change treatments and, at the same time, helps to economize on healthcare.

- In Chapter 13, "Use of Machine Learning in Healthcare," V. Lakshman Narayana, R. S. M. Lakshmi Patibandla, B. Tarakeswara Rao and Arepalli Peda Gopi focus on AI-assisted healthcare. Quotient Health has developed a program designed to reduce the cost of EMR structures by strengthening and standardizing the structuring of these frames. This chapter discusses healthcare AI, various implementations of AI, certifiable healthcare benefits, the morality of AI computations and opportunities to improve quality of healthcare skills.

- In Chapter 14, "Methods of MRI Brain Tumor Segmentation," Amit Verma discusses the requirements for and importance of using MRI imaging in brain tumor segmentation and the basic methods of doing it. Furthermore, a region-based generative model with weighted aggregation methods for performing brain tumor segmentation using MRI images is also discussed.

- In Chapter 15, "Early Detection of Type 2 Diabetes Mellitus Using a Deep Neural Network-Based Model," Varun Sapra and Luxmi Sapra focus on implementing a deep neural network for early identification of diabetes mellitus. For this purpose, benchmark dataset available on the UCI Machine Learning Repository and Kaggle are explored. This chapter suggests a deep neural network-based framework for early detection of disease that can be used as an adjunct tool in clinical practices.

- In Chapter 16, "A Comparative Analysis of Implementation Framework for Masked Face Detection," Pranjali Singh, Amitesh Garg and Amritpal Singh discuss quick and accurate approaches for the difficult task of face recognition resulting from certain facial features being hidden by the masks used during the current pandemic. This study uses deep learning-related techniques to resolve the issues of detecting facial features hidden by a mask. Another method of face mask detection is through TensorFlow, YOLOv5, SSDMNV2, SVMs, OpenCV, and Keras. The first step is to discard the masked face region. Next, a pre-trained deep convolutional neural network (CNN) is applied to extract the best features from the obtained regions. Labeled image data is used to train the CNN model. With 98.7% accuracy, a face mask is identified by the proposed system. By using the SVM classifier, the dataset of RMFD had a testing accuracy of 99.64%, SMFD achieved a 99.49% testing accuracy, and LFW achieved 100% testing accuracy. The SSDMNV2 approach used in the study in this chapter yields a 92.64% accuracy score and a 93% F1 score.

- In Chapter 17, "IoT-Based Automated Healthcare System," Dr. Darpan Anand and Mr. Ashish Kumar give an overview of the SDN and NFV types of sensors used in IoT devices. Apart from that, the views of various researchers are also given. The challenges of an SDN-based IoT device for healthcare architecture are also discussed.

The seventeen chapters of this book were written by eminent professors, researchers, and those in the industry from different countries. The chapters were initially peer reviewed by the editorial board members, reviewers, and those in the industry who also span many countries. All chapters have been designed to include basic introductory topics and advancements as well as future research directions, which will enable budding researchers and engineers to pursue their work in this area.

The topic of intelligent IoT for advanced healthcare system(s) is so diversified that it cannot be covered in a single book. However, with the encouraging research contributed by the researchers in this book, we (contributors), editorial board members, and reviewers tried to sum up the latest research domains, developments in the data analytics field, and other applicable areas. First and foremost, we express our heartfelt appreciation to all the authors. We thank them all for considering and trusting this edited book as the platform for publishing their valuable work, and for for the kind co-operation extended by them during the various stages of processing this manuscript. We hope this book will serve as a motivating factor for those researchers who have spent years working as crime analysts, data analysts, statisticians, and budding researchers.

Dr. Rohit Tanwar
School of Computer Science,
University of Petroleum and Energy Studies, Dehradun, India

Dr. S. Balamurugan
Director of Research and Development,
Intelligent Research Consultancy Service (iRCS), Coimbatore, India

Dr. Rakesh Kumai Saini
School of Computing, DIT University, Dehradun, India

Dr. Vishal Bharti
School of Computing, DIT University, Dehradun, India

Dr. Premkumar Chithaluru
School of Computer Science,
University of Petroleum and Energy Studies, Dehradun, India

Internet of Medical Things—State-of-the-Art

Kishor Joshi[1] and Ruchi Mehrotra[2*]

[1]Mahavir Heart Hospital, Patna, India
[2]University of Petroleum & Energy Studies, Dehradun, India

Abstract

Technological innovations have helped in early diagnosis and disease management, thereby preventing long-term complications of various diseases which contribute to morbidity and mortality. Internet of Things used in the healthcare industry and is the Internet of Medical Things (IoMT). The chapter compiles seminal research about IoMT. The paper elaborates the growth of the IoMT market in the last decade from in-hospital and clinics and having reached to home segment as well. With every second, 127 IoT devices adding in the market, and by 2021, it is expected that 35 billion devices will be connected to web, and by 2026, this market will touch almost one trillion US dollars. There are virtual clinics and telehealth for remote monitoring of patients both in rural areas and even where immediate access to clinicians by severely sick patients is always needed like cardiac and obstetric care. There is personal emergency response system (PERS) becoming highly popular in case of chronic critical diseases and is life-saving. The paper covers latest technological advancements for the on-body segment like the consumer health wearables. The traditional approach in healthcare being more personalized and touch-based system is not replaceable for diagnosis. The old-age, chronically ill patients need remote monitoring and medial management services that ensure the nurses or local healthcare assistants connect to doctors in urban or super-speciality fields for better services. The conclusion indicates that there is already a steep rise in IoMT products, but there is still a huge potential for growth in the IoMT industry.

Keywords: Technology, innovations, healthcare, mortality, diagnosis

*Corresponding author: uniqueruchi@rediffmail.com

Rohit Tanwar, S. Balamurugan, R. K. Saini, Vishal Bharti and Premkumar Chithaluru (eds.) Advanced Healthcare Systems: Empowering Physicians with IoT-Enabled Technologies, (1–20) © 2022 Scrivener Publishing LLC

1.1   Introduction

Early diagnosis and timely management of diseases through technological interventions prevents long-term complications and mortalities. The critical diseases like heart disease and stroke are leading cause of various forms of disability and death across the world. The burden of disease is extremely high in both developed and developing countries and least developed countries (LDCs). One of the main difference lies is with technology embedded systems and usage of Internet of Things (IoT) in entire medical treatment plans and even used later for monitoring of patients. This incredible change in the medical industry has been established with application of technology and specifically IoT in healthcare. IoT is defined as "Sensors and actuators embedded in physical objects are linked through the wired and wireless networks" [1]. Infrastructure facilities, optimal resource utilization, quality of service delivery, regular monitoring, timeliness of reporting, and resource mobilization have strengthened healthcare systems. It is more interactive and quick responsive system which is necessary for medical services.

1.2   Historical Evolution of IoT to IoMT

Kevin Ashton who worked for Procter & Gamble in the year 1999 attempted to invent new technology to apply in his work space which led to the idea of linking radio-frequency identification (RFID) to "IoT". Hence, this game changer technology was also known as embedded internet or pervasive computing. The year 2000 marked the beginning of internet in industries and almost all enterprises for information storage and retrieval of data. However, the accuracy being a concern so human to things and things to things interaction became more popular gradually. So, this slow development until 2010 suddenly saw a boom after the Gartner report in 2011. According to them, IoT is the network of physical objects which comprise of embedded technology for communication and interact with their internal states or the external environment [2]. IoT has helped in generation and utilization of huge data for rapid data processing. IoT utilizes cloud computing–enabled applications like consumer file storage. For leading company, Compaq, it was start of annually 2 billion USD turnover to sell servers to internet providers [3].

Though few aspects are non-replaceable by any form technology, still, digital interventions have penetrated in almost every component of all industries. Like in cases of libraries where, conventionally, these are in physical form of services and infrastructure, but it is now replaced with digital data storage and sharing to remotely access the intellectual content by anyone, anytime [4].

Healthcare has been traditionally more popular in its physical form of interaction between patient and nurses, pathologist, pharmacist, or clinicians. Hence, the emerging technology is transforming lives by replacing the human touch in partial mode in banking and financial markets, retail shopping, education, security systems, and many other sectors. Healthcare sector has seen massive change by reducing the number of visits to the hospital due to technological developments [5, 6]. In true sense, the leverage for power of IoT is to eliminate the burden of healthcare sector by enabling patients to connect with the medical facility providers by transferring their data in a secured embedded system.

The internet has been rebranded and is now referred to as "the cloud". The IoT device requires a unique identification enabled by the RFID. Device has sensors for monitoring various parameters and can send the data through a wired or wireless communication to the cloud where this data is stored and can be converted into information. The procession of the enormous amount of data continuously generated (Big Data) requires immense computing power which is available in the cloud servers.

Now, with technological advancements, the medical devices are enabled to collect, analyze, and send data across the web using these advancements. They can now connect both digital and non-digital heart monitor like the heart monitor with patient beds directly to internet. Internet of Medical Things (IoMT) is going to bring a paradigm shift and will alter the future of healthcare by providing smart digital solutions with ease, comfort, availability, and accessibility of quality healthcare anywhere, anytime.

Most of the healthcare professionals and hospitals are now using IoT devices to optimally use their resources. Almost 70% of such hospitals and organizations use patient monitoring and maintenance of patient records. Patient data record is to be kept safely but industry is not tamper-proof, and hence, data leakage is still an issue in case of IoT. But still, in IoMT, there is an upper hand in as it has smart solutions which include endpoint security, internal segmentation, standard policies, and practices to authenticate end users and real-time monitoring which safety measures to prevent data breaches.

1.2.1   IoT and IoMT—Market Size

With half of the IoT market, IoMT constitutes the largest part IoT market. In 2017, IoT market was at $41 billion and expected to increase to $158 billion in 2022 with connected medical devices contributing to one-third of the market by 2022 [7]. The statistics indicate the gradual penetration of IoT technology. Almost 7 billion IoT devices were there in 2018, and in 2019, it jumped to 26.66 billion active IoT devices. Every second, 127 new IoT devices are connected to web, and by end of 2021, there will be almost 35 billion IoT devices installed worldwide. In terms of revenue generation for IoT market, the global spending on IoT in 2016 was $737 billion, and by 2021, it is expected to reach $124 billion, and only by 2026, it will reach $1.1 trillion. This indicates the enormity of IoT markets as global IoT healthcare market should reach 14 billion USD by 2024 [8].

Electronic patient records and patient monitoring are the largest usage of IoT in the present situation. Security in usage of IoMT is a major challenge. IoMT has improved the efficiency of healthcare delivery while lowering the cost of delivery per patient along with rapid implementation, thereby saving time and further lowering costs. The major challenge in IoMT is non-standardization of devices being in various platforms and inability for devices of one manufacturer to communicate with software or hardware of another. Multiple platform results in inefficiency. New devices and software need capital in terms of development and Food and Drug Administration (FDA) approval. Data privacy and security are factors that are to be kept in mind during its development and implementation. But implementation of IoMT increases cost of healthcare for devices, apps, cloud storage, and security. Data bandwidth required for the Big Data generated continuously by IoMT devices strains internet networks.

1.3   Smart Wearable Technology

The on-body segment or smart wearables can be broadly divided into consumer health wearables and medical- or clinical-grade wearables. Medical-grade smart wearables are high quality and are FDA approved for use in hospital or home use. But recently, high-grade consumer wearables have taken on the quality of medical-grade wearables and have been validated in studies to be useful.

1.3.1   Consumer Fitness Smart Wearables

The most popular ones are wearable devices which are also called as lifestyle devices which include activity trackers like bands, wristwatches, chest strap, and shoes. These devices are worn by patients as well as healthy people who are fitness conscious. Such devices have sensors that regularly monitor, record, and collect data based on the health parameters based on physical activities.

Consumer smart wearables generate data which can help provide feedback to the individual regarding his/her health and thereby modify their lifestyle accordingly. But these devices are plagued with issues of reliability, safety, and security of this data [9]. A 2017 study by Apple and Stanford University in 400,000 users of Apple watch series 1, 2, and 3 and its mobile app used data generated by the pulse sensors to identify hearth rhythm abnormality called atrial fibrillation. Atrial fibrillation is an irregularity of the heart beat with the pulse generated described as irregularly irregular. This can initially be intermittent with intervening normal heart rhythm or become chronic with continuous AF. The results of this study showed that 0.5% of the subjects received a notification of an irregular pulse. These subjects were sent a telemetry ECG patch to directly detect and monitor the electrical activity of the heart. Results showed that that the Apple watch diagnosed an episode of AF correctly 84% of the time and one-third were diagnosed with AF by the ECG patch. In addition, 57% of those who received an AF notification by the mobile app consulted a doctor. The Apple Heart Study shows that consumer wearable technology can help in detecting serious medical conditions like atrial fibrillation [10]. Consumer smart wearables can sense and continuously record some vital bodily functions and therefore provide feedback regarding health and help in modifying behaviour and lifestyle [11]. But more than half of the technology used in consumer smart wearables has not been certified or validated independently. Only 1 in 10 technologies has been validated with clinical research. Therefore, quality of data smart consumer wearables is debatable and interpretation of such data is questionable [12]. In contrast, clinical- or medical-grade wearables are approved or certified by health regulatory authorities like the FDA and are used with the advice of healthcare professionals or on prescription of a doctor. Accuracy of these devices can enable diagnosis and management of diseases.

1.3.2   Clinical-Grade Wearables

Medical-grade or clinical-grade wearables are those certified by the regulatory authorities like FDA for use by healthcare professionals. They can be used at home or in a clinic or hospital and expected to improve quality of life in chronic diseases and reduce the cost of long-term care.

With advances in technology, consumer wearables are slowly moving to the accuracy of medical-grade devices. A study by the Stanford University using the Apple watch with 4lac users showed that atrial fibrillation could be detected in accurately to a high degree. The users were alerted about the arrhythmia by the smart watch and resulted in half of them consulting a doctor [13]. But this study was not ideal as it was not controlled and subjects were not randomized [14]. Increasing number of high quality Medical-grade wearables are slowly turning the focus of smart wearables from fitness and activity trackers to clinical-grade devices which can be used by medical professionals [15]. The Apple Watch 4 has a medical-grade sensor approved by the FDA [16].

Current Health (Edinburgh, Scotland) has created a wireless AI device for monitoring patients in hospital and also at home. This device monitors patient's vital parameters like pulse rate, respiratory rate, oxygen saturation, temperature, and patient mobility. It provides doctors with continuous data regarding health of their patient in real time. Current Health uses machine learning for analysis of this data and generates useful information and detect any significant changes [17]. An insertable cardiac monitor named Confirm Rx developed by Abbott healthcare can monitor ECG continuously for up to 2 years and can connect to a smartphone app (myMerlin) wirelessly through Bluetooth. It can also automatically send information to the doctor who can correlate symptoms with the heart rhythm [18]. Wrist-worn wearable devices as developed by researchers at the University of Michigan can also can detect circulating cancer cells in the blood, thereby revolutionizing cancer care [19].

A **wearable cardiac defibrillator** (WCD) is a portable device which is worn on the body and can deliver life saving shocks to terminate life-threatening ventricular arrhythmias. This can be used in lieu of an implantable cardioverter defibrillator (ICD) in patients who are not candidates for an ICD or early after a Myocardial infarction or are on the cardiac transplant list. In a study on uninsured patients with ischemic or nonischemic cardiomyopathy, WCD was shown to prevent unnecessary ICD implants in the subgroup of patients whose cardiac function subsequently improves following recovery thereby saving costs [20]. WCD can also be used in patients who are at high risk of ventricular arrhythmias and sudden cardiac death early after myocardial infarction. In a study of more than 8000 patients who had a WCD, 1.6% received shocks and 91% were revived from a cardiac arrhythmia. There was high rate of successful shock resulting in survival of 84%–95% of patients who received shocks [21]. WCD can also reduce the implantation rate of ICD in patients with heart failure who are diagnosed with cardiomyopathy, listed for transplant or on inotropic support. In a study on 89 patients with congestive heart failure with the above criteria, it was seen that 34% received an ICD, while 41.5% patients improved with a WCD who would have otherwise received an ICD [22].

Wearable waterproof sensors can also monitor the electrolytes in sweat and can analyze an athlete even underwater and monitor state of hydration and need for electrolytes. This can help enhance athletes performance [23]. Data from devices monitoring the mechanics of walking and the speed, symmetry of gait, and the length of stride can predict the development Alzheimer's disease in patients. Patients can be monitored remotely by such mobile devices [24].

1.4   Smart Pills

Smart pills are medications that have minute sensors incorporated inside which can be ingested and can be used to monitor patient compliance. The sensors are activated by the acid in the stomach and connect to a smart wearable device which relays data to a smartphone application. The Abilify MyCite was a revolutionary smart pill which ultimately failed commercially. This contained aripiprazole (Abilify, Otsuka Pharmaceuticals) an antipsychotic medication used in psychiatric disorders like schizophrenia and was approved by the FDA in 2017 [25]. It incorporated the Proteus ingestible event marker (IEM) made from dietary minerals in very small quantities. The integrated circuit is the size of a grain of sand and is embedded in each medication tablet [26]. Activation of the sensor results in emission of a signal to the tablet computer indicating successful ingestion of the medication and ticks the checklist for dosing along with the time of ingestion. This ensures that the elderly are compliant with much needed medications. But the smart pill also necessitates wearing a smart device using a tablet computer which the elderly may find difficult. This smart pill was supposed to revolutionize medication dosage but the company Proteus Digital Health ran into financial troubles and filed for bankruptcy in 2020 after being unable to find funds due to the COVID-19 crisis after the drug major Otsuka pharmaceutical withdrew financial support from the project [27]. This may indicate that smart pills may not be financially viable despite their promise of technology and medicine merging to offer better compliance [28].

Studies of medications with sensors in chronic diseases like diabetes and hypertension demonstrate that digital health improves compliance by reminding patients to take their dose of medication at the appropriate time and also improve medication safety [29]. Newer ingestible or injectable nanosensors may one day be the early warning systems for diseases. But such embedded wearables also raise legal and ethical issues regarding privacy and security. An implantable chip containing medical records of a patient which were implanted in some Alzheimer's patients in 2002 raised several issues resulting in banning of forced implants resulting in the technology being shelved [30].

1.5   Reduction of Hospital-Acquired Infections

Control of hospital-acquired infections is very important in hospital setting and hand hygiene plays a vital role. The monitoring of compliance to hand hygiene practices has been automated by AeroScout solution by Stanley Healthcare which monitors hand washing by each staff and can identify breaks in infection control practices. This can potentially save billions of dollars spent in combating hospital-acquired infections every year [31]. In a study which compared automated hand hygiene compliance system with human observers, it was found that automated system collected better data and resulted in compliance goals being met although the reduction in hospital-acquired infections was not significant [32]. Automated compliance systems have also resulted in better health for the hospital staff resulting in less employee absenteeism [33].

1.5.1   Navigation Apps for Hospitals

Patients getting lost in huge hospital complexes result in thousands of cancelled appointments and millions of dollars in cost in big hospitals. Data from the National Health Service from the UK in 2013 shows that about 7 million appointments were messed every year due to visitors and patients losing their way in and around hospitals [34]. In a study at the University of Nottingham, all junior doctors reported to have got lost on the way to in an emergency and crucial time was wasted [35]. Children's Hospital Boston has developed a GPS-based app named MyWay which guides patients and even staff to their location in the shortest way and has reduced stress for visitors and patients in navigating through the hospital [36]. There is a need for the healthcare facilities to plan configuration of design and use technology and characteristics of future users in developing navigation facilities in healthcare centers with special emphasis on people who are challenged visually or cognitively with a need to develop a universal symbol system for healthcare [37].

1.6   In-Home Segment

Technology can also be used to increase the rapidity of emergency response to a patient or person by the use of a personal emergency response system

(PERS). The PERS uses a wearable smart device which connects to a call center or emergency medical service available round the clock to respond to any activation of the device Bridgera Rescue is an emergency response application which provides security personnel with the touch of a button. It is useful for any person who is in immediate need for security such as elderly at home [38]. These systems can also be a substitute for monitoring safety for aging patients by personal care workers. It has been shown that such PERS has reduced healthcare costs, saved lives, and has been accepted well by the patients [39]. But usage of PERS system despite availability has been low. The push-button device activator needs to be worm constantly or should be immediately accessible. In a study with persons with disabilities, only 16% of participant used it with concerns about falling was the most common reason for PERS usage and 3 out of 4 users felt greater security using it [40, 41]. Moreover, despite availability, PERS was not activated 83% of the time by the elderly after a fall while they were on the floor for more than 5 minutes [42]. High rate of non-usage has led to evaluation of newer PERS systems; hands-free automated speech recognition system utilizing ceiling mounted microphone array system may be more effectively usable but is still under research [43].

1.7 Community Segment

Health kiosks are devices which can provide services like connecting patients to healthcare providers or dispense products such as medicines. Kiosks are a useful way to decrease the burden on human healthcare workers and reduce the time spent by patients and healthcare workers in obtaining data. It is seen that the tasks performed and data obtained by kiosks are valid but not all data collected is usable with many users inputting data which was random and not usable or not related [44]. Installation of digital kiosks has been associated with various patterns of use as time passes with an initial rapid increase in the first 5 months followed by a rapid reduction in usage thereafter. This rapid initial rise seen is due to enthusiastic usage by patients older than 15 years [45]. Kiosk usage is determined by user friendliness but it is seen that older users and are less likely to be at ease at using the Kiosk system while skilled workers are more likely to use it compared to other groups [46].

1.8 Telehealth and Remote Patient Monitoring

The notable revolution came through the medical industry being more of physical and touch-based system when partial replacement gradually started with the virtual mode. Though this industry still remains more a touch-based sector where no replacement for personal visits is possible in cases of physical examination, surgical needs, and health emergency as well. But virtual consultations are getting popular and patients as well as their attendants are able to manage the health conditions and acquire medicaments timely. Few examples include video consultations, telecalling, video observations, digital tests, and reporting systems. There are few areas where telehealth has creeped in and has made things easy and more accurate.

The developments include the vital sign parameter (VSP) measurement and the virtual visit being quite popular through the audio/video consultations. The most common usage is among the patients with chronic diseases, elderly populations, disabled patients, and paediatrics as well. Data analysis from Medline since 2003–2004 indicates that telesystems prevailed that time as well but lack of standard practices and lack of evaluation framework for legal, ethical, clinical, and technical aspects lacked for practical implementation [47].

Virtual visits and telehealth are also cost effective in monitoring chronically ill patients. Studies indicate that virtual visits between trained home healthcare nurse and chronically ill patients have improved patient outcome at a much lower cost in comparison to the traditional method of skilled personal interaction of home healthcare visits [48]. In cases of chronic acute respiratory illness, the result seemed to be different. Increased convenience may tap into unmet demand of healthcare and new utilization increased overall healthcare spending in case of such diseases. Net annual healthcare spending increased in respiratory disease which showed direct-to-consumer telehealth increased access for many patients but increased utilization of services and healthcare overall spending also increases [49].

Similar kind of tool for children with special healthcare needs program called as the U Special Kids (USK) by University of Minnesota made families was launched. The program connected virtually both the children with special healthcare needs and nurses at USK also from rural and urban backgrounds. These virtual visits through video conferencing provided more information than telephone call as management of such special children became far better [50].

Virtual clinic systems have transformed even the rural India healthcare scenario. The virtual e-clinics expand the outreach of healthcare facilities in rural regions by connecting the local medical practitioners and health workers who connect patients with the qualified specialist doctors in the city through video conferencing technologies. These virtual modes consisted of smart phones, laptop/computers, medical monitors, and other assisted devices and under supervision of local health worker in lines with the standard protocols. This becomes need of the hour as qualified doctors are not available in remote areas but quality healthcare consultations can still be offered through virtual e-clinics [51].

Remote patient monitoring can monitor data, reduce readmissions, and improve patient outcomes after discharge from hospital. Remote monitoring can help healthcare workers address issues which could be managed without hospitalization. This can decrease the number of readmissions and also lead to better outcomes. Patients on remote monitoring are discharged with wearable smart devices which monitor vital signs like blood pressure, pulse rate, oxygen saturation, and weight and when used with video conferencing can help diagnose and save time while preventing confusion. Any concern can be detected early and treated early and complications prevented. Surveys have shown that a majority of patients over 40 are willing to use a remote health monitoring device if it reduced their physical visits to the hospital or doctor [52]. A meta-analysis of 13 studies with more than 3,000 patients of patients with chronic heart failure between 2003 and 2013 showed that remote patient monitoring reduced mortality significantly in comparison to the usual care with the group which had the quickest intervention having the lowest mortality rate. It was also seen that groups of patients with the high frequency of monitoring and those on remote medication management had a lower mortality [53]. Remote patient monitoring inpatients with chronic heart failure can greatly enhance care of such patients by anticipating episodes of decompensation. This can improve communication between patients and their doctors and can increase independence of patients. A handheld device called Blue Box developed at the University of Houston with three biosensors to monitor two lead ECG, bioimpedance, and photoplethysmography was used on healthy subjects. The ECG sensor measured the RR interval and the QRS duration, and heart rate. Data from the BlueBox obtained from healthy subjects was compared to the cardiac output measured by Echocardiography and was found to have a linear correlation. Such devices may in the future be useful to remotely monitor patients with heart failure [54]. A new wearable peritoneal dialysis device developed by AWAK Techologies, Singapore, can remotely monitor automated peritoneal devices on patients and was associated with significant decrease in the number of hospitalizations per patient year and also reduced the number of days patients were hospitalized. In a study, the device showed that remote monitoring reduced the rate of hospitalization compared to those not remotely monitored with fewer days spent in hospital [55]. Remote patient monitoring also helped reduce hospitalization costs in Medicare patients with heart failure due to shorter duration of hospitalization from early diagnosis and treatment [56]. Remote patient monitoring not only can reduce costs of healthcare but also has shown to be efficient in patient management but more prospective studies with economic analysis are needed [57].

Ethical issues hold the key in telehealth due to privacy and confidentiality. The ethical challenge lies with the data leakage and abuse which has potential to harm both the patient and healthcare providers. Aspects relating to relationships, trust building during virtual visits, telehealth influences healthcare service delivery, treatments costs, quality of life, and fear of identity exploitation are some interconnected dots which highlight the ethics of telehealth [58].

1.9   IoMT in Healthcare Logistics and Asset Management

Transportation and delivery of healthcare products and services include pharmaceuticals, surgical supplies, medical devices, consumables, and equipment used in medical field. Here, IoMT in transportation and shipment of medicines is used in monitoring temperature sensors, humidity content, end-to-end visibility solutions to track customized medicines for cancer patients using RFID including bar codes, drones, and many more other new developments. The RFID technology for logistics management in IoMT is contactless, fully automatic technology. With almost negligible manual interventions, this can work in toughest of harsh environmental issues. An automatic identification technology such as an Auto-ID system based on RFID technology is an important asset for inventory systems for two reasons. First of all, the visibility provided by this technology allows an accurate knowledge of inventory level by eliminating the discrepancy between inventory record and physical inventory. Secondly, RFID technology can prevent or reduce sources of errors. Benefits of using RFID technology include the reduction of labor costs, the simplification of business processes, and the reduction of inventory inaccuracies [59].

IoT can improve efficiency of equipment use in healthcare. Hospitals have thousands of equipment in inventory and managing them efficiently is a major concern. It is seen that only one-third of the equipment is being utilized was about 32%–38% while hospitals are spending a huge amount of money on assets that are not properly utilized. IoT can also efficiently help track and sterilize surgical equipment, thereby reducing hospital-acquired infections. Tracking of equipment by healthcare workers becomes easier and makes workflow more efficient. IoT can remind of timely service of equipment, thereby increasing their lifespan. The materials management is quite crucial to maintain the timely supplies of medical devices, stock, and consumables, devices like pacemaker or lenses or implants should be not overstocked but also not get expired. Hence, long-term inventory management can help in stock planning and efficient scheduling of supplies which further reduces cost and warehousing burden [60]. Inventory management can be optimized through technology and use of IoT for tracking and data to create models for ideal inventory management using Artificial Neural Networks and Fuzzy Logic [61]. IoT using RFID technology can automate the process of health asset management by tracking medical equipment spread across various departments or hospitals. It can help reduce the volume of inventory by improving utilization of existing assets and help in planning acquisition of new assets more efficiently. Pilferage and loss of equipment can also be reduced and the weak spots of inventory management can be located using smart devices and software applications [62]. IoT can thereby greatly benefit healthcare by optimizing workflow leading to faster response during emergencies, improve utilization of existing assets, and make resource allocation more efficient [63]. Patient flow management systems can improve patient transport in hospitals between units or different buildings by booking the travel and automatically sending request for transport and sending real-time monitoring information of the trip. This can save costs by timely delivery of patient to the operating room or a CT scan or MRI unit and avoid delays and prevent inconvenience to patients [64]. In addition, IoT can also increase efficiency of healthcare staff and productivity by managing personnel.

1.10   IoMT Use in Monitoring During COVID-19

A continuous patient monitoring wearable called the VitalPatch received emergency use authorization from the United States FDA. This device can continuously monitor QT interval ECG in patients undergoing COVID-19 treatment with hydroxychloroquine and chloroquine which are known to prolong the QT interval. Such monitoring can decrease the adverse events due to these drugs in hospital and after discharge [65].

Another clinical wearable device from Northwestern University and Shirley Ryan AbilityLab which features a flexible device, the size of a postage stamp placed on the skin of the notch above the sternal bone paired with a flexible pulse oximeter, allows doctors to monitor the three symptoms of fever, breathlessness, and cough by measuring the temperature and tiny vibrations from the skin and along with oxygen levels in the body in patients without any symptoms allowing for monitoring of patients progress and treatment response. Development of an algorithm to distinguish COVID from non-COVID causes of the symptoms is in progress by collecting thousands of hours of data from such devices by remote monitoring of patients [66]. Although wearable devices in medicine reduce the need for healthcare workers in chronic diseases and allow the elderly to live independently while improving the quality of care, they are still significant challenges [67]. The LifeVest by Zoll is a wearable cardioverter defibrillator device, which is worn around the waist and collects ECG data and informs and alerts the patient in case of a life-threatening arrhythmia. Conductive gel is deployed automatically by dry electrodes attached to the device before giving a shock to the patient. This can be lifesaving to patients who are at high risk for sudden cardiac death due to such arrhythmias. The device can also automatically deliver a shock if the patient has been rendered unconscious [68].

The model of telehealth has been quite prevalent in pandemic times of COVID-19 especially for high-risk obstetric patients. In order to prevent them from exposure of corona virus at the personal visit at the healthcare centre, the Columbia University Irving Medical Centre efficiently and effectively implemented a telehealth process. Covering important aspects of close patient surveillance, engagement, escalation protocols, effective communication, and coordination through easy-to-follow algorithms reduced the virus exposure risk to all concerned. In the last decade, telehealth including the various healthcare apps and remote monitoring equipment have emerged as quite cost effective and convenient to those class of patients who had limited healthcare service accessibility due to pandemic scare [69]. During COVID-19 pandemic, telehealth rapidly took over almost in specialities like even prenatal care at Irving Medical Centre. Super specialized domain like high-risk pregnancies prenatal screening, surveillance, and examinations to reduce personal visits was made possible through telehealth and virtual visits. This reduced patient travel, virus-risk exposure for obstetric patients who had underlying medical or fetal conditions, and being tailor made for specific patients was fruitful [70].

1.11   Conclusion

Information Technology (IT) has not only been an engine of growth for economies of many nations but has also resulted in quality of life improvement in these countries bringing about improvements in healthcare and education among other sectors. The proliferation of healthcare-specific

IoT products opens up immense opportunities, and the huge amount of data generated by these connected devices holds the potential to transform healthcare. IT has resulted in better patient-doctor contacts and saved lives by enabling early diagnosis and treatment resulting in a better quality of life. The IoMT devices are now moving from clinic, hospitals to home and making healthcare accessible for all. It helps in better healthcare management of chronic and critically ill patients. The virtual healthcare systems include telehealth, virtual clinics, telemedicine, and remote monitoring and most easy to manage daily life style are the wearable devices. The wearable devices segments is gaining huge popularity due to its user-friendly structures like fitness bands, chest strap, and smart watch with blood pressure, heart rate, oxygen level, saturation, and glucose levels monitoring, which is indicative of better lifestyle management practices and increased level of awareness for better health. The ray of hope still lies with new technological advancements in IoMT daily penetrating our household and making lives easier and better accessibility to healthcare services. The future of IoMT indicates an optimistic outlook despite a lot needs to be achieved; still, there is huge potential further in market which remains untapped.

References

1. Lueth, K.L., Why the Internet of Things is called Internet of Things: Definition, history, disambiguation, IoT Analytics.com, 2014, https://iot-analytics.com/internet-of-things-definition/#:~:text=A brief history of the Internet of Things&text=But the actual term "Internet, new exciting technology called RFID (accessed Aug. 23, 2020).

2. Gartner Glossary, Internet of Things, Gartner, https://www.gartner.com/en/information-technology/glossary/internet-of-things (accessed Aug. 27, 2020).

3. Regalado, A., Who Coined 'Cloud Computing'?, MIT Technology Review, 2011, https://www.technologyreview.com/2011/10/31/257406/who-coined-cloud-computing/ (accessed Aug. 23, 2020).

4. Kaladhar, A. and Rao, K.S., Internet of things: a route to smart libraries. *J. Adv. Lib. Sci.*, 4, 1, 29–34, 2018.

5. Litan, R., Vital signs via broadband: Remote health monitoring transmits savings, enhances lives, Better Healthcare Together, 2008, [Online]. Available: http://www.broadbandillinois.org/uploads/cms/documents/litan.pdf.

6. Atkinson, R.D. and Castro, D., Digital Quality of Life: Understanding the Personal and Social Benefits of the Information Technology Revolution,

SSRN Electron. J, no. October, 2011, https://papers.ssrn.com/sol3/papers. cfm?abstract_id=1278185

7. Taylor, K., Sanghera, A., Steedman, M., Thaxter, M., Medtech and the internet of medical things: How connected medical devices are transforming healthcare, *Deloitte,* no. July, 2018, [Online]. Available: https://www2.deloitte. com/content/dam/Deloitte/global/Documents/Life-Sciences-Health-Care/ gx-lshc-medtech-iomt-brochure.pdf.

8. Mayaan, D.G., The IoT Rundown For 2020: Stats, Risks, and Solutions, Security today, 2020, https://securitytoday.com/Articles/2020/01/13/The-IoT-Rundown-for-2020.aspx?Page=2 (accessed Aug. 28, 2020).

9. Piwek, L., Ellis, D.A., Andrews, S., Joinson, A., The Rise of Consumer Health Wearables: Promises and Barriers. *PLoS Med.,* 13, 2, pp. 1–9, 2016.

10. Stanford Medicine, Apple Heart Study demonstrates ability of wearable technology to detect atrial fibrillation, Stanford Medicine News Centre, 2019, http://med.stanford.edu/news/all-news/2019/03/apple-heart-study-demonstrates-ability-of-wearable-technology.html (accessed Aug. 27, 2020).

11. Garge, G.K., Balakrishna, C., Datta, S.K., Consumer Healthcare: Current Trends in Consumer Health Monitoring. *IEEE Consum. Electron. Mag.,* 7, 1, 38–46, 2018.

12. Peake, J.M., Kerr, G., Sullivan, J.P., A critical review of consumer wearables, mobile applications, and equipment for providing biofeedback, monitoring stress, and sleep in physically active populations. *Front. Physiol.,* 9, JUN, 1–19, 2018.

13. Perez, M.V. *et al.,* Large-Scale Assessment of a Smartwatch to Identify Atrial Fibrillation. *N. Engl. J. Med.,* 381, 20, 1909–1917, Nov. 2019.

14. Garvin, E., What's the Difference: A Look at Consumer and Medical-Grade Wearables in Healthcare, HIT Consultant, 2019, https://hitconsultant. net/2019/07/08/whats-the-difference-a-look-at-consumer-and-medical-grade-wearables-in-healthcare/#.X0UaU9MzbfY (accessed Aug. 25, 2020).

15. Frost & Sullivan, Wearables: Differentiating the Toys and Tools in Healthcare, Alliance of Advanced BioMedical Engineering, 2017, https://aabme.asme. org/posts/wearable-technologies-and-healthcare-differentiating-the-toys-and-tools-for-actionable-health-use-cases (accessed Aug. 25, 2020).

16. Cooper, L., Medical-grade devices vs. consumer wearables, electronic specifier, 2019, Electronic specifier, https://www.electronicspecifier.com/ products/wearables/medical-grade-devices-vs-consumer-wearables (accessed Aug. 25, 2020).

17. Current health, Transition healthcare from the hospital to the home, Current health, 2020, https://currenthealth.com/ (accessed Aug. 27, 2020).

18. Abbott, Confirm Rx ICM ICapturing the Rhythm of Life, Abbott, 2019, https://confirmyourrhythm.com/.

19. Kim, T.H. *et al.,* A temporary indwelling intravascular aphaeretic system for *in vivo* enrichment of circulating tumor cells. *Nat. Commun.,* 10, 1, 1478, 2019.

20. Mitrani, R.D., Mcardle, A., Slane, M., Cogan, J., Myerburg, R.J., Wearable defibrillators in uninsured patients with newly diagnosed cardiomyopathy or recent revascularization in a community medical center. *Am. Heart J.*, 165, 3, 386–392, 2013.

21. Epstein, A.E. *et al.*, Wearable Cardioverter-Defibrillator Use in Patients Perceived to Be at High Risk Early Post-Myocardial Infarction. *J. Am. Coll. Cardiol.*, 62, 21, 2000, LP – 2007, Nov. 2013.

22. Kao, A.C. *et al.*, Wearable defibrillator use in heart failure (WIF): results of a prospective registry. *BMC Cardiovasc. Disord.*, 12, 1, 123, 2012.

23. Seshadri, D.R. *et al.*, Wearable sensors for monitoring the physiological and biochemical profile of the athlete. *NPJ Digit. Med.*, 2, 1, 72, 2019.

24. Del Din, S. *et al.*, Gait analysis with wearables predicts conversion to Parkinson disease. *Ann. Neurol.*, 86, 3, 357–367, Sep. 2019.

25. U. F. and D. Administration, FDA approves pill with sensor that digitally tracks if patients have ingested their medication, FDA News Release, 2017, https://www.fda.gov/news-events/press-announcements/fda-approves-pill-sensor-digitally-tracks-if-patients-have-ingested-their-medication (accessed Aug. 24, 2020).

26. Plowman, R.S., Peters-Strickland, T., Savage, G.M., Digital medicines: clinical review on the safety of tablets with sensors. *Expert Opin. Drug Saf.*, 17, 9, 849–852, 2018.

27. Muoio, D., Digital pill' maker Proteus Digital Health files for bankruptcy, Mobi health news, 2020, https://www.mobihealthnews.com/news/digital-pill-maker-proteus-digital-health-files-bankruptcy (accessed Aug. 24, 2020).

28. Kent, C., *Proteus Digital Health: A Sharp Lesson for Smart Pills?*, Pharma Technology Focus, 2020, https://pharma.nridigital.com/pharma_apr20/proteus_digital_health_a_sharp_lesson_for_smart_pills.

29. Moorhead, P., Zavala, A., Kim, Y., Virdi, N.S., Efficacy and safety of a medication dose reminder feature in a digital health offering with the use of sensor-enabled medicines. *J. Am. Pharm. Assoc.*, 57, 2, 155–161.e1, 2017.

30. Eunjung Cha, A., Smart pills' with chips, cameras and robotic parts raise legal, ethical questions, The Washington Post, 2014, https://www.washingtonpost.com/national/health-science/smart-pills-with-chips-cameras-and-robotic-parts-raise-legal-ethical-questions/2014/05/24/6f6d715e-dabb-11e3-b745-87d39690c5c0_story.html?utm_term=.643b662a8a7a (accessed Aug. 25, 2020).

31. Healthcare, S., AeroScout Hand Hygiene Compliance Monitoring, Stanley Healthcare, 2020, https://www.stanleyhealthcare.com/hospital-clinics/rtls/hand-hygiene-compliance-monitoring (accessed Aug. 27, 2020).

32. McCalla, S., Reilly, M., Thomas, R., McSpedon-Rai, D., An automated hand hygiene compliance system is associated with improved monitoring of hand hygiene. *Am. J. Infect. Control*, 45, 5, 492–497, 2017.

33. Strauch, J., Braun, T.M., Short, H., Use of an automated hand hygiene compliance system by emergency room nurses and technicians is associated with decreased employee absenteeism. *Am. J. Infect. Control*, 48, 5, 575–577, 2020.

34. Pinchin, J., Getting lost in hospitals costs the NHS and patients, *The Guardian*, 2017.

35. Brown, M., Shaw, D., Sharples, S., Le Jeune, I., Blakey, J., A survey-based cross-sectional study of doctors' expectations and experiences of non-technical skills for Out of Hours work. *BMJ Open*, 5, 2, e006102, Feb. 2015.

36. Ashton, K., Internet of Things case study: Boston Children's Hospital and smarter healthcare, IoT News, 2017, https://iottechnews.com/news/2017/feb/28/internet-things-case-study-boston-childrens-hospital-and-smarter-healthcare/ (accessed Aug. 25, 2020).

37. Devlin, A.S., Wayfinding in healthcare facilities: contributions from environmental psychology. *Behav. Sci. (Basel, Switzerland)*, 4, 4, 423–436, Oct. 2014.

38. Bridgera, Personal Emergency Response System (PERS) Bridgera Rescue-Personal Security Anywhere-You-Go, Bridgera, 2020.

39. Hyer, K. and Rudick, L., The Effectiveness of Personal Emergency Response Systems in Meeting the Safety Monitoring Needs of Home Care Clients. *JONA J. Nurs. Adm.*, 24, 6, pp. 39–44, 1994, [Online]. Available: https://journals.lww.com/jonajournal/Fulltext/1994/06000/The_Effectiveness_of_Personal_Emergency_Response.10.aspx.

40. Mann, W.C., Belchior, P., Tomita, M.R., Kemp, B.J., Use of Personal Emergency Response Systems by Older Individuals With Disabilities. *Assist. Technol.*, 17, 1, 82–88, Mar. 2005.

41. McKenna, A.C., Kloseck, M., Crilly, R., Polgar, J., Purchasing and Using Personal Emergency Response Systems (PERS): How decisions are made by community-dwelling seniors in Canada. *BMC Geriatr.*, 15, 1, 1–9, 2015.

42. Heinbüchner, B., Hautzinger, M., Becker, C., Pfeiffer, K., Satisfaction and use of personal emergency response systems. *Z. Gerontol. Geriatr.*, 43, 4, 219–223, 2010.

43. Hamill, M., Young, V., Boger, J., Mihailidis, A., Development of an automated speech recognition interface for personal emergency response systems. *J. Neuroeng. Rehabil.*, 6, 1, 1–11, 2009.

44. Mackrill, J., Marshall, P., Payne, S.R., Dimitrokali, E., Cain, R., Using a bespoke situated digital kiosk to encourage user participation in healthcare environment design. *Appl. Ergon.*, 59, 342–356, 2017.

45. Nicholas, D., Huntington, P., Williams, P., Three years of digital consumer health information: a longitudinal study of the touch screen health kiosk. *Inf. Process. Manage.*, 39, 3, 479–502, 2003.

46. Nicholas, D., Huntington, P., Williams, P., Chahal, P., Determinants of Health Kiosk Use and Usefulness: Case Study of a Kiosk Which Serves a Multi-Cultural Population. *Libri*, 51, 2, 102–113, 2001.

47. Koch, S., Home telehealth—Current state and future trends. *Int. J. Med. Inform.*, 75, 8, 565–576, 2006.

48. Finkelstein, S.M., Speedie, S.M., Potthoff, S., Home Telehealth Improves Clinical Outcomes at Lower Cost for Home Healthcare. *Telemed. e-Health*, 12, 2, 128–136, Apr. 2006.

49. Ashwood, J.S., Mehrotra, A., Cowling, D., Uscher-Pines, L., Direct-To-Consumer Telehealth May Increase Access To Care But Does Not Decrease Spending. *Health Aff.*, 36, 3, 485–491, Mar. 2017.

50. Cady, R., Kelly, A., Finkelstein, S., Home telehealth for children with special healthcare needs. *J. Telemed. Telecare*, 14, 4, 173–177, Jun. 2008.

51. Angrish, S. *et al.*, How effective is the virtual primary healthcare centers? An experience from rural India. *J. Family Med. Prim. Care*, 9, 2, 465–469, Feb. 2020.

52. Hennick, C., How Remote Patient Monitoring Programs Are Beneficial, HealthTech, 2020, https://healthtechmagazine.net/article/2020/04/how-remote-patient-monitoring-programs-are-beneficial (accessed Aug. 25, 2020).

53. Nakamura, N., Koga, T., Iseki, H., A meta-analysis of remote patient monitoring for chronic heart failure patients. *J. Telemed. Telecare*, 20, 1, 11–17, Dec. 2013.

54. Pollonini, L., Rajan, N.O., Xu, S., Madala, S., Dacso, C.C., A Novel Handheld Device for Use in Remote Patient Monitoring of Heart Failure Patients—Design and Preliminary Validation on Healthy Subjects. *J. Med. Syst.*, 36, 2, 653–659, 2012.

55. Sanabria, M. *et al.*, Remote Patient Monitoring Program in Automated Peritoneal Dialysis: Impact on Hospitalizations. *Perit. Dial. Int.*, 39, 5, 472–478, Sep. 2019.

56. Pekmezaris, R. *et al.*, The Impact of Remote Patient Monitoring (Telehealth) upon Medicare Beneficiaries with Heart Failure. *Telemed. e-Health*, 18, 2, 101–108, Jan. 2012.

57. Klersy, C. *et al.*, Economic impact of remote patient monitoring: An integrated economic model derived from a meta-analysis of randomized controlled trials in heart failure. *Eur. J. Heart Fail.*, 13, 4, 450–459, 2011.

58. Fleming, D.A., Edison, K.E., Pak, H., Telehealth Ethics. *Telemed. e-Health*, 15, 8, 797–803, Sep. 2009.

59. Ajaz, K., The Importance of Equipment Efficiency for the Healthcare Sector, Electronic Health Reporter, 2018, https://electronichealthreporter.com/the-importance-of-equipment-efficiency-for-the-healthcare-sector/ (accessed Aug. 25, 2020).

60. Matityaho, S., LogiTag System, The IoT Streamlines Healthcare Supply Chains, 2015, https://irp-cdn.multiscreensite.com/1fd06f20/files/uploaded/IoTInHealthcare_FINAL.pdf.

61. Man, L.C.K., Na, C.M., Kit, N.C., IoT-Based Asset Management System for Healthcare-Related Industries. *Int. J. Eng. Bus. Manage.*, 7, 19, Jan. 2015.

62. Shiklo, B., RFID and IoT: A smart symbiosis for hospital asset tracking and management, ScienceSoft, 2018, https://www.scnsoft.com/blog/smart-hospital-asset-tracking.

63. BEHRTECH, 3 Great Benefits of IoT for Healthcare Asset Management, BehrTech Blog, 2020, https://behrtech.com/blog/iot-for-healthcare-asset-management/ (accessed Aug. 25, 2020).

64. Hanne, T., Melo, T., Nickel, S., Bringing Robustness to Patient Flow Management Through Optimized Patient Transports in Hospitals. *INFORMS J. Appl. Anal.*, 39, 3, 241–255, Mar. 2009.

65. DAIC, FDA Grants Emergency Use Authorization to Vital Connect for Cardiac Monitoring in COVID-19 Patients, Diagnostic and Interventional Cardiology, 2020, https://www.dicardiology.com/content/fda-grants-emergency-use-authorization-vitalconnect-cardiac-monitoring-covid-19-patients (accessed Aug. 25, 2020).

66. Science Daily, Clinical-grade wearables offer continuous monitoring for COVID-19, ScienceDaily, 2020, https://www.sciencedaily.com/releases/2020/07/200701125410.htm (accessed Aug. 25, 2020).

67. Darwish, A. and Hassanien, A.E., Wearable and implantable wireless sensor network solutions for healthcare monitoring. *Sensors*, 11, 6, 5561–5595, 2011.

68. Zoll, Zoll Life Vest, Zoll Cardiac Diagnostics, 2020, https://lifevest.zoll.com/medical-professionals.

69. Spiegelman, J., Krenitsky, N., Syeda, S., Sutton, D., Moroz, L., Case Study Rapid Development and Implementation of a Covid-19 Telehealth Clinic for Obstetric Patients, NEJM Catal, no. May 15, 2020.

70. Aziz, A. *et al.*, Telehealth for High-Risk Pregnancies in the Setting of the COVID-19 Pandemic. *Am. J. Perinatol.*, 37, 8, 800–808, Jun. 2020.

2

Issues and Challenges Related to Privacy and Security in Healthcare Using IoT, Fog, and Cloud Computing

Hritu Raj, Mohit Kumar, Prashant Kumar*, Amritpal Singh
and Om Prakash Verma

Dr. BR Ambedkar National Institute of Technology Jalandhar (Punjab), India

Abstract

In today's era, the IoT (Internet of Things) introduced a new way to create a bond between devices and humans for enhancing and making life quite easy. The main purpose of attraction toward improving the healthcare industry with the latest technology is because IoT has proven great opportunity in smart offices, warehouses, smart homes, etc. So, IoT can also improve the healthcare industry very well. The healthcare sensor generates health-related data like blood pressure, blood glucose, blood temperature, ECG, and much more. These devices produce very large amounts of data, which need to be processed, filtered, and stored securely and efficiently. In this paper, we will discuss the complete architecture with various challenges and security risks of the next-generation healthcare industry with healthcare IoT sensor and fog computing. This paper also consists of some methodology used in various research papers to address the security and privacy related in IoT, fog, and cloud computing environment.

Keywords: Internet of Things, healthcare, fog computing, cloud computing, security, privacy

Corresponding author: prashantk@nitj.ac.in

Rohit Tanwar, S. Balamurugan, R. K. Saini, Vishal Bharti and Premkumar Chithaluru (eds.) Advanced Healthcare Systems: Empowering Physicians with IoT-Enabled Technologies, (21–32) © 2022 Scrivener Publishing LLC

2.1   Introduction

IoT (Internet of Things) is very trending system consists of a variety of sensors, networking devices, microcomputer or microprocessor, optimized software, and different objects. To exchange data among each other, IoT devices, computers servers, and even cloud for data processing Apat *et al.* [24]. The demand of IoT devices is increasing day by day, and this will create a large opportunity for the IoT industry and researchers. Figure 2.1 illustrates healthcare using IoT. From the last few years, the sensor industry has evolved from making tiny sensors like photodetectors, temperature sensors, and hall sensors to more advanced sensors like blood glucose sensor, oxygen saturation level sensor, and ECG. With integration of fog computing and cloud, it facilitates the disease prediction of certain kinds and can get future insights of different diseases. The IoT system comprises various things like wearable IoT sensors, adaptive network interfaces, and optimized software integration module to cloud. Sensors are used to collect health-related data of sick patient with devices like oximeter for measuring oxygen saturation percentage in blood, blood pressure meter for measuring systolic blood pressure as well as diastolic blood pressure in arteries, blood glucose meter for measuring concentration of blood glucose using tiny drop of blood taken from human body, weight sensor for periodic measurement of patient weight for further analysis, and temperature sensor for monitoring real-time body temperature data.

Fall detection sensor for detection of accidental fall is using accelerometer and gyroscope and more advanced sensors like ECG for measuring electrical heart activity at rest. Adaptive networking interface provides support for a large number of networking protocols to easily integrate with different networking devices and software with enhanced algorithms to process health-related data efficiently and accurately Multag *et al.* [25]. There are a number of other uses of IoT devices. There are, like in fitness, a variety

Figure 2.1 Healthcare using IoT.

of fitness trackers available in the market for measuring daily activity like heart rate, sleep time, and running and walking time and also provide an interface for calling and messaging from right to the wrist. Companies offering these types of devices are Apple, Samsung, Fitbit, Xiaomi, etc. Next use of IoT devices is in smart homes, where the smart home Ghosh *et al.* [31], consists of a variety of a smart sensors like smart lock for keyless entry in car and homes, photo-director for turning garden light on at night and off at the day, sensor for detecting movement in room and triggering alarm when an intrusion happens, wireless camera with internet access to remotely monitor home and other premises, smart thermostat for controlling temperature according to human need, and smart fire alarm system for triggering alarm when a thing catches fire; IoT sensors can also be used in smart traffic management system for monitoring vehicle tracking on roads and switching traffic light according to traffic need. IoT sensors can also be used in warehouses for tracking workers activities. The increasing demand of smart devices in various fields creates huge amount of data and these data falls under various risk and challenges, if does not handled properly (especially health-related data). Patient data generated by smart heath sensors are very sensitive and critical, and management of these data is quite challenging Alihamidi *et al.* [32]. Every healthcare system must be provided security mechanism to handle five major factors in data handling: availability, integrity, confidentiality, authentication, and non-repudiation.

2.1 Related Works

A paper proposed by Sun *et al.* [1] named "Security and Privacy in the Medical Internet of Things: A Review" was published in March 2018. In this paper, various security issues are discussed about health-related data which are traveling over the internet. Their main focus was data usability, integrity, and auditing.

They also talked about different existing techniques available like encryption and access control.

A survey paper by Zhang *et al.* [2] on "Security-Aware Measurement in Software-Defined Networking (SDN)" consists of SDN basic architecture, issue in security, performance analysis, bandwidth analysis, topologies, and future scope.

A paper named "Privacy-Preserving and Multifunctional Health Data Aggregation With Fault Tolerance for Cloud Assisted WBANs" written by Han *et al.* [3] discusses privacy preserving technique in wireless body area networks.

Abuwardih *et al.* [5] presented a paper on privacy preserving in healthcare data; in this paper, they discussed various types of attacks and privacy issues related to patient data. They also proposed some architectures and procedures to handle different type of attacks related to patient data. The paper was named "Privacy Preserving Data Mining on Published Data in Healthcare", and it was proposed in 2016.

Anwar *et al.* [6] proposed a paper in 2015 named "Anytime Anywhere Access to Secure Privacy-Aware Healthcare Services: Issues Approaches and Challenges"; this paper consists of various approaches and challenges arises in healthcare industry for providing anytime and anywhere access of health-related resources. In this paper, they have shown approaches that are currently available and also discussed different policies made by government for information and technologies–related and international data–related security issues. The issues are generated by human, machine, and some other factors. All the security-related concern is discussed in detailed manner.

Rahman *et al.* [18] published a paper in ICOST (International Conference on Smart Homes and Health Telematics) naming "Inclusive Society: Health and Wellbeing in the Community and Care at Home". In this paper, they have proposed a generic model "PriGen" for securing patient health-related data with the help of cloud storage. PriGen facilitates access of patient health-related data without involvement of any other party from the cloud as well as hiding highly sensitive data. PriGen uses homomorphic function for encryption of data that needs very high security and which is critical. This algorithm preserves the highly sensitive health-related personal data in public cloud environment and maintains confidentiality of the patient data.

Bindahman *et al.* [19] proposed a paper in 2011 ICIEIS (Informatics Engineering and Information Science: International Conference) in which they talked about general concept of privacy problem related to patient health data. They discussed various available security measures and its performance comparison related to healthcare data. Based on that, they also suggested some techniques for those security-related problems.

Next is the paper written by Dubovitskaya *et al.* [20] entitled "ICT Systems Security and Privacy Protection: 30th IFIP TC 11 International Conference SEC 2015". In this paper, they have discussed various problems in building of health-related database for heterogeneous environment, where data are coming from various sources of different network environment of different hospitals. The integration of data comes from different locations. They introduced scaling and securing techniques for patient e-health data. They have used an algorithm called RSDB (Representative Protein Sequence Database) for collecting patient data efficiently and securely that are coming from various sources.

A paper by Idoga *et al.* [22] has discussed different issues related to privacy in the application e-healthcare environment.

2.3   Architecture

In this section, we will discuss three-layer architecture of next-generation healthcare industry with smart sensors, fog node, and cloud computing. The new healthcare industry will change the way hospital staff or doctors treat the patient. This IoT-driven healthcare industry will get highly efficient environment at very low cost, which decreases the workload and increases the throughput. The layered architecture will do different tasks at different layer. The three layers are device layer, fog layer, and cloud layer as shown in Figure 2.2.

2.3.1   Device Layer

At this layer, a very large number of smart sensors are involved, which are gathering tons of health-related data in near real-time. Any patient or healthcare specialist can access these data using any web-enabled device like phone, tablet, or computers. What they require is a secure and stable communication protocol to next layer in this case (fog layer). There is various communication are available for the wireless sensor nodes for communication within each other or propagating information to next layer. But selection of best protocol from the pool of various protocols is a tedious task. There are some protocols which are widely adopted for some general data transfer tasks are Low-Energy Bluetooth and High-Fidelity Wi-Fi.

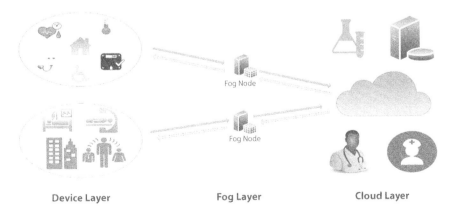

Figure 2.2 Three-layer architecture.

Low-Energy Bluetooth is good for beacon type signal and where power constrains matter too much or battery is irreplaceable (like in heart pacemaker). On the other hand, Wi-Fi is used where long-range and high-data rate required (like transferring raw ECG data).

2.3.2 Fog Layer

This layer consists of high-end processors, large and high-speed data storage, and Network Interface Card for communication over internet. The patient health data are very critical data a normal considerable amount of latency can cost lives, example of such type of data is Myocardial Infarction where latency of seconds can cause serious damage Singh *et al.* [26]. So, we cannot rely only on cloud for data processing and analyzing critical time sensitive data. In handling these types of data, we require analysis, processing, and storage as close as possible to the devices where data is generated Badidi *et al.* [23]. Thus, need of fog computing arises here, and it processes, analyzes, and stores (for further use) health-related data which is very time-sensitive in nature Kraemer *et al.* [28]. This layer also filters, compresses high volume raw data, and passes to next layer (cloud computing layer) for big data analytics purposes.

2.3.3 Cloud Layer

The cloud layer integrates data from various fog nodes and does analysis using deep learning, generates pattern, and gets future insights for the disease prediction. The cloud layer provides various connectivity protocols to address variety of users across the world Akintoye *et al.* [27]. The fog node across different geographical areas uses different communication channel like optical fibers, twisted pair, co-axial cable, satellite communication, and sometimes LTE. The cloud provides best data management techniques to health-related user for better management of large amount of patient data. The cloud healthcare system incorporates set of rules through which it can analyze patterns and can trigger alarm when any risky pattern detected. The cloud layer uptime should be as high as possible (very near to 100%). So, it can always be there for help when ever any request arises from persons involved in healthcare institutions.

2.4 Issues and Challenges

Integration of IoT and fog computing can take the healthcare industry to the next level. The smart health sensors of wearable IoT devices stays with the patient all the time and it monitors patient heart rate, blood pressure, body temperature, blood glucose, oxygen saturation, and much more in real time and passes these whole data to the fog node for the processing and storage and then to the cloud for deep learning Khan *et al.* [29]. All this data plays an important role in the healthcare industry. So, it should be protected from various threats and vulnerabilities. There are a number of security challenges that we should care about. Generally, the patient care industry invests very less amount of money on privacy and security of healthcare data. But in a smart healthcare system, security and privacy plays a very important role Hamid *et al.* [30]. The data produced by medical e-health sensors are very large and very sensitive. These data also contain patient private information. The patient data can be hampered on different stages like in data gathering from sensors and transfer it to fog nodes and sometimes on clouds also.

Some of the data risks that should be taken into account are integrity of data, authenticity of data, and auditing of data and private data of patients. Various mechanisms are shown in Table 2.1.

Integrity of Patient Data: It refers to availability of the same data in the whole system without change. Or you can say no modification in data throughout its life cycle. This means accuracy of data should not be tempered. There should be no unintentional change in data. Any intention should reflect immediately in the whole system. The main purpose of maintaining integrity is to ensure accuracy and reliability of the health data. Integrity can be sub-categorized in four categories: integrity defined by user, integrity of reference, integrity of various domains, and integrity of data entity.

Usability of Patient Information: Information usability refers to no unauthorized access of patient data generated or stored by smart healthcare systems. The use of deep learning on patient data can generate unique patterns and provide different solutions. The data generated by the system also comes at data privacy risks. The little bit of unwanted modification in data can cause serious issues.

Audition of Healthcare Data: Access of healthcare devices needs to be auditioned properly for monitoring of various mechanisms and techniques for identifying unwanted patterns. The integration of cloud computing resources may also create some trouble in security concerns because the cloud providers generally are usually unreliable in case of privacy terms. So, it requires a good audition procedure, the audition procedure consists of records used in operation, the service provider (in this case the cloud provider) and the user which is involved in patient care.

Privacy of Patient: Privacy of users plays a very important role in any digital technology. In the e-health system, patient information is the most

Table 2.1 Security and privacy mechanism prosed in some papers.

Paper	Techniques	Domain	Characteristic
[4]	Machine Learning	Smart Healthcare Health Decision	Support System
[7]	Attribute Based-Encryption	Personal Healthcare	Encrypting Personal Healthcare Records
[8]	Ciphertext Policy-Attribute Based-Encryption	Wireless Network for Healthcare Sensors	Preserving integrity and confidentiality of health-related data
[9]	Attribute Based-Encryption	Patient Data sharing	Resolving key escrow problem
[10]	KMS	e-health systems	Lightweight end to end key management
[11]	IoT sensors based on Cloud	Senior citizen health data management	Providing medical assistance to elder people
[12]	Ciphertext Policy-Attribute Based-Encryption	Encrypted cloud data	Resolving APKS problem in Cloud computing
[13]	m2-ABKS	Encrypted e-health data	Authorized access of records and collusion attacks are addressed
[14]	Laplace guided KR	Image Compression	Achieving high compression ratio with low computational cost
[15]	PASStree	Matching of string	Providing good string matching without privacy hampering
[16]	Authentication techniques	Patient Supervision	Promising patient's privacy while preserving confidentiality of system
[17]	Homomorphic Encryption	Privacy of Data	Preserving privacy of data generated by IoT devices

valuable resource. So, we need to be very careful in keeping data safe. The patient data can be divided into two kinds: general records and the critical personal information. General records do not require any good privacy like name, age, sex, height, weight, and color. But critical personal information needs special attention in terms of security and privacy [21]. Critical information includes genetic info data, allergy from some kind medicine, addiction to drugs, certain kinds of infections, color blindness data, fertility information, sexual orientation, and some others. This information needs to be encrypted before storing and sending it to the cloud.

There are some threats available related to security and privacy.

Fake Identity Attack: In this, attacker can create false identity of authorized persons in the system and can do certain things like changing the entries and deleting some important records; attackers can also downgrade the system performance by consuming system resources unnecessarily.

Data Tampering Attack: In this, attacker can tamper health-related data by changing, editing, manipulating, and destroying.

Spamming: In this attack, fake data of patients is created and flooded in the system which induces unnecessary entry in data tables which leads to inaccurate results.

Denial-of-Service Attack: In this, attacker creates a large number of fake packets to flood the network, and then, the system engages in fulfilling the request generated by the fake packets and denies the request generated by genuine packets. This results in poor system performance and uptime.

Eavesdropping: In this, attackers take access of the communication channel and start snooping the packet traveling in that channel. If a very strong encryption technique is not applied, then it is very easy for attackers to read and understand those data.

Location Privacy: In this, attacker can gain live location access of the patient, generated form the wearable IoT devices attached to the patient or the mobile phone.

Usages Privacy: In this, attacker can gain usage information of the patient or the person involved in the healthcare to find the useful and predict some sensitive information.

2.5   Conclusion

Technological advancement in the healthcare industry is increasing rapidly, and a variety of wearable devices are available for gathering health-related patient data. Data gathered from these smart devices are very huge.

The high volume of important data invites attackers to steal and manipulate it. To maintain integrity, security and privacy of health-related data. In this paper we have discussed architecture of the next generation healthcare system with latest available IoT devices, use of fog computing for local processing and storing, then for pattern recognition sends it to the cloud. Here, deep learning and data mining are done on that data. There are many security privacy issues, and challenges are there that need to be addressed very carefully.

References

1. Sun, W., Cai, Z., Li, Y., Liu, F., Fang, S., Wang, G., Security and Privacy in the Medical Internet of Things: A Review. *Secur. Commun. Netw.*, 2018, 9, 2018.
2. Zhang, H., Cai, Z., Liu, Q. *et al.*, A survey on security-aware measurement in SDN. *Secur. Commun. Netw.*, 2018, 2018. https://doi.org/10.1155/2018/2459154.
3. Han, S., Zhao, S., Li, Q., Ju, C.-H., Zhou, W., PPM-HDA: privacy-preserving and multifunctional health data aggregation with fault tolerance. *IEEE Trans. Inf. Forensics Secur.*, 11, 9, 1940–1955, 2016.
4. Yin, H. *et al.*, Smart Healthcare. *Found. Trends R Electron. Des. Autom.*, 1, 1–67, 2018.
5. Abuwardih, L.A., Shatnawi, W., Aleroud, A., Privacy preserving data mining on published data in healthcare: A survey. 1–6, 2016. https://ieeexplore.ieee.org/document/7549444
6. Anwar, M., Joshi, J., Tan, J., Anytime anywhere access to secure privacy-aware healthcare services: Issues approaches and challenges. *Health Policy Technol.*, 4, 4, 299–311, 2015.
7. Lounis, A., Hadjidj, A., Bouabdallah, A., Challal, Y., Secure medical architecture on the cloud using wireless sensor networks for emergency management, in: *Proceedings of the 2013 IEEE 8th International Conference on Broadband, Wireless Computing, Communication and Applications, BWCCA 2013*, pp. 248–252, October 2013.
8. Lounis, A., Hadjidj, A., Bouabdallah, A., Challal, Y., Healing on the cloud: secure cloud architecture for medical wireless sensor networks. *Future Gener. Comput. Syst.*, 55, 266–277, 2016.
9. Li, M., Yu, S., Zheng, Y., Scalable and secure sharing of personal health records in cloud computing using attributebased encryption. *IEEE Trans. Parallel Distrib. Syst.*, 24, 1, 131–143, 2012.
10. Abdmeziem, M.R. and Tandjaoui, D., A cooperative end to end key management scheme for e-health applications in the context of internet of things, in: *Ad-hoc Networks and Wireless*, pp. 35–46, Springer, Berlin Heidelberg, 2014.

11. Hu, J.-X., Chen, C.-L., Fan, C.-L., Wang, K.-H., An intelligent and secure health monitoring scheme using IoT sensor based on cloud computing. *J. Sens.*, 2017, Article ID 3734764, 11 pages, 2017.

12. Li, M., Yu, S., Cao, N., Lou, W., Authorized private keyword search over encrypted data in cloud computing, in: *Proceedings of the 31st International Conference on Distributed Computing Systems (ICDCS '11)*, IEEE, Minneapolis, Minn, USA, pp. 383–392, July, 2011.

13. Miao, Y., Ma, J., Liu, X., Wei, F., Liu, Z., Wang, X.A., m2-ABKS: attribute-based multi-keyword search over encrypted personal health records in multi-owner setting. *J. Med. Syst.*, 40, 11, 246, 2016. https://link.springer.com/article/10.1007/s10916-016-0617-z

14. Song, C., Lin, X., Shen, X. *et al.*, Kernel regression based encrypted images compression for e-healthcare systems, in: *Proceedings of the International Conference on Wireless Communications and Signal Processing*, pp. 1–6, 2013.

15. Bezawada, B., Liu, A.X., Jayaraman, B., Wang, A.L., Li, R., Privacy Preserving String Matching for Cloud Computing, in: *Proceedings of the 35th IEEE International Conference on Distributed Computing Systems, ICDCS '15*, pp. 609–618, July 2015.

16. Li, C.-T., Lee, C.-C., Weng, C.-Y., A secure cloud-assisted wireless body area network in mobile emergency medical care system. *J. Med. Syst.*, 40, 5, 1–15, 2016.

17. Gong, T., Huang, H., Li, P., Zhang, K., Jiang, H., A Medical Healthcare System for Privacy Protection Based on IoT, in: *Proceedings of the 7th International Symposium on Parallel Architectures, Algorithms, and Programming, PAAP '15*, pp. 217–222, December 2015.

18. Rahman, F., Ahamed, S., II, Yang, J.-J., Wang, Q., nclusive Society: Health and Wellbeing in the Community and Care at Home. *11th International Conference on Smart Homes and Health Telematics ICOST 2013*, June 19–21, 2013.

19. Bindahman, S. and Zakaria, N., Informatics Engineering and Information Science. *International Conference ICIEIS 2011*, November 14–16, 2011.

20. Dubovitskaya, A., Urovi, V., Vasirani, M., Aberer, K., ICT Systems Security and Privacy Protection. *30th IFIP TC 11 International Conference SEC 2015*, May 26-28, 2015.

21. Farahani, B., Firouzi, F., Chang, V., Badaroglu, M., Constant, N., Mankodiya, K., Towards fog-driven IoT eHealth: Promises and challenges of IoT in medicine and healthcare. *Future Gener. Comput. Syst.*, 78, Part 2, 2018. https://digitalcommons.uri.edu/ele_facpubs/79

22. Idoga, P.E., Agoyi, M., Coker-Farrell, E.Y., Ekeoma, O.L., Review of security issues in e-Healthcare and solutions. *2016 HONET-ICT*, Nicosia, pp. 118–121, 2016.

23. Badidi, E. and Moumane, K., Enhancing the Processing of Healthcare Data Streams using Fog Computing. *2019 IEEE Symposium on Computers and Communications (ISCC)*, Barcelona, Spain, pp. 1113–1118, 2019.

24. Apat, H.K., Bhaisare, K., Sahoo, B., Maiti, P., Energy Efficient Resource Management in Fog Computing Supported Medical Cyber-Physical System. *2020 International Conference on Computer Science, Engineering and Applications (ICCSEA)*, Gunupur, India, pp. 1–6, 2020.

25. Mutlag, A.A., Ghani, M.K.A., Arunkumar, N., Mohammed, M.A., Mohd, O., Enabling technologies for fog computing in healthcare IoT systems. *Future Gener. Comput. Syst.*, 90, 62–78, 2019.

26. Singh, S., Bansal, A., Sandhu, R., Sidhu, J., Fog computing and IoT based healthcare support service for dengue fever. *Int. J. Pervasive Comput. Commun.*, 14, 2, 197–207, Jun. 2018.

27. Akintoye, S.B., Bagula, A.B., Isafiade, O.E., Djemaiel, Y., Boudriga, N., Data Model for Cloud Computing Environment. *e-Infrastructure and e-Services for Developing Countries. AFRICOMM 2018. Lecture Notes of the Institute for Computer Sciences Social Informatics and Telecommunications Engineering*, vol. 275, 2019.

28. Kraemer, F.A., Braten, A.E., Tamkittikhun, N., Palma, D., Fog Computing in Healthcare-A Review and Discussion. *IEEE Access*, 5, 9206–9222, 2017.

29. Khan, S., Parkinson, S., Qin, Y., Fog computing security: a review of current applications and security solutions. *J. Cloud Comput.*, 6, 1, 19, 2017.

30. Al Hamid, H.A., Rahman, Sk Md M., Shamim Hossain, M., Almogren, A., Alamri, A., A Security Model for Preserving the Privacy of Medical Big Data in a Healthcare Cloud Using a Fog Computing Facility With Pairing-Based Cryptography. *IEEE Access*, 5, 22313–22328, 2017.

31. Ghosh, A.M., Halder, D., Hossain, S.A., Remote health monitoring system through iot. *2016 International Conference on Informatics Electronics and Vision (ICIEV)*, pp. 921–926, 2016.

32. Alihamidi, I., Ait Madi, A., Addaim, A., Proposed Architecture of e-health IoT. *2019 International Conference on Wireless Networks and Mobile Communications (WINCOM)*, Fez, Morocco, pp. 1–7, 2019.

3

Study of Thyroid Disease Using Machine Learning

Shanu Verma*, Rashmi Popli and Harish Kumar

J.C. Bose University of Science and Technology, Faridabad, India

Abstract

Thyroid problems occur due to the deficiency of iodine. It is a major health problem among the population living with iodine deficiency, and this endocrine disorder has seen common problems everywhere. Thyroid function test based on the value of TSH, T3 and T4, may indicate thyroid dysfunction and may indicate symptoms and signs that are diagnostic of hyperthyroidism or hypothyroidism. Hyperthyroidism in the gland that contains a high amount of thyroid hormone. Hypothyroidism is a gland that does not fabricate thyroid hormone that perform impaired metabolic functions. Graves is the biggest disease in hypothyroidism which is associated with eye disease. An exceptional type of cancer occurring in the thyroid is a thyroid cancer that infects the gland at the base of the neck. Thyroid cancer disease has been increasing for the past few years. Endocrinologists believe that this is due to the use of new technology, i.e., machine learning, intensive learning allows the detection of thyroid cancer that may not have been detected in the past. According to the Cancer Registry, thyroid cancer is the second more common cancer among women of all cancers, with cancer in thyroid occurring at only 3.5%. This chapter studies thyroid disease using machine learning algorithm.

Keywords: Thyroid, thyroid cancer, hypothyroidism, hyperthyroidism, machine learning, classification algorithm

---

*Corresponding author: shanu.verma56@gmail.com

Rohit Tanwar, S. Balamurugan, R. K. Saini, Vishal Bharti and Premkumar Chithaluru (eds.) Advanced Healthcare Systems: Empowering Physicians with IoT-Enabled Technologies, (33–42) © 2022 Scrivener Publishing LLC

3.1 Introduction

In India, thyroid disorder is the most common endocrine diseases. About 42 lakh population in India is affected by thyroid disorders. The type of thyroid disorder depends on various characteristics such as sex, iodine levels, age, and more [1]. Hyperthyroidism is one of the primary causes of thyroid cancer, although some researchers suggest that up to 20% of people with hyperthyroidism may be prone to thyroid cancer [15].

Thyroid cancer occurs when the thyroid produces hormones that control your heart rate, blood pressure, weight, and body temperature. It shows no signs or symptoms, and when it grows a lump on the neck that can be felt through the skin, the voice has changed and it has become hoarse. There are various classes of thyroid cancer. Some are growing very gradually and others can be very violent. Globally, thyroid cancer accounts for 32% and the incidence of new cases is 3 lakh per year. In addition, 32,000 thyroid cancer patients die annually.

3.2 Related Works

Over the years, many researchers worldwide worked in machine learning, deep learning, artificial intelligence, predictive analytics, and data science in health-related illness about future challenges and opportunities. Although some research works have been done to determine these possible causes, effects, and solutions, yet it is still a global problem. This chapter will study of thyroid disease using machine learning. Various researchers has studied research work basis for our research and understanding. There are some research papers in this regard are described below.

Parry and Kripke [11] have discussed thyroid effect on women mood disorders. Women have a higher risk of premenstrual, peripartum, and perimenopause that may occur in puberty with oral contraceptive onset and depressive illness. This paper study case reports of various persons and suggest some treatment guidelines such as Treatment-Resistant Unipolar Depression and Rapid Cycling Mood disorders. The conclusion of this paper is that, as compared to men, women have high number of depression.

Razia *et al.* [20] have studied various machine learning algorithms and comparison between them to achieve better accuracy in the prediction of thyroid disease. The conclusion of this paper is that the decision trees has better accuracy as compared to the naïve Bayes, SVM, and, multi-linear regression.

Pakdel and Ghazavi [12] have described selenium effect on Thyroid disorders. This paper conducts literature survey over the past 20 years' (1995–2014) papers and discussed that this topic has increased in recent years. This literature paper was restricted to two index such as Social Science Citation Index and Science Citation Index Expanded and performing searching using keyword. The conclusion of this research is that similar studies have to be carried within next 5 years.

Priyanka *et al.* [1] have studied thyroid disease among women from rural and urban populations in Bangalore. It is described in this letter that every eight women in Bangalore are suffering from thyroid disease. This study was done at the actual hospital in Bangalore.

Godara [17] have predicted thyroid disease using machine learning technique. The method used to detect thyroid disease such as support vector machine and logistic regression on basis of recall, F-measure, error, ROC, and precision. To compare these techniques, Weka version is used.

Mathew [16] have studied thyroid cancer in South India. This study based on population taken from the Registry Program of National Cancer from 2005 to 2014. This paper studies the thyroid cancer patient in Thiruvananthapuram district and compares it with the other four regions Delhi, Mumbai, Bangalore, and Chennai. This paper found that Thiruvananthapuram has a higher rate of thyroid cancer in patients than in the other four regions.

3.3   Thyroid Functioning

Thyroid gland is a predominant organ of human body. Cardiovascular complications include an extreme thyroid condition, increased blood pressure, increased cholesterol levels, depression, and decreased fertility [2]. The thyroid gland has become an important disease in this endocrine region which is an endocrine gland located in the neck, in case of severity the patient may die [3]. There are two traditional diseases of the thyroid that are hyperthyroidism and hypothyroidism that release hormones in the thyroid that control the rate of metabolism of the body. The thyroid glands are made up of two active thyroid hormones that are Triiodothyronine Total (T3) and Thyroxine Total (T4) to control the metabolism of body [4]. From these two thyroid hormones T3 and T4, the main building part of the thyroid glands is iodine which prevails in some problems that are highly potent. To the prediction of disease, machine learning has played a decisive role and provides better accuracy. There are different classification algorithms for prediction whether the patient has thyroid disease or not.

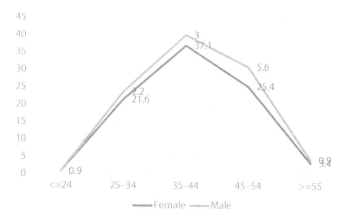

Figure 3.1 Analysis of thyroid.

A machine learning model was trained with a data set of 1,300 benign thyroid nodules and trained with following variables: Name, Age, Triiodothyronine Total (T3), Thyroxine Total (T4), TSH (4th Generation), and Serum [5]. Serum are present in about 60% of patients with autoimmune thyroid disease and are more frequent in females. This research paper has analyzed thyroid disease among different ages in years as shown in Figure 3.1.

3.4   Category of Thyroid Cancer

There are various categories of thyroid cancers that are found in tumours based on cells. These are papillary thyroid cancer, follicular thyroid cancer, anaplastic thyroid cancer, and medullary thyroid cancer, as shown in Figure 3.2.

There are various categories of thyroid cancers.

- **Papillary Thyroid Cancer:** Papillary thyroid cancer occurs mostly in children and women and grows very slowly. The common type of thyroid cancer is papillary thyroid cancer. This type of cancer occurs at any stage but is mostly affected between the ages of 30 and 50 [6].
- **Follicular Thyroid Cancer:** This is the second most common type of cancer caused by the thyroid and is less common than papillary thyroid cancer. This type of cancer mostly affects people above the age of 50 years. It is also

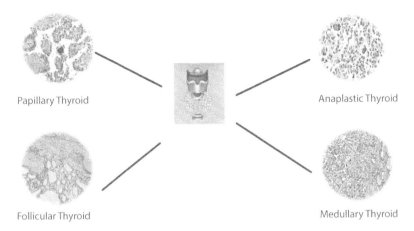

Figure 3.2 Categories of thyroid cancer.

a type of behavioral thyroid cancer but the thyroid has a slightly higher risk of spreading than papillary cancer [6].

- **Anaplastic Thyroid Cancer:** Anaplastic thyroid cancer has rapidly developing, poorly differentiated thyroid cancer that can begin with differentiated thyroid cancer or a benign thyroid tumor. It is often seen in patients who have prolonged thyroid inflammation. It spreads rapidly to both local and distant organs [6].
- **Medullary Thyroid Cancer:** Medullar thyroid cancer spreads more than other types of cancer. It is a special type of thyroid cancer that is hereditary in many patients. This type of cancer occurs in young children and can be treated well with adequate surgery [6].

3.5 Machine Learning Approach Toward the Detection of Thyroid Cancer

Machine learning is the technology of a new era, and it is the field that is used to construct models and is helpful in prediction of diseases. Machine learning algorithms are used to identify hidden patterns and relationships in historical data. Data are needed to support medical decision-making to predict accurate, robust, and efficient models. The use of machine learning in modern healthcare systems is increasing and necessary [7]. By 2025, CAGR has raised machine learning targets in the healthcare sector from

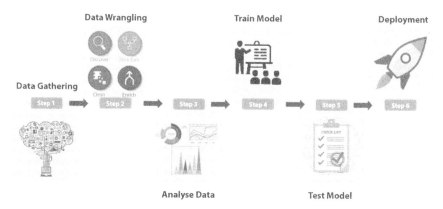

Figure 3.3 Machine learning life cycle model.

$2.1 billion to $50.2% in 2018 to $36.1 billion. In fact, machine learning has an important part of patient data compared to improving healthcare delivery systems, cutting costs and developing, and monitoring and handling treatment processes and medicines. As we all know that maintaining and updating and recording the patient's medical history is a very expensive process. These problems are solved by the use of machine learning technologies to reduce time, effort, and money.

To build an efficient machine learning project in healthcare, there are various steps to do such as data gathering, data wrangling, analyze data, train the model, test the model, and deployment, as shown in Figure 3.3. Sickness treatment has ordinary influence for healthcare physicians, and impeccable diagnosis at the right time is very important for a patient [2]. Compared to the previous approach, machine learning first builds the model and then presents the first reliable and accurate predictions for model construction without defining patient characteristics.

There are various machine learning algorithms for thyroid detection, some of which are as follows.

3.5.1   Decision Tree Algorithm

This algorithm used the divide-and-conquer method to construct a decision tree to solve the classification problem using decision-making trees [8]. These form a model based on decisions that relate to features in the data set and very fast to train. Examples of these types of models include random forests and conditional decision trees. The goal is to create a model that predicts the accuracy of thyroid disease using target variables, i.e., TSH by using simple decision rules derived from data features, i.e., T3 and T4.

This algorithm works on the basis of input and output variable (x, y) that is specified in a label set of pairs as follows.

The algorithm is to learn the mapping function from the input variable x to the output variable y, which is given the label set of the input output pair

$$T = \{(x, y)\}n \qquad (3.1)$$

In Equation (3.1), T represents the training set and n represents the number of training samples.

3.5.2   Support Vector Machines

This is machine learning algorithm that is used for text categorization, image segmentation that uses classification algorithm, and regression and detection of outlier. To implement this in healthcare, sampling is divided among training and testing [9]. This algorithm aims to isolate diseases and then work through a hyperplane. This algorithm used the training data as input and separated the graph of the data in the class as output in the hyperplane [10]. Let us consider classification task such as $\{u_i, v_i\}$ where $i = 1....n$ u_i are data points, $u_i \in S^d$ and v_i are labels. The data points and labels are displaced through the hyperplane with $wtx + b = 0$, where w represents a D-dimensional coefficient vector that is normal to the hyperplane and b represents an offset from the origin.

3.5.3   Random Forest

This machine learning algorithm is used to estimate hierarchical variables using a classification algorithm and to assess disease risk that evaluates a function that helps doctors to make medical decisions. The training time of random forest is less as compared to other algorithms. In healthcare, this algorithm is used for disease trends and disease risks that can be identified by analyzing the patient medical records.

3.5.4   Logistic Regression

Logistic regression is a supervised learning algorithm that is used to estimate target variables. The nature of the target or dependent variable is dichotomous, meaning that yes or no, there will be only two possible classes. In healthcare, logistic regression is used to predict a patient's readmitted whether a patient is readmitted to a hospital or not. It can be divided into two classes: either the patient is not admitted or is not readmitted. Logistic regression can be used to classify whether a person will be prone to cancer due to environmental variables such as smoking habit, highway, and drinking alcohol [18].

3.5.5   Naïve Bayes

Naïve Bayes algorithm is used for prediction of disease. This algorithm trains label data sets and for this they must be trained on label data sets. This algorithm works on the basis of prior probability. The prior probability is the probability of disease that is based on its symptoms and is conducted on a data set.

$$X(T = Thyroid) = (TSH, T3 \& T4)/(Overall\ Symptoms)$$

This algorithm is used to predict the disease based on the maximum value between classes and that class will represent its disease or will be selected [19].

ML has contributed a considerable number of disciplines in recent years including healthcare, vision, and natural language processing. There are several machine learning approaches that are analyzed and used for the diagnosis of thyroid disease. The analysis shows that all the papers use different machine learning technologies and show different accuracy. In most research paper, it suggests that logistic regression and decision tree have obtained better accuracy than other algorithms, as shown in Figure 3.4.

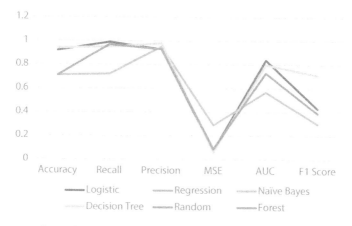

Figure 3.4 Analysis of machine learning approach on thyroid.

3.6   Conclusion

The prevalence of thyroid disease in the Earth is still worrisome today, which is seen as a major threat to human life and leading to increased research. Thyroid and thyroid cancers occur mostly in women with a ratio of 3:1 compared to men. Various machine learning approaches have been implemented to predict or detect thyroid disease so that treatment for it is less complex and will increase the patient's chances of recovery. There is a need to develop machine learning algorithms to analyze the effects of thyroid and thyroid cancer which require the minimum parameters of an individual to detect the thyroid and keeps both the time and money of the patient.

References

1. Priyanka, A prevalence of thyroid dysfunction among young females of urban and rural population in and around Bangalore. *Indian J. Appl. Res.*, 9, 11, 37–38, November – 2019.
2. Chaubey, G., Bisen, D., Arjaria, S., Yadav, V., Thyroid Disease Prediction Using Machine Learning Approaches. *Natl. Acad. Sci.*, 44, 3, 233–238, 2020.
3. Ma, L., Ma, C., Liu, Y., Wang, X., Thyroid Diagnosis from SPECT Images Using Convolutional Neural Network with Optimization. *Comput. Intell. Neurosci.*, Article ID 6212759, 11 pages, https://doi.org/10.1155/2019/6212759, 2019.
4. Yadav, D.C. and Pal, S., Discovery of Hidden Pattern in Thyroid Disease by Machine Learning Algorithms. *Indian J. Public Health Res. Dev.*, 11, 1, 61–66, 2020.
5. Reverter, J.L., Rosas-Allende, I., Puig-Jove, C., Zafon, C., Megia, A., Castells, I., Pizarro, E., Puig-Domingo, M., Luisa Granada, M., Prognostic Significance of Thyroglobulin Antibodies in Differentiated Thyroid Cancer. *J. Thyroid Res.*, Article ID 8312628, 6 pages, https://doi.org/10.1155/2020/8312628, 2020.
6. Thyroid cancer, Patient Care & Health Information Diseases & Conditions, 2020, https://www.mayoclinic.org/diseases-conditions/thyroid-cancer/symptoms-causes/syc-20354161.
7. Beam, A.L., Big Data and Machine Learning in Healthcare, American Medical Association, 2018.
8. Jongboa, O.A., Development of an ensemble approach to chronic kidney disease diagnosis. *Sci. Afr.*, 8, 1–8, 2020, https://doi.org/10.1016/j.sciaf.2020.e00456.

9. Shailaja, K., Machine Learning in Healthcare: A Review. *Proceedings of the 2nd International conference on Electronics, Communication and Aerospace Technology (ICECA 2018) IEEE Conference Record #42487*, IEEE Xplore.

10. Duggal, P., Prediction Of Thyroid Disorders Using Advanced Machine Learning Techniques. *International Conference on Cloud Computing, Data Science & Engineering.*

11. Parry, B.L. and Kripke, D.F., Antidepressant and Stabilizing Effects of Thyroid Hormone Augmentation in Women's Mood Disorders. *JETR*, 5, 3, 59–67, March 2020.

12. Pakdel, F. and Ghazavi, R., Effect of Selenium on Thyroid Disorders: Scientometric Analysis. *Iran J. Public Health*, 48, 3, 410–420, Mar 2019.

13. Mathew, I.E. and Mathew, A., Rising Thyroid Cancer Incidence in Southern India: An Epidemic of Overdiagnosis? *J. Endocr. Soc.*, 1, 5, 480–487, 2017.

14. Alhozali, A., Al-Ghamdi, A., Alahmadi, J., Pattern of Thyroid Cancer at King Abdulaziz University Hospital, Jeddah: A 10-Year Retrospective Study. *Open J. Endocr. Metab. Dis.*, 6, 121–125, 2016.

15. Mofit Cancer Center, Cancer Types & Treatments, *Can Hyperthyroidism Be a Thyroid Cancer Symptom?*, 2018, https://moffitt.org/cancers/thyroid-cancer/faqs/can-hyperthyroidism-be-a-thyroid-cancer-symptom/

16. Mathew, I.E., Rising Thyroid Cancer Incidence in Southern India: An Epidemic of Over diagnosis? *J. Endocr. Soc.*, 1, 5, 480–487, May 2017.

17. Godara, S., Prediction of Thyroid Disease Using Machine Learning Techniques. *Int. J. Electron. Eng.*, 10, 2, 787–793, June 2018, www.csjournals.com.

18. Packt, Healthcare Analytics: Logistic Regression to Reduce Patient Readmissions, 2017, https://hub.packtpub.com/healthcare-analytics-logistic-regression-to-reduce-patient-readmissions/

19. Bohra, H., Health Prediction and Medical Diagnosis using Naive Bayes. *Int. J. Adv. Res. Comput. Commun. Eng.*, 6, 4, 32–35, April 2017.

20. Razia, S., Kumar, P.S., Rao, A.S., Machine learning techniques for thyroid disease diagnosis: A systematic review. *Modern Approaches in Machine Learning and Cognitive Science: A Walkthrough*, pp. 203–212, 2020.

4

A Review of Various Security and Privacy Innovations for IoT Applications in Healthcare

Abhishek Raghuvanshi[1]*, Umesh Kumar Singh[2] and Chirag Joshi[3]

[1]Department of CSE, MIT, Ujjain, India
[2]Institute of Computer Sciences, Vikram University, Ujjain, India
[3]Department of CSE, DIT University, Dehradun, India

Abstract

The Internet of Things (IoT) provides a wide variety of healthcare uses, including assistance for independent living and well-being and illness control. Furthermore, IoT healthcare has the goal of helping patients control their own condition and connect and interact with healthcare professionals. IoT is making daily life easy by facilitating in routine work. The IoT has a variety of applications in the real world including mining, energy, medicine, intelligent towns, agriculture, and transport. This paper provides an analysis of numerous security and privacy technologies in healthcare, clever communities, and intelligent homes available for IoT applications. Roughly two-thirds of respondents said that the main issue was interoperability and protection according to the findings of the industrial internet poll, commissioned by the World Economic Forum. IoT security is a major issue of concern and it is required to be dealt carefully to make IoT a companion of human in daily routine works and to make life of common people comfortable.

Keywords: IoT, vulnerability, IoT healthcare, smart city, smart homes

*Corresponding author: abhishek14482@gmail.com

Rohit Tanwar, S. Balamurugan, R. K. Saini, Vishal Bharti and Premkumar Chithaluru (eds.) Advanced Healthcare Systems: Empowering Physicians with IoT-Enabled Technologies, (43–58) © 2022 Scrivener Publishing LLC

4.1   Introduction

4.1.1   Introduction to IoT

For the health industry, the Internet of Things (IoT) can be a game changer. By concentrating on better patient care, improving efficiency, and reducing costs, IoT can transform the healthcare sector. You can collect unique real-time critical data by developing an intelligent system. The intelligent, real-time internet services can analyze the crucial data collected to make smart choices for health management, the collection of information, and surgical assistance.

IoT is "A world where physical objects are seamlessly integrated into the information network and where the physical objects can become active participants in the business process" [1].

The proximity of all IoT objects is the ability to access the internet and business knowledge. The highlight of the available method allows the article to be operated remotely over the present system base, thus creating more incorporation and less human intercession of this actual fact.

IoT transforms objects from ancient to intelligent by introducing the foundational developments, e.g., coding, mailing, internet conventions, and applications [2].

Figure 4.1 represents major components in IoT. Sensors are a lot of diodes equipped for detecting natural physical boundaries, for example, temperature and pressure. Sensors are responsible for acquisition of data. They can be configured to collect data continuously. Sensors are capable of capturing humidity, temperature, motion, and many more. IoT platform is a middleware. IoT platform is a bridge between IoT devices and the cloud server. It is responsible for the transmission between IoT devices and cloud server. Many quality IoT platforms are available nowadays such as Microsoft Azure IoT and AWA IoT. Actual data is stored in cloud server. In cloud, data analytics applications are applied and relevant data is shared with stakeholders using mobile applications.

Figure 4.1 Conceptual framework of IoT.

4.1.2   Introduction to Vulnerability, Attack, and Threat

To comprehend IoT security, the threat, the vulnerabilities, and attack must be characterized. A threat is any potential vindictive event that could hurt an advantage. To understand IoT protection, the threat, the vulnerabilities, and the attack must be identified. A risk is any potential vindictive event that could hurt an advantage. Vulnerability is a vulnerability that makes imaginable a hazard. Faulty arrangements, configuration botches, or incomplete and ambiguous coding protocols can be due to this.

An attack is an operation that exploits a threat from vulnerability or authorizes it. The submission of a vindictive contribution to an application or the flooding of a system attempting to refuse assistance is an instance of an assault.

In the 2014 World Economic Forum Industrial Internet Survey (WESWS), the obstacles or hurdles in IoT adaptation are identified, as in Figure 4.2 [3]. Around two-thirds of respondents said that interoperability and stability are the main issue. IoT security is therefore the hour-need for today's network media to provide safe and streamlined services in an enterprise web app environment.

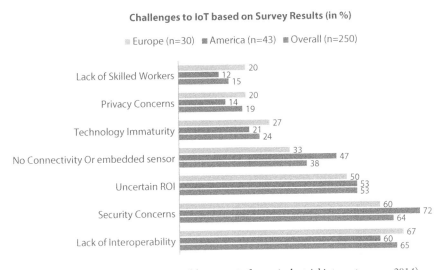

Figure 4.2 Barriers of IoT (Source: world economic forum industrial internet survey, 2014).

4.2   IoT in Healthcare

Most of the developing countries have already been started using smart healthcare. The patient's information is put away on virtual stage so that it very well may be effortlessly gotten to by well-being administrations from anyplace and whenever. As the sensors are being conveyed across nearly territories in clinical gears, this prompts tremendous advantages to the well-being part from IoT.

The challenge of increasing the use of IT frameworks in healthcare is probably security concerns when systems are supposed to have health information [2].

Safety: It belongs to a system which is safe from outside of the framework for deliberate attacks and control. The system includes the information security component. Researchers in [3] mention common healthcare security concerns such as privacy, approval, and honesty.

4.2.1   Confidentiality

Privacy is one of the medical provider's core tasks. The health data are confidential information that must be protected against unauthorized users. The system gives the approved user access to the information and requires the creation of a trusted environment for the patient to seek care. According to the 1997 HIPAA, the patient's health information had to be protected.

4.2.2   Integrity

Keeping e-health record integrity is important because it is used to locate patients and pursue them when moving from one provider to another. In order to decide on patient care, the honesty of information about medical services is required. It delivers precise and unaltered health information throughout the life cycle. It maintains the data precision, consistency, and confidence. Some random numbers are used to monitor data integrity.

4.2.3   Authorization

The EHR system agrees to access the record and store by physicians, thereby enhancing the process of medical recording for an approved user. The organizations of medical services are seeking to alleviate these risks and are responsible for authorization. It is important to mention the access control mechanisms to protect the privacy of the patient. The authorization process is limited to external users. It is a process; the system needs to determine e-health data access privileges.

4.2.4 Availability

The availability is an element that is the property of a framework that allows authorized users to open, use and access a record. It means that, if required by an approved user, then the information is constantly accessible to customers. You must ensure that health records are available through the prevention of interruption to service due to hardware failures, improvements to the framework, and power failures. It is more important than to safeguard the availability of health records.

IoT must have the solution in the health industry:

- Monitor hand hygiene to minimize hospital-acquired infection transmission to patients.
- Providing the core practices for clinicians, headquarters, and billing staff.
- The precise composition of proteins to be analyzed, provided, and supported.
- To allow operations to be asset and optimized, machines, data, and people connected and deployed on the machines.

So as to improve the personal satisfaction, late advances in the advances of WSN have picked up consideration toward different fields like social insurance, amusement, industry, retail, travel, and crisis of the executives. The contextual analysis examines about the social insurance application as it is a developing field. In the ongoing years, human services frameworks run over a difficult issue of the expansion in the number of inhabitants in older individuals and furthermore the cash spent for social insurance issues. Another innovation that meets both quality and moderateness is the need of the day. The highlights, for example, consistent checking with ready instruments and relative data, are added bit of leeway to the social insurance frameworks when WSN advancements are applied. Besides, the WSN advances additionally give a practical arrangement as far as quality and furthermore are more affordable contrasted with other potential innovations [4]. WSN likewise assumes a job in interfacing wearable gadgets. The wearable gadgets can give a constant and close checking of the people with the goal that immaculate well-being status is kept up. At the point when these frameworks are joined to telemedical frameworks, they can caution when an unusual circumstance happens. Such an incorporated wearable gadget centers around long haul checking that assists with following the recuperation and conclusion of medical problems. For instance, patients with heart issues have been found checked effectively with this innovation [4].

Electronic healthcare is patient data that store information on health in digital format. Patient-centered data enables an authorized user to access the data at any time or from anywhere. Annual savings of over $81 billion from the electronic healthcare system. E-healthcare provides increasing social benefits and health benefits and reduced medical errors. The most difficult aspect of improving the use of IT frameworks in healthcare is likely to be security issues when systems are supposed to contain health information. In the health sector, the blockchain is a revolution. Changes in health services may bring about by blockchain. It solves the issue of adapting and building a healthcare system in the healthcare community, pharmaceutical industry, and insurance companies.

The incorporated framework can be utilized for different observing activities, for example, medicate treatment, knee medical procedure, and cerebrum injury recovery [5]. These days, the wearable gadgets have been utilized for straightforward heartbeat screens, to screen everyday exercises [6–8]. A few applications center around fall recognition, area location, and stance discovery. As of late, research works are concentrating to create small sensors to coordinate with certain substances to implant in the body.

4.3   Review of Security and Privacy Innovations for IoT Applications in Healthcare, Smart Cities, and Smart Homes

The rising population of the planet is posing a number of challenges for traditional health systems. The cost of healthcare has increased because of the rising aging population in developed countries. An extension of the age demographic has provided politicians, healthcare professionals, insurance firms, and patients in hospitals with substantial obstacles. Few financial and human capitals are one of the main obstacles for growing millions of people to deliver better healthcare.

This paper [9] sets out a short outline of the nuts and bolts Machine Learning and its standards and calculations submissions. We will begin with a more extensive machine definition study and afterward consolidating various types of getting the hang of including methods administered and uncontrolled and profound learning perfect standards. We will examine usage, in the remainder of the paper, of Machine Learning calculations in various territories including design recognition, sensor systems, identification of irregularities, and the IoT, and checking of well-being.

This paper [10] features a system that incorporates the IoT and some generally utilized AI calculations to make a prescient model that can be utilized to gauge indoor temperature of shrewd structures. This prescient model was prepared to build up practicality to a totally new dataset utilizing online learning system. To approve the methodology, the paper leads a Machine Learning that puts together test with respect to recorded genuine sensor data [11]. The paper at that point recommends that the accompanying procedure ought to be incorporated into an IoT design dependent on edge computing to empower the structure to work in a vitality productive manner.

Arsalon Mohsen Nia *et al.* (2016) [11] gave an inside and outside examination of potential assaults and weaknesses. Mohamed Abomhara *et al.* (2014) [12] gave security dangers and difficulties in IoT. They likewise tended to that there are four interconnected segments, in particular individuals, article, equipment, and programming, which speaks with one another over untrusted private system. Cart Das *et al.* (2016) [13] gave an insightful and inside and outside investigation of future problems in IoT.

Salim Elbouanani [14] demonstrated that there is at present no norm or system which covers all security perspectives in the IoT. They found that confirmation is a genuine test in IoT.

Krishna Kanth Gupta *et al.* (2016) [15] anticipated that there will be 25 billion IoT gadgets by 2020. They likewise recognized difficulties in IoT.

Gurpreet Singh Matharu *et al.* (2014) [16] explained that interoperability; normalization and security are the regions which require a ton of examination so web of things can flourish.

Hui Suo *et al.* (2012) [17] introduced encryption-based methodology to enhance security features in IoT solutions.

C. Flügel *et al.* (2009) [18] introduced a review over a portion of the specialized provokes that should be defeated to assemble such system. L. Atzori *et al.* (2012) [19] promoted the idea of using IoT in social platforms.

IEEE Range 2014 [20] established Java as the prominent design tool for IoT solutions. World Financial Gathering Modern Web Overview (2014) [21] set up a more clear comprehension of the extraordinary chances and new dangers emerging from the industrial internet.

Hammi *et al.* (2018) [22] proposed a unique decentralized framework called air pockets of trust, which guarantees a powerful recognizable proof and verification of gadgets. Authors in [23–25] proposed different blockchain-based solutions for IoT ecosystem.

Javaid *et al.* (2018) [26, 27] introduced a PUF and blockchain-based arrangement called BlockPro for information provenance and information respectability for secure IoT conditions.

M. Anwer *et al.* (2020) [28] proposed course of action of different masters' procedures of blockchain to make IoT check and discussion about their limitations.

Yu *et al.* (2015) [29] introduced distinctive known feeble gadgets to encounter DDOS attack. Zhang *et al.* (2015) [30] showed by various authorities a noteworthy perspective in IoT landscape.

Authors in [31, 32] played out a wide examination on the powerless IoT devices, including thousands of interesting contraptions. A large portion of them were transparently accessible by methods for the internet requiring no unmistakable evidence.

Authors in [33] proposed the idea of checking information so as to permit that information security, just as moving sensor data over the populace. It adds an additional tag to the reality change to guarantee dependent correspondence, with the goal that the distinguishing proof of the client can be secured.

Authors in [34] acquainted one strategy with secure client personality. This strategy is named as zero-information evidence. This strategy gives extraordinary specialists to sender that the individual in question can communicate data so that their character is not unveiled.

Work done in [35] contains a square chain–based IoT structure. This system is likewise fit for ensuring client's personality in heterogeneous system. It likewise encourages encryption and decoding of information on IoT organization.

Authors in [36] have assessed the presentation of a grouping method (K-namelessness) to shroud the area of detecting hubs. This proposed strategy expresses that the information will be gathered from various situations without revealing the area of sensor hubs.

Presently, IPV6 convention will be fundamental for IoT. In any case, IPV6 has some security traps. IPV6 is helpless against Denial-of-Service assault [38]. Authors in [37] proposed a standard-based philosophy to alleviate IPV6 weaknesses. This proposed technique is utilized for assault location. Authors in [39] have additionally proposed an encryption-based strategy. This procedure is appropriate for forestalling Denial-of-Service assault in IPV6.

Cryptography is additionally vital in securing client information in IoT applications identified with social insurance. Work done in [37] gave a productive start to finish key administration plot. This proposed conspiracy is lightweight and it is equipped for performing key trade activity with least assets. This plan gives solid security arrangements utilization of least assets. The vast majority of the overwhelming cryptographic tasks are performed by the outsiders.

Work in [38] talked about all the issues identified with IoT applications in social insurance. At that point, authors proposed a proficient plan. This plan is likewise lightweight. A mix of homomorphism calculation alongside improved DES is utilized.

Authors in [39] have introduced another cryptography-based answer for the given security in various IoT applications in social insurance. This plan utilizes advanced signature, open key cryptography, and timestamps. This plan is more adaptable and exact.

Authors in [40] proposed a cloud-based model for get to control in various human services applications. Plan depends on characteristic-based encryption. It forestalls unapproved access up by and large. It is likewise productive and versatile. Authors have likewise evolved dynamic security arrangements. Authors in [41] likewise proposed a characteristic-based encryption-based structure for get to control in IoT applications. It additionally ensures a further extent of protection of patient's information.

Authors in [42] proposed a symmetric key–based strategy to help security protecting in string coordinating. They built up a proficient and secure ordering plan. This plan is a decent double tree, and made so that lone information identified with watchwords is unveiled to patient and every single other datum is covered up.

Work in [43] proposed an answer. This arrangement utilizes code examination to recognize various weaknesses in the framework. It is guaranteed that the proposed procedure is equipped for recognizing all the weaknesses referenced in NVD. Authors in [44] arranged informational indexes of assaults. At that point, characterization is applied on informational collections. This classifier helps in identifying weaknesses.

Authors in [45] introduced a web crawler. This web crawler utilizes report bunching. It depends on TF-IDF. Authors in [46] presented a source code investigation technique. This strategy depends on the information mining ideas. Scientists in [47] have acquainted new strategies with separate weaknesses in web applications.

Authors in [48] have acquainted a cutting edge technique with identify weaknesses in web apps. It likewise utilizes information mining and static examination of source code. These analysts [49] found that XML infusion is a significant weakness in all web applications. It is additionally found that practically all current web apps experience XML infusion issue.

An assessment has been lead [50] on different International Standards like ISO-27002, OWASP, COBIT, and PCI/DSS, that portray the degree of joining of countermeasures, which center around the security of web applications from the point of view of upsetting web application ambushes dominatingly from code implantations. The producers imparted that the chance of underwriting is huge developed and extensively canvassed in basically all the international standard rules, yet ambushes are at an ascending because of Code combination shortcomings. There is an urgent need to make fashioners and clients mindful of the security checks and to request that they execute the norms warily, in order to confine such assaults.

Examiners in [51] talked about the brisk outcomes of the nonappearance of security and the meaning of huge worth on the thing that improves life cycle and the essential examinations that influence them. Furthermore, the creators have proposed a lot of security robotized instruments and approaches that can be utilized all through the SDLC as a way to deal with improve fundamental electronic applications' security and quality. Additionally, they mentioned that any web improvement alliance should offer preparing and care, on web application prioritization, risk classification, security requirement definition, threat modeling, architecture arrangement audits, secure coding, and post-sending security assessment.

Instead of the information base driver in the SDriver, a middle person was organized [52], the so-called SQLProb (SQL Proxy-based Blocker), which could debilitate the SQL imbuement in web applications, by setting a go-between blocker in the framework. The SQLProb eliminates client responsibility from the application that created demand; in any case, when the client input information has been implanted into the request, it supports the solicitation's syntactic construction made. It asserts client responsibilities by eliminating and adjusting them against huge responsibilities and by utilizing and improving the hereditary check. The SQLProb is a finished revelation approach that does not need adjusting the application or information base code, along these lines keeping up a key decent ways from the multifaceted thought of dirtying, learning, or code instrumentation. Likewise, the information support strategy does not need metadata or learning. The SQLProb is independent of the programming language utilized in the web application. In any case, the impediment of the design is the mix of the center individual framework, which will be the overhead for the web application to ruin the SQL implantation. In like way, it does not strengthen the astounding requests which are semantically correct yet lead to SQL implantation.

Authors in [53] gathered web service estimations into two rule characterizations as assistant estimations and quality estimations. The maker has outlined most of the current web service estimations which are found in the composition. A large portion of the estimations fall all through beneath normal, which joins execution, endures quality and flexibility, and limits life, with the exception of dealing with precision, uprightness, receptiveness, openness, interoperability, and security.

The direct and future effect or seriousness of damages was investigated by researchers in [54]. The producer arranged the ambushes for numerous undeniable classes at the time. They also regularly clustered ambushed mechanical assemblies so that safety authorities can be figured out. They also provided a detailed and structured survey of current devices and frameworks that can improve the two aggressors and the defensive system. For a greater understanding of their capabilities, the manufacturers addressed the positives and detrimental signs of mechanical assemblies.

- Summary of Literature Review

IoT is saving life, saving money, and making treatment available to people in remote areas by predicting the disease through continuous collection of health-related data using smart devices and gadgets and processing this collected data to predict disease in a patient and providing timely treatment. Major challenges to IoT healthcare such as privacy security and identification are also discussed. Authors have provided solutions in parts. These solutions are based on the concept of artificial intelligence, machine learning, blockchain, and cryptography. These solutions provide some sort of privacy and security solutions to various IoT applications. But still, there is a need of a lot of research to address certain issues related to IoT network. These issues are discussed as follows:

- It is found that authentication is a real challenge in IoT. The fact behind this is that appropriate authentication infrastructure is not available in IoT.
- Distribution of keys is another challenge.
- Security is the biggest worry for most industries.
- Man-in-the-middle assault is a serious problem because of the architecture.
- DDOS attack is also a major problem with IoT network. But a universal mitigation plan is not available.
- Vulnerability in IoT device is a dangerous issue. It is needed to be classified and predicted. Vulnerable device is a real threat to IoT network. Such devices are required to be identified.

4.4   Conclusion

IoT is saving lives, saving money, and making treatment available to people in remote areas by predicting the disease through continuous collection of health-related data using smart devices and gadgets and processing this collected data to predict disease in a patient and providing timely treatment. Expectations from IoT healthcare are also elaborated in this chapter. Issues related to IoT are also available based on scientific studies. Major challenges to IoT healthcare such as privacy security and identification are also discussed.

IoT is buzzing everywhere. IoT has established its necessity in many areas of our daily life including healthcare, smart cities, smart homes, smart agriculture, logistics, transportation, education, and various manufacturing industries. But, it is observed that security is a major barrier in adaption of IoT. Security is needed at IoT device level, where data is collected, at network level, where data is transmitted, and at the end at the cloud level, where data is stored. This paper has presented a review of various security and privacy solutions for IoT applications in healthcare, smart cities, and smart homes.

References

1. Gartner, Hyper Cycles Research, 2014, https://www.gartner.com/en/research/methodologies/gartner-hype-cycle
2. Oxford Economics, https://www.oxfordeconomics.com/forecastsand-models/industries/data-and forecasts/global-industry-databank/benefits-and-uses.
3. www3.weforum.org/docs/WEFUSA_IndustrialInternet_Report2015.pdf
4. Kakria, P., Tripathi, N.K., Kitipawang, P., A Real- Time Health Monitoring System for Remote Cardiac Patients Using Smartphone and Wearable Sensors. *Int. J. Telemed. Appl.*, 2015. https://pubmed.ncbi.nlm.nih.gov/26788055
5. Milenkovic, A., Otto, C., Jovanov, E., Wireless sensor networks for personal health monitoring: Issues and an implementation. *Comput. Commun.*, 29, 2521–2533, 2006.
6. Anliker, U., Ward, J.A., Lukowicz, P., Troster, G., Dolveck, F. *et al.*, AMON: a wearable multi- parameter medical monitoring and alert system. *IEEE Trans. Inf. Technol. Biomed.*, 8, 415–27, 2004.
7. Darwish, A. and Hassanien, A.E., Wearable and Implantable Wireless Sensor Network, Solutions for Healthcare Monitoring Sensors. *Sensors,* 12, 12375–12376, 2012.
8. Aminian, M. and Naji, H.R., A Hospital Healthcare Monitoring System Using Wireless Sensor Networks. *J. Health Med. Inform.*, 4, 2, 1–6, 2013.

9. Shanthamallu, U.S., Spanias, A., Tepedelenlioglu, C., Stanley, M., A brief survey of machine learning methods and their sensor and IoT applications. *2017 8th International Conference on Information, Intelligence, Systems & Applications (IISA)*, Sensors, Larnaca, pp. 1–8, 2017.

10. Paul, D., Chakraborty, T., Datta, S.K., Paul, D., IoT and Machine Learning-Based Prediction of Smart Building Indoor Temperature. *2018 4th International Conference on Computer and Information Sciences (ICCOINS)*, Kuala Lumpur, pp. 1–6, 2018.

11. Nia, A.M. and Jha, N.K., Fellow, A Comprehensive Study of Security of Internet of Things. *IEEE Trans. Emerging Top. Comput.*, 5, 4, 586–602, 2016.

12. Abomhara, M. and Køien, G.M., Security and Privacy in the Internet of Things: Current Status and Open Issues. *IEEE Conference on Privacy and Security in Mobile Systems (PRISMS)*, 2014.

13. Das, D. and Sharma, B., General Survey on Security Issues on Internet of Things. *Int. J. Comput. Appl.*, 139, 23–29, 2016.

14. Elbouanani, S. and El Kiram, M.A., Introduction To The Internet Of Things Security Standardization and research challenges. *11th International Conference on Information Assurance and Security*, IEEE, pp. 32–37, 2015.

15. Gupta, K. and Shukla, S., Internet of Things: Security Challenges for Next Generation Networks. *1st International Conference on Innovation and Challenges in Cyber Security*, IEEE, pp. 315–318, 2016.

16. Matharu, G.S., Upadhyay, P., Chaudhary, L., The Internet of Things: Challenges & Security Issues. *International Conference on Emerging Trends*, IEEE, pp. 54–59, 2014.

17. Suo, H. and Wan, J., Security in the Internet of Things: A Review. *International Conference on Computer Science and Electronics Engineering*, IEEE, pp. 648–651, 2012.

18. Flügel, C. and Gehrmann, V., Scientific workshop 4: intelligent objects for the Internet of Things: Internet of Things-application of sensor networks in logistics. *Communications in Computer and Information Science*, vol. 32, pp. 16–26, 2009.

19. Atzori, L., Iera, A., Morabito, G., Nitti, M., The social Internet of Things (SIoT) when social networks meet the Internet of Things: concept, architecture and network characterization. *Comput. Networks*, 56, 16, 3594–3608, 2012.

20. http://spectrum.ieee.org/computing/software/top-10-programming-languages

21. www3.weforum.org/docs/WEFUSA_IndustrialInternet_Report2015.pdf

22. Hammi, M.T. *et al.*, Bubbles of Trust: A decentralized blockchain-based authentication system for IoT. *Comput. Secur.*, 78, 126–142, 2018.

23. Banerjee, M., Lee, J., Choo, K.-K.R., A blockchain future for internet of things security: A position paper. *Digital Commun. Networks*, 4, 3, 149–160, 2018.

24. Khan, M.A. and Salah, K., IoT security: Review, blockchain solutions, and open challenges. *Future Gener. Comput. Syst.*, 82, 395–411, 2018.

25. Agrawal, R., Verma, P., Sonanis, R., Goel, U., De, A., Kondaveeti, S.A., Shekhar, S., Continuous security in IoT using Blockchain, in: *2018 IEEE International Conference on Acoustics, Speech and Signal Processing (ICASSP)*, IEEE, pp. 6423–6427, 2018.

26. Javaid, U., Siang, A.K., Aman, M.N., Sikdar, B., Mitigating IoT Device based DDoS Attacks using Blockchain, in: *Proceedings of the 1st Workshop on Cryptocurrencies and Blockchains for Distributed Systems*, ACM, p. 7176, 2018.

27. Javaid, U., Aman, M.N., Sikdar, B., BlockPro: Blockchain based Data Provenance and Integrity for Secure IoT Environments, in: *Proceedings of the 1st Workshop on Blockchain-enabled Networked Sensor Systems*, ACM, pp. 13–18, 2018.

28. Anwer, M., saad, A., Ashfaque, A., Security of IoT Using Block chain: A Review. *2020 International Conference on Information Science and Communication Technology (ICISCT)*, KARACHI, Pakistan, pp. 1–5, 2020.

29. Yu, T., Sekar, V., Seshan, S., Agarwal, Y., Xu, C., Handling a trillion (unfixable) flaws on a billion devices. *Proceedings of the 14th ACM Workshop on Hot Topics in Networks - HotNets-XIV*, ACM Press, pp. 1–7, 2015.

30. Zhang, Z.-K., Cho, M.C.Y., Shieh, S., Emerging Security Threats and Countermeasures in IoT. *Proceedings of the 10th ACM Symposium on Information, Computer and Communications Security - ASIA CCS '15*, ACM Press, pp. 1–6, 2015.

31. Patton, M., Gross, E., Chinn, R., Forbis, S., Walker, L., Chen, H., Uninvited Connections: A Study of Vulnerable Devices on the Internet of Things (IoT). *IEEE Joint Intelligence and Security Informatics Conference*, IEEE, pp. 232–235, 2014.

32. Airehrour, D., Gutierrez, J., Ray, S.K., Secure routing for internet of things: A survey. *JNCA*, 66, 198–213, 2016.

33. Lazarescu, M.T., Design of a WSN platform for long-term environmental monitoring for IoT applications. *IEEE J. Emerging Sel. Topics Circuits Syst.*, 3, 1, 45–54, 2013.

34. Fleisch, E., What is the Internet of Things? An economic perspective, in: *Economics, Management, and Financial Markets*, no. 2, pp. 125–157, 2010.

35. Chatzigiannakis, I., Pyrgelis, A., Spirakis, P.G., Stamatiou, Y.C., Elliptic curve based zero knowledge proofs and their applicability on resource constrained devices, in: *2011 IEEE Eighth International Conference on Mobile Ad-Hoc and Sensor Systems*, October 2011, pp. 715–720.

36. Henze, M., Hermerschmidt, L., Kerpen, D., Häußling, R., Rumpe, B., Wehrle, K., A comprehensive approach to privacy in the cloud-based internet of things. *Future Gener. Comput. Syst.*, 56, 701–718, 2016.

37. Abdmeziem, M.R. and Tandjaoui, D., A cooperative end to end key management scheme for e-health applications in the context of internet of things, in: *Ad-hoc Networks and Wireless*, pp. 35–46, Springer, Berlin Heidelberg, 2014.

38. Gong, T., Huang, H., Li, P., Zhang, K., Jiang, H., A Medical Healthcare System for Privacy Protection Based on IoT, in: *Proceedings of the 7th International Symposium on Parallel Architectures, Algorithms, and Programming, PAAP '15*, December 2015, pp. 217–222.

39. Hu, J.-X., Chen, C.-L., Fan, C.-L., Wang, K.-H., An intelligent and secure health monitoring scheme using IoT sensor based on cloud computing. *J. Sens.*, 2017, Article ID 3734764, 11 pages, 2017.

40. Lounis, A., Hadjidj, A., Bouabdallah, A., Challal, Y., Healing on the cloud: secure cloud architecture for medical wireless sensor networks. *Future Gener. Comput. Syst.*, 55, 266–277, 2016.

41. Li, M., Yu, S., Zheng, Y., Scalable and secure sharing of personal health records in cloud computing using attribute- based encryption. *IEEE Trans. Parallel Distrib. Syst.*, 24, 1, 131–143, 2012.

42. Bezawada, B., Liu, A.X., Jayaraman, B., Wang, A.L., Li, R., Privacy Preserving String Matching for Cloud Computing, in: *Proceedings of the 35th IEEE International Conference on Distributed Computing Systems, ICDCS '15*, July 2015, pp. 609–618.

43. Li, Z. *et al.*, VulPecker: an automated vulnerability detection system based on code similarity analysis. *ACM, Proc. of the 32 Annual Conference on Computer Security Applications*, p. 201213, 2016.

44. Uwagbole, S.O., Buchanan, W.J., Fan, L., Applied machine learning predictive analytics to SQL injection attack detection and prevention. *Symposium on Integrated Network and Service Management (IM), 2017 IFIP/IEEE*, IEEE, pp. 1087–1090, 2017.

45. Guojun, Z., Design and application of intelligent dynamic crawler for web data mining, in: *Automation (YAC), 2017 32nd Youth Academic Annual Conference of Chinese Association*, IEEE, pp. 1098–1105, 2017.

45. Medeiros, I., Neves, N., Correia, M., Detecting and removing web application vulnerabilities with static analysis and data mining, IEEE. *IEEE Trans. Reliab.*, 65, 1, 54–69, 2016.

47. Masood, A. and Java, J., Static Analysis for Web Service Security – Tools & Techniques for a Secure Development Life Cycle. *International Symposium on Technologies for Homeland Security*, pp. 1–6, 2015.

48. Medeiros, I. and Neves, N., Detecting and Removing Web Application Vulnerabilities with Static Analysis and Data Mining. *IEEE Transactions on Reliability*, pp. 1–16, 2015.

49. Salas, M., II, de Geus, P.L., Martins, E., Security Testing Methodology for Evaluation of Web Services Robustness - Case: XMLInjection. *IEEE World Congress on Services*, pp. 303–310, 2015.

50. Madan, S., Security Standards Perspective to Fortify Web Database Applications from Code Injection Attacks. *International Conference on Intelligent Systems, Modeling and Simulation*, pp. 226–233, 2010.

51. Teodoro, N. and Serrao, C., Web application security: Improving critical web-based applications quality through in-depth security analysis, in:

International Conference on Information Society (i-Society), pp. 457–462, 2011.

52. Liu, A., Yuan, Y., Wijesekera, D., Stavrou, A., SQLProb: a proxy based architecture towards preventing SQL injection attacks, in: *Proceedings ACM Symposium on Applied Computing (SAC'09)*, pp. 2054–2061, 2009.

53. Ladan, M.I., Web Services Metrics: A Survey and A Classification. *J. Commun. Comput.*, 9, 7, 824–829, 2012.

54. Hoque, N., Bhuyan, M.H., Baishya, R.C., Bhattacharyya, D.K., Kalita, Network Attacks: Taxonomy, tools and systems. *J. Comput. Netw. Appl.*, 40, 307–324, 2013, http://dx.doi.org/10.1016/j.jnca.2013.08.001.4

5

Methods of Lung Segmentation Based on CT Images

Amit Verma* and Thipendra P. Singh

School of Computer Science, UPES, Dehradun, Uttarakhand, India

Abstract

Considering the ground truth of most of the hospitals, today, also the doctors are manually observing the computed tomography (CT) images of lungs based on their experience and knowledge. CT images of lungs have major applications in the analysis of functioning, structure, and many more information about the pulmonary images. Lung airways, parenchyma of lungs, and breathing mechanism are majorly analyzed on the basis of CT images. So, for better analysis and to avoid manual method of analysis of CT images by the doctor, automatic and almost accurate analysis of CT images is very important for better diagnosis for any lung problem. In this chapter, automatic and semi-automatic methods of segmentation of lungs CT images are discussed.

Keywords: Segmentation, CT image, machine learning, medical image, lung, seed pixel, knowledge-based

5.1 Introduction

Image segmentation is the process of dividing an image into multiple parts according to the interest, as it is less efficient to analyze the whole image despite analyzing the interesting part of the image only. Segmentation helps to analyze the particular area of the image in a much better way [1]. The main objective of any segmentation technique is to make images more informative and useful for the analyst.

Corresponding author: amit.uptu2006@gmail.com

Rohit Tanwar, S. Balamurugan, R. K. Saini, Vishal Bharti and Premkumar Chithaluru (eds.) *Advanced Healthcare Systems: Empowering Physicians with IoT-Enabled Technologies*, (59–68) © 2022 Scrivener Publishing LLC

Therefore, segmentation plays a vital role in investigating the pulmonary computed tomography (CT) image, which provides high-resolution images of lungs depending on the hardware used. Pulmonary CT image can be considered as a compulsory precursor for the analysis of any lung disorder related to functional tissues of lungs, analysis of lung airways, and the functioning of diaphragm and lungs in the breathing process [2–6].

Pulmonary CT images are manually visualized by the doctors to get the information about the anatomy of the lungs of a patient and this manual analysis is a tedious process. So, there is a great need for automatic and accurate analysis of CT images for better diagnosis of the patient. This requires pulmonary CT image segmentation to get information about the particular portion of the image. Multiple semi-automated and automated methods have been developed for segmenting the pulmonary CT images. These methods are based on region growing process [9–11], which include the selection of seed pixels and adjust pixels are compared on the basis of threshold. If the value of the pixel lies within the range of the threshold, then the particular pixel is considered with in the region. The major difference in semi-automatic and fully automatic approach of performing lung (or other organ) segmentation is the selection of seeds and threshold value. In case of fully automatic methods, optimal threshold value is selected automatically [29]. Whereas in semi-automatic methods, seed pixels and threshold values are selected with manual interaction [7, 8]. Some of the methods of lung segmentation in pulmonary CT images have been discussed in this chapter.

5.2   Semi-Automated Algorithm for Lung Segmentation

In this topic, some state-of-the-art methods for segmenting lung CT images, which can have human intervention, are discussed.

5.2.1   Algorithm for Tracking to Lung Edge

The algorithm for segmenting the left and right lung in the CT image consists of mainly four steps [8], as shown in the flow diagram in Figure 5.1.

For calculating the center of mass M, all pixels of CT images within the threshold of range −800 to −500 are determined for both rights and left lung. Now, starting point S is determined concerning M as an outermost point of the lung contour, that is, S can be considered on the boundary of the lung as shown in Figure 5.2. Further, for tracing the lung contour

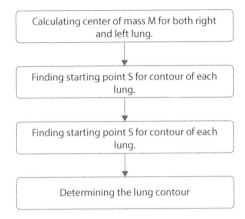

Figure 5.1 Flow of step for semi-automated way of segmenting both the lungs in CT image.

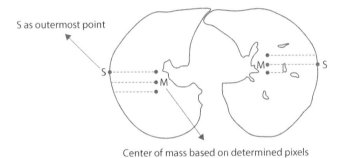

Figure 5.2 The positions of S and M.

separate for both right and left lung, the standard algorithm has been used, in which starting from point S, three adjacent pixels are determined in the searching direction and pixel values are compared with a threshold value, T. The first pixel with a value less than T is considered as the next contour pixel. If the first among the three neighbor pixels find to be the contour point, then we change the search direction to the right. If all the three neighboring pixels are having values greater than T, then the search direction would be changed to left. In the rest of the cases, the direction of the search remains the same. In all the above three steps, humans can intervene in determining seed pixel for the algorithm if considering S or M as a starting point for finding the lung contour algorithm is not giving a better result. Even if the operator wants to include or exclude any particular region in the CT image, the operator can draw lines that will not be crossed by the algorithm in segmenting the right and left lung.

After determining the pixels belonging to the lung contour, the rest of the pixels are erased from the image to get more information about the interesting region.

5.2.2   Outlining the Region of Interest in CT Images

Manually outlining the region of interest in CT image by using some graphical tool always depends on the effort and working experience of the operator. This process is slow and tedious for the operator and more dependent on the quality or resolution of the CT image to outline the informative area by the operator. So, there is a great requirement to automate with or without human interaction the process of outlining the interesting area. This method is based on segmenting the CT image using the region growing method that is starting from seed pixels and growing the region based on similar characteristics [9–11]. This method is divided into three processes that are locating the region of interest, identifying the seed pixels on the boundary of the region, and finding the next outline point from the seed pixels [12].

5.2.2.1   Locating the Region of Interest

Here, the properties are decided (world model) based on which the region is located in the CT image. Based on this world model, the pixel is considered to belong to the region if it falls within the decided threshold range (upper and lower). So, for finding the lung outline in the CT image, the associated CT number of the pixel should satisfy the world model to be considered within the region of interest.

5.2.2.2   Seed Pixels and Searching Outline

Here, the selection of the seed pixels can be automatic or interactive, four pixels are identified on the lung boundary, and the search moves toward the center of the region. The search is carried out in four directions that are top to bottom, bottom to top, left to right, and vice versa as shown in Figures 5.3a and 3b. Here, the motive is to identify the seed pixels within the area of interest to be outlined. If the interactive mode is adopted, then the seed pixels are identified by the operator and assumed to lie within the world model. Now, the pixels are examined in four directions as mention above until the boundary of the region is identified (transition) based on the difference in the threshold.

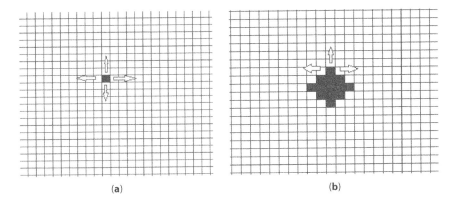

Figure 5.3 (a) Searching in four directions. (b) Region growing based on seed.

5.3   Automated Method for Lung Segmentation

This section contains an overview of the fully automatic methods for performing organ segmentation based on the CT images dataset.

5.3.1   Knowledge-Based Automatic Model for Segmentation

To study the anatomy of the lungs, manual CT images are segmented for measuring spleen volume [13], finding the variation in the lung attenuation [14] and tumors [15] which require the efforts of operators. To improve the process of CT image segmentation, various semi-automatic methods were also proposed, which are majorly based on the thresholding. For the identification of various functional tissues, pixels are clustered based on the specified threshold range using gray-level CT images [16–19]. The threshold range can be manually set [20] or can be specified automatically based on some parameters. Further, pixel-based 2D/3D region growing–based semi-automated approach of segmentation of CT images [2, 21–23] was also followed. In this section, fully automated method of CT image segmentation has been discussed. A knowledge-based system has been developed for pixel-based automatic segmentation of CT images, and the structure knowledge is used to guide the segmentation algorithm for better results [24]. By the term knowledge, we mean the anatomical information which includes the organ size, shape, volume, and position for performing organ segmentation based on pulmonary CT images [25, 26]. The system has used an external knowledge-based model, interface engine, and image processing connected with the blackboard [27] for controlled interaction.

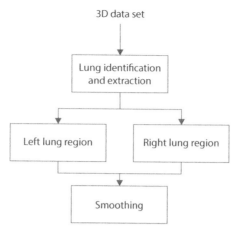

Figure 5.4 Step for lung segmentation using CT images.

5.3.2   Automatic Method for Segmenting the Lung CT Image

In this method, both the lungs that are right and left have been identified in the CT images. The approach is based on three major steps that are identifying the outline of lungs based on thresholding over CT images, detecting the connecting tissues (junction) of lungs for separating the right and left lung and smoothing [28]. As many methods discussed previously have used an interactive way of selecting the fixed threshold value for segmenting the image, in this approach, optimal threshold value is selected automatically [29]. A brief overview of the process for segmenting the lung in the CT image is shown in Figure 5.4.

For extracting the lung from the CT image, 3D datasets have been used and the optimal threshold value is selected automatically for separating the region of interest from the background.

5.4   Advantages of Automatic Lung Segmentation Over Manual and Semi-Automatic Methods

Manually identifying the organ and anatomical structure from a CT image is tedious work for an operator which requires a very good experience and potential. Based on the CT image, operator used to identify the region of interest to see the disorder (if applicable) in the functioning of the organ. Moreover, to reduce the work of the operator, to improve the efficiency, and to improve the accuracy of the results, various researchers propose semi-automatic methods for segmenting the region of interest from CT image. In this semi-automatic approach, the operator has to only decide the outline pixels using some graphical tools, and the interested region gets segmented automatically. These methods have remarkably reduces the work of the operator and improve the accuracy of results so that doctors can diagnose the patient in a much better way instead of wasting time in doing manual analysis of CT images. The process further improved with the contribution of various automatic methods in which the seed and optimal threshold selection are done automatically without any interaction of the operator. The organs can be automatically segmented in the CT images for doctors to take much better decisions and follow a better diagnosis process.

5.5 Conclusion

In this chapter, we discuss the ways and importance of analyzing the CT images using the segmentation process. The segmenting of the organs in the CT images is the process of separating the organ region in the CT image from the background. Much work has been done in the field of CT image segmentation, broadly, which can be categorized into two main categories: semi-automatic and fully automatic approach of segmentation. These approaches are used by various researchers in segmenting the CT images of various organs; in this chapter, we mainly consider the pulmonary images. The importance of automatic and accurate segmentation of regions of interest in CT images is also discussed in the chapter.

References

1. Khan, W., Image segmentation techniques: A survey. *J. Image Graph.*, *1*, 4, 166–170, 2013.
2. Hedlund, L.W., Anderson, R.F., Goulding, P.L., Beck, J.W., Effmann, E.L., Putman, C.E., Two methods for isolating the lung area of a CT scan for density information. *Radiology*, *144*, 2, 353–357, 1982.
3. Uppaluri, R., Mitsa, T., Sonka, M., Hoffman, E.A., McLennan, G., Quantification of pulmonary emphysema from lung CT images using texture analysis. *Am. J. Respir. Crit. Care Med.*, *156*, 248–254, 1997.
4. Amirav, I. S. R. A. E. L., Kramer, S.S., Grunstein, M.M., Hoffman, E.A., Assessment of methacholine-induced airway constriction by ultrafast high-resolution computed tomography. *J. Appl. Physiol.*, *75*, 5, 2239–2250, 1993.

5. Shojaii, R., Alirezaie, J., Babyn, P., Automatic lung segmentation in CT images using watershed transform, in: *IEEE International Conference on Image Processing 2005*, 2005, September, vol. 2, IEEE, pp. II–1270.

6. Hoffman, E.A., Behrenbeck, T. H. O. M. A. S., Chevalier, P.A., Wood, E.H., Estimation of regional pleural surface expansile forces in intact dogs. *J. Appl. Physiol.*, 55, 3, 935–948, 1983.

7. Boriek, A.M., Liu, S. H. A. O. B. O., Rodarte, J.R., Costal diaphragm curvature in the dog. *J. Appl. Physiol.*, 75, 2, 527–533, 1993.

8. Pavlidis, T., *Algorithms for graphics and image processing*, Springer Science & Business Media, Springer-Verlag, Berlin Heidelberg, 2012.

9. Rosenfeld, A., *Digital picture processing*, Academic press, Morgan Kaufmann Publishers Inc., San Francisco CA United States, 1976.

10. Gonzalez, R.C. and Wintz, P., *Digital image processing*, Reading, Mass., Addison-Wesley Publishing Co., Inc, *Appl. Math. Comput.*, Addison-Wesley Longman Publishing Co., Inc. 75 Arlington Street, Suite 300 Boston, MAUnited States, 13, 451, 1977.

11. Nevatia, R. and Price, K.E., Locating structures in aerial images. *IEEE Trans. Pattern Anal. Mach. Intell.*, 4, 5, 476–484, 1982.

12. Keller, J.M., Edwards, F.M., Rundle, R., Automatic outlining of regions on CT scans. *J. Comput. Assisted Tomogr.*, 5, 2, 240–245, 1981.

13. Breiman, R.S., Beck, J.W., Korobkin, M., Glenny, R., Akwari, O.E., Heaston, D.K., Ram, P.C., Volume determinations using computed tomography. *Am. J. Roentgenol.*, 138, 2, 329–333, 1982.

14. Robinson, P.J. and Kreel, L., Pulmonary tissue attenuation with computed tomography: comparison of inspiration and expiration scans. *J. Comput. Assisted Tomogr.*, 3, 6, 740–748, 1979.

15. Ettinger, D.S., Leichner, P.K., Siegelman, S.S., Fishman, E.K., Klein, J.L., Order, S.E., Computed tomography assisted volumetric analysis of primary liver tumor as a measure of response to therapy. *Am. J. Clin. Oncol.*, 8, 5, 413–418, 1985.

16. Pache, J.C., Roberts, N., Vock, P., Zimmermann, A., Cruz-Orive, L.M., Vertical LM sectioning and parallel CT scanning designs for stereology: application to human lung. *J. Microsc.*, 170, 1, 9–24, 1993.

17. Rössner, S., Bo, W.J., Hiltbrandt, E., Hinson, W., Karstaedt, N., Santago, P., Crouse, J.R., Adipose tissue determinations in cadavers–a comparison between cross-sectional planimetry and computed tomography. *Int. J. Obes.*, 14, 10, 893–902, 1990.

18. Borkan, G.A., Gerzof, S.G., Robbins, A.H., Hults, D.E., Silbert, C.K., Silbert, J.E., Assessment of abdominal fat content by computed tomography. *Am. J. Clin. Nutr.*, 36, 1, 172–177, 1982.

19. Archer, D.C., Coblentz, C.L., Dekemp, R.A., Nahmias, C., Norman, G., Automated *in vivo* quantification of emphysema. *Radiology*, 188, 3, 835–838, 1993.

20. Pfefferbaum, A., Zatz, L.M., Jernigan, T.L., Computer-interactive method for quantifying cerebrospinal fluid and tissue in brain CT scans: effects of aging. *J. Comput. Assisted Tomogr.*, *10*, 4, 571–578, 1986.

21. Denison, D.M., Morgan, M.D., Millar, A.B., Estimation of regional gas and tissue volumes of the lung in supine man using computed tomography. *Thorax*, *41*, 8, 620–628, 1986.

22. Hoffman, E.A., Sinak, L.J., Robb, R.A., Ritman, E.L., Noninvasive quantitative imaging of shape and volume of lungs. *J. Appl. Physiol.*, *54*, 5, 1414–1421, 1983.

23. Olson, L.E. and Hoffman, E.A., Lung volumes and distribution of regional air content determined by cine X-ray CT of pneumonectomized rabbits. *J. Appl. Physiol.*, *76*, 4, 1774–1785, 1994.

24. Brown, M.S., Mcnitt-Gray, M.F., Mankovich, N.J., Goldin, J.G., Hiller, J., Wilson, L.S., Aberie, D.R., Method for segmenting chest CT image data using an anatomical model: preliminary results. *IEEE Trans. Med. Imaging*, *16*, 6, 828–839, 1997.

25. Sonka, M., Sundaramoorthy, G., Hoffman, E.A., Knowledge-based segmentation of intrathoracic airways from multidimensional high-resolution CT images, in: *Medical imaging 1994: physiology and function from multidimensional images*, vol. 2168, pp. 73–85, International Society for Optics and Photonics, Newport Beach, CA, United States, 1994, May.

26. Kanazawa, K., Kubo, M., Niki, N., Satoh, H., Ohmatsu, H., Eguchi, K., Moriyama, N., Computer aided screening system for lung cancer based on helical CT images, in: *International Conference on Visualization in Biomedical Computing*, Springer, Berlin, Heidelberg, pp. 223–228, 1996, September.

27. Nii, H.P., The blackboard model of problem solving and the evolution of blackboard architectures. *AI Mag.*, *7*, 2, 38–38, 1986.

28. Hu, S., Hoffman, E.A., Reinhardt, J.M., Automatic lung segmentation for accurate quantitation of volumetric X-ray CT images. *IEEE Trans. Med. Imaging*, *20*, 6, 490–498, 2001.

29. Sonka, M., Hlavac, V., Boyle, R., *Image processing, analysis, and machine vision*, Nelson Education, Springer US, 2014.

6

Handling Unbalanced Data in Clinical Images

Amit Verma

School of Computer Science, UPES, Dehradun, Uttarakhand, India

Abstract

Manual detection of abnormalities accurately in the clinical images like MRIs by the operators is tedious work that requires good experience and knowledge, specifically manually segmenting the brain tumor in the MRI for further diagnosis by the doctor. So, multiple automatic and semi-automatic approaches were developed to automate the process of segmenting the malignant area of the tumor. The major problem which arises to train the model for automatic segmentation of clinical images is the imbalanced data set. An imbalanced clinical data set means the healthy tissues are always far greater than the cancerous tissues. This difference between the majority and minority data in the data sets reduces or adversely affects the accuracy of predicting model due to biased training data sets. So, it becomes a major concern for the various researchers to balance the data before using it to train a particular prediction model, and various data-level and algorithm-level–based approaches were developed to balance the imbalance data for improving the accuracy of the trained model. In this chapter, the concept and problem of imbalanced data are discussed and various approaches for balancing the data are also highlighted in which one of the state-of-the-art method bagging is discussed in detail.

Keywords: Bagging, unbalanced data, boosting, MRI, deep learning, medical, brain tumor

Email: amit.uptu2006@gmail.com

Rohit Tanwar, S. Balamurugan, R. K. Saini, Vishal Bharti and Premkumar Chithaluru (eds.) Advanced Healthcare Systems: Empowering Physicians with IoT-Enabled Technologies, (69–80) © 2022 Scrivener Publishing LLC

6.1 Introduction

Magnetic Resonance Images (MRIs) play a vital role in detecting brain tumors; in India, it is a fast-growing disorder and mainly in children [1]. In India, Glioblastoma Multiforme (GBM), Meningioma, Astrocytoma, etc., are some of the most common categories of a malignant brain tumor [2–6]. MRIs are clinical images that can be considered pre-diagnosis for any patient with brain abnormality in size, functioning, detecting tumor, or anatomy. MR imaging allows operators to take brain pictures on various radio frequencies for better analysis of the area of interest [7]. But it always remains a challenging task to manually segment the brain tumor due to its uneven or irregular size and shape [33, 34]. Operators manually segment the tumor size using some graphical tools to make the report, and further, the doctor manually analyzes the MRI based on the report of the operator for diagnosis. Semi-automatic and automatic segmentation of MRI remains a matter of concern for various researchers, and many state-of-the-art methods [8–15] have been developed to automate the procedure of segmenting the brain tumor on MR images with higher accuracy so that doctor can diagnose the patient in a much better way. The most common problem for applying machine learning or deep learning to train the model for automating the process of segmenting MR images is imbalanced data.

Imbalanced data means when the data is biased to one or more specific class [16, 17], let say an MRI of the brain with malignant tumor will have far more pixels representing the healthy tissues than the cancerous one. Therefore, the model, directly train based on MRI images with such data, will get biased toward the healthy tissues and can predict cancerous tissues as healthy. The imbalanced data set trained model drastically decreases the performance of the predictor, and the class imbalance is one of the common problems in segmenting the clinical images (MRIs). For solving the problem of imbalanced data set, many algorithm-level and data-level–based methods were introduced. The approach of data-level–based methods is to re-sampling and under-sampling of a positive and negative class of data [18, 19]. Whereas in algorithm-level–based methods [20–22], modifications were done in learning algorithm to handle imbalanced data in learning data set to train the predictor. Cluster-based under-sampling [23] is one of the state-of-the-art methods under data-level–based methods for handling imbalanced data. Bagging (Bootstrap aggregating) [24] is one of the most popular approaches for handling the problem of imbalanced data, which is an algorithm-based technique.

In this chapter, the problem of imbalanced data and the consequences of training the model based on imbalanced data are explained in simple language. Further, two main approaches that are cluster-based and bagging considering the clinical data are discussed. The objective of this chapter is to make the reader understand the problem of imbalanced data in segmenting the MR images mainly for brain tumor detection and to get the knowledge about the two state-of-the-art methods for solving the problem of making a biased model.

6.2   Handling Imbalance Data

The problem of class imbalance is one of the major concerns in segmenting the clinical images majorly like segmenting the brain tumor. As the data sets containing the spatial resolution information based on the MRIs of the brain with tumor mostly have large data (pixels) representing the healthy tissues of the brain as compare to the malignant area. In simple words, Figures 6.1 and 6.2 represent the distribution of imbalanced and balanced data over a 2D graph [25]. As we can see that blue dots which are in majority in Figure 6.1 can be considered as pixels representing the healthy tissues and red dots representing the cancerous ones, and blue dots are far more than red which is representing the biased data for creating the predictor model. So, the trained model based on imbalanced data will have low accuracy and can misclassify the cancerous tissue as health which could be more costly for the patient than the wrong classification of healthy tissue as cancerous [26]. So, it is important to balance the data before using it for training the model. The example of balanced data is shown in Figure 6.2 where blue dots representing the healthy tissues are almost the same as the malignant tissues represented by red dots. A variety of state-of-the-art methods have been developed to improve the efficiency of the predictor model by correcting the problem of imbalanced data. Majorly, the overall work by various researchers for balancing the data set can be classified into two main categories that are performing over-sampling or under-sampling on the data that is called at data-level–based technique [18], and modifying the learning algorithm according to the biased data is called the algorithm-level–based technique [19]. Some of the notified approaches under data-level–based techniques are random cluster–based under-sampling [27], random over-sampling–based method [28], SMOTE [29], and MSMOTE [30], and major algorithm-level–based techniques are bootstrap aggregation method [24], boosting approach [31], and adaptive

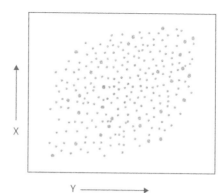

Figure 6.1 Typical example of imbalanced data.

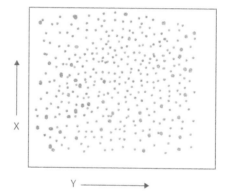

Figure 6.2 Typical example of balanced data.

booting [32], which are some of the notable techniques for handling the imbalance data. Cluster-based under-sampling and bagging are discussed in detail in the following subsections.

6.2.1   Cluster-Based Under-Sampling Technique

Classification of a class is the process of predicting the class for unknown data with the help of trained model; it is well-known technique in machine learning [37–39]. Classifier is trained with the training data set and the hypotheses model is prepared to get the result for some new inputs. There are vast application of classification analysis. Any classification model broadly involve four major steps that are collection of sample data, distribute the data in training data and testing data keeping in mind that training data instances should always be greater than the testing data, train the model using training data, and now model is ready to predict the result for some new data. But the major concern is always the accuracy of the predictor model which majorly depends on the uniformity of the training samples. If the training data is not uniform, this means uniform distribution of labeled data than the model (predictor) could be get biased toward majority data. This arises the problem of imbalance class distribution.

For balancing the data, under-sampling approach is adopted by many researchers for its better accuracy as compare to the over-sampling approach. Considering the data of brain tumor MR images for segmenting the malignant part in the image. Assuming that HT is the majority data of healthy tissue in the data set and MT, the data with minority data represent the malignant tissues. Now to maintain the uniformity in the data, HT is randomly divided into several subsets of data as shown below.

$HT = \{HT_{0, HT1} \dots HT_n\}$, where $n \in N$, N is the set of natural numbers.

The number of distributed subsets depends on the variance between the size of HT and MT; let the size of HT be H and the size of MT be L. Then, the number of subsets would be S according to the equation below.

$$S = \frac{H}{L}$$

where

$S = \{S_0, S_1 \dots S_m\}$, where $m \in N$, N is the set of natural numbers.

With each subset, L will be concatenated.

$S_f = \{S_i \cup L\}$, where $i \rightarrow \{N\}$, N is the set of natural numbers.

For example, if $H = 1,000$ and $L = 10$, then the recommended number of subsets S would be 100 and with each set S_i, L would be concatenated for final set S_f.

Now, the data is balanced and can be used to train the predictor using any modeling technique for segmenting the brain tumor in the MR images.

For more detailed specification, let the total size of the data D be 1,100 in which HT = 1,000 and MT = 100. Now, we make four clusters of the data

Table 6.1 Cluster distribution.

Cluster ID	HT	MT	$S_i = HT_i/MT_i$
1	300	30	10
2	300	30	10
3	200	20	20
4	200	20	10

set D as shown in Table 6.1, showing the data in majority HT and minority MT data sets.

Now, according to the equation below, the majority samples are selected randomly and concatenated with the minority sample for final data sets to train the model [40].

$$S_K^{HT} = (m * MT) * S_i / \sum_{i=0}^{k} S_i$$

where m is the ratio of HT:MT and k is the total number of clusters. So, the final number of majority data sample to be selected in each cluster and concatenated with the minority samples are shown in Table 6.2.

Now, each cluster with the majority sample is concatenated with minority samples MT.

$$S_f = \sum_{i=0}^{k} \{HT_i, MT\}$$

Table 6.2 Numbers of majority sample in each cluster.

Cluster ID	HT_i
1	1 * 100 * 10 / (10 + 10 + 20 + 20) = 17
2	1 * 100 * 10 / (10 + 10 + 20 + 20) = 17
3	1 * 100 * 10 / (10 + 10 + 20 + 20) = 34
4	1 * 100 * 10 / (10 + 10 + 20 + 20) = 34

With the above equation, we get the final balanced data set to train the model for the prediction.

6.2.2   Bootstrap Aggregation (Bagging)

Bagging [24] is one of the notable algorithm-level–based approaches for handling unbalanced data, majorly used for clinical data such as MRI data of brain tumor segmentation. For classifying the tissues with higher accuracy, considering the BRATS2015 data set [35] tissues can be segmented as either healthy or cancerous with four different categories. The four different categories (labeled) of malignant tissues are edema, non-enhancing (solid), non-enhancing (core), and necrotic [36]. Bagging technique can be used with imbalanced data D for better classification accuracy. In the process of bagging, multiple data sets {d1, d2, ..., dm} are dragged from the given unbalanced data D as shown in Figure 6.3, and in each data set, data is randomly drawn from the data D with replacement. By the term with replacement, we mean that already drawn elements from D can be drawn again. It is recommended that training instances in data sets should be 60% of training instances in D. Now, on various data sets from d1 to dm, training models either same or different are applied on their data sets. Each model gives an output from y1 to ym, and an average of all outputs are taken for better accuracy or the process of voting is adopted to get the class of data, which is given as output by a maximum number of models.

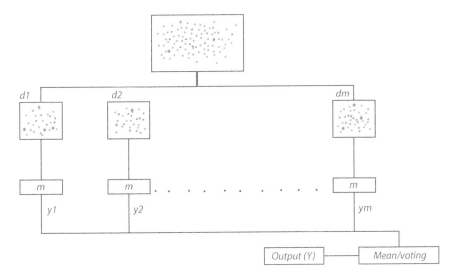

Figure 6.3 The process of bootstrap aggregation.

Bagging is more effective with unstable models like classification and linear regression as in unstable procedures small changes in D can result in a larger change in the predictor model, whereas bagging degrades the performance with the stable procedure like k-nearest neighbor method.

6.3   Conclusion

In this chapter, we discuss the importance of balancing the imbalanced data and how the model trained using imbalance data can affect the performance of the predictor. Imbalanced data is the common and major problem with clinical data like the MRI data for brain tumor segmentation. Considering the problem of imbalanced data, data with the high variance between the majority and minority data. In the case of MRI data for brain tumor segmentation, data representing the healthy tissues are mostly always much higher than the data representing the malignant tissues. So, for making a predictor model to automatic segmentation, the balancing of data is required. The process of bagging is discussed in the chapter for handling imbalanced data.

References

1. Hndu, Over 2,500 indian kids suffer from brain tumour every year, The Hindu, New Delhi, India, 2018, www.thehindu.com/sci-tech/health/Over-2500-Indian-kids-suffer-from-brain-tumour-every-year/article14418512.ece (2018). LastAccessed: June 2019.
2. Drevelegas, A. and Nasel, C., *Imaging of brain tumors with histological correlations*, Springer Science & Business Media, New York, 2010.
3. Dupont, C., Betrouni, N., Reyns, N., Vermandel, M., On image segmentation methods applied to glioblastoma: state of art and new trends. *IRBM*, 37, 3, 131–143, 2016.
4. Bauer, S., Wiest, R., Nolte, L.P., Reyes, M., A survey of mri-based medical image analysis for brain tumor studies. *Phys. Med. Biol.*, 58, 13, R97, 2013.
5. Menze, B.H., Jakab, A., Bauer, S., Kalpathy-Cramer, J., Farahani, K., Kirby, J., Burren, Y., Porz, N., Slotboom, J., Wiest, R. *et al.*, The multimodal brain tumor image segmentation benchmark (brats). *IEEE Trans. Med. Imaging*, 34, 10, 1993–2024, 2015.
6. Mohan, G. and Subashini, M.M., Mri based medical image analysis: survey on brain tumor grade classification. *Biomed. Signal Process. Control*, 39, 139–161, 2018.
7. Drevelegas, A. and Nasel, C., *Imaging of brain tumors with histological correlations*, Springer Science & Business Media, New York, 2010.

8. Agn, M., Puonti, O., Law, I., af Rosenschöld, P., van Leemput, K., Brain tumor segmentation by a generative model with a prior on tumor shape, in: *Proceeding of the multimodal brain tumor image segmentation challenge*, pp. 1–4, 2015.

9. Corso, J.J., Sharon, E., Dube, S., El-Saden, S., Sinha, U., Yuille, A., Efficient multilevel brain tumor segmentation with integrated bayesian model classification. *IEEE Trans. Med. Imaging*, 27, 5, 629–640, 2008.

10. Menze, B.H., Van Leemput, K., Lashkari, D., Weber, M.A., Ayache, N., Golland, P., A generative model for brain tumor segmentation in multimodal images, in: *International conference on medical image computing and computer-assisted intervention*, Springer, pp. 151–159, 2010.

11. Prastawa, M., Bullitt, E., Ho, S., Gerig, G., A brain tumor segmentation framework based on outlier detection. *Med. Image Anal.*, 8, 3, 275–283, 2004.

12. Bauer, S., Nolte, L.P., Reyes, M., Fully automatic segmentation of brain tumor images using support vector machine classification in combination with hierarchical conditional random field regularization, in: *International conference on medical image computing and computer-assisted intervention*, Springer, pp. 354–361, 2011.

13. Hamamci, A., Kucuk, N., Karaman, K., Engin, K., Unal, G., Tumor-cut: segmentation of brain tumors on contrast enhanced mr images for radiosurgery applications. *IEEE Trans. Med. Imaging*, 31, 3, 790–804, 2012.

14. Lun, T. and Hsu, W., Brain tumor segmentation using deep convolutional neural network, in: *Proceedings of BRATS-MICCAI*, 2016.

15. Pratondo, A., Chui, C.K., Ong, S.H., Integrating machine learning with region-based active contour models in medical image segmentation. *J. Vis. Commun. Image Represent.*, 43, 1–9, 2017.

16. He, H. and Garcia, E.A., Learning from imbalanced data. *IEEE Trans. Knowl. Data Eng.*, 21, 9, 1263–1284, 2009.

17. López, V., Fernández, A., García, S., Palade, V., Herrera, F., An insight into classification with imbalanced data: Empirical results and current trends on using data intrinsic characteristics. *Inf. Sci.*, 250, 113–141, 2013.

18. Shelton, C.R., Balancing multiple sources of reward in reinforcement learning, in: *Advances in Neural Information Processing Systems*, T.K. Leen, T.G. Dietterich, V. Tresp (Eds.), vol. 13, pp. 1082–1088, MIT Press, Cambridge, MA, USA, 2001.

19. Jang, J., Eo, T., Kim, M. *et al.*, Medical image matching using variable randomized undersampling probability pattern in data acquisition, in: *International Conference on Electronics, Information and Communications*, pp. 1–2, 2014.

20. Sudre, C.H., Li, W., Vercauteren, T. *et al.*, Generalised dice overlap as a deep learning loss function for highly unbalanced segmentations, in: *Deep Learning in Medical Image Analysis and Multimodal Learning for Clinical Decision Support*, New York, pp. 240–248, Springer, 2017.

21. Rezaei, M., Yang, H., Meinel, C., Deep neural network with l2-norm unit for brain lesions detection, in: *International Conference on Neural Information Processing*, Springer, pp. 798–807, 2017.

22. Hashemi, S.R., Salehi, S.S.M., Erdogmus, D. *et al.*, Tversky as a loss function for highly unbalanced image segmentation using 3d fully convolutional deep networks. *CoRR*, 1–8, abs/1803.11078, 2018.

23. Yen, S.J. and Lee, Y.S., Cluster-based under-sampling approaches for imbalanced data distributions. *Expert Syst. Appl.*, 36, 3, 5718–5727, 2009.

24. Breiman, L., Bagging predictors. *Mach. Learn.*, 24, 2, 123–140, 1996.

25. Small, H. and Ventura, J., *Handling unbalanced data in deep image segmentation*, University of Colorado, Boulder, CO 80309, United States, 2017.

26. López, V., Fernández, A., García, S., Palade, V., Herrera, F., An insight into classification with imbalanced data: Empirical results and current trends on using data intrinsic characteristics. *Inf. Sci.*, 250, 113–141, 2013.

27. Yen, S.J. and Lee, Y.S., Cluster-based under-sampling approaches for imbalanced data distributions. *Expert Syst. Appl.*, 36, 3, 5718–5727, 2009.

28. Moreo, A., Esuli, A., Sebastiani, F., Distributional random oversampling for imbalanced text classification, in: *Proceedings of the 39th International ACM SIGIR conference on Research and Development in Information Retrieval*, pp. 805–808, 2016, July.

29. Chawla, N.V., Bowyer, K.W., Hall, L.O., Kegelmeyer, W.P., SMOTE: synthetic minority over-sampling technique. *J. Artif. Intell. Res.*, 16, 321–357, 2002.

30. Hu, S., Liang, Y., Ma, L., He, Y., MSMOTE: Improving classification performance when training data is imbalanced, in: *2009 second international workshop on computer science and engineering*, 2009, October, vol. 2, IEEE, pp. 13–17.

31. Guo, H. and Viktor, H.L., Learning from imbalanced data sets with boosting and data generation: the databoost-im approach. *ACM Sigkdd Explor. Newsl.*, 6, 1, 30–39, 2004.

32. Taherkhani, A., Cosma, G., McGinnity, T.M., AdaBoost-CNN: An adaptive boosting algorithm for convolutional neural networks to classify multi-class imbalanced datasets using transfer learning. *Neurocomputing*, 404, 351–366, 2020.

33. Shivhare, S.N., Kumar, N., Singh, N., A hybrid of active contour model and convex hull for automated brain tumor segmentation in multimodal MRI. *Multimedia Tools Appl.*, 78, 24, 34207–34229, 2019.

34. Shivhare, S.N. and Kumar, N., Brain tumor detection using manifold ranking in flair mri, in: *Proceedings of ICETIT 2019*, Springer, Cham, pp. 292–305, 2020.

35. Kistler, M., Bonaretti, S., Pfahrer, M., Niklaus, R., Büchler, P., The virtual skeleton database: an open access repository for biomedical research and collaboration. *J. Med. Internet Res.*, 15, 11, e245, 2013.

36. Havaei, M., Davy, A., Warde-Farley, D., Biard, A., Courville, A., Bengio, Y., Larochelle, H., Brain tumor segmentation with deep neural networks. *Med. Image Anal.*, 35, 18–31, 2017.

37. del-Hoyo, R., Buldain, D., Marco, A., Supervised classification with associative SOM, in: *International Work-Conference on Artificial Neural Networks*, pp. 334–341, Springer, Berlin, Heidelberg, 2003, June.

38. Lee, T.S. and Chen, I.F., A two-stage hybrid credit scoring model using artificial neural networks and multivariate adaptive regression splines. *Expert Syst. Appl.*, 28, 4, 743–752, 2005.

39. Li, X., Ying, W., Tuo, J., Li, B., Liu, W., Applications of classification trees to consumer credit scoring methods in commercial banks, in: *2004 IEEE International Conference on Systems, Man and Cybernetics (IEEE Cat. No. 04CH37583)*, vol. 5, pp. 4112–4117, IEEE, 2004, October.

40. Yen, S.J. and Lee, Y.S., Under-sampling approaches for improving prediction of the minority class in an imbalanced dataset, in: *Intelligent Control and Automation*, pp. 731–740, Springer, Berlin, Heidelberg, 2006.

7

IoT-Based Health Monitoring System for Speech-Impaired People Using Assistive Wearable Accelerometer

Ishita Banerjee and Madhumathy P.*

Department of ECE, Dayananda Sagar Academy of Technology and Management, Bangalore, India

Abstract

In modern life, with the advent of technology, many difficulties are overcome to make life more convenient. But the situations are much more different for people who are physically impaired and still communication to the world is a challenging job for them. The support of sign language and its uses have extended helping hands toward speech-impaired persons but still it is difficult to understand for the common people. This proposed project aims toward implementation of a wearable electronic glove which serves as an electronics speaking system for the speech-impaired persons. The communication is done in the form of audio signals which can be understood by common people. There is also a provision of LCD display which helps the information to convey to be displayed for communication with the hearing-disabled persons. Using real-time operating systems and embedded systems, these technological advances are brought into reality. We also propose to update and track health related information like heartbeat and body temperature using cloud-based storage in Internet of Things (IoT). This will enable to establish an effective communication for those suffering from any kind of communication disorders. For the implementation, we need to depend on accelerometers and sensors so that the movements can be read accurately and transformed to the required audio or visual form. Using this approach, the hindrance of communication will be reduced. We also approach for a microcontroller-based reconfigurable smart device that can collect, process, and transmit data and store it into the cloud for further monitoring. IoT-based wireless

---

Corresponding author: sakthi999@gmail.com

Rohit Tanwar, S. Balamurugan, R. K. Saini, Vishal Bharti and Premkumar Chithaluru (eds.) Advanced Healthcare Systems: Empowering Physicians with IoT-Enabled Technologies, (81–100) © 2022 Scrivener Publishing LLC

communication systems with network devices that are connected to each other will communicate through open source internet access and establish connection between apps and devices for communication between the person under supervision and the medical supervisor. This also can help in keeping track of real-time records and emergency alerts. To handle the storage and analysis of data related issues, IoT analytics is implemented.

Keywords: Healthcare monitoring, IoT, wearable accelerometer, gesture recognition, cloud-based storage, speech impairment

7.1   Introduction

Sign language is the communication method here for speech- and hearing-disabled people to communicate with each other [1–4]. The representation of sign language differs in each corner of the world due to diversities in language. This makes it difficult for global communication. The major difficulties for speech- and hearing-disabled people occur due to lack of expression of their emotions, mental health, and behavioral issues with normal people. This causes a mental set back as well as social obstacles for them and they get discouraged to open up about their problems in public as well as personal places or even in emergency situations. Due to language diversity in different regions in the world, the communication needs a stronger bond to thread all the possibilities of interaction. Even if we consider only India, different regions have different languages for communication. This finally resulted in the advent of Indian Sign Language which is the most widely used sign language in India [5, 6]. Even if there is a common thread for speech- and hearing-impaired people to interact among them, it still lacks the common platform to interact with normal people since this ISL is not known to them and it cannot be interpreted by them so easily.

The difficulties mentioned here became the research areas over the years to give a common platform for speech- and hearing-impaired people and normal people to express their thoughts with each other [7]. The research areas concentrate on detection the hand gestures [8–10]. This hand gesture detection is even widely used in the field of robotics and even medical support field that deal with artificial or prosthetic hands.

When we make any kind of gesture by moving our hands, the gesture can be interpret to convey information in digital form. As we can express our information through gestures to a large extend, this leads toward the improvement of sign languages [11–13]. This can surely convey information, facts, and emotions effectively.

The proposed project aims toward designing an electronic speaking system or an electronic glove for the purpose of ease of communication [14–16]. This helps a speech- and hearing-impaired person to communicate to each other and even to the outer world. One accelerometer tracks the movements made by hand gestures and this mounted on a wearable glove. The main control unit is handled by Arduino Mega which captures user inputs. Thus, this is a command basis control unit. This proposed work is based on the concept of embedded systems which contains application-specific integrated circuit or microcontroller-based platform to address intended application. These are mostly pre-programmed with many functionalities for addressing a general group of queries and then can be used by the users according to their programs or applications. It needs other parts of the electronic system to incorporate with itself to achieve the task. Most of the microprocessors are used as components of the embedded systems. The embedded system comes with advantages of lesser power consumption, compact size, and low cost units. The processing resources are limited, thus interacting with other units and programming the components is a real challenge here. The embedded systems hold common purpose microprocessors and/or specific purpose microcontrollers ranging from a huge variety. For example, if we consider Digital Signal Processors, these are used for very specific application-oriented purposes; thus, it can also be optimized for increasing performance and reduction of size and cost. The real-time operating systems and embedded system serve the purpose together to solve and answer many critical real-life scenarios.

After capturing and processing the data which is majorly done by the embedded system, the real challenge comes when the data is to be communicated to the network connected devices. Here comes the importance of IoT where sharing of data happens between the network connected devices via secure service layer. For storing and analyzing the data that are transferred by the connected network components, Internet of Things (IoT) analytics is used. The raw data received is converted to more usable form by means of data extraction and data analytics. We collect data from several sources and share through the network after required level of processing. The robustness and reliability of IoT have extended its application widely into the healthcare fields [17–20]. Smart sensors can be implemented for patient health monitoring and the related data that are pulse rate, blood sugar level, blood pressure, etc., can be precisely monitored time to time without much human intervention. These collected data can be sent to the medical team for proper monitoring and call for any changes in medication or treatment if required. This ensures healthy living with wearable electronic health monitoring devices.

7.2   Literature Survey

With the technological development and adaptation of technology in day-to-day life, the need of imposing technology to make life easier for the physically disabled people also came into the minds of the researchers. Technology and medical field came hand in hand to minimize the difficulties in speech- and hearing-impaired people as well as critical patients who face hurdles to communicate their thoughts and feelings to the outer world. The use of Electronic Hand Glove is a strong support to such people.

S. F. Ahmed *et al.* elaborated their work in this field [21]. Here, the researchers have implemented electronic speaking gloves for dumb people for the ease of communication. The concept of synthesized speech is used to facilitate effective communication which acts as a virtual tongue to the speech disabled people. Here, the author made use of touch phone to make different gestures for analyzing the data from the made gestures. The inbuilt application software makes audio sound by interpreting the various gestures. This needs user awareness about the technology so that the user can make use of the smart phones and apps properly which may not be a real scenario always. Therefore, this system limits its usefulness to a limited group of technologically aware people.

R. R. Itkarkar and A. V. Nandi present their work in [22]. The purpose of the proposed work was to understand and interpret the gestures made by the speech-impaired people and convert it to a common interpretation form so that it can be understood easily by all. The proposed system is termed as Gesture to Speech system or G2S system that can be used to build the basic concept of image processing by skin color segmentation. The camera implemented for the purpose of capturing the hand gestures takes images of the movements, and then, the image processing part takes place. After various steps of image segmentation and image extraction, the hand gesture is interpreted. This can now help to play the prerecorded sound track corresponding to that particular hand gesture.

A five-fingered underactuated prosthetic hand controlled by surface EMG (electromyographic) signals acts as a supporting device for artificial hand movements [23]. The device proposed here is light weight and simple and serves the requirements of prosthetic hands. The theory of self-adaptivity helps to limit the excess use of hardware, thus reducing the size and weight of the system. The size and shape is kept similar to an adult hand. The hand movement is controlled by EMG motion pattern classifier. This makes use of VLR (variable learning rate) along with neural network. The signal processing part uses wavelet transform. Sample entropy is also used here. As the thumb moves, the pattern classifier senses its motion. It also traces the motions made by the middle finger and the index finger along with the thumb. The three electrodes help to record the EMG signals produced by the movements of the fingers. By continuous movement of single finger, the underactuated prosthetic hand can even make various postures such as power grasp. This application, if used properly, can be a great help to treat hand imputation cases.

Kuldeep Singh V Rajput implemented a speaking hand glove [24]. This paper described design of gloves that can translate the gestures made by speech impaired. A speech-impaired person who needs to communicate through sign language faces many difficulties since the sign language used by them is not understood by normal people. The authors propose to give a solution to the problem. The voice chip used here is a 8-bit MCU (4-bit ADPCM with sampling rate 6KHz).

G. Marin and *et al.* suggested a system for recognizing hand gesture using leap motion device and Kinect devices [25]. The invention of leap motion devices is of great help toward gesture recognition. Once data is gathered from the sources, the feature extraction is done which could be given to SVM classifier for the purpose of gesture recognition. Data is acquired by lead motion from where feature extraction takes place. These extracted features are then fed to the SVM classifier where the gesture is recognized. The sixth sense technology helps to interact with the digital information using only hand gesture using a wearable interface to the physical world. Wearable sensors, motion sensors, accelerometers, etc., are used to interface humanmachine interaction [26].

S. Apte and *et al.* work on the sixth sense technology [27]. The authors propose the use of a smart glove embedded with flex sensors or transducer where the physical movement or physical energy is transformed into electrical energy. The voltage output of transducers is processed by microcontrollers and other circuits to control and drive home appliances. Such wearable devices have many other applications such as making call, multimedia applications, ticket booking updates, operating maps, and tracking vehicles and flights [28, 29]. To identify the gestures, a marker detection technique can be fast enough for its usability in Augmented Reality (AR) [30].

Geetha M. and Menon R. proposed a gesture control method [31]. They proposed a method to represent some static symbolic form of alphabets (A-Z). The proposed work uses polygon approximation method with Douglas-Peucker algorithm. This approximates the boundary of gesture image. As the gesture edge is approximated, chain code direction is assigned to it. So, firstly, the finger count is detected and later the gesture is read. This is done using Canny edge algorithm. This can also make a difference between open finger and closed finger gesture making it a complex system.

S. U. N. Praveenkumar and S. Havalagi proposed a system of driving gloves with sensors implanted on its fingers and thumb is made to capture the gestures made by the fingers and then translate it to a speech form so that everyone can understand the information to be communicated made through hand gesture. This work definitely is an added advantage for the biomedical field [32].

Y. Li proposed a work on sign language translation [33]. In this paper, sign language recognition is extended to a newer level by identifying the components of the gestures made during interpretation of sign languages. The skeletal muscles show some movements while performing activities that are transformed into electrical signals and sensed by accelerometers and surface electromyography. Right hand and left hand dictate the main words and supported words, respectively. The expression of a sentence can also be done by the hand shape, finger, or palm orientation or their movement. The estimated word is calculated by averaging the left side channels. Knowing the threshold levels are also of great importance for this calculation. The algorithm that approximates the values is fuzzy k-means algorithm.

7.3   Procedure

As we can see that there are different research works done on the field of electronic gloves, most of the existing models use flex sensors. As the flex sensors can be mounted one in each fingers, so it limits the number commands that can be set. The existing model has difficulties in setting centralized health parameters [34, 35]. To overcome these difficulties, we propose for designing an electronic speaking glove with LCD. This is a portable device thus gives the user flexibility to use it. Patients will get on time services from doctors and family. It will reduce the processing time and human intervention as well as accuracy will be increased. This patient assistance system can be used in hospitals as well as in homes. This wearable device is usually placed in the hand of paralyzed patient so patient get the on time services from the doctor and family member for bending hand in the different position.

This electronic speaking system communicates either through the speaker or through LCD.

Hand gestures are interpreted with glove consists of accelerometer. Initially, all the audio and display forms are stored in the SD card. The block diagram is shown in Figure 7.1. Accelerometer is fixed to the patient hand for his assistance. APR300 kit and speaker is used for voice announcement purpose. Different voices are recorded and these voices are enabled by bending the hands.

Each wrist position indicates different service which patient need as shown below.

1.	Washroom	- Bend the wrist toward left side
2.	I need food	- Bend the wrist toward right side
3.	I need tablets	- Palm facing upwards
4.	I need water	- Wrist at 90°
5.	Regular checkup	- Wrist at −90°

We have different sensors to monitor the different parameters of the patients, e.g., temperature sensor, heartbeat sensor, and respiration sensor.

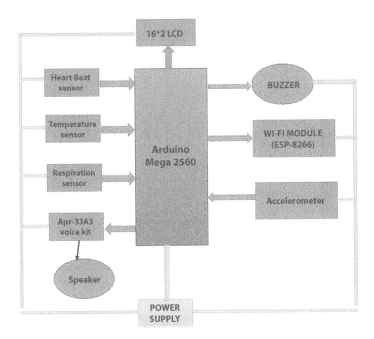

Figure 7.1 Block diagram of proposed system.

Each sensor monitors the parameters if anything below or above the threshold the system will send monitored data to the web application using IoT. Each patient will have the profile in the cloud. Each patient health parameters can be read on web portal. Each parameters plot will be appear separately. We can take report from the website. If any of the parameters go below or above the threshold level, then alarm will be set ON.

The hardware used are Arduino Mega 2560 microcontroller, accelerometer, 16x2 LCD display, APR 33A3 voice kit, Wi-Fi module, buzzer, speaker, respiration sensor, heartbeat sensor, and temperature sensor. The Arduino sketch is done in Embedded C. The Arduino Mega 2560 board can be depicted as shown in Figure 7.2. It is a microcontroller-based platform. It operates at a voltage of 5 V. 256 KB of flash memory and 4 KB of RAM is used to store and so the data processing.

The voice kit saPR33A series Q7.0 can trigger circuits to store and playback audio signals. This is shown in Figure 7.3. Out of all eight channels associated with this kit, each can record for 1.3 m of audio message. It runs on supply of 12 V AC/DC. Let us see how recording is done here. First, the board is powered on and jumper is fixed in JP1. Selection of J5 helps for recording in a particular channel. To record in M0, we shall make M0 Grounded and we can directly initiate the voice recording for storage purpose. After the segment is completed, LD2 will interpret that no

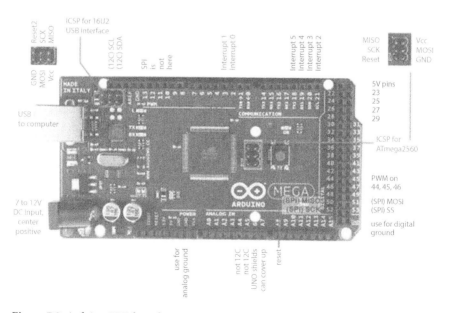

Figure 7.2 Arduino 2560 board.

Figure 7.3 Voice kit APR 33A3.

place for storage is available in this channel any more. During play back, J4 is activated. If we connect M0 to Ground, we can see that the LD2 will remain ON and play the recordings in the channel M0. The process can be repeated for other channels also.

The temperature sensor used is LM35. The circuit diagram shown in Figure 7.4 has two transistors: one having 10 times more emitter region of the other. Thus, current intensity varies for both the transistors. The voltage across R1 resistor can be said proportional to the absolute temperature and they have a linear relationship. The amplifier at the top of the circuit makes the base region voltage of Q1 transistor to be proportional to the

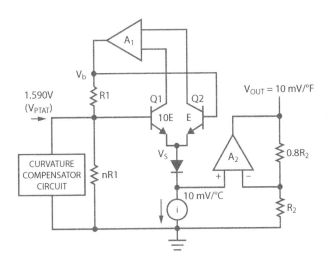

Figure 7.4 Working circuit diagram of LM35.

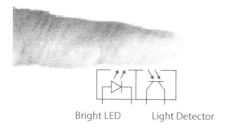

Bright LED   Light Detector

Figure 7.5 Working of heartbeat sensor.

absolute temperature. Another amplifier at the right of the circuit shown is used to convert the temperature scale from Kelvin to Celsius (for LM 35).

The heartbeat sensor helps to measure heartbeat based on the light intensity changes due to scattered or absorbed light during its path through the blood for each heartbeat. A light detector and a LED can perform this work very well. The intensity of the LED matters a lot since the brightness of the LED determines whether there is passing blood through the finger during heartbeat once its place on the LED. As the blood is pumped by the heart, the finger becomes nontransparent and the brightness of light falling on the detector is low. Thus, per heartbeat, the detector can receive the signal through the LED which is later converted to electrical signal. This converted signal after amplification gives the measure of heart beats. The process how heartbeat sensor works is shown in Figure 7.5.

The respiration sensor is kind of a stretch which is sensitive to movements. The strap is tied around the patient's chest or upper abdomen to measure the expansion and contraction of rib cage due to inhale and exhale and converted into signal form to show on the screen. The sensor is shown in Figure 7.6.

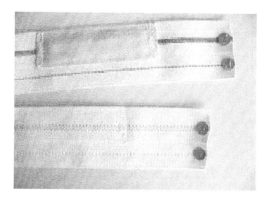

Figure 7.6 Respiration sensor.

The information collected by the sensors is shared among the network components by ThingSpeak open source IoT application. This stores and retrieves data using HTTP protocol via Internet or LAN. After successful login in the web portal, the channels are created. For the application shown here, three channels are created for temperature, heartbeat, and respiration monitoring, respectively, as shown in the Figure 7.7.

The following is the algorithm of the health monitoring system is as follows:

Step1: Initialization of pins to which the accelerometer, sensor, buzzer, voice kit, and LCD are connected.

Step2: Declare the pins of LCD connections with Arduino.

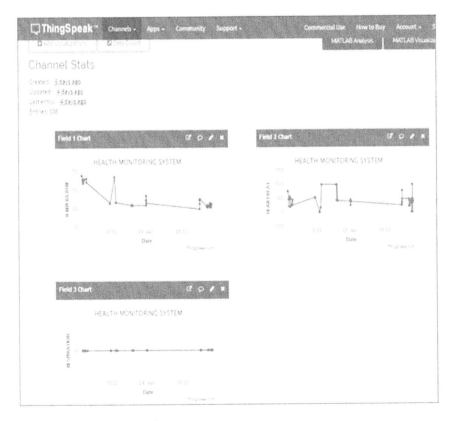

Figure 7.7 Channels for heath monitoring.

Step3: Set the baud rate.

Step4: Assigning pins as input and output pins.

Step5: Set all the channels to high initially.

Step6: Assign accelerometer reading to variables.

Step7: Calling accelerometer function.

Step8: Temperature and heartbeat measurement and corresponding output.

Step9: Uploading the measurements into cloud.

Step10: Analyze values of accelerometer for different positions.

Step11: Using if, else if statements with the values of accelerometer to produce output.

The input and output pins of the microcontroller are initialized, and then, conditions are set by programming. There are three parameters on which conditions are imposed, i.e., X, Y, and Z. Let us see the first condition. If X ≥ 300 and Y < 300 and Z ≥ 300, then LCD will flash a message as "I need Water" and the speaker will play the same message as "I need Water". Then, after this message delivery, the temperature will be checked again. In case the first condition fails, then the second condition will be checked and so one. One any of the one condition is set true the sensor checks the temperature. If it is greater than 37°C, then temp is displayed as high and buzzer is ON. If temperature is lesser than 37°C, then it will check heartbeat. Each time any value is displayed on the LCD, it is simultaneously uploaded in cloud. Again for heartbeat, the condition of alert is heartbeat lesser than 470 or greater than 900. The heartbeat measured is also uploaded into the cloud. Next, the checking for accelerometer is done. This working is described in terms of flowchart in Figure 7.8.

When the gesture is made, the accelerometer sends the x, y, z coordinates for that gestures into the Arduino. The Arduino processes and sends the corresponding test command of that gesture that is sent to LCD and APR 33A3 voice kit. The LCD displays the test command and voice kit receives the signal and sends the corresponding voice into speaker. Heartbeat sensor, temperature sensor, and respiration sensor are the input to the Arduino and Wi-Fi module and buzzer are the output of the Arduino. Whenever the heartbeat and body temperature is higher than the threshold value, the buzzer is on and LCD displays the corresponding command.

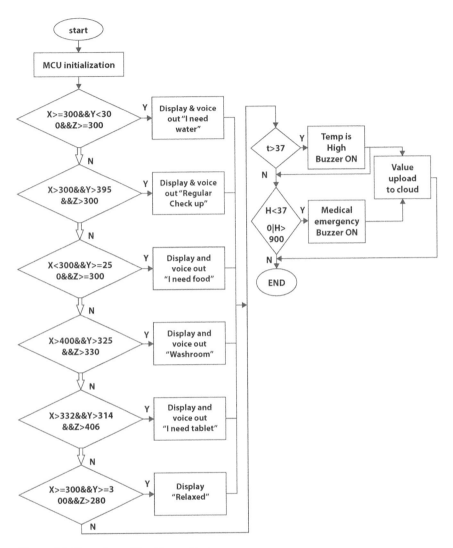

Figure 7.8 Flow chart of health monitoring.

7.4 Results

The hardware shown here is mounted with accelerometers that collect data which are simulated through software tool. The glove is used to make sign gestures that can be interpret through the accelerometer. Hardware circuit for measuring the gestures is shown in Figure 7.9.

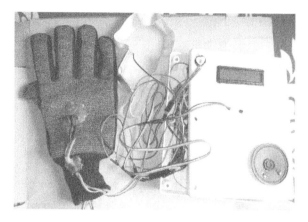

Figure 7.9 Hardware circuit for hand gesture recognition.

The different gestures and the corresponding commands are displayed on LCD. As we have already stored recorded voice messages for each gesture, when a gesture is interpreted by an accelerometer, we can play the corresponding message from the recordings. The text for that command can also be displayed simultaneously. Figure 7.10 shows the "Temp is High" on the LCD display whenever the body temperature is high and "Medical Emergency" on the LCD display whenever the heartbeat is high.

Let us see the graphical analysis now. Whenever the body temperature and heartbeat are greater than the threshold value, then the corresponding measured value of temperature, heartbeat, and respiratory measures are uploaded to cloud as shown in Figures 7.11, 7.12, and 7.13, respectively.

If we look into the graph shown in Figure 7.11, it shows that the temperature of the patient is varying with respect to time and is well plotted as shown.

Figure 7.12 depicts the heartbeat rate during a given time slot and shows that there is a sudden rise at around 17.35 which might need medication. After which the graph becomes much stable.

Figure 7.13 shows the number of times the patient inhales and exhales in the given time.

The device used here has portability, convenience in terms of ease of usage, cost, and weight. This device will help persons those have normal communication disability. Patients will get on time services from doctors and family.

Hand Gesture   **Command on LCD Display**

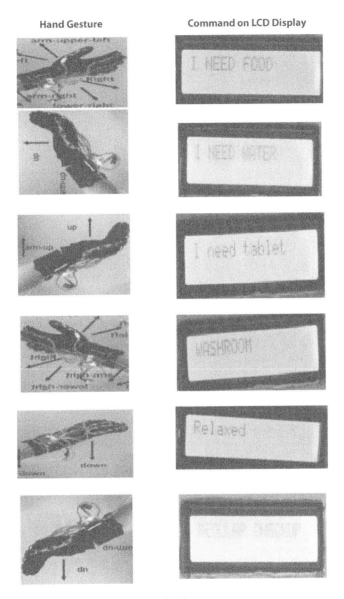

Figure 7.10 Gesture and commands accordingly.

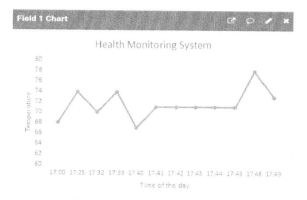

Figure 7.11 Field chart for body temperature.

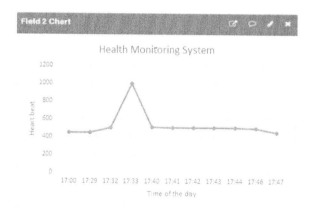

Figure 7.12 Field chart for heartbeat.

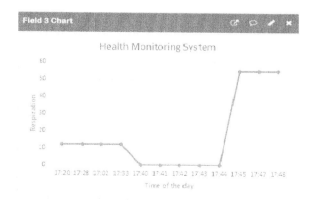

Figure 7.13 Field chart for respiration rate.

7.5   Conclusion

The advent of sign language is a miraculous change in the lives of speech- and hearing-impared people. The main aim of the project was to provide support to the speech-impaired people to express themselves with the outer world and also for the paralyzed persons to convey their needs to their supervisors. The project aims on feeding the inputs taken from the accelerometer to the Arduino Mega for different gestures which can be communicated to others via LCD display and speaker in the form of audio output. Depending on the three axes of the accelerometer, the program is built. Along with the existing gesture control system, this proposal adds value to the work by uploading the values to the cloud through IoT and heath care monitoring is also proposed simultaneously. So, this project acts as a dual purpose prototype that can be used either by just speech-impaired person or by bed-ridden patients. As extension of future work this Arduino is reconfigurable and coding extension options are always available. Hence, this concept can be extended for adding different voice for different gestures.

References

1. Karmel, A., Sharma, A., Pandya, M., Garg, D., IoT based assistive device for deaf, dumb and blind people. *International Conference on Recent Trends in Advanced Computing*, vol. 165, *Procedia Comput. Sci.*, pp. 259–269, 2019.

2. Spender, A., Bullen, C., Altmann-Richer, L., Cripps, J., Duffy, R., Falkous, C., Farrel, M., Horn, T., Wigzell, J., Yeap, Wearables and the internet of things: considerations the life and health insurance industry. *Br. Actuar. J.*, 24, 1–31, 2019.

3. Ghotkar, A.S., Khatal, R., Khupase, S., Asati, S., Hadap, M., Hand gesture recognition for indian sign language. *Indian conference on computer communication and informatics*, pp. 1–4, 2012.

4. Rekha, J., Bhattacharya, J., Majumder, S., Shape, texture and local movement hand gesture features for indian sign language recognition. *International conference on trendz in information sciences and computing (TISC2011)*, IEEE, pp. 30–35, 2011.

5. Singha, J. and Das, K., Indian sign language recognition using eigen value weighted euclidean distance based classification technique. *Int. J. Adv. Comput. Sci. Appl.*, 4, 2, pp. 188–195, 2013.

6. Subha Rajam, P. and Balakrishnan, G., Real time indian sign language recognition system to aid deaf-dumb People. *IEEE International Conference on Communication Technology*, pp. 737–742, 2011.

7. Kishore, P.V.V. and Rajesh Kumar, P., A video based indian sign language recognition system (INSLR) using wavelet transform and fuzzy logic. *IACSIT Int. J. Eng. Technol.*, 4, 5, pp. 537–542, 2012.

8. Zhu, C. and Sheng, W., Wearable sensor-based hand gesture and daily activity recognition for robot-assisted living. *IEEE Transactions on Systems, man and cybernetics, Part A*, 41, 3, 2011.

9. Sanna, K., Juha, K., Jani, M., Johan, M., Visualization of hand gestures for pervasive computing environments. *Proceedings of the working conference on advanced visual interfaces*, ACM, pp. 480–483, 2006.

10. Juha, K., Panu, K., Jani, M., Sanna, K., Giuseppe, S., Luca, J., Sergio, D.M., *Accelerometer-based gesture control for a design environment*, Springer, Finland, 2005.

11. Garcia-Ceja, E., Galvn-Tejada, C.E., Brena, R., Multi-view stacking for activity recognition with sound and accelerometer data. *Inf. Fusion*, 40, 45–56, 2018.

12. Erdau, B., Atasoy, I., Koray, H., Ofuul, Integrating features for accelerometer-based activity recognition. *Proc. Comput. Sci.*, 98, 522–527, 2016.

13. Hui, S. and Zhongmin, W., Compressed sensing method for human activity recognition using tri-axis accelerometer on mobile phone. *J. China Univ. Posts Telecommun.*, 24, 2, 31–71, 2017.

14. Mirri, S., Prandi, C., Salomoni, P., Fitting like a GlovePi: a wearable device for deaf-blind people. *14th IEEE Annual Consumer Communications & Networking Conference (CCNC)*, pp. 1057–1062, 2017.

15. Jani, M., Juha, K., Panu, K., Sanna, K., Enabling fast and effortless customization in accelerometer based gesture interaction. *Proceedings of the 3rd international conference on Mobile and ubiquitous multimedia*, ACM, Finland, pp. 25–31, 2004.

16. Malik, S. and Laszlo, J., Visual touchpad: A two-handed gestural input device. *Proceedings of the ACM International Conference on Multimodal Interfaces*, p. 289, 2004.

17. Anliker, U. *et al.*, MON : a wearable multiparameter medical monitoring and alert system. *IEEE Trans. Inf. Technol. Biomed.*, 8, 4, 415–427, 2004.

18. Sareen, S., Sood, S.K., Gupta, S.K., IoT-based cloud framework to control ebola virus outbreak. *J. Ambient. Intell. Humaniz. Comput.*, 9, 1–18, 2016.

19. Yang, Z., Zhou, Q., Lei, L., Zheng, K., Xiang, W., An IoT-cloud based wearable ECG monitoring system for smart healthcare. *J. Med. Syst.*, 40, 12, 1–11, 2016.

20. Verma, P., Sood, S.K., Kalra, S., Cloud-centric IoT based student healthcare monitoring framework. *J. Ambient. Intell. Humaniz. Comput.*, 116, 1–17, 2017.

21. Ahmed, S.F., Muhammad, S., Ali, B., Saqib, S., Qureshi, M., Electronic speaking glove for speechless patients A tongue to the dumb. *IEEE Conference on Sustainable Utilization and Development in Engineering and Technology*, pp. 56–60, 2010.

22. Itkarkar, R.R. and Nandi, A.V., Hand gesture to speech conversion using Matlab. *Fourth International Conference on Computing, Communications and Networking Technologies (ICCCNT)*, pp. 1–4, 2013.

23. Zhao, J., Jiang, L., Shi, S., Cai, H., Liu, H., Hirzinger, G., A five-fingered underactuated prosthetic hand system. *Proceedings of IEEE International Conference on Mechatronics and Automation*, pp. 1453–1458, 2006.

24. Singh, K. and Rajput, V., Design and implementation of Talking hand glove for the hearing impaired. *IEEE*, 2014.

25. Marin, G., Dominio, F., Zanuttigh, P., Hand gesture recognition with leap motion and kinect devices. *IEEE*, 2014.

26. Mannini, A. and Sabatini, A.M., Machine Learning Methods for Classifying Human Physical Activity from On-Body Accelerometers. *Sensors*, 10, 2, pp. 1154–1175, 2010.

27. Apte, S., Sawant, D., Dubey, M., Pandole, M., Vengurlekar, P., Gesture based home automation using sixth sense technology. *Int. J. Comput. Appl.*, 5, pp. 179–186, 2017.

28. Desale, R.D. and Ahire, V.S., A study on wearable gestural interface-- A sixth sense technology. *IOSR J. Comput. Eng.*, 10, 5, 1016, 2013.

29. Mistry, P., Meas, P., Chang, L., WUW -Wear Ur World -A wearable gesture interface. *Proceedings of the 27th International Conference extended abstracts on Human factors Computing Systems*, Association for Computing Macinery/Special Interest Group on Computer-Human Interaction, MIT Open Access Article, 2009.

30. Hirzer, M., Marker Detection for Augmented Reality Applications, Technical Report, ICG Publications, ICG-TR-08/05, 2008.

31. Geetha, M. and Menon, R., Gesture Recognition for American Sign Language with Polygon Arroximation. *IEEE International Conference on Technology for Education*, 2011.

32. Praveenkumar, S.U.N. and Havalagi, S., The amazing digital gloves that give voice to the voiceless. *IJAET*, 6, 1, 471–480, 2013.

33. Li, Y., A Sign-Component-Based framework for chinese sign language recognition using accelerometer and sEMG data. *IEEE Trans. Biomed. Eng.*, 59, 10, 2695–2704, 2012.

34. Yuan, Y.S. and Cheah, T.C., A study of internet of things enabled healthcare acceptance in Malaysia. *J. Crit. Rev.*, 7, 3, 25–32, 2020.

35. Noah, B., Keller, M.S., Mosadeghi, S., Stein, L., Johl, S., Delshad, S., Spiegel, B.M.R., Impact of remote patient monitoring on clinical outcomes: an updated meta-analysis of randomized controlled trials. *NPJ Digital Med.*, 1, Article no. 20172, pp. 1–12, 2018.

8

Smart IoT Devices for the Elderly and People with Disabilities

K. N. D. Saile[1]* and Kolisetti Navatha[2]

[1]Department of Computer Science and Engineering, CMR Institute of Technology, Hyderabad, India
[2]Department of Computer Science and Engineering, Sreyas Institute of Engineering and Technology, Hyderabad, India

Abstract

The increasing growth in technology is reducing human effort day by day. The advent of the Internet of Things (IoT) is making human lives much easier with the help of automation, which is a helping hand to people in many ways. Especially, for elderly and differently abled people the technology of IoT is a boon. The global population of people above the age of 60 is about 962 million and it is expected to reach a count that is double to the existing by 2050. The physical and cognitive health of individuals decreases with age, and hence, there a need to take care of such individuals. Apart from them, we also have differently abled people who come across day-to-day challenges to be faced. The revolution in the paradigm of IoT brought a huge change by making devices for the elderly and people with disabilities like health management, sensors, wearable devices, audio, and video assistance. All these are possible with the help of the IoT. In this chapter, we will discuss the technology trends and devices made during the IoT era.

Keywords: Internet of Things, smart devices, elderly people, differently abled people

8.1 Introduction

Internet of Things also known as IoT is a fusion of digitally connected physical devices over the network. The devices are embedded with sensors,

---

**Corresponding author:* saileknd3@gmail.com

Rohit Tanwar, S. Balamurugan, R. K. Saini, Vishal Bharti and Premkumar Chithaluru (eds.) Advanced Healthcare Systems: Empowering Physicians with IoT-Enabled Technologies, (101–114) © 2022 Scrivener Publishing LLC

actuators, and other hardware components along with internet connectivity. The advent of IoT made lives easier by reducing human efforts. The network devices are implemented in such a way that the human-to-human interaction and human-to-computer interaction has reduced gradually. IoT is used widely in our day-to-day lives like smart home, transport, enterprise automation, medical, and healthcare.

Automation of things has touched humans in all walks of life in various ways, especially for the elderly and differently abled people. The world's population is aging. As per the statistics of 2017, it is expected that the population of people above the age of 60 is expected to reach 2.1 billion by 2050 [1]. As age increases the physical and cognitive health of people reduces gradually, and hence, special care is to be taken for those individuals. Apart from those, many people with disabilities face challenges to make their day-to day work done. The innovations and advancements in the paradigm of IoT made a huge change by making devices for them like healthcare [2] monitoring devices, wearable devices, and audio assistance.

In this chapter, we shall discuss the technology trends that are made available during the era of IoT particularly for the elderly and differently abled, which are a hope for their survival.

8.2   Need for IoT Devices

Of all the population across the globe, we have people who are growing older, as well as differently abled people [3]. It is often observed that they find it difficult to do their day-to-day chores without an assistance [4]. IoT

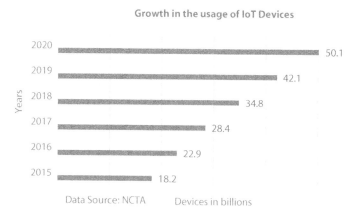

Figure 8.1 Chart showing growth in the usage of IoT devices.

is a boon to such kinds of people which helps them to make their tasks easier and making lives smarter. The use of mobile technology and wireless technology can help people to have a better livelihood. The market of IoT is increasing drastically, and it is assumed to have more than 50 billion IoT products in the market in the near future (Figure 8.1).

8.3   Where Are the IoT Devices Used?

In the last few years, home automation has been a common implementation in the field of IoT, which has a tremendous advantage for the elderly and people with disabilities which includes security and safety. Along with home automation, we have smart appliances for making their tasks easier and also healthcare devices which help in monitoring the regular health conditions and many more [5]. Let us have a look at the automation techniques which is making lives easier and simpler. Figure 8.2 shows the areas where IoT devices are used.

8.3.1   Home Automation

One of the home automation techniques [6] includes automatic light controlling systems. They work on the mechanism of turning on and off the light with a remote control or apps on smartphones. Few controlling systems work on motion-based recognition [7] where, depending upon the motion of the person, if he is not available the lights turn off and turn on when the person is available. This automation technique majorly is helpful for people with disabilities in movement and cannot reach the switches.

Another important home automation system is an automated home security and safety. Cognitive intelligence is a major challenge for elderly people. Automated doors and locks are very useful so that they do not fear missing locking of doors. When someone is outside the doors, these automatic locking systems which are available help the people with disability to unlock the doors with a single touch on the app on their smartphone.

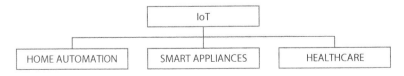

Figure 8.2 Areas of IoT devices used.

8.3.2   Smart Appliances

Different from home automation which consists of lights, fans, sensors, and automated smart appliances are the appliances that we use in our day-to-day lives and are connected to the smart phones via a Bluetooth. Generally, elderly people tend to forget turning off devices such as toasters, stoves, and oven, which may be very dangerous. Automation of these appliances [8] will help them and make the task easier just with a click of a button. Apart from home appliances we have wearable devices like text readers, braille watches, and hearing aids for differently abled people.

8.3.3   Healthcare

Healthcare plays a vital role for any individual. Extra care is needed, particularly concerning the healthcare of elderly people. There are many healthcare devices like medicine dispenses and remainder systems for the medicines that are to be taken regularly. These medicine dispensers will help to have appropriate doses for them. The remainder systems help in maintaining a schedule and popping a remainder based on the schedules to avoid missing meetings and schedules.

Now, let us have a detailed look at the smart IoT devices for elderly and differently abled people.

8.4   Devices in Home Automation

8.4.1   Automatic Lights Control

The automatic lights controlling systems come with inbuilt sensors in it. An automatic light control device turns on when it detects an object. When the person enters the location, the sensor detects the motion of the object and puts on the light. There is a time limit that to be set to the sensors when to put off when no object is detected. Based on the time set, the light automatically puts off when there is no object identified in its location. There are advanced sensors that can check for a certain range of distance and when no object is identified it turns off. This technology is mainly helpful for people who have movement disabilities and cannot reach the switches.

8.4.2   Automated Home Safety and Security

Home security is always challenging when the elderly and differently abled people who lead a single life. There are many home security devices where the mobile applications have the option to unlock the doors based on the control given by the user. Any person sitting inside the home can unlock the doors of his home without moving. In this automation technique, the home is installed with a device that displays the image of the person who has arrived. The app installed in the smartphone of the user can unlock the door or speak to the person outside the door with the help of the mobile device. These kinds of devices are mainly helpful for people with mobility challenges.

Another automatic locking system for elders is the smart lock mechanism which works on thumb impressions and also smartphone unlock. These devices make their task easier to avoid using keys and slipping the keys from their hands. When the user wants to lock the door, he can do it with the help of a smartphone, and when he wants to unlock it, he can use the fingerprint scanner.

8.5   Smart Appliances

Smart appliances are always helpful to all groups of people. But, these appliances with much more customization can be used for elderly and differently abled people. Few of the smart appliances are as below.

8.5.1   Smart Oven

A smart oven is a home appliance that integrates with a smart home network through Wi-Fi or Bluetooth. The app should be installed on our smartphone to get connected to a smart oven [9]. It allows users to control the oven remotely or to set automatic functions. The smart oven has different functions from preheating, adjusting the cooking temperatures, etc. This smart oven also sends alerts when the oven is preheated properly, when the timer expires, or if there is a problem with the oven.

8.5.2   Smart Assistant

Engaging a caretaker or an assistant to an elderly and disabled people to help in their daily activities is a difficult task. Finding and affording them is not much easy. An IoT offers them with a completely smart device called a smart assistant (virtual assistant). It gets connected to a Wi-Fi network to operate. It takes voice commands as input and internally designed with a speaker to give the audio as a reply. It performs numerous tasks and services that include the answering of queries like what is the date today, temperature right now, history of diseases, and playing of songs from movies by searching on the internet. It can be operated from the place where we are sitting without any difficulty.

8.5.3   Smart Washers and Dryers

The elderly and people with some disabilities cannot roam many times in their homes for their daily activities. Washing or laundry is one of them. To make it simpler, smart washers and dryers [10] are an IoT device connected to the internet that can operate from the place of sitting. An intended app should be maintained in a smartphone to give operative commands like the type of fabric, time as well as to get notifications like number of cycles to finish, time left, water sufficiency, and power problems if any from it.

8.5.4   Smart Coffee Machines

Fifty percent of the population drinks coffee at least once in a day to get rid of tiredness. The majority of the elderly and some disabled persons are not able to make themselves by standing or sitting 5–10 minutes continuously. For such people, IoT helps with a smart coffee machine [11] that is connected to the internet can operate from their smartphone by installing its intended app from the place of sitting to give instructions like turns on/off, milk, and number of spoons of coffee powder and sugar. It notifies the user when it is ready or when it requires assistance.

8.5.5   Smart Refrigerator

A refrigerator is used to store daily essentials like milk, eggs, bread, fruits, vegetables, and many more. It cannot detect when the items stored in it are spoiled or expired. The elderly and some disabled people cannot go through it daily. A smart refrigerator [12] is an IoT-programmed device. It can able to recognize and manage items stored inside it and keep track of important details such as usage and expiry. These refrigerators work on a RFID or barcode system to collect the batch and manufacture detail directly from the internet.

8.6   Healthcare

Today's healthcare system has also recognized the advantages of IoT to improve the quality of healthcare, by changing the traditional healthcare systems to smart healthcare [13], smart automated tools that lead to better diagnostics, and enhancing treatment for patients.

The mobile health is a practice supported by mobile devices, such as mobile phones, patient monitoring devices, personal digital assistants (PDAs), and other wireless devices [13].

There are few IoT devices for elderly people and differently abled people. First, let us have a look at devices for elderly people which are as follows.

8.6.1 Smart Watches

Smart watches are digital watches with enhanced features that display the heart rate, steps count, number of miles of walk, remainders systems, answering the calls when the mobile is away from the person, etc.

8.6.2 Smart Thermometer

A smart thermometer is a wearable device with Bluetooth connection to smartphones, which has improved features to the traditional medical thermometer. This smart thermometer [14] is worn to the hand which keeps track of the body temperatures every 16 seconds in real time and sends an alert. It also keeps track of the time when a medicine is taken and also prompts alerts when the next dosage of medicine is to be taken. The merits of this thermometer are that there is no discomfort and it can be readable at any time and self-measurable.

8.6.3 Smart Blood Pressure Monitor

Monitoring the blood pressure in elderly people is a very important task, to maintain proper health conditions. In the olden days, whenever the people need to check the blood pressure, they always used to rush to a doctor. But now, with the emerging technologies, everything is at the click of the button.

Smart blood pressure monitor system [14] is a digital device which displays the graph of the heartbeat. It calculates the systolic and diastolic blood pressures. As it is a known fact that the healthy blood pressure ranges from 90/80 to 120/80 mmHg, any change from the normal blood pressure will be displayed on the device screen and prompted to the user.

8.6.4 Smart Glucose Monitors

A smart glucose monitor is a very helpful device for diabetic patients to identify their blood sugar level and take appropriate injections. The device is equipped with a test strip bottle. These strips are used to detect blood sugar levels. To perform the test, we need to insert test strip and prick your finger and place the test strip into the blood. This glucose monitor device [14] can be connected to the smartphone similar to that of an OTG device. Once the test is performed, the results are displayed on the screen as well as on the smart phone.

8.6.5   Smart Insulin Pump

Approximately 422 million people have diabetes worldwide. They need insulin all day. To take insulin easily, an IoT-based device called insulin pump can operate through a smartphone with its intended app using the internet to specify instructions and to get notifications.

Insulin pumps are small, computerized devices used to deliver small doses and variable doses of insulin before and after the meal. Insulin pumps release insulin almost the way our body naturally does.

The insulin pump is about the size of a smartphone and attaches it to your body using an infusion set: thin plastic tubing and either a small tapered tube called a cannula or a needle put under the skin is called infusion site. This can be placed on the buttock, thigh, or belly. Insulin pumps [14] use rapid acting and short acting insulin, but not long acting since the pump is programmed to deliver a small amount of insulin continuously to keep blood sugar levels even.

8.6.6   Smart Wearable Asthma Monitor

An automated device for asthma monitoring [14] is a wearable patch type device that helps to detect respiration patterns, tracking cough rate, temperature, heartbeat, and other asthma symptoms. It comes with a rechargeable battery and can be worn anywhere in the upper torso, back, or front. It has a voice journaling feature. For this, just press the wearable and it can start recording relevant journal entries such as behavior, feelings, or any changes needed to notice and to record. All this data gets transferred to your smartphone for long term records and doctor's review.

Performing the daily chores for the differently abled people is always a challenging task. There are different people like visually impaired, deaf, and movement disabilities. There are different IoT devices developed and manufactured which are helpful to them in many ways. Now, we shall see the smart IoT devices for differently abled.

8.6.7   Assisted Vision Smart Glasses

People with disabilities in vision require help from others to always carry out tasks. Partially sighted have the ability to detect light and motion. Smart glasses are useful for people with partial vision difficulties and help them to find what they want independently and avoid obstacles. This was developed by the researchers of Oxford University; smart glasses [16] use object detection and help the visually challenged to navigate on their own. Smart glasses are a pair of glasses which collects visual information using sensors and relays it back to the wearer using OLED (Organic Light Emitting Diode) screens and headphones.

8.6.8   Finger Reader

This is a wearable device designed by the researchers at MIT's Media Lab, which is helpful for visually impaired to read the text. This device needs to be worn on the index finger which is embedded with a camera. This camera on the top of the device scans the text with the moments of the finger and reads the text aloud. This finger reader is very advantageous because the visually impaired people can read the normal text also apart from the braille. A vibration motor present prompts an alert when the reader moves away from the script.

8.6.9   Braille Smart Watch

This is a wearable device similar to that of a smart watch but useful for visually challenged people. This type of watch is first developed by DOT. This braille smart watch monitor features like heart rate and footsteps. All the features of a smart watch are imbibed in this braille watch. It works on the wireless Bluetooth technology to connect the smartphones. It is a very fashionable device with comfort.

8.6.10   Smart Wand

The smart wand is an improvised version of a traditional stick that is used by visually impaired people. This works on smart sensor technology. It is a handheld device that was created by Jin-Woo Han. This wand comprises a sensor strip that tells about how far is the person from an object and helps in moving them forward without any obstacles [15].

8.6.11   Taptilo Braille Device

Taptilo Braille device is a wireless device that syncs to a smartphone using the internet with the use of the intended application to teach and learn Braille reading and writing.

8.6.12   Smart Hearing Aid

Smart hearing aids are the most popular and effective treatment option for hearing loss. The aim of smart hearing aids is to make the hearing restoration process feel as natural as possible by removing wires and other physical connectivity. The automatic functionality in smart hearing aids allows users to interact with their environment naturally while the device's functionality enhances sound by reducing noise. Smart hearing aids use Bluetooth technology to connect wirelessly to smartphones, doorbells, smoke alarms, and more.

8.6.13   E-Alarm

E-alarm is a small electronic hand-held device with the functionality to expend a loud siren like alarming sound. It gets activated either by pressing a button or when pulled. The E-alarm siren will sound continuously for 30 minutes or unless the pin is returned to the device. It is used to attract attention to scare off an aggressor.

8.6.14   Spoon Feeding Robot

The elderly and people with some disabilities cannot do their work by themselves. They need some caregiving people to feed their food. There is a spoon-feeding robot to make you live independently by feeding food. A grab arm picks up the desired food in a food container, and it releases the food on the spoon of a spoon arm. The spoon arm keeps the spoon to the user's mouth. Then, the user can eat the food on the spoon.

8.6.15   Automated Wheel Chair

An automated wheel chair is mechanically controlled device that works with user command. This chair provides an opportunity for people with mobility challenges to move from one place to another. The automated wheelchair is also provided with an obstacle detection system which reduces the chance of clash while on the journey.

There is a lot of advancement in the field of IoT in the last 2–3 years. The IoT-enabled devices are making the differently abled and elderly people's lives easier. Smart vehicles are one of the greatest achievements in the field of IoT-based devices. An intelligent car with voice assistance and obstacle detector to aid the disabled [17] is a smart vehicle that is developed to move as well as to detect the obstacles and stop the movement of the vehicle. This works with the help of Google Voice–based search and Amazon's speech services. This smart vehicle is mainly useful for people who are physically challenged.

Physically disabled people always need the support of others in every walks of life. Sometimes, leaving them unattended may even cost their lives. It is particularly with people using wheelchairs and other support devices to keep them in movements. Authors in [18] demonstrated a smart device automatic pose detection to avoid dangerous situations, which prompts an emergency bell based on the posture of the individual. The machine learning algorithm used in this will identify the posture, and if there is any change in the posture, it will prompt the user to avoid accidents.

A smart glove for the visually impaired helps in identifying the obstacles in their path. The motor in the glove starts vibrating if it encounters an obstacle in the way. Authors in [19] described the architecture which is low cost and effective glove for the visually impaired. Nikola Kristic, who is a graduate from Belgrade, developed a prototype for a smart glove that not only vibrates and occurrence of an obstacle but also performs several other functions. The name of the smart glove is ANORA which performs that tasks like spatial orientation, identifying the currency, detection of lights in the room, color recognition, and panic buttons which sends the message when the user is lost in his direction [20]. This panic buttons send messages to the dear ones the location of the user where he is situated. This is one of the advances which help the visually impaired people to perform several other tasks.

There are situations where elderly people need to stay alone, and it is challenging for them to keep track of their daily activities because of their cognitive abilities. Researchers have been working in different areas where there could be a better monitoring system for elderly people. One among them is the ICE, i.e., IoT cares for elders which work on the Intel Edison platform [21]. This checks and prompts and alarm on finding any abnormalities in the functioning of the elderly people. All the data is stored in the cloud so that the family can track the health conditions of the individual.

The authors in [22] made use of a smartphone and a wearable smart watch to find and prompt an alert message to the family when the Alzheimer's patient is lost and is unaware of his location. Authors in [23] developed sensors that measure blood pressure, heartbeat, and body temperature on a mesh network while [24] developed a mobile application which with the help of activities performed predicts the health condition of the elderly person and also prompts the necessary actions that need to be taken.

Home automation is been very well advanced and is been used in everyone's daily routine and in particular for the elderly and people with disabilities. The automation of home has been extended to all areas and appliances in the entire home right from controlling the lights to the temperature sensors, gas emission detection system, etc. This automation system [25] uses transceivers and RF wireless communication between the user and the control board.

There are wide varieties of IoT devices that are being manufactured the home automation systems for the elderly and people who are living alone. Some of the companies that help in home automation are Legrand home automation, Philips, Leviton, Elk, Qolsys, etc. Most of the devices are accompanied by Amazon's Alexa, Google Assistant, and Apple Homekit. Another technology that makes the lives of the differently abled easier is the usage of RFIDs (Radio Frequency Identifications). RFID has the tags and sensors through which wireless communication can be established and measure the data. This is much useful to visually impaired people for purchasing things from a Walmart or identifying the location they are present [26].

8.7   Conclusion

Smart IoT devices are helpful for the elderly and differently able people, which provide good monitoring features and make their task easier and simpler. They save manual tasks and time. The quality of life also increases with the usage of IoT devices. As every technology has pros and cons, using IoT devices by elderly and differently abled people suffer few demerits as the person who is using the devices need to be aware of the technology and usage of the devices. There is also a security breach that is to be handled using the IoT devices.

References

1. United Nations, Department of Economic and Social Affairs, Population Division, World Population Ageing 2017-Highlights (ST/ESA/SER.A/397), 2017.

2. Dang, L.M., Piran, M.J., Han, D., Min, K., Moon, H.A., Survey on Internet of Things and Cloud Computing for Healthcare. *Electronics*, 8, 768, 2019, https://doi.org/10.3390/electronics8070768.

3. World Health Organization and the World Bank Group, World Report on Disability, 2008, Available at: https://www.unicef.org/protection/World_report_on_disability_eng.pdf

4. Sasaki, J., Yamada, K., Tanaka, M., Fujita, H., Pisanelli, D.M., Rasconi, R., Tiberio, L., De Lazzari, C., Improving Safety and Healthy Life of Elderly People: Italian and Japanese Experiences, in: *Proceedings of the 2009 conference on New Trends in Software Methodologies, Tools and Techniques*, The Netherlands, pp. 585–598, 2009.

5. Ibarra-Esquer, J.E., González-Navarro, F.F., Flores-Rios, B.L., Burtseva, L., Astorga-Vargas, M.A., Tracking the Evolution of the Internet of Things Concept Across Different Application Domains. *Sensors*, 17, 1379, 2017, https://doi.org/10.3390/s17061379.

6. Eriksson, H. and Timpka, T., The potential of smart homes for injury prevention among the elderly. *Inj. Control Saf. Promot.*, 9, 2, 127–131, 2002, https://doi.org/10.1076/icsp.9.2.127.8694.

7. Castillo, J.C., Castro-González, Á., Fernández-Caballero, A., Latorre, J.M., Pastor, J.M., Fernández-Sotos, A., Salichs, M.A., Software architecture for smart emotion recognition and regulation of the ageing adult. *Cogn. Comput.*, 8, 357–367, 2016, https://doi.org/10.1007/s12559-016-9383-y.

8. Misbahuddin, S., Orabi, H., Fatta, R., Al-Juhany, M., Almatrafi, A., IoT Framework Based Healthcare System for Elderly and Disabled People. *International Conference on Recent Advances in Computer Systems (RACS 2015)*, pp. 99–102, 2015.

9. Lifewire, https://www.lifewire.com/smart-oven-range-4159902.

10. Lifewire,https://www.lifewire.com/what-is-a-smart-washer-and-dryer-4159824.

11. Lifewire, https://www.google.com/amp/s/www.androidauthority.com/best-smart-coffee-makers-945813/amp/.

12. Lifewire, https://www.lifewire.com/smart-refrigerator-4158327.

13. Islam, S.M.R., Kwak, D., Kabir, M.D.H., Hossain, M., Kwak, K.-S., The Internet of Things for Healthcare: A Comprehensive Survey. *IEEE Access*, 3, 678–708, 2015, https://doi.org/10.1109/ACCESS.2015.2437951.

14. Celler, B., Lovell, N., Chan, D., The Potential Impact of Home Telecare of Clinical Practice. *Med. J. Aust.*, 171, 10, 518–521, 15 Nov. 1999.

15. https://www.engineering.com/Education/EducationArticles/ArticleID/65Help-the-Blind-Navigate.aspx

16. Gulati, U., Ishaan, I., Dass, R., Intelligent Car with Voice Assistance and Obstacle Detector to Aid the Disabled. *Proc. Comput. Sci.*, 167, 1732–1738, 2020. 10.1016/j.procs.2020.03.383, https://doi.org/10.1016/j.procs.2020.03.383.

17. Guerra, B.M.V., Ramat, S., Beltrami, G., Schmid, M., Automatic Pose Recognition for Monitoring Dangerous Situations in Ambient-Assisted

Living. *Front. Bioeng. Biotechnol.*, 8, 415, 2020. https://doi.org/10.3389/fbioe.2020.00415.

18. Linn, T., Jwaid, A., Clark, S., Smart glove for visually impaired. *2017 Computing Conference*, London, pp. 1323–1329, 2017, https://doi.org/10.1109/SAI.2017.8252262.

19. https://www.forbes.com/sites/rebeccabanovic/2019/04/20/anora-the-smart-glove-helping- the-blind/#61c79e18173e.

20. David Chung Hu, B., Fahmi, H., Yuhao, L., Kiong, C.C., Harun, A., Internet of Things (IoT) Monitoring System for Elderly. *2018 International Conference on Intelligent and Advanced System (ICIAS)*, Kuala Lumpur, pp. 1–6, 2018. https://doi.org/10.1109/ICIAS.2018.8540567.

21. Rodrigues, D., Luis-Ferreira, F., Sarraipa, J., Goncalves, R., Behavioural Monitoring of Alzheimer Patients with Smartwatch Based System, in: *Proceedings of the 2018 International Conference on Intelligent Systems (IS)*, IEEE, Funchal-Madeira, Portugal, 25–27 September 2018, pp. 771–775.

22. Stavropoulos, T.G. *et al.*, IoT Wearable Sensors and Devices in Elderly Care: A Literature Review. *Sensors (Basel, Switzerland)*, 20, 10 2826, 16 May. 2020.

23. Karakaya, M., Sengül, G., Bostan, A., Remotely Monitoring Activities of the Elders Using Smart Watches. *Int. J. Sci. Res. Inf. Syst. Eng.*, 3, 56, 2017, https://doi.org/10.3390/s20102826.

24. Ghazal, B. and Khatib, K., Smart Home Automation System for Elderly, and Handicapped People using XBee. *Int. J. Smart Home*, 9, 203–210, 2015, https://doi.org/10.14257/ijsh.2015.9.4.21.

25. Chaturvedula, K., U.P., RFID Based Embedded System for Vehicle Tracking and Prevention of Road Accidents. *Int. J. Eng. Res. Technol.*, 1, 6, 2012.

9

IoT-Based Health Monitoring and Tracking System for Soldiers

Kavitha N.* and Madhumathy P.

Department of ECE, RV Institute of Technology and Management, Bangalore, India

Abstract

In the present era, securing our nation soldiers' health is one of the primary duties of an army for securing our nation from enemy warfare. The nationwide protection is primarily dependent on the ground army, air-force, and navy. The soldiers play a significant role in securing our nation. Our country's defense department must be equipped with the requirement to secure our soldier's health. Hence, we propose an IoT-based system to monitor and track the soldier's health; mainly, it is required for army persons who take part in unusual mission activity. The soldier's health has been monitored by IoT-based system and located through GPS (Global Positioning Systems). This is feasible by using the temperature sensor, heartbeat sensor, and technologies involved in communication required for health related issues. Here, initially, soldier's body temperature is measured using LM35, and pulse rate using a heartbeat sensor and the values obtained are being compared with the threshold value kept on the basis of standard human body value; once the monitored value of the soldier exceeds that threshold value, automatically, control room will receive the information by specifying value obtained on the sensor.

Depending on that value, the doctors being present in the control room will take immediate action based on the severity of the patient. The immediate medication will be started by tracking the soldier's location in the war field by attaching the smart sensors to the soldier's body. For complete mobility with a personal server, it has been implemented. It would, in turn, through wireless mode give a message to the server base station. Depending on unique IP address, soldiers have been identified at the earliest.

Corresponding author: kavithaprashanthn@gmail.com

Rohit Tanwar, S. Balamurugan, R. K. Saini, Vishal Bharti and Premkumar Chithaluru (eds.) *Advanced Healthcare Systems: Empowering Physicians with IoT-Enabled Technologies,* (115–136) © 2022 Scrivener Publishing LLC

Keywords: Health monitoring system, IoT, wireless health sensors, embedded processor, GPS, temperature sensor, cloud computing

9.1   Introduction

Indian army is one of the largest standing armed forces in the world with 255 active troops counting 1,200,255 and reserve troop counting nearly 990,960 [2]. The unavailability of information about the injuries of army people would lead to permanent disability/death, and majorly causalities are not due to direct assaults in the battle field but due to injuries.

The control room will be having real-time information which includes exact location of the soldier and health is made immediately available then immediate medication can be provided and soldier's safety issues can be taken care. The main cause for army suffering is due to unavailability of information regarding health and unable to track the position of soldiers. The soldier's safety has many drawbacks such as failure in providing continuous communication about current location of soldiers in-par with the control room, requires instant medical interest, and operations underneath various geographical conditions, which are the some important safety issues.

Improving country's security, several relief funds are released for disasters caused due to natural or man-made; Armed Forces have been strengthened by providing financial support to the defense equipment by taking the initiative of Make-in-India. In latest IT scenarios, cloud computing is becoming an imagined paradigm shift. Cloud computing provides a centralized virtual environment for users without any active physical infrastructure investment. Clients can store cloud data and run internet applications. Computing is a massive pool of services that can provide customers with a system and a small-to-large hardware platform. The server that stores data from a specific user is leased/rented to the user on a monthly basis. This use can be increased or reduced and the customer will only be charged according to the use [7].

The conventional techniques for monitoring soldiers' health in battle field were tracking systems based on GSM and ZigBee, walkie-talkie. These methodologies had few drawbacks such as signal loss, noisy signals, and bulky in nature with higher installation cost. Hence, we need a system to overcome these drawbacks, wherein we aim at a system which is at lower cost, wireless system, portable, and highly reliable in tracking the soldier's life on the battlefield. In addition to that, the system should be in such a way that it can be used in real-time scenarios for providing immediate medication for the needy soldiers. There is no single mechanism to provide all of the specified services. However, we can identify a very important mechanism that is cryptographic technique that supports all forms of information integrity. Information encryption is the most common way of providing security. The anticipated is an IoT system which would continuously communicate about the soldiers' health condition and also the location.

Here, GPS can be used with proposed system for monitoring temperature of body and pulse rate of each and every individual. The monitored health parameters have been conveyed through IoT-based system to control room for further actions, wherein as soon as the location and position of the soldiers have been tracked, they have been guided to medication centers for further actions.

9.2   Literature Survey

Literature survey is the reference of some of the approaches already used. So, any new approach should be developed by the reference of some of the old and existing approaches.

GPS-based system for tracking and monitoring solders health [1]: The primary challenges that exist in military operations are to provide continuous communication with base (control room). It requires vigilant preparation and synchronization for appropriate routing among soldier's organizations. Hence, GPS is used to track the soldier location which has been communicated to control room station for further action, wherein communicating the relay information within short-range at high speed using bio-medical sensor, mainly by implementing M-Health system. Such implementation secures soldiers' health and, in turn, country will be secured. In addition to that, real-time video is also provided. These real-time information helps in reducing the casualties caused due to war, and also warnings are given to soldiers by providing critical information.

A real-time autonomous soldier health monitoring [2]: The main motivation for this is Indo-Pak War that took place on 1971, in that 54 soldiers families were declared missing. Over 160 million people died in wars. This is mainly due to the fact of incessant warfare which took place in modern times. Hence, a wireless sensor network has been used wherein multifunctional sensor nodes have been used which consumes less power, cheap, and multifunctional with miniaturization to communicate for short distances, which are integral part of military C4ISRT system. It would ensure safety of every soldier in the armed forces by making them to wear a device which would periodically update pulse rate value of the of the wearer, which has transmitter at source in GPS module which would track the location of the wearer during difficult situations, such as intimating immediately when pulse rate falls below the threshold.

An IoT-based patient monitoring system using Raspberry Pi [3]: The Raspberry Pi is one of the major platforms to learn IoT, since it provides low cost and tiny platform with Linux server. On Raspberry Pi, general purpose I/O pins and actuators have been interfaced. Here, patient's body temperature and heart rate are monitored using specialized sensor. Few sensors such as temperature, respiration, accelerometer, and heartbeat have been connected to Raspberry Pi which acts as small clinic. The data collected through Raspberry Pi has been transferred through wireless mode to IoT website through internet, since MAC address has been already registered to the internet and also been added to the board. After connecting Raspberry Pi and sensors, on the monitor screen, output is obtained when we connect all system terminals to Raspberry Pi board.

Cloud computing–based smart system to connect e-health sensors [4]: Cloud computing is one of the technological services providing various computing resources which are compatible, namely, services and application. Since cloud computing is flexible and modern technique to manage with less effort, automated techniques with high storage capacity and low cost. Raspberry Pi and wireless health sensors are connected to accumulate the data being sent from sensors, further the accumulated data has been transmitted through wireless mode to the cloud through platform services. This combination of Raspberry Pi with cloud computing and wireless sensor networks would result in novel generation of technology in terms of monitoring the patient, and efficiency of medical staff performance has been improved and also a range of data mining method are applied to take out and analyze patients data in minimal cost.

Hence, a system is designed to accurately monitor soldiers' health accurately with system architecture.

9.3   System Requirements

The process of dividing a multipart topic into minor blocks for enhanced understanding is called analysis. In engineering field, the parameters that we consider are dimensions of the system, involved mechanism, and also structures for investigating the activity called analysis. The life cycle of the task starts at this analysis phase. In this phase, only a multipart task has been divided into exhaustive requirements of business. It also guides us in collecting the required entities on the basis of application complexity and also the path to be followed when task documents have been created. The entire procedure has a repetitive involving a method to gather the required documents, and effective communication and requirements are being managed.

9.3.1 Software Requirement Specification

A prerequisite requirement of system software to be developed is called software requirements. Software Requirement Specification (SRS) consists of non-functional requirements and also software functions. Software engineering is composed of specification, elicitation, validation, and analysis of software requirements.

9.3.2 Functional Requirements

- The system must send a message to the owner whenever a soldier is in danger.
- Each sensor senses respective input, processes, and gives desired output.
- Basically, to track any soldier, we need latitude and longitude which will be obtained from GPS and in microcontroller memory it is being stored.
- The tracked coordinates of soldier's position have been displayed on LCD screen along with status of their health is also been displayed.

9.4 System Design

Designing of a system is a process of defining system architecture which has a modules defined for a system requirements being specified as shown in Figure 9.1. It is a technique to develop application oriented product "blends the perspective of marketing, design, and manufacturing into a single approach to product development"; further, product which is to be manufactured has been designed by considering the information about marketing.

System Architecture

The ARM7 TDMI core is 32-bit RISC embedded processor which yields in preeminent arrangement and also the characteristics of area and power. The processor is of smaller size, consumes less power, and yields good results.

- The 32-bit ARM processor operates with higher flexibility and maximum performance.
- Both instructions and data are of 32-bit.
- It supports pipelining in three-stages.
- The operation is fully static.
- It has a coprocessor-type interface.
- It has an embedded ICE debug facilities.
- Specific process technologies have been ported to generic layout.
- SoC integration process has been simplified by unified memory bus.

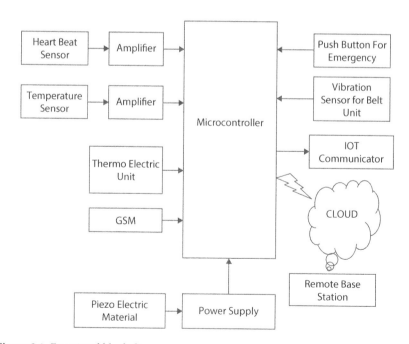

Figure 9.1 Functional block diagram.

- ARM7TDMI-S is binary-compatible family such as ARM9, ARM9E, and ARM10 where higher level microcontroller or microprocessor is used to port design.
- The devices which are battery-powered should consume less power and design is static.
- Coprocessors are used for extending the instruction set with specific requirements.
- Debug facilities in real-time is carried out by embedded ICE-RT and optional ETM units.

The performance of ARM's processor is advantageous compared to conventional 16-bit processor because density standard ARM code is twice. This is probable only when Thumb code act as ARM code on 32-bit register. Since Thumb code is equivalent to 65% code size of ARM due to which the performance is equivalent to 160 % of ARM processor. This yields in full speed execution of flash implementation in ARM mode.

9.4.1   Features

- ARM7TDMI-S is 16-bit/32-bit microcontroller comprising in-built flash memory of 32 to 512 KB, static RAM of 8 to 40 KB with LQFP64 package. It operates at 60 MHz having interface/accelerator of 128-bit wide.
- It has boot loader software which is in-built with In-System Programming/In-Application Programming (ISP/IAP), and it also includes 400-ms single flash sector and 256 bytes programming in 1 ms.
- It has a capability of tracing instruction execution at a higher speed rate and also offers on-chip Real Monitor software by embedded ICE RT.
- It has endpoint RAM which is 2-KB device controller with full-speed compliant.
- LPC2146/48 uses DMA in-built RAM of 8 KB to USB.
- LPC2142/44/46/48 provides variable analog output by DAC of single 10-bit.
- It has PWM unit, watchdog having two timers/external events counters of 32 bit.
- It has a clock input of 32 kHz Real-Time Clock (RTC) consumes less power.

- It has SSP with variable data length and buffering capabilities, 16C550, two UARTs, 400 kbit/s, two I2C-bus, and SPI.
- Vectored Interrupt Controller (VIC) is used to configure the priorities and has vector addresses.
- Tiny LQFP64package has 5 V tolerant I/O pins out of 45.
- On the whole 21 external interrupt pins exist.
- It has in-built 60-MHz CPU clock with operating range from 1 to 25 MHz.
- It has power-down and idle as the power saving modes.
- The power optimization is carried out by either enabling or disabling the peripheral functions and clock scaling.
- Through external interrupt, processor can be switched from power-down mode to power-on mode.
- CPU operates at a voltage 3 to 3.6 V using POR and BOD circuits on a single power supply chip.

9.4.1.1   On-Chip Flash Memory

There are different types of flash memory system, namely, LPC2141/42/44/46/48 include a 32, 64, 128, 256, and 512 KB, respectively. To store data as well as code and flash memory is used. There are several ways to program flash memory such as through serial port programming system. When application is running, flash may be erased by application program, which is flexible for storing data, upgrading field firmware, etc. Here, 100,000 erase/write minimum cycles have been provided for a data-retention of 20 years.

9.4.1.2   On-Chip Static RAM

In-built static RAM is used to store code and data. It uses 8-, 16-, and 32-bit SRAM in LPC2141, LPC2142/44, and LPC2146/48, respectively. Suppose LPC2146/48 is used as 8-KB SRAM, then it is used for storing code, execution, and data, and USB is mainly used for the block intended to.

9.4.2   Pin Control Block

Most of the microcontroller pins are multifunctional. The on-chip peripherals and pin connection is controlled through multiplexers by configuration registers. To specific pin, peripherals are connected and activated by enabling interrupts. In a hardware environment, few pin peripheral functions are not assigned; those pins are considered as undefined. The microcontroller functionality is to have a pin select registers in a Pin Control Module. Ports 0 and 1 are constituted as input when we reset all pins with few exceptions: JTAG is assumed to be functional by JTAG pin when we enable debug pin; Trace is assumed to be functional by Trace pin when we enable trace. The open drain interface pins are I2C0 and I2C1.

9.4.3   UARTs

There exist two UARTs in LPC2141/42/44/46/48. Handshake interface with full modem control is provided along with standard transmit and receive data lines compared to other microcontrollers such as LPC2000. For both UARTs, i.e., PC2141/42/44/46/48 fractional baud rate has been generated to enable the microcontroller with standard rates such of 115,200 for more than 2-MHz crystal frequency. Hardware has been fully implemented with flow-control functions using auto-CTS/RTS.

9.4.3.1   Features

- Based on FIFO, 16-byte data has been received and transmitted.
- FIFO receiver triggering points are at 1, 4, 8, and 14 bytes.
- Without external crystal frequency baud rate has been generated by built-in fractional baud rate generator.
- Transmission flow control is implemented on FIFO basis using XON/XOFF software on both UARTs
- Interface signals in standard modem are equipped in LPC2144/46/48 UART1 module providing hardware flow control using auto-CTS/RTS.

9.4.4   System Control

A control loop is being used for regulating other devices behavior, directs, and manages the control system.

9.4.4.1   Crystal Oscillator

External crystal frequency ranges from 1 to 25 MHz is used as oscillator. Here, fosc is referred as oscillator output frequency and CCLK is referred as ARM processor clock frequency. Until and unless PLL is running and connected, both clock frequencies have same value.

9.4.4.2   Phase-Locked Loop

The clock frequency is given as an input to phase-locked loop (PLL) which ranges from 10 to 25 MHz. The Current Controlled Oscillator (CCO) is multiplied with input frequency which ranges from 10 to 60 MHz, which ranges from 1 to 32 but the microcontroller family which we have considered here to which integer value cannot exceed 6 because of the CPU's upper frequency limit. Since desired output frequency is provided by PLL due to the CCO frequency ranges from 156 MHz to 320 MHz, hence no additional divider is required in the loop. The PLL chip which is reset can be enabled by software. The PLL is activated and configured by programming; PLL is connected to a clock source after it has been locked then 100 μs is given as settling time.

9.4.4.3   Reset and Wake-Up Timer

Watchdog reset and RESET pin are two sources on the LPC2141/42/44/46/48. The glitch filter is present along with Schmitt trigger input in RESET pin. Wake-up timer has been reset using chip reset assertion which would be present until it de-assert external reset, and initialization of on-chip flash controller will be completed, passing of specific number of clocks and working of the oscillator.

The processor will start executing at address 0 when we remove internal reset which is nothing but reset vector. Predetermined values are used for initialization of all peripheral registers.

It verifies whether chip operation and oscillator are functional before instructions are executed. It mainly plays a major role; when we turn off aforementioned functions due to some reasons, wake-up timer is used for processor wake-up from power-down mode caused due to turning off oscillator and other functions.

Before executing any code, wake-up timer will monitor crystal oscillator. The oscillator yields a significant amplitude signal for driving the clock signal if there is a power-down mode. There are many factors that are dependent on amount of time taken such as value of VDD ramp during power on mode and also crystal type such as quartz crystal behavior during the present ambient conditions and also there signal depending on external circuitry.

9.4.4.4   Brown Out Detector

There exist two levels of voltage monitoring on VDD pins such as LPC 2141/42/44/46/48. The BOD interrupt signal is asserted to the VIC, if the voltage is less than 2.9 V, where VIC is connected to BOD interrupt signal. Using interrupt signal, it can be enabled otherwise software is used to read the signal being monitored and will be stored in the specific register. In next stage, detecting low voltage is carried out if voltage on VDD pin is less than 2.6 V which would, in turn, deactivate LPC 2141/42/44/46/48. This low voltage would make the chip unreliable and also avoid changes in the flash memory. The reset down voltage less than 1 V is maintained by BOD circuit simultaneously overall reset is maintained by POR circuitry. Hysteresis is maintained for threshold voltages of 2.9 and 2.6 V. During the typical process, 2.9-V detection is allowed by hysteresis which will be reliable interrupt or it can be an event loop for sense the condition which has been regularly executed.

9.4.4.5   Code Security

The applications can be controlled or debugged from LPC2141/42/44/46/48 feature. When valid checksum is detected after on-chip boot loader is reset from flash, it has been read from address 0x1FC as 0x8765 4321 in flash, and the flash code has been protected when debugging has been disabled. We can enable the disabled debugging by using the ISP for full chip erase.

9.4.4.6   External Interrupt Inputs

There are few selectable pin functions which are level sensitive external interrupt inputs in LPC 2141/42/44/46/48. We can have four interrupt signals which are independent with respect to external events when we combine the pins. From power-down mode, we can make the processor to power-up mode by using inputs of external interrupt. For external interrupts, few capture input pins are used.

9.4.4.7   Memory Mapping Control

The interrupt vectors mapping will be changed by Memory Mapping Control from address 0x00000000. To flash memory or to static RAM interrupt, vectors have been mapped which helps in controlling the interrupts for uninterrupted code execution at different memory spaces.

9.4.4.8   Power Control

The idle and power-down modes are two reduced power modes in LPC2141/42/44/46/48. Until and unless either reset or interrupt occurs, instruction execution will be suspended. In idle mode, processor resumes execution based on interrupt generation and peripheral function operation will be continued. Usage of power by the processor will be eliminated during idle mode. Chip does not receive any internal clocks since oscillator is shut down during power-down mode. During power-down mode, the values of peripheral registers, SRAM, and processor state registers have been conserved and chip output pins logic levels remain static. Using either specific interrupts or reset, normal operation can be restarted from the power-down mode which can function without the intervention of clocks. RTC can be kept active during power-down mode by selecting clock source of 32-kHz external clock as an alternative to PCLK to ensure that RTC is active even in the power-down mode by enabling microcontroller. Keeping RTC active, we can increase power-down current. It will be lesser than idle mode.

In certain application, several individual peripherals need to be in off state if it is not used; it has been controlled by peripherals power control which would save the power both in active and idle mode.

9.4.5   Real Monitor

Real-time debugging is carried out by Real Monitor manufactured by ARM Inc., which is one of the configurable software modules. It is one of the backgrounds running in lightweight debug monitor where user will be debugging their foreground application. In presence of embedded ICE logic, DCC is used to communicate with the host. Here, Real Monitor software with specific configuration is programmed into on-chip flash memory. In the on-chip flash memory, Real Monitor software has been programmed containing specific configuration in LPC2141/42/44/46/48.

9.4.5.1   GPS Module

In most of the electronic gadgets and automobiles, GPS module has been used for tracking the commerce all over the globe. This module would give specific position and time of the device instantaneously. To get the tracking details, mainly, we require a GPS receiver which is cheaper and tiny.

It took decades of research to create GPS module to get exact location from any point to anywhere. Since 1970 till date, several GPS satellites are launched for tracking the device. Through dedicated radio frequencies (RFs), satellites will be continuously transmitting the data down to earth. In turn, tiny GPS receivers will have antennas and tiny processors for receiving the data through the antenna directly from GPS satellites which help in estimating the position and time. Ground stations and constellation of satellites are used by the GPS receivers to estimate location and time from any point on earth. All the time, there will be a minimum of 24 active satellites orbiting above earth over12,000 miles. The satellites positions are built in such a way that there will be at least 12 satellites above your location.

The RF which ranges from 1.1 to 1.5 GHz is used for transmitting the information to the earth through visible satellites. GPS module is used for estimating time and position by performing mathematical calculation on data transmission and reception.

GPS receivers were able to accurately estimate time and position based on information being forwarded to earth through satellite. Due to the presence of accurate atomic clock, GPS satellite was able to estimate the time accurately. Mainly, time has been estimated accurately by the combination of arrival times of various points on the sky and atomic clock timing at which it has been moved to earth. That is from the visible satellites, time stamp and data will be received by the GPS module, and this would give the each satellite distance to GPS receiver.

Through serial interface in various formats, GPS data has been exhibited. There are two types of message formats such as standard and nonstandard. NMEA data is given as output from all GPS receivers. The lines of data formatted in NMEA standard are called sentences. The various data bits in each sentence are organized in such a way that data has been separated by commas.

9.4.6 Temperature Sensor

- The temperature measured by estimating the ratio between electrical output to temperature by LM35 which has temperature sensor
- It accurately measures the temperature than thermistor.
- The sensor circuitry is not subjected to oxidation it is sealed.
- LM35 is more efficient than thermocouples in generating higher output voltage and output voltage need not be amplified.

9.4.7   Power Supply

The power supply of electronic circuits and other devices are designed for converting AC mains with high voltage to appropriate less supply voltage. Each block executes a specific function. Regulated DC power supply is one which preserves constant output voltage irrespective of load variations or AC mains fluctuations. Power supply block diagram is shown in Figure 9.2.

9.4.8   Regulator

Fixed voltage such as 5V, 12V and 15V and also output voltages which are a variable are also present in voltage regulator ICs. It has been rated based on the upper limit current is passed. Most regulators has overload protection and thermal protection. Unlike power transistors fixed voltage regulator also has 3 leads such as 7805 +5V 1A regulator. For regulating the power supply positive lead needs to be connected to your unregulated DC power supply.

9.4.9   LCD

In today's market, 1 Line, 2 Line, or 4 Line LCDs are most commonly available, it holds up to 80 characters with a single controller, whereas 2 HD44780 controllers is used if we want to hold up more than 80 characters. This would help in creating animated text scripts and so on other than

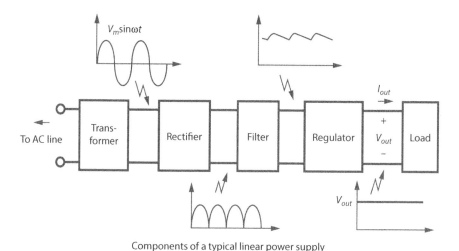

Components of a typical linear power supply

Figure 9.2 Functional block diagram of power supply.

Figure 9.3 Heartbeat sensor.

displaying simple static characters. Usually, the LCD switch 1 controller has 14 Pins and 16 Pins, i.e., additional pins are connections with backlight LED.

9.4.10   Heart Rate Sensor

The heartbeat is measured through sensor by placing finger on it. To determine heartbeat, the microprocessor is interfaced to sensor showing digital output as shown in Figure 9.3. Depending on each pulse in the finger blood flow, it has been measured on light modulation principle. Usual quiescent heart rate for adults ranges between 60 and 100 beats per minute (bpm). Therefore, 60 to 100 bpm is the threshold kept for measurement. Hence, if the soldier heartbeat exceeds, the threshold value automatically information will broadcast to control room.

9.5   Implementation

A specific algorithm is implemented through computer programming and deployment of computer system. World Wide Web Consortium is implemented through web browsers and programming languages are implemented through software development tools.

When an interface is implemented through concrete class object-oriented programming occurs as special case, the interface has concrete class implementation and it includes implementations methods precise by the interface.

In many industries, clients have been guided regarding the purchase of hardware or software which is referred as the implementation of post-sales process. It mainly requires systems integrations, analysis of scope, customizations and policies of user, and training and delivery of users. Task management methodologies are used by task manager for overseeing the steps. Several professionals are unaware of business and technical analysts and so on in the knowledge-based economy for implementations of software.

For successful implementation of a system in a systematic way, a huge number of tasks are required to be carried out which are inter-related. Making use of methodology which is well-proven for implementation and combining the professional recommendation will aid but often it leads to deprived planning and insufficient resourcing would mainly leads to many problems during task implementation which would hinder in achieving the desired results.

9.5.1   Algorithm

1. Pulse rate sensor is used for computing the soldier pulse rate. The pulse rate will be tracked once it traverses threshold level then automatically sends attentive message to control room and also the pulse rate being displayed on LCD.
2. LM35 temperature sensor used for measuring soldier body temperature, and if it exceeds entry level, then automatically attentive note is being forwarded to control room.
3. Further using GPS receiver, exact location of soldier has been tracked and information is passed to control room.
4. In case of emergency situation, panic button will be pressed by the soldiers to intimate the control room.

9.5.2   Hardware Implementation

ARM Microcontroller: It is one of the Acorn RISC Machine, and it has a fewer instruction set for computation in a various environments of a computer processors. It has been developed by ARM Holdings, and to other companies, licenses are provided. The products are designed by their own which as either systems-on-chips (SoC) or systems-on-modules (SoM) architectures which integrates interfaces, memory, radios, etc. Keeping this instruction set, core has been designed and licenses are provided to other companies to implement in their own products.

Universal Asynchronous Receiver-Transmitter (UART): It is a device which provides asynchronous serial communication where transmission speeds and data format are configurable. Outside the UART, driver circuit being present manages the electrical signals. For serial communications, UART is used as IC in serial port to connect computer or peripheral device. Similarly synchronous operation is also supported by Universal Synchronous and Asynchronous Receiver-Transmitter (USART).

Controller: The controller controls the working and mechanisms of heartbeat sensor, vibration sensor, and GPS.

Heartbeat Sensor: It measures the soldier heart rate per minute and soldiers' health conditions have been monitored by keeping threshold value as the reference. If it exceeds or decreases the set threshold value, then it is considered that soldier is in critical condition.

Temperature Sensor: Body temperature is measured by this sensor. The temperature range at which it is operated ranges from −55°C to 150°C. The standard human temperature is around 370°C [6]. Hence, 300°C to 400°C is considered as threshold value.

GPS: This tracks soldier movements in the battlefield. This module uses a geostationary satellite where it is possible to know the location of the soldier.

Wi-Fi Module: EPS Wi-Fi 8266 module offer a flash memory of 512K. It is one of the user friendly module in terms of configuration and set up with lesser cost. Each and every soldier is identified through unique IP address of every module being present with soldier. To control room, every soldier is connected with EPS8266 module IP address.

9.5.3   Software Implementation

Embedded C: It is the C programming language extensions used for addressing commonality issues in extensions for different embedded systems. Historically, to maintain interesting features which includes fixed-point arithmetic, I/O operation basic, and numerous different memory banks, nonstandard extensions to the C language are used in embedded C programming.

Keil μVision3: It is one of the IDE (Integrated Development Environment) which eases to write and compile embedded programs. It sums up tool configuration, a task manager, a powerful debugger, a make facility, and editor. Several example programs such as printing the string "Hello World" uses Serial Interface; for analog and digital systems, data acquisition system MEASURE is used; for traffic light controller, TRAFFIC with RTX is used with Tiny operating system.

Table 9.1 Test case for monitoring the soldiers' health.

Test Case ID #1	Test Case Description—Communication			
S#	**Prerequisites**	**S#**	**Test Data Requirement**	
1	Soldier must establish communication with base station.	1	IP address of soldier should be valid	
Test Condition				
Sending and Analyzing Health Parameters				
Step #	**Step Details**	**Expected Results**	**Actual Results**	**Pass/Fail/ Not Executed/ Suspended**
1	Receiving GPS signal	Communication Between soldier and base station	Got GPS Signal	Pass
2	Monitoring body temperature (T)	Popping of value in degree Celsius	Soldier is normal or Soldier is freezing.	Pass
3	Monitoring of heart rate (H)	Popping of value in beats/min	Display of heart rate	Pass
4	Emergency situation	Popping of alert message to base station	Display of word "EMERGENCY"	Pass
5	Tracking location of soldier	Popping of message of GPS location along with emergency alert	Popping of message of soldiers GPS location	Pass

9.6   Results and Discussions

The quality of the application has been analyzed by testing the software in development stage by providing cessation utilizer, and by undergoing several stages of testing, the application has been developed and implemented.

Test cases have been validated on the basis of functionality features of software application as shown in Table 9.1. Various test scenarios considered are indistinct and cover an extensive range of possibilities.

The wireless sensors are embedded into the jacket and connection is established between soldier and the base station. The threshold range is set for every parameter and with respect to the threshold value appropriate action will be taken.

9.6.1   Heart Rate

The heartbeat sensor is designed to measure heartbeat when finger is placed on it. It works on the principle of light modulation by blood flow through finger at each pulse. A normal heart rate depends on the individual's age and body size. For adults 18 and older, a normal resting heart rate is between 60 and 100 beats per minute (bpm), depending on the person's physical condition and age and the output heart rate is shown in Figure 9.4. Hence, the measurement threshold is set from 60 to 100 bpm. Whenever heartbeat of soldier will deviate from the threshold value, the system will transmit information to control room.

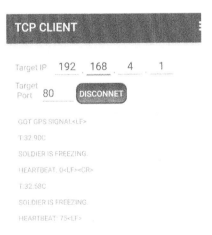

Figure 9.4 Output for heart rate.

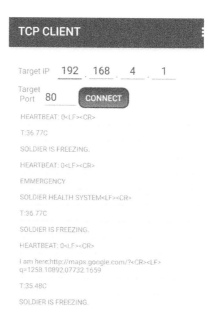

Figure 9.5 Output for temperature sensor.

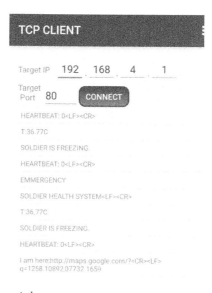

Figure 9.6 Output for panic button.

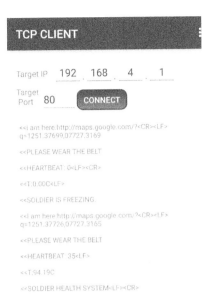

Figure 9.7 Output for GPS services.

9.6.2   Temperature Sensor

LM35 is a temperature sensor which is widely used to measure body temperature. This device is rated to operate over a −55°C to 150°C temperature range. The normal human temperature is around 370°C [5]. Hence, a threshold value in the range of 300 to 400 C is considered. The output of temperature sensor shown in Figure 9.5.

9.6.3   Panic Button

Panic button is one kind of switch which is provided to soldiers to help in panic situation. If soldier presses panic button, then system will generate an alert by which the base camp will come to know if soldiers are in difficult situation. The output of panic button shown in Figure 9.6.

9.6.4   GPS Receiver

The GPS unit is installed in addressing system so that base camp can track their movements and real-time information in all weather, at all times form anywhere on globe. The output of GPS services shown in Figure 9.7.

9.7 Conclusion

This chapter reports on an IoT-based system for the health monitoring and tracking of soldiers. Biomedical sensors provide heartbeat, body temperature, and environmental parameters of every soldier to control room. This technology can be helpful to provide the accurate location of missing soldier in critical condition and overcome the drawback of soldiers missing in action. The addressing system is also helpful to improve the communication between soldier to soldier in emergency situation and provide proper navigation to control room. Thus, we can conclude that this system will act as a lifeguard to the army personnel of all over the globe. In future, a portable handheld sensor device with more sensing options may be developed to aid the soldiers. In addition to that, Grove gas sensors can be placed which measures oxygen concentration in environment, medical instruction can be given to the soldiers to overcome the situation, and ZigBee technology can be used for extending the range of network for communication.

References

1. Kumar, P., Rasika, G., Patil, V., Bobade, S., Health Monitoring and Tracking of Soldier Using GPS. *Int. J. Res. Advent Technol.*, 2, 4, 291–294, Apr. 2014.
2. Sharma, S., Kumar, S., Keshari, A., Ahmed, S., Gupta, S., Suri, A., A Real Time Autonomous Soldier Health Monitoring and Reporting System Using COTS Available Entities. *Second International Conference on Advances in Computing and Communication Engineering (ICACCE)*, Deharadun-India, pp. 683–687, May 2015.
3. Kumarand, R. and Rajasekaran, M., An IoT based patient monitoring system using raspberry Pi. *International Conference on Computing Technologies and Intelligent Data Engineering*, Kovilpatti-India, pp. 1–4, Jan. 2016.
4. Jassas, M., Abdullah, A., Mahmoud, H., A Smart System Connecting e-Health Sensors and the Cloud. *IEEE 28thCanadian Conference on Electrical and Computer Engineering Halifax*, Canada, pp. 712–716, May 2015.
5. Shaikh, R., Real Time Health Monitoring System of Remote Patient Using Arm7. *Int. J. Instrum. Control Autom. (IJICA)*, 1, 3–4, 102–105, 4, 2012.
6. Kumar, D. and Repal, S., Real Time Tracking and Health Monitoring of Soldiers using ZigBee Technology: a Survey. *Int. J. Innov. Res. Sci. Eng. Technol.*, 4, 7, 5561–5574, Jul. 2015.
7. Raj, G. and Banu, S., GPS Based Soldier Tracking And Health Indication System With Environmental Analysis. *Int. J. Enhanc. Res. Sci. Technol. Eng.*, 2, 12, 46–52, Dec. 2013.

10

Cloud-IoT Secured Prediction System for Processing and Analysis of Healthcare Data Using Machine Learning Techniques

G. K. Kamalam* and S. Anitha†

Department of Information Technology, Kongu Engineering College, Perundurai, Erode, Tamilnadu, India

Abstract

Data analysis converts raw data into information useful for decision-making. In recent years, the most promising research area is healthcare data analysis. For efficient analysis of data, the critical tool emerged is machine learning (ML) that uses various statistical techniques and algorithms like supervised, unsupervised, and reinforcement to predict the results of data analysis on healthcare data more precisely. In ML, various algorithms, such as supervised learning, unsupervised learning, and reinforcement learning algorithms, are used for analysis. For analyzing different healthcare data, the chapter describes varied categories of ML techniques and commonly used probability distributions in Data Science like Bernoulli, Uniform, Binomial, and Normal (Gaussian) Distribution. In the healthcare field, cloud technology and Internet of Things (IoT) offer several opportunities to clinical IT. It improves healthcare services by identifying the disease caused by the human body and contributing its non-stop methodical innovation in a massive information domain. To manipulate patient records in cloud-IoT environments is still a big challenge because of extensive data. A new model does not require the intervention of human to analyze large volume of data received from numerous origins and also sensor data is presented. Fuzzy temporal neural classifier is applied in the cloud-IoT environment to optimize the secured storage and easy handling of a vast amount of patient records. Presented work pursuits the healthcare system's performance in reducing the execution time of patient's request, optimizing desired

---

**Corresponding author*: kamalamparames@gmail.com
†Corresponding author: anithame.it@kongu.edu

Rohit Tanwar, S. Balamurugan, R. K. Saini, Vishal Bharti and Premkumar Chithaluru (eds.) Advanced Healthcare Systems: Empowering Physicians with IoT-Enabled Technologies, (137–172) © 2022 Scrivener Publishing LLC

garage of patient's massive facts, and imparting records retrieval process for those applications. The experimental analysis outcome of the presented method performs better than existing benchmark systems considering parameters like disease prediction accuracy, sensitivity, specificity, F-measure, and computational time.

Keywords: Fuzzy neural classifier, disease prediction and accuracy, probability distribution, data analysis

10.1   Introduction

Healthcare is regard as a significant determinant in supporting the universal physical and mental health and comfort of people around the world. So, handling a large amount of patient's health data in manual and electronic form is essential and challenging. An Electronic Health Record (EHR) contains a patient's paper chart in a digitized format. EHRs were real time, containing patient records that easily and securely make information to the authorized users. The healthcare industry is generating a large amount of data that includes information about patients and their disease diagnosis reports. As the patient's data is large, machine learning (ML) techniques are using for implementation. The data are pre-processed and used for further analysis and prediction.

ML, a powerful transformative technology, transforms human society lifestyle. ML algorithms and techniques help in predicting the disease accurately and efficiently. ML takes part a critical position in healthcare mainly for clinical decision-making. It makes the system automatically learn and develop the programs to grow and change when exposed to the new data. The application of ML in hospitals is to analyze heterogeneous data, visualize, and predict diseases. In medical domains, to identify and diagnose diseases and predict future outcomes, ML techniques and tools are used. Learning medical data encounters several difficulties since the datasets are characterizing incompleteness, noisy data (incorrect), sparseness, and inappropriate data [1]. Since 80% of healthcare data is unstructured and consists of a multitude of patient databases, ML techniques integrated with soft computing yields performance and accuracy a better one [2].

In terms of efficiency and accuracy, Internet of Things (IoT) and cloud-based applications work better than ordinary applications. Medical, military, and banking were some of the applications based on cloud and IoT applications. Cloud-based IoT applications provide services to access patient records in remote areas. Healthcare applications collect the data timely and update medical parameters severity.

Integration of cloud technology and IoT brings an improvement over processing, achieving scalability due to distributed environment, and networking capacity provides a new space to address healthcare applications. AI (Artificial Intelligence), ANN (Artificial Neural Network), ACO (optimization algorithm, Ant Colony Optimization), etc., mine large volume of data, mine the information, and extract and perform processing of real-time data in the domain of healthcare. Cloud technology offers various services to the massive cloud users with diverse and dynamic environment.

ML algorithms in the decision-making process for handling large amounts of data play a major role. The model, such as neural network clustering method, effectively identifies the disease. In this work, a large amount of data of different types such as text, image, and audio are collected through IoT devices. Cloud storage system stores the collected data. The ML algorithm groups data into normal and abnormal.

Hospitals maintain the health record for all the patients. This information is beneficial to predict all kinds of diseases. The datasets of various diseases contain the attributes and values of the particular disease needed for the prediction. ML algorithms take place a prominent part in diagnosis and prediction. The doctors use outcome gained from this to provide better medical care and increase the patient's satisfaction. Medical data is classified into training data and test data. The algorithm uses training data to train model, and test set to measure accuracy of the model accuracy.

The chapter flow is organized as follows: Section 10.2 summarizes review on literature and Section 10.3 summarizes three different classifications of medical data. Section 10.4 proposes the various data analysis techniques used to analyze the diversified medical data. Section 10.5 describes the ML methods used in healthcare. Section 10.6 describes the probability distribution. Section 10.7 presents the various evaluation metrics to evaluate the ML model's performance accuracy builds to solve a problem. Section 10.8 explains the function of the proposed architecture. Section 10.9 briefs the experimental results. Section 10.10 provides conclusion.

10.2   Literature Survey

Verma and Sood [3] proposed a methodology which monitors, diagnose, and predicts the severity of the disease using cloud-integrated IoT technology. It mostly pays attention on student healthcare data. Using the standard UCI Repository, systematic health data in terms of student perspective has been generated. Various classification algorithms and sensors predict the diseases affecting the students with severity. Evaluation criteria like F-measure, specificity and sensitivity, and the prediction accuracy were calculated, but the system lacks security.

Li *et al.* [4] presented new energy model which analyzes video stream data in cloud- IoT domain, which is produced by vehicle cameras. Both real testbeds and simulations are performed for a specific application. The main drawback is that a large number of video streams cannot be stored in IoT devices.

Stergiou *et al.* [5] presented fuzzy c-means segmentation technique to predict the disease and reviewed various security issues encountered in using cloud-based IoT technologies. Also, the task of cloud computing in IoT functions is demonstrated. But, the method produces less prediction accuracy.

In the work of Avinash Golande *et al.* [6], the accuracy of using different techniques is compared. Training data is trained using ML algorithms like decision tree, KNN, K-means clustering, and support vector machine (SVM).

In the work of Seyedamin Pouriyeh *et al.* [7], the ML algorithm's performance is studied through 10-fold cross-validation method, implemented using decision tree algorithm. This algorithm is popularly used because it is fast, easy, and straightforward to interpret. Internal nodes in a decision tree represent the dataset attributes, and branches denote the outcome of each node. The SVM model is defined as a finite-dimensional vector in which each dimension represents the features. The limitation is that the response time is more.

In the work of Sellappan Palaniappan *et al.* [8], ML algorithms classified as supervised and unsupervised algorithms. Naive Bayes provides a new way of understanding and processing of data. The algorithm learns by calculating the correlation between the attributes (variables) and the target. The drawback is that accuracy of prediction is less and limited data is stored.

Kumar and Gandhi [9] build up three-tier architecture which handles an enormous amount of data. Firstly, the data collection process is taken care of by Tier-1. Secondly, storing a massive volume of sensor data in cloud computing is concentrated in Tier-2. Thirdly, a model is developed that identifies the symptoms of heart diseases using ROC analysis. But, the system needs security.

Gelogo *et al.* [10] explained different directions of applying IoT in u-healthcare applications. For IoT-based u-healthcare service, a new framework has been introduced. The results improve the performance of the healthcare service but need continuous data for diagnosis.

Gope and Hwang [11] proposed IoT-based medical device. Tiny, light-weight sensor networks monitor patients' health remotely. Moreover, the security need is also considered in designing the healthcare system. The drawback is that the system requires security.

Hossain and Muhammad [12] proposed a healthcare industrial IoT system for online monitoring of patient health. The system analyzes health records of patients with sensors and medical devices to adverse death circumstance. The system incorporates procedures to build security like watermarking, signal enhancements to circumvent clinical errors, and identity thefts. But, it takes more resources for the processing of data.

In IoT-based healthcare environment, risks are minimized using the Intelligent and Collaborative Security Model, proposed by Islam *et al.* [13]. The drawback is that the response time is very high.

To predict and diagnose the various deadly diseases, Sethukkarasi *et al.* [14] introduced model named Neuro-Fuzzy Temporal Knowledge Representation. But, the limitation is that accuracy and specificity is smaller than existing method.

In the work of Takayuki Katsuki *et al.* [15], current advances in the area of the medical field developing nowadays have been discussed. Based on patient data, ML techniques play a vital role in diagnosing diseases. Presently, all health institutions are adapting to EHRs. Health information about the patient is included in EHR. These records are useful for better results and the victory of the healthcare revolution.

Ganapathy *et al.* [16] proposed a classifier named Temporal Fuzzy Min-Max (TFMM). It classifies medical features for effective decision-making. Also, PSO-based rule extractor agent added which brings an improvement in accuracy of disease detection. But, security components are not included.

Mohan *et al.* [17] proposed Hybrid Random Forest with a Linear Model (HRFLM) that uses multiclass variables and binary classification for detecting heart disease with high prediction accuracy. But, the technique does not take into account the age factor.

10.3   Medical Data Classification

Specialized analytical technique extricates valuable information and converts into a form suitable for computation. The healthcare system generates enormous patient-related data that includes X-rays, diagnostic reports, signals like ECG, laboratory records, and MRI in either documents or Electronic Medical Records (EMR). These data are classified as structured data, unstructured data, and semi-structured data [18].

10.3.1   Structured Data

It is stored in relational database. Structured healthcare data include lab test results, a hierarchy of different kinds of diseases and their symptoms, information about a diagnosis, and patient medication prescriptions such as admission history and drug.

10.3.2   Semi-Structured Data

Data that do not meet the formal structure has been stored by self-describing identity. It consists of data generated from sensors and is intentionally provides as a source for monitoring the behavior of patient.

10.4   Data Analysis

Structured and unstructured medical datasets have unexplored, plenty of information that can be exploited using AI methods to diagnose diseases. ML techniques provide a pathway for the professionals of healthcare to analyze such data for irregularities [20]. The regimen of health analytics currently takes a path toward sophisticated level of prescriptive analysis instead of simple descriptive level analysis. Analytics in healthcare domain apply mathematical tools which analyze a large data volume to make decisions that help improve care for every patient. The need of data analytics will improve the quality of healthcare by providing efficient medicine that reduces readmission rate, earlier detection of diseases to avoid spreading and improving treatment methods. A healthcare organization incorporates descriptive and diagnostic analytics to improve the quality of treatment. But, for tangible benefits, predictive and prescriptive health analytics can be followed [21].

10.4.1   Descriptive Analysis

Descriptive analytics are used to quantify events and generate reports. Descriptive analytics is often utilized and effectively acknowledged a variety of analytics. Descriptive health analytics has been applied to medical data in many healthcare organizations. Healthcare analytics begins with descriptive analytics that considers events occurred, consumed resources, or patient's diagnosis charts. It helps to categorize, cluster, and classify the data, converting it into meaningful information that can enhance continuous monitoring and improve performance. Data summarization might be in the form of graphs and reports that illustrate how many patients were hospitalized, who are high-risk patients and should be treated first, the performance of surgeon, cost and facilities, etc. More number of envisioning is used by descriptive analytics [22].

10.4.2   Diagnostic Analysis

Diagnostic analytics takes the perception from descriptive analytics and dig into data, to understand the causes of those outcomes. Diagnostic analytics works on the investigation of historical data and discovers why it happens. For example, why the patient went to the hospital, and why he dropped the treatment. Diagnostic analytics needs more investigations and analysis of the health data to identify the problem cause and helps to understand the consequence faced due to that problem. In healthcare, diagnostic analytics will explore the data and make correlations [23].

10.4.3   Predictive Analysis

Predictive analytics uses historical data to train models and makes predictions on future outcomes. It tells what is likely to happen. Predictive analytics could be the advanced style of analytics and increases the accuracy of diagnosis. Predictive analytics will find the hidden patterns from large quantities of data, group the data into well-organized sets to predict the behavior, and discover the changes [24]. Predictive analytics in healthcare will accurately assess the early diagnosis of disease, risk scores for each patient by determining patterns, etc. Predictive analytics will help the health professionals by answering questions like which drugs should be used for treatment, who is likely to get the same symptoms, which patient will have the highest risk of hospitalization, and identify which patients may need additional attention [25].

10.4.4   Prescriptive Analysis

Prescriptive analytics integrates insight from all previous analyses leading to optimized decision-making. It determines what action to be taken in the future for the current problem or decision. The need for prescriptive analytics comes into picture when health problems involve too many choices to consider descriptive or predictive effectively. Prescriptive analytics identifies the problem. Prescriptive analytics predicts not only what will happen but also why it happens. For example, one can determine the drug dosage to achieve maximal cure in treatment. Alternatively, surgical choices are taken by considering the advantages and disadvantages of the surgical output. Prescriptive analytics supports both personalized medication and evidence-based medication area [26].

10.5   ML Methods Used in Healthcare

ML tools and methodology help in predicting as well as diagnosing diseases at early stages. The types of learning in ML can be classified into supervised, semi-supervised, and unsupervised learning.

10.5.1   Supervised Learning Technique

Supervised or prediction technique maps the available set of input data to a different labeled output. Build a model that can make predictions based on the relationship, which has been learned from past datasets [27]. It requires a training dataset with labels and trains the model to generate predictions for new data. If the output variable is categorical/discrete from a finite set, then the problem is called classification or pattern recognition. Predicting one of two classes, then it is a binary classification—for example: disease prediction of a patient. Suppose prediction is for more than two types, then multi-class classification [28]. The classification method helps in solving real-world problems. Supervised learning algorithms used in medical care detects lung diseases [29] and identifies different body parts from medical images [30]. It is used to predict a benign or malignant tumor to distinguish between healthy and non-healthy images in the future. It is also used to foretell the chance of heart attack within a year by analyzing earlier patients' data. Regression is like classification used to classify if the output is a continuous value. Logistic regression predicts the patient is affected by the diseases or not because of environmental factors. Regression technique foretells patient's life expectation [31].

ML methodologies naive Bayes classifier, C4.5 decision tree, ANNs, random forest, gradient boosted classification tree, etc., have been found to provide a different accuracy rate in disease prediction. A SVM is used to predict dementia, and its performance can be validated by statistical analysis. A supported vector machine can be used to identify rheumatoid arthritis with the patient's prescription records and improves the accuracy of predictive models of disease [32].

Decision trees identify the unhealthy condition of patient from healthcare data [33]. Risk level prediction during pregnancy and identification of the cardiovascular problem can be performed through decision trees.

The selection of feature subset in the Bayesian classifier is used to predict the survival of cirrhotic patients [34].

10.5.2   Unsupervised Learning

Unsupervised or descriptive learning finds hidden pattern. Unsupervised algorithms do not have output categories or labels on the data. Clustering is the standard unsupervised learning method for grouping data on similarity or dissimilarity measures. Phenotyping algorithms can be implemented on EMR data to identify the disease status of a group of patients who have a common diagnosis. Unsupervised learning method in healthcare includes detecting heart diseases by identifying carotid plaques and predicting hepatitis disease [35, 36]. K-means clustering algorithm predicts illness by identifying similarities in the attributes forming clusters [37]. It is used to distinguish different types of patients having more probability of being readmitted [38].

10.5.3   Semi-Supervised Learning

It learns from labeled and unlabeled data. In addition to labeled training images, it is applied for medical image segmentation [39]. A semi-supervised learning technique is used to patient's EHR for phenotype extraction [40].

10.5.4   Reinforcement Learning

Reinforcement learning learns from the opinion gathered through environment interaction and generates evaluative feedback. Feedback is provided as a reward to actions performed over time. With noisy, multi-dimensional, and incomplete data, RL provides solutions to optimal decision-making in various healthcare domains. RL approach advances toward some healthcare domains like dynamic treatment policies in chronic disease, automated medical diagnosis, i.e., mapping patient treatment history and symptoms to accurate classification of disease and other general domains like drug discovery and development, health management, etc. [41].

10.6   Probability Distributions

The two categories of probability distribution are discrete and continuous. Random variable is one which is obtained from statistical experiment outcome. Discrete random variable represents a finite set of positive integers, whereas continuous specifies infinite range values. It deals with a discrete random variable, whereas continuous probability distribution deals with a continuous random variable [42–44].

10.6.1   Discrete Probability Distributions

- Binary Random Variable: x is either 0 or 1.
- Continuous Random Variable: x ranges over 1, 2, 3 till m, where "m" is the total count of unique outcomes.

Each outcome of the discrete random variable contains probability. Discrete probability constitutes the association between outcome and probability. Probability Mass Function (PMF) specifies the probability of an inevitable outcome. Cumulative Distribution Function (CDF) returns probability value equal to else a value lower than a specified outcome. Percent-Point Function (PPF) provides discrete value, and the value is equal to otherwise less than given probability [42–44].

10.6.1.1   *Bernoulli Distribution*

The two outcomes are 0 or 1. It has only one trial. The random variable "X" takes a numeric input "one" for success probability (say, t), and input "zero" for failure (say $1 - t$). Equation (10.1) shows the PMF of a Bernoulli distribution [42–44].

$$P(x) = \begin{cases} 1-p, & x=0 \\ p, & x=1 \end{cases} \tag{10.1}$$

E(X) and V(X), expected and variance of "X", are defined in Equations (10.2) and (10.3), respectively.

$$E(X) = 1 * p + 0 * (1 - p) = p \tag{10.2}$$

$$V(X) = E(X^2) - [E(X)]^2 = p - p^2 = p(1 - p) \tag{10.3}$$

10.6.1.2   Uniform Distribution

In uniform distribution, infinite outcomes are possible [42–44]. Each outcome holds an identical probability. "X" follows uniform distribution if PDF is as shown in Equation (10.4):

$$f(x) = 1/(b - a) \quad for -\infty < a \leq x \leq b < \infty \tag{10.4}$$

E(X) and V(X), mean and variance of "X", are defined in Equations (10.5) and (10.6), respectively.

$$E(X) = \frac{(a+b)}{2} \tag{10.5}$$

$$V(X) = \frac{(b-a)^2}{12} \tag{10.6}$$

10.6.1.3   Binomial Distribution

The binomial distribution is a distribution with only two possible outcomes 0 or 1, where probability, success (p), and failure (q) are identical on all trials, and the outcomes need not be equally likely. Events whose outcome is binary use the binomial distribution [42–44].

Equation (10.7) shows the mathematical representation for a binomial distribution.

$$P(x) = \frac{n!}{(n-x)!x!} p^x q^{n-x} \tag{10.7}$$

The mean (μ) and variance Var(X) are shown in Equations (10.8) and (10.9), respectively.

$$\mu = n * p \tag{10.8}$$

$$Var(X) = n * p * q \tag{10.9}$$

If the success (p) and the count of trials (n) are known, then the formula for calculating success probability (x) among n trials is shown in Equation (10.10).

$$P(X=x)=\frac{n!}{x!(n-x)!}p^x(1-p)^{(n-x)} \tag{10.10}$$

10.6.1.4 Normal Distribution

PDF defined on "X" for a normal distribution is shown in Equation (10.11).

$$f(x)=\frac{1}{\sqrt{2\pi}\sigma}e^{\left(-\frac{1}{2}\left(\frac{x-\mu}{\sigma}\right)^2\right)} \quad for -\infty<x<\infty, \tag{10.11}$$

E(X) and Var(X), mean and variance of "X", are shown in Equations (10.12) and (10.13), respectively.

$$E(X)=\mu \tag{10.12}$$

$$Var(X)=\sigma^2 \tag{10.13}$$

Value of mean is zero and standard deviation is one [42–44]. For such a case, PDF becomes as shown in Equation (10.14).

$$f(x)=\frac{1}{\sqrt{2\pi}}e^{-x^2/2} \quad for -\infty<x<\infty, \tag{10.14}$$

10.6.1.5 Poisson Distribution

Events occur in time and space of random nature [42–44]. The PMF of "X" occurring distribution that is Poisson is outlined in Equation (10.15).

$$P(X=x)=e^{-\mu}\frac{\mu^x}{x!} \quad for\ x=0,1,2,\ldots\ldots \tag{10.15}$$

Mean (μ) is defined as shown in Equation (10.16).

$$\mu = \lambda * t \tag{10.16}$$

where
λ represents the rate at which an event occurs;
t represents the length of a time interval;
X represents the number of events in the time interval "t".
E(X) and Var(X) are shown in Equations (10.17) and (10.18), respectively.

$$E(X) = \mu \tag{10.17}$$

$$Var(X) = \mu \tag{10.18}$$

10.6.1.6   Exponential Distribution

Variable "X" having exponential distribution models the time occurrences among different events. Equation (10.19) shows the PDF of an exponential distribution [42–44].

$$f(x) = \{\lambda e^{-\lambda x}, \quad x \geq 0 \tag{10.19}$$

$\lambda > 0$ represents the rate parameter. E(X) and Var(X), mean and variance of "X" following exponential distribution, are shown in Equations (10.20) and (10.21), respectively.

$$E(X) = \frac{1}{\lambda} \tag{10.20}$$

$$Var(X) = \left(\frac{1}{\lambda}\right)^2 \tag{10.21}$$

10.7   Evaluation Metrics

To build an effective ML model, evaluating a model is essential. To focus on estimating the generalization accuracy of new and unseen data, assessing a ML model is critical. The evaluation model helps in model creation and selection that provides greater accuracy in unseen data. Evaluation metrics quantify the performance of a model. Different metrics that are available evaluates the model accuracy. Some of them are listed below [45–47].

10.7.1   Classification Accuracy

It is termed as ratio of correct and input sample predictions (the total input samples in the test set) [45–47]. Classification accuracy measures how often the classifier carries out the correct predictions, which is defined as shown in Equation (10.22).

$$Accuracy = \frac{number\ of\ correct\ predictions}{total\ number\ of\ predictions\ made} \qquad (10.22)$$

10.7.2   Confusion Matrix

A confusion matrix specifies the model performance. It depicts the detailed estimation of correct and incorrect predictions for each class. Its size is an N*N. In confusion matrix, "N" specifies number of predicted classes [45–47]. The binary classification problem consists of two classes, YES or NO, as shown in Table 10.1. Terms are defined as follows:

- Accuracy: the proportion of sum of correct predictions.
- Positive Predictive Value or Precision: proportion of correctly recognized positive cases.
- Negative Predictive Value: proportion of correctly recognized negative cases.
- Sensitivity or Recall: proportion of correctly recognized actual positive cases.
- Specificity: It is the proportion of correctly recognized actual negative cases.

True Positive (TP): Model precisely foretells positive class. That is, the predicted and actual output was YES.

Table 10.1 Confusion matrix.

Confusion Matrix		Target			
		Positive	Negative		
Model	Positive	a	b	Positive Predictive Value	a/(a + b)
	Negative	c	d	Negative Predictive Value	d/(c + d)
		Sensitivity	Specificity	Accuracy = (a + d)/ (a + b + c + d)	
		a/(a + c)	d/(b + d)		

True Negative (TN): Model precisely foretells the negative class. That is, the predicted and actual output was NO.

False Positive (FP): Model precisely foretells the positive class. That is, the predicted and actual output is YES and NO, respectively.

False negative (FN): Model precisely foretells the negative class. That is, the predicted output is No, and the actual output was YES.

10.7.3   Logarithmic Loss

It suits classification for multi-class problems. To calculate Log Loss for N samples and M classes is shown in Equation (10.23).

$$LogarithmicLoss = \frac{-1}{N} \sum_{i=1}^{N} \sum_{j=1}^{M} y_{ij} * \log(p_{ij}) \qquad (10.23)$$

where

y_{ij} represents that sample data i belongs to class j or not.

p_{ij} represents that the probability of sample data i belonging to class j.

Upper bound is not specified for Log Loss. Its range is [0, 8]. It leads to greater accuracy when value is nearer to 0, whereas it achieves lower accuracy if it is away from 0. Classifier achieves greater accuracy by minimizing Log Loss. Model is estimated as better one when Log Loss value is lower [45–47].

10.7.4   Receiver Operating Characteristic Curve, or ROC Curve

It is representation of a graphical plot exemplifying diagnostic ability. It exemplifies binary classification system by varying the discrimination threshold value. The curve is created by plotting sensitivity against (1-specificity) for different threshold values [45–47].

10.7.5   Area Under Curve (AUC)

Evaluating binary classification problems is done using this metric [45–47]. The critical fundamental terms are as follows:

True Positive Rate (Sensitivity): TP/(FN + TP) gives the value of TPR. TPR refers to the proportion of TP and the sum of FN and TP [Equation (10.24)].

$$TruePositiveRate = \frac{TruePositive}{FalseNegative + TruePositive} \quad (10.24)$$

True Negative Rate (Specificity): TN/(FP + TN) gives the value of TNR. TNR refers to the proportion of TN and the sum of FP and TN [Equation (10.25)].

$$TrueNegativeRate = \frac{TrueNegative}{TrueNegative + FalsePositive} \quad (10.25)$$

False Positive Rate: The formula FP/(FP + TN) is used to find the value of FPR. FPR refers to the proportion of FP and the sum of FP and TN [Equation (10.26)].

$$FalsePositiveRate = \frac{FalsePositive}{TrueNegative + FalsePositive} \quad (10.26)$$

False Positive Rate (FPR) and True Positive Rate (TPR) range is [0, 1]. AUC ranges within 0 and 1.0. AUC created by plotting FPR vs. TPR varying values in the range [0, 1].

AUC is expedient for two reasons:

Scale-invariant: AUC is scale-invariant. Instead of considering absolute values, it evaluates the prediction accuracy.

Classification-threshold–invariant: AUC is classification-threshold–invariant. Irrespective of the threshold value chosen for classification, it measures the model's prediction quality.

10.7.6   Precision

Precision provides the proportion of TP to the sum of TP and FP predicted by the classifier, as shown in Equation (10.27).

$$Precision = \frac{TruePositives}{TruePositives + FalsePositives} \qquad (10.27)$$

Greater precision value represents that algorithm brings an output a substantially more relevant results compared to that of the irrelevant ones [45–47].

10.7.7   Recall

Recall provides the proportion of correct positive samples, and all relevant identified positive samples are shown in Equation (10.28).

$$Precision = \frac{TruePositives}{TruePositives + FalseNegatives} \qquad (10.28)$$

The high recall represents that the algorithm returns the most relevant results [45–47].

10.7.8   F1 Score

F1 score provides test's accuracy. It ranges between [0, 1]. The best value is 1, which represents perfect precision value and recall value, and the worst is 0 specifies that how robust the classifier is. Precision represents the number of samples the classifier classifies correctly, and robust represents the classifier never omits a notable count of samples. Greater value of precision and lower recall value provides an exceedingly accurate, but the classifier omits a significant count of samples that are hard to classify. The performance of the model is better for the greater F1 score value [45–47]. Mathematically, the F1 score is defined as shown in Equation (10.29).

$$F1 = 2 * \cfrac{1}{\cfrac{1}{precision} + \cfrac{1}{recall}} \qquad (10.29)$$

F1 score is an effective evaluation metric for the following classification scenarios:

- False Positives and False Negatives are equally costly—it represents that the classifier misses on true positives or false positives.
- Adding more data does not effectively change the effectiveness of the outcome.
- True Negatives are high.

10.7.9   Mean Absolute Error

It defines as the average of the difference between the original and the predicted values. The measure specifies how far the predictions were away from the actual output. It does not give an idea of whether under prediction or over prediction of the data is performed [45–47]. Mathematically, it is defined as shown in Equation (10.30).

$$MeanAbsoluteError = \frac{1}{N} \sum_{j=1}^{N} |y_j - \hat{y}_j| \qquad (10.30)$$

10.7.10   Mean Squared Error

Similar to Mean Absolute Error, Mean Squared Error takes the average of the square of the difference between the original and the predicted values, as shown in Equation (10.31).

Advantage of MSE:

- It is easier to compute the gradient.
- Effect of larger errors becomes more pronounced then smaller errors.

$$MeanSquaredError = \frac{1}{N} \sum_{j=1}^{N} (y_j - \widehat{y_j})^2 \qquad (10.31)$$

10.7.11   Root Mean Squared Error

For solving regression problems, Root Mean Squared Error (RMSE) is a widely used metric. The assumption that is followed is that the error is unbiased and normal distribution is performed [45–47]. The important points are as follows:

- The power of "square root" provides a large number of deviations.
- The "squared" outcome of this metric provides more robust results. It prevents neglecting of the positive and negative error values and displays the plausible error term magnitude.
- Use of absolute error values is avoided
- Reconstructing the error distribution using RMSE is more reliable for a large number of samples.
- RMSE is highly affected by outlier values. Outliers to be pulled out of the data set before using this metric.
- Compared to mean absolute error, RMSE provides higher weightage and punishes large errors.

Mathematically, the RMSE metric is defined as shown in Equation (10.32).

$$RMSE = \sqrt{\frac{\sum_{i=1}^{N} (Predicted_i - Actual_i)^2}{N}} \qquad (10.32)$$

10.7.12   Root Mean Squared Logarithmic Error

In Root Mean Squared Logarithmic Error (RMSLE), the log of the predictions and actual values are calculated, as shown in Equation (10.33). RMSLE is mainly used when both predicted, and true values are huge numbers, when the value of RMSE decreases, the performance of the model is improved [45–47].

$$RMSLE = \sqrt{\frac{1}{n} \sum_{i=1}^{n} (\log(p_i + 1) - \log(a_i + 1))^2} \qquad (10.33)$$

RMSE and RMSLE are the same if predicted, and actual values are small. RMSE is lesser than RMSLE when predicted, or the actual value is larger. RMSE is greater than RMSLE when both predicted, and the actual value is larger.

10.7.13   R-Squared/Adjusted R-Squared

R-squared is defined as shown in Equations (10.34) and (10.35).

$$R^2 = 1 - \frac{MSE(model)}{MSE(baseline)} \qquad (10.34)$$

$$\frac{MSE(model)}{MSE(baseline)} = \frac{\sum_{i=1}^{N}(y_i - \hat{y}_i)^2}{\sum_{i=1}^{N}(y_i - \widehat{y}_i)^2} \qquad (10.35)$$

MSE(model): Mean Squared Error of the predictions opposed to the actual values.

MSE(baseline): Mean Squared Error of mean prediction opposed to the actual values.

10.7.14   Adjusted R-Squared

The formula for adjusted R-squared is as shown in Equation (10.36).

$$\bar{R}^2 = 1 - (1 - R^2)\left[\frac{n-1}{n-(k+1)}\right] \qquad (10.36)$$

k represents the number of features.

n represents the number of samples.

When a feature is added, if R-squared value increases, the feature added brings value to the model: otherwise, the feature need not be considered [45–47].

10.8   Proposed Methodology

The Cleveland dataset is taken from the UCI repository to identify and predict the disease, and it contains 14 attributes and 304 records. The target attribute gives the result 0 or 1. If 1, then the effect is positive and indicates the presence of disease. Otherwise, it means the absence of disease.

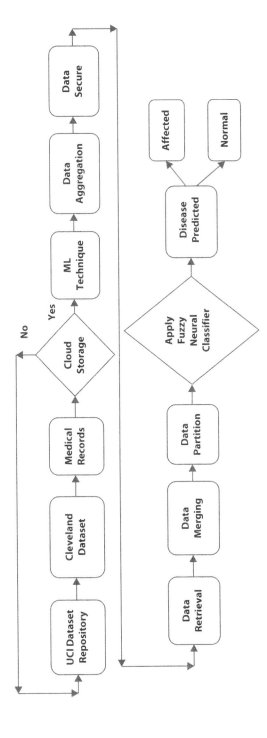

Figure 10.1 Overall classification framework.

In the proposed work, whether the person has a disease or not is predicted using one ML algorithm, fuzzy neural classifier. The proposed system is carried out into four stages, which include (1) data preprocessing, (2) cloud storage, (3) applying fuzzy neural classification algorithm, and (4) disease prediction.

Figure 10.1 illustrates that using IoT devices, details about the patient were gathered from remote areas. The UCI repository was also used for the diabetes dataset. Patient records were stored in medical records and collected from hospitals. The above process is called a data collection module. The data collection module collects the data and stores it in the cloud, and a secure storage mechanism is used to secure the data. There are five different stages in secure data mechanisms like storage, aggregation, merging, partition, and retrieval. Fuzzy neural–based classification algorithm classifies patients affected by disease and not affected by disease.

10.8.1   Neural Network

The components of neuron include inputs like hidden layer x_i and output layer y_i. The activation function [Equation (10.37)] like sigmoid and constant bias bc obtain the result.

$$f\left(bc + \sum_{i}^{n} x_i\, u_i\right) \tag{10.37}$$

10.8.2   Triangular Membership Function

The three vertices of the triangular function $\Delta_s(x)$ in a fuzzy set S are k, l, and m which are at lower, center, and upper boundaries, respectively. The membership function as shown in Equation (10.38) has lower and upper limits, which is 1, and at the centre, it is 0.

$$\Delta_S(x) = \begin{cases} 0 & \text{if } x \leq k \\ \dfrac{x-k}{l-k} & \text{if } k \leq x \leq l \\ \dfrac{m-x}{m-l} & \text{if } l \leq x \leq m \\ 0 & \text{if } x \geq m \end{cases} \tag{10.38}$$

10.8.3   Data Collection

In the Cleveland dataset, a total of 303 clinical records are present, of which, six records have missing values. So, excluding it, 297 records are considered for solving a single objective fitness function. The data collected from different sources are shown in Figure 10.2.

10.8.4   Secured Data Storage

One of the popular optimization algorithms, PSO, is used to select and extract the feature with temporal constraints. Among 76 attributes of different data types with 303 patient records in the Cleveland dataset, only 13 relevant attributes are selected. The attributes used for personal identification are age and sex; it is called as primary attributes. Other remaining attributes, cp, testbps, chol, fbs, restecg, thalach, exang, olpeak, slope,

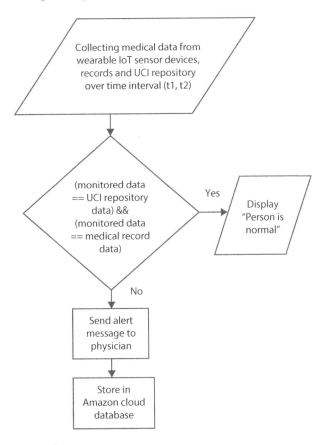

Figure 10.2 Data collection.

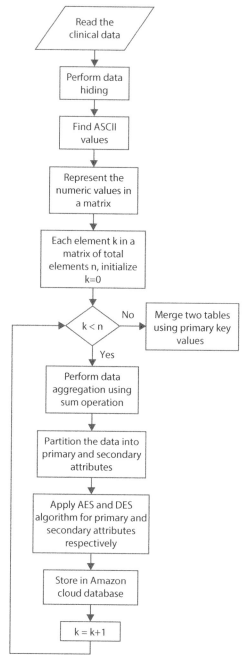

Figure 10.3 Secured data storage.

ca, and thal, are called sensitive attributes as they are of high importance. "num" attribute is the target.

Apache HBase implemented in Hadoop Distributed File System (HDFS) accumulates massive data. As data security is the main issue in cloud storage, security algorithms such as DES and AES are used for the table of records and are depicted in Figure 10.3.

10.8.5   Data Retrieval and Merging

After retrieval of data form cloud, merging operation is performed. To restore the original values, the reverse operation of aggregation is performed as shown in Figure 10.4.

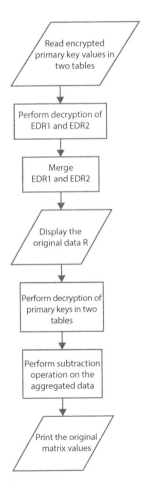

Figure 10.4 Data retrieval and merging.

10.8.6   Data Aggregation

The summation operation is used as the aggregation function to the data stored in the table after decrypting it. Then aggregation function is applied to both row and column values as indicated in Figure 10.5.

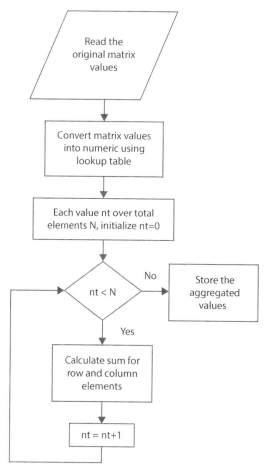

Figure 10.5 Data aggregation.

10.8.7   Data Partition

A decision tree–based split is used for partitioning the data as shown in Figure 10.6. Inputs for training samples for constructing trees are of high entropy [Equation (10.39)]. Using Divide-and-Conquer (DAC) approach in a top-down recursive manner, trees are built quickly and straightforwardly. For removing irrelevant samples on D, tree pruning is performed.

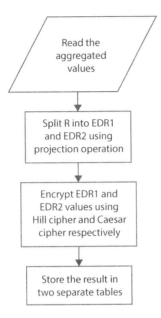

Figure 10.6 Data partition.

$$Entropy = -\sum_{j=1}^{m} p_{ij} \, log_2 \, p_{ij} \qquad (10.39)$$

10.8.8   Fuzzy Rules for Prediction of Heart Disease

Rule 1:
$if((age < 45)\&(cp == 0)\&(exang == 0)\&(restecg == 0)\&(slope == 1))$
    $num = 0;$
This indicates the person is normal.
Rule 2:
$if((45 \leq age < 55)\&(cp == 1)\&(exang == 0)\&(restecg == 1)\&(slope == 2))$
    $num = 1;$
This indicates the person has low severity of heart disease.
Rule 3:
$if((55 \leq age < 65)\&(cp == 2)\&(exang == 1)\&(restecg == 1)\&(slope == 2))$
    $num = 2;$
This indicates the person has moderate level of disease symptom.
Rule 4:

if((60 ≤ *age* < 70)&(*cp* == 2)&(*exang* == 1)&(*restecg* == 1)&(*slope* == 3))
            num = 3;
This indicates the person has high level of disease symptom.
Rule 5:
if((age > 70)&(*cp* == 3)&(*exang* == 1)&(*restecg* == 1)&(*slope* == 3))
            num = 4;
This indicates the person has very high level of disease symptom.

10.8.9   Fuzzy Rules for Prediction of Diabetes

if(*fbs* < 120)
The person does not require insulin dosage
Diabetes_symptom=type0(low):
if((120 ≤ *fbs* ≤ 150))
                if(*age* < 18)
        3–4 units of insulin dosage before pre-breakfast and pre-dinner
    else
        4–5 units of insulin dosage before pre-breakfast and pre-dinner
Diabetes_symptom=type1(medium):
if((150 ≤ *fbs* ≤ 200))
                if(*age* < 18)
        5–6 units of insulin dosage before pre-breakfast and pre-dinner
    else
        6–7 units of insulin dosage before pre-breakfast and pre-dinner
Diabetes_symptom=type2(high):
if((200 ≤ *fbs* ≤ 250))
        7 units of insulin dosage before pre-breakfast and pre-dinner
Diabetes_symptom=type2(very high):
if((250 ≤ *fbs* ≤ 300))
        8 units of insulin dosage before pre-breakfast and pre-dinner
Diabetes_symptom=type2(severe):
if((*fbs* > 300))
                9 units of insulin dosage before pre-breakfast and pre-dinner

10.8.10   Disease Prediction With Severity and Diagnosis

Training phase

For diagnosing the disease, fuzzy rules are used with Neural classifier. In training phase, most relevant features contributing to the disease are selected. Then neural tree is constructed and weights are applied to the features at Timestamp (t1,t2) for accurate decision-making as depicted in Figure 10.7.

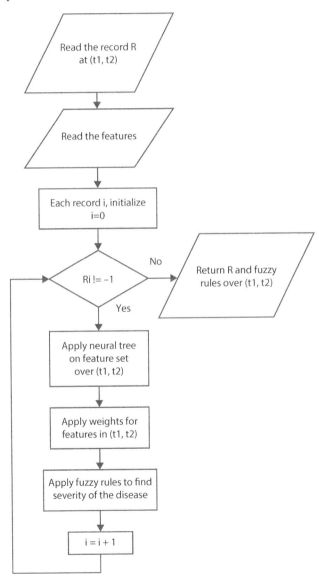

Figure 10.7 Training phase.

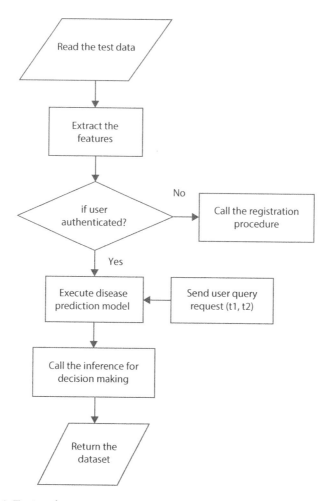

Figure 10.8 Testing phase.

Testing phase

In the testing phase, inference and expert advice are considered for decision-making as specified in Figure 10.8.

10.9   Experimental Results

The UCI repository dataset is first loaded as shown in Figure 10.9.

A security algorithm encrypts the data and stored in the cloud. Figure 10.10 lists the encrypted data.

Based on the attribute range of values, fuzzy rules are applied to find the normal and abnormal state of a person. Fuzzy temporal neural

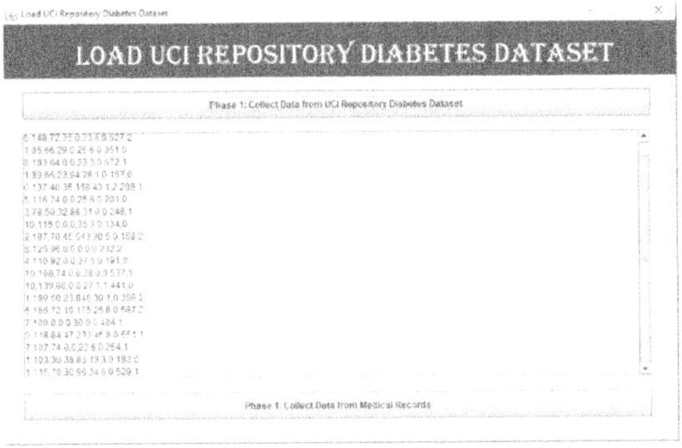

Figure 10.9 Collect data from UCI repository dataset.

Figure 10.10 Secured data storage.

classification classifies the normal and abnormal states of a person and is shown in Figure 10.11.

For each record, based on the class value obtained using target attribute, type of disease and its severity level is obtained and is shown in Figure 10.12.

The classification factors such as accuracy, sensitivity, specificity, precision, and F-measure are improved by using temporal attributes with fuzzy rules and providing security for cloud storage compared to existing method HRFLM, and the graphical representation is shown in Figure 10.13.

Even though additional computation is required for offering protection, decision-making is done on the right time with reduced overall computational time compared to TFMM by applying useful and smart rules, and the illustration is shown in Figure 10.14.

Figure 10.11 Fuzzy temporal neural classification.

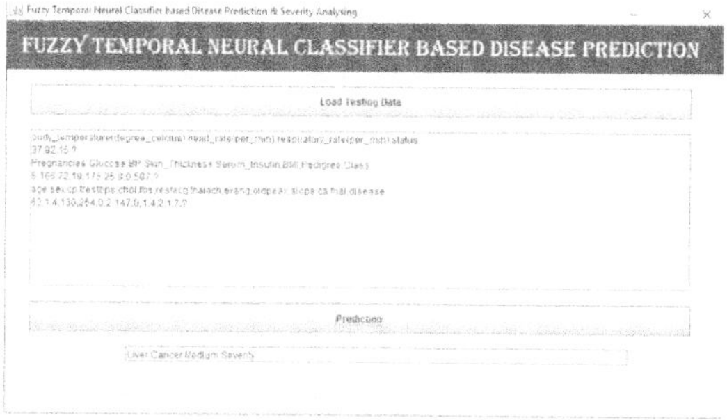

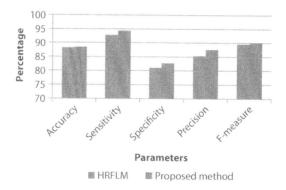

Figure 10.12 Disease prediction.

Figure 10.13 Parameters vs. percentage.

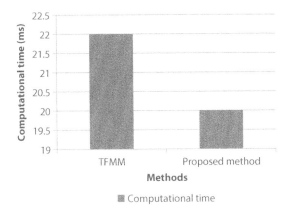

Figure 10.14 Methods vs. computational time.

10.10   Conclusion

Different forms of IoT devices such as smartphone, digital sensor, PC, laptop, and tablet are used by stakeholders to send medical requests efficiently. Cloud technology offers a reliable service in healthcare domain. The services include obtaining patent's data, telemedicine, disease diagnosing, and storing, securing, and retrieving EMR. IoT endpoints submit massive volume of medical data in the cloud environment through internet and help to perform intelligent operations to predict valuable information from the medical data and enhance the medical services to the mankind.

Integration of cloud technology and IoT brings an improvement over processing; achieving scalability due to distributed environment, networking capacity provides a new space to address healthcare applications. ML algorithms play a significant role in predicting diseases. The proposed ML algorithm performs very well. The classification algorithms give training and testing accuracy. In the future, more experiments will be conducted to increase the performance by using other feature selection algorithms.

References

1. Magoulas, G.D. and Prentza, A., Machine Learning in Medical Applications. In: Paliouras G., Karkaletsis V., Spyropoulos C.D. (eds) Machine Learning and Its Applications, ACAI 1999, Lecture Notes in Computer Science, Springer, Berlin, Heidelberg, vol. 2049, pp 300-307, 2001. https://link.springer.com/chapter/10.1007/3-540-44673-7_19
2. Kaura, P. and Sharmab, M., MamtaMittalc, Big Data and Machine Learning Based Secure Healthcare Framework. *Proc. Comput. Sci.*, 132, 1049–1059, 2018.

3. Verma, P. and Sood, S.K., Cloud-centric IoT based disease diagnosis healthcare framework. *J. Parallel Distrib. Comput.*, https://doi.org/10.1016/j.jpdc.2017.11.018, 116, 27–38, 2018.

4. Li, Y., Orgerie, A.-C., Rodero, I., Amersho, B.L., Parashar, M., Menaud, J.-M., End-to-end energy models for Edge Cloud Based IoT platforms: Application to data stream analysis in IoT. *Future Gener. Comput. Syst.*, https://doi.org/10.1016/j.future.2017.12.048, vol. 87, 667–678, 2018.

5. Stergiou, C., Psannis, K.E., Kim, B.-G., Gupta, B., Secure integration of IoT and cloud computing. *Future Gener. Comput. Syst.*, https://doi.org/10.1016/j.future.2016.11.031, 78, 964–975, 2018.

6. Golande, A. and Kumar, T.P., Heart Disease Prediction Using Effective Machine Learning Techniques. *Int. J. Recent Technol. Eng. (IJRTE)*, 944–950, 2019.

7. Pouriyeh, S., Vahid, S., Sannino, G., De Pietro, G., Arabnia, H., Gutierrez, J., A comprehensive investigation and comparison of Machine Learning Techniques in the domain of heart disease. *2017 IEEE Symposium on Computers and Communications (ISCC)*, pp. 204–207, 2017.

8. Palaniappan, S. and Awang, R., Intelligent heart disease prediction system using data mining techniques. *2008 IEEE/ACS International Conference on Computer Systems and Applications*, pp. 108–115, 2008.

9. Kumar, P.M. and Gandhi, U.D., A novel three-tier Internet of Things architecture with machine learning algorithm for early detection of heart diseases. *Comput. Electr. Eng.*, https://doi.org/10.1016/j.compeleceng.2017.09.001, vol. 65, 222–235, 2018.

10. Gelogo, Y.E., Hwang, H.J., Kim, H., Internet of things (IoT) framework for u-healthcare system. *Int. J. Smart Home*, http://dx.doi.org/10.14257/ijsh.2015.9.11.31, vol. 9, 11, 323–330, 2015.

11. Gope, P. and Hwang, T., BSN-Care: A Secure IoT-Based Modern Healthcare System Using Body Sensor Network. *IEEE Sens. J.*, 16, 5, 1368–1376, 2016.

12. Hossain, M.S. and Muhammad, G., Cloud-assisted industrial internet of things (IIoT)–enabled framework for health monitoring. *Comput. Networks*, https://doi.org/10.1016/j.comnet.2016.01.009, 101, 192–202, 2016.

13. Islam, S.M.R., Kwak, D., Kabir, M.H., Hossain, M., Kwak, K., The Internet of Things for Healthcare: A Comprehensive Survey. *IEEE Access*, 3, 678–708, 2015.

14. Sethukkarasi, R., Ganapathy, S., Yogesh, P., Kannan, A., An intelligent neuro fuzzy temporal knowledge representation model for mining temporal patterns. *J. Intell. Fuzzy Syst.*, 10.3233/IFS-130803, 26, 3, 1167–1178, 2014.

15. Katsuki, T., Ono, M., Koseki, A., Kudo, M., Haida, K., Kuroda, J., Makino, M., Yanagiya, R., Suzuki, A., Feature Extraction from Electronic Health Records of Diabetic Nephropathy Patients with Convolutional Autoencoder. *Association for the Advancement of Artificial Intelligence*, 2018.

16. Ganapathy, S., Sethukkarasi, R., Yogesh, P., An intelligent temporal pattern classification system using fuzzy temporal rules and particle swarm optimization. *Sadhana*, https://doi.org/10.1007/s12046-014-0236-7, 39, 283–302, 2014.

17. Mohan, S., Thirumalai, C., Srivastava, G., Effective Heart Disease Prediction Using Hybrid Machine Learning Techniques. *IEEE Access*, 7, 81542–81554, 2019.

18. Martin-Sanchez, F. and Verspoor, K., Big data in medicine is driving big changes. *Article Yearb. Med. Inform.*, 9, 1, 14–20, 2014.

19. Shailaja, K., Seetharamulu, B., Jabbar, M.A., Machine Learning in Healthcare: A Review. *Second International Conference on Electronics, Communication and Aerospace Technology (ICECA)*, 2018.

20. Dash, S., Shakyawar, S.K., Sharma, M., Kaushik, S., Big data in healthcare: management, analysis and future prospects. *J. Big Data*, 6, Article number: 54, 1–25, 2019.

21. Groves, P., Kayyali, B., Knott, D., Van Kuiken, S., *The Big Data Revolution in Healthcare: Accelerating Value and Innovation*, Asia-Pacific McKinsey & Company, URI: http://hdl.handle.net/11146/465, 2013.

22. Raghupathi, W. and Raghupathi, V., An Overview of Health Analytics. *J. Health Med. Inform.*, 4, 3, 1–11, 2013.

23. Khalifa, M. and Zabani, I., Utilizing health analytics in improving the performance of healthcare services: A case study on a tertiary care hospital. *J. Infection Public Health*, 9, 6, 757–765, 2016.

24. Rueckel, D. and Koch, S., Application Areas of Predictive Analytics in Healthcare. *Twenty-third Americas Conference on Information Systems*, Boston, 2017.

25. Winters-Miner, L.A., Seven ways predictive analytics can improve healthcare, https://www.elsevier.com/connect/seven-ways-predictive-analytics-can-improve-healthcare, Elsevier, Netherlands, 2014.

26. Kuttappa, S., Optimize healthcare delivery and reduce costs with Prescriptive analytics, IBM, United States. https://www.ibmbigdatahub.com, 2020.

27. Sidey-Gibbons, J., Sidey-Gibbons, C. Machine learning in medicine: a practical introduction. *BMC Med. Res. Methodol.*, 19, 64, 1–18, 2019.

28. Murphy, K.P., *Machine Learning: A Probabilistic Perspective*, p. 3, The MIT Press, Cambridge, London, 2012.

29. Shen, W., Zhou, M., Yang, F., Yang, C., Tian, J., Multi-scale Convolutional Neural Networks for Lung Nodule Classification. *International Conference on Information Processing in Medical Imaging*, Springer, pp. 588–599, 2015.

30. Yan, Z., Zhan, Y., Peng, Z., Liao, S., Shinagawa, Y., Zhang, S., Metaxas, D.N., Zhou, X.S., Multi-instance deep learning: Discover discriminative local anatomies for body part recognition. *IEEE Trans. Med. Imaging*, 35, 5, 1332–1343, 2016.

31. Qayyum, A., Qadir, J., Bilal, M., Al-Fuqaha, A., Secure and Robust Machine Learning for Healthcare: A Survey, in *IEEE Reviews in Biomedical Engineering*, US, vol. 14, pp. 156–180, 2021.

32. Battineni, G., Chintalapudi, N., Amenta, F., Machine learning in medicine: Performance calculation of dementiaprediction by support vector machines (SVM). *Inf. Med. Unlocked*, 16, 1–8, 2019.

33. Kelarev, A.V., Stranieri, A., Yearwood, J.L., Jelinek, H.F., Empirical Study of Decision Trees and Ensemble Classifiers for Monitoring of Diabetes Patients in Pervasive Healthcare. *IEEE*, 441–446, 2012.

34. Blanco, R., Inza, I., Merino, M., Quiroga, J., Larranaga, P., Feature selection in Bayesian classifiers for the prognosisof survival of cirrhotic patients treated with TIPS. *J. Biomed. Inf.*, 38, 5, 376–388, 2005.

35. Pandey, A.K., Pandey, P., Jaiswal, K.L., Sen, A.K., DataMining Clustering Techniques in the Prediction of Heart Disease using Attribute selection method, *International Journal of Science, Engineering and Technology Research, (IJSETR)*, 2, 10, 16–17, 2013.

36. Polat, K. and Güneş, S., Prediction of hepatitis disease based on principal component analysis and artificial immune recognition system. *Appl. Math. Comput.*, 189, 2, 1282–1291, 2007.

37. Paul, R., Sayed Md., A., Hoque, L., Clustering medical data to predict the likelihood of diseases. *Fifth International Conference on Digital Information Management (ICDIM)*, IEEE Xplore, 2010.

38. Jothi, N., Rashid, N.A., Husain, W., Data Mining in Healthcare – A Review. *Proc. Comput. Sci.*, 72, pp. 306–313, 2015.

39. Bortsova, G., Dubost, F., Hogeweg, L., Katramados, I., de Bruijne, M., Semi-supervised Medical Image Segmentation via Learning Consistency Under Transformations. *International Conference on Medical Image Computing and Computer-Assisted Intervention*, pp. 810–818, 2019.

40. Beaulieu-Jones, B.K. and Greene, C.S., Semi-supervised learning of the electronic health record for phenotype Stratification. *J. Biomed. Inf.*, Cornell University, 64, pp. 168–178, 2016.

41. Yu, C., Liu, J., Fellow, IEEE, Nemati, S., Reinforcement Learning in Healthcare: A Survey, arXiv:1908.08796v4 [cs.LG], 2020.

42. https://www.analyticsvidhya.com/blog/2017/09/6-probability-distributions-data-science

43. https://towardsdatascience.com/probability-distributions-in-data-science-cce6e64873a7

44. https://machinelearningmastery.com/discrete-probability-distributions-for-machine-learning/

45. https://towardsdatascience.com/metrics-to-evaluate-your-machine-learning-algorithm-f10ba6e38234

46. https://www.analyticsvidhya.com/blog/2019/08/11-important-model-evaluation-error-metrics/

47. https://heartbeat.fritz.ai/evaluation-metrics-for-machine-learning-models-d42138496366

11

CloudIoT-Driven Healthcare: Review, Architecture, Security Implications, and Open Research Issues

Junaid Latief Shah[1]*, Heena Farooq Bhat[2] and Asif Iqbal Khan[3]

[1]Department of Information Technology, Sri Pratap College, Cluster University Srinagar, J&K, India
[2]Department of IT & SS, University of Kashmir, Srinagar, J&K, India
[3]Department of Computer Science, Jamia Millia Islamia University, New Delhi, India

Abstract

The blending of Cloud Computing and IoT or CloudIoT provides an efficient paradigm to connect varied medical resources and dispense efficient, reliable, agile, and intelligent healthcare services to the patients with chronic illness. With CloudIoT, healthcare systems have been augmented with ubiquitous health monitoring and critical care services. The popularity of CloudIoT-driven healthcare applications has only surged in today's world due to minimal cost implications and pervasive feature of sensor-based computing. Since IoT devices have constrained storage and processing power, as such are unable to provide efficient e-health facilities and process or store humongous volume of collected medical data. Thus, integrating IoT with Cloud provides a seamless platform for bridging the gap among dissimilar objects and regulating escalating resource requirements in healthcare sector. Although CloudIoT architecture contributes toward effective patient care, yet it is challenging, given the issue of reliability and security of the patient information. The framework also lacks an established and secure healthcare architecture. The CloudIoT involves disparate networks through which sensitive medical data gets transacted. This data could be abused by malicious users and pervasive healthcare service operations could be rendered ineffective. The healthcare systems require robust security in order to avoid data tampering and privacy of user data is not compromised.

Corresponding author: junaidlatiefshah@gmail.com

Rohit Tanwar, S. Balamurugan, R. K. Saini, Vishal Bharti and Premkumar Chithaluru (eds.) Advanced Healthcare Systems: Empowering Physicians with IoT-Enabled Technologies, (173–254) © 2022 Scrivener Publishing LLC

In this chapter, we survey the available CloudIoT papers and showcase overall scenario on CloudIoT-driven healthcare services. The chapter contemplates discussion on background elements that drive CloudIoT-health paradigm and discusses various security protocols and enabling technologies powering CloudIoT-health platform. We also present a conceptual healthcare monitoring architecture that takes into account diverse tasks which include data analysis, communication, and computation involving cloud storage. A use case scenario is also presented that recognizes various elements that underpin and convert IoT data and transmit it to cloud. Also, we highlight design considerations for the architecture. The chapter discusses security loopholes inherent in IoT architecture and the Cloud platform. The chapter also elaborates discussion on various security countermeasures that have been proposed in literature highlighting their strengths and limitations. Also, a discussion on possible defense measures has been provided. Finally, the chapter culminates by underlining some burning research problems and security issues that need to be addressed for seamless healthcare services.

Keywords: Cloud, IoT, sensor, RFID, CloudIoT

11.1   Introduction

The Internet of Things (IoT) points to small interconnected objects that communicate data using internet autonomously without any human intervention. These objects use sensor communication that generates data at an exponential rate and arduous to manage, given the constrained computational power and data services embedded in these devices [3, 6]. To vanquish this, blending of Cloud into IoT, also referred to as CloudIoT, proves to be panacea for enabling transmission between varied dissimilar devices and managing exponential data generation rate [42, 138]. CloudIoT model allows flawless service deployment and application access hinged on various cloud supported models [3, 39]. As depicted in Figure 11.1, the seamless integration of two heterogeneous technologies has allowed for the design of rational and well-organized healthcare monitoring systems, surveillance systems, environment monitoring, smart city, smart homes, intelligent energy management systems, etc. [3, 66].

The recent times have seen a surge in aged population globally resulting in serious health ailments which, in turn, increases hospitalization and clinical care cost for people around the world [7, 95, 137]. Periodic health checks and monitoring play a significant role in minimizing healthcare costs and enhancing Ambient Assisted Living for elder people having chronic ailments [24, 35]. Traditional healthcare setup is quite monotonous and inappropriate which does not scale up to the current demand of our

Figure 11.1 CloudIoT applications.

hospitals and healthcare institutions [8, 10]. The increase in ageing population has driven the necessity for designing coherent and structured healthcare systems which aim to minimize clinical costs and load on healthcare
institutions and, in turn, improve the quality of life for older people [9].

The CloudIoT framework enables varied IoT services to interconnect
and transact information within the network for yielding robust healthcare solutions [98, 136]. There are number of factors and issues that drive
further research work in this area, some of which include increase in aged
people globally, rise in chronic and high-risk diseases, and soaring increase
in daily health system [98]. The application of CloudIoT in health systems
can augment medical infrastructure and can significantly improve patient
healthcare with resolute and tenacious innovation [9, 42]. The implementation of CloudIoT system offers flexibility for patients to carry on with
their usual business and day-to-day work while medical practitioners are
tracking their activities in the background and providing them with expert
advice and consultation [98]. With profound rise in chronic and severe
health ailments, the application of enabling technologies like CloudIoT
play a vital part in diagnosis and treatment that notably influences hospital
costs and healthcare budget of average people [5, 60, 106].

To assist common people and ease daily life of patients having chronic
medical ailments, the idea of ambient-based living has developed gradually

with time [13, 14]. The application of CloudIoT in healthcare has supplemented diverse range of application which include deployment of wireless sensor network for collecting patient data, communication of data to the cloud, processing and data analytics, Artificial Intelligence–based services and application rendering [102, 130, 135]. One among the novel concepts of employing CloudIoT in health-based system is its ubiquitous nature of dispensing clinical services that have minimum service deployment costs associated with it [42, 86]. However, with ubiquitous nature and exponential data generation rate, healthcare systems demand high-end data storage systems with mining and analytics [150]. The cloud offers a robust system to serve the need and facilitate secure healthcare data transaction with concealing implementation part from the end system [28]. Also, it grants autonomy with respect to data transfer and storage and allows mobile devices of users to receive health updates and analysis [92]. The CloudIoT framework is being adopted on a global scale in order to collaborate and connect geographically separated medical infrastructures and also provide ubiquitous, scalable and economical healthcare solutions to patient community [1, 11, 116]. Implementation of CloudIoT framework in healthcare includes integration and collaboration of various state-of-the-art technologies, mobile apps, sensor nodes, and end users that transact and communicate information as one integrated system to analyze, track, and monitor data [14, 49]. Majority of CloudIoT healthcare models have three primary components. These include wearable body sensors and devices for data perception, communication device for real-time updates including data transfer to warehouse and cloud-based archival space for data inference and processing including mining [42, 104]. A large number of wearable body sensors including implantable clinical bio-markers are readily available in stores that carry out minute and precise data collection [133]. Majority of these sensors record vital patient data that helps in prior disease diagnosis and timely delivery of associated medical treatment [64, 121]. Some bio-sensors record electrocardiography (ECG) data of patients which gets transmitted to persistent storage in the cloud via wireless medium such as internet. The medical data is then studied and analyzed and relevant actions are undertaken [48, 51, 77]. The models can also include backend clinical care systems that continuously monitor and pull out information from the cloud storage [40].

The cloud also offers medical practitioners and health experts, on-demand and seamless access to varied range of data including E-Medical Records (EMRs), doctor recommendations, and laboratory test results aggregated from heterogeneous sources [45, 141]. Handling chronic health cases and ailments such as asthma and diabetes and follow up drug regimens can be done automatically, as the system can notify healthcare team in case of disparate or follow up appointments [2, 133]. The CloudIoT model also offers tools for data analysis that will update medical or clinical experts to observe and keep record of people at any time period [41, 96, 130].

Old age care and monitoring using CloudIoT has permitted aged persons to have an individualistic and vibrant quality of life [64, 121]. Providing timely and ubiquities medical attention to the aged people is one of the arduous tasks. CloudIoT-driven healthcare has been instrumental in alerting patients of their periodic medical attention and scheduled medication [49]. The CloudIoT platform also supports critical care applications that sense emergency situations so that real-time decisions could be taken with respect to providing healthcare facilities [71].

Although CloudIoT model augments healthcare framework substantially, its technical and implementation bottlenecks impede the vision of its expeditious and structured development [49, 141]. The CloudIoT model suffers inherent security challenges and privacy issues that compromise the validity of medical data [3]. Using CloudIoT infrastructure, sensitive, and personal patient data gets transacted over unsecured networks which could be abused by malevolent users raising concerns regarding its security and privacy [41, 145]. Ensuring security means protection and safeguarding IoT and Cloud infrastructure including applications from malicious intrusions [120]. For example, if the network layer in IoT gets compromised, then the attacker can gain control over the entire IoT network and leverage attack on other devices via the compromised node. Similarly, if the cloud fails to authenticate access to its interface, then the sensitive data might get leaked and exposed. In general, the devices that maintain online presence are susceptible to attacks from malevolent users [122]. A report from International Data Corporation points that by the year 2020, more than 200 million devices will be internet ready and most of these devices will be easy target for attackers. The attacks which include Denial of Service, harmful Trojans, and Worms would be mostly directed toward home appliances [82]. A study by Hewlett Packard (HP) indicates that about 70% of IoT devices are susceptible to attacks. As per recent analysis by HP, about 90% of Internet-enabled devices collected at least some minimal user information via the device product, cloud, or some mobile application. This personal user information is vulnerable to abuse and unauthorized access by attackers. This will, in turn, question the confidentiality and integrity of the personal data. As such, users will be hesitant to embrace this new technology paradigm [75, 82].

As of today, Machine-to-Machine (M2M), sensor networks, and Human-to-Machine (H2M) systems have become intrinsic components of CloudIoT-based healthcare framework; as such, security issues associated with sensor, M2M, and H2M continue to be persistent in CloudIoT platform with Internet Protocol (IP) being the underlying connectivity protocol [108]. Thus, entire CloudIoT health architecture needs to be protected from threats that may obstruct the rendered services as well as challenge the integrity, privacy, and authenticity of data. Since CloudIoT involves interconnection of heterogeneous networks, it automatically inherits the security flaws present in conventional computer networks [49, 138]. The limited computational resources in sensor objects further add to the complexity because the traditional security solutions cannot be applied. Therefore, extensive research has to be carried to provide seamless and robust security solutions for the CloudIoT platform [49, 75]. A majority of these security solutions are applied either at distinct IoT layers or Cloud, whereas other solutions dispense end-to-end (E2E) security for CloudIoT. For example, a recent survey research carried by authors in [4, 17] segregate security threats into four categories: application, communication, architecture, and data. This segregation of security threats is different from traditional layered network architecture. Also, threats for hardware, network, and application components are briefly discussed. Similar to this research, another survey in [57] elaborates discussion on security protocols for IoT and analyzes its security issues. The security issues highlighted in [37, 117] consider and contrast various key management frameworks and encryption algorithms. In [3, 6, 152], the authors present a holistic comparison of intrusion detection systems. Authors in [124] present a survey and debate on contributions dispensing confidentiality, security, authentication, and user privacy for IoT along with the security for intermediate layers. The authors also highlight on trust management, authentication issues, data privacy, and security of the network. A survey highlighting privacy preserving mechanisms for IoT has presented in [100]. In [157], the researchers pinpoint various security threats and their possible solutions for CloudIoT platform. The authors discuss user identity and privacy, sensor object compromise, and key exchange security implications for CloudIoT. A similar survey carried by authors in [5, 154] discuss vital security threats related to object identity, access authentication, user privacy, and demand for light weight encryption mechanisms.

In contrast to the existing work found in the literature, we follow the research methodology as depicted in Figure 11.2.

Our main significant contribution in this chapter is summarized as follows:

Figure 11.2 Research methodology.

- Discussion on background elements that drive CloudIoT-health integration.
- Review of security protocols and enabling technologies powering CloudIoT-health platform.
- Presents a conceptual architecture for healthcare monitoring system. The architecture includes a real-life model that presents actors and flow of data that achieve transformation IoT data to cloud platform. Also, we highlight some architectural design considerations of the platform.
- Summarizes and highlights various security vulnerabilities hampering seamless IoT model including issues persistent in the Cloud platform.
- Holistic vision on varied security countermeasures that have been proposed in literature highlighting their strengths and limitations. Also, a discussion on possible defense measures has been provided.
- Underlines some open research issues and security implications that demand robust solutions for seamless healthcare services.

The segregation of the other sections of this chapter is as follows:

Section 11.2 points out the background elements that drive the CloudIoT health paradigm and highlights underlying reason for their seamless integration. Section 11.3 elaborates discussion on security protocols and various enabling technologies for CloudIoT healthcare. Section 11.4 presents a conceptual architecture for healthcare monitoring system and includes a real-life model that presents actors and flow of data. Also, a brief overview on design elements has been provided. Section 11.5 presents various security vulnerabilities associated with IoT architecture including issues persistent in the Cloud platform. Section 11.6 points out security countermeasures that have been proposed in literature highlighting their strengths and limitations. Also, a discussion on possible defense measures has been provided. Section 11.7 presents some open research issues and security challenges impeding development of a secure framework for CloudIoT health paradigm. Section 11.8 presents discussion and analysis. Finally, Section 11.9 concludes the chapter.

11.2   Background Elements

The CloudIoT platform serves remote healthcare monitoring applications and offers flexible services to patients having chronic health situations and disabilities [139]. Implementing health monitoring with Cloud and IoT assists in early disease diagnosis, and as such, feasible healthcare options could be made available to ascertain patient comfort and easement [102].

The "Internet of Things (IoT)" offers a computational platform to healthcare architecture where healthcare objects are deployed with sensors, tiny microchips having data transmission capability and state-of-the-art communication protocols for interfacing and interacting with communication network including the physical environment [49, 110, 129]. IoT-driven healthcare systems include disparate sensor network that perceive, monitor, and collect information from the surroundings and transmit this information in real time to the cloud warehouse using internet as the medium [43, 66]. This helps in archiving, analytics, and mining of large data volumes and trigger alert signals and message events. The IoT-driven health system dispenses a seamless data production service that allows medical information extraction from a remote system using internet as underlying medium [26]. Thus, IoT-driven health system has played a pivotal role in enhancing ambient medical service with vigorous surveillance and minimal costs [9].

The IoT in itself involves heterogeneous devices that transmit data over the network using diverse interconnecting protocols [3]. "Things" represent small sensor objects that have the capability to interact with similar devices over the network. For communication, these devices use standards such as "Bluetooth" and "Zigbee" that have small data signaling radius and minimal power gobbling features [144]. The IoT has led to the genesis of personalized Healthcare by recording medical history of each patient in the backend database [33]. As pervasive healthcare systems are not so common, several health complications go unnoticed in traditional healthcare models [24]. The IoT-based healthcare tries to bridge this gap by implementing active health surveillance and analytics of medical data [150]. IoT platform dispenses countless solutions for managing healthcare; however, the feasible one hinges on limitations and requirements of a particular implementation [66, 141]. The feasible layout aids in designing seamless and economical healthcare model that supplements existing medical infrastructure, hospital systems, and online patient check [10, 130]. As an example, to monitor patients physically in hospitals over a period of time, we utilize services of healthcare workers. However, IoT eliminates such liability by providing ubiquitous patient monitoring systems wherein sensors, control nodes, and cloud platform work in conjunction and transmit data wirelessly to medical team [139].

Even though the emergence of IoT-based healthcare has only increased in recent years, however no formal or precise architecture is yet originated for the concept framework. As illustrated in Figure 11.3, the fundamental architecture of IoT is partitioned into four layered hierarchy: "Perception or Physical layer", "Network or Transport layer", "Middleware layer", and "Application or Service layer". Each level in the hierarchy carries out a predefined function and offers service to the layer above it.

The first layer, i.e., perception or physical layer, consists of tiny physical sensors, "RFID"-based objects, actuators, etc. The basic function performed at this level is to perceive, monitor and record data and communicate this data to a predetermined destination system. The second layer, i.e., network layer, is assigned the task of transmission of collected information to a remote destination. The third layer, i.e., middleware layer, acts as an intermediary connecting the network interface and application and offers diverse analytical processes. The topmost layer, i.e., application layer, provides application interface and control panel to the user.

Although IoT is applied in varied application areas ranging from online health surveillance, smart e-healthcare, smart living, autonomous traffic system, and environment surveillance; however, these applications produce humongous volume of data that entail for pliable network

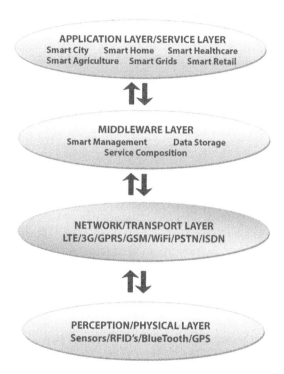

Figure 11.3 IoT layered architecture.

infrastructure that can underpin such high traffic volumes [30, 153]. As already discussed, that IoT-based systems have limited space, thus it is not feasible to archive this data locally. IoT devices have inherent constrained computational power which degrades its performing capabilities [104, 105]. Earlier solution was to migrate data and computation to server computers which were stocked with requisite processing infrastructure. But, this process had some limitations [20, 126]. First, processing applications and archiving data on mainframe computers was a cumbersome process and costly. Second, in case the mainframe computers failed, the whole system would shut which was not desirable. Therefore, shifting data and computation to Cloud data center seems to be a robust solution [30, 104]. The Cloud offers a flexible, on-request, and supple infrastructure for health-based system hosting and dispenses accessibility to vast computational infrastructures that are connected to each other [39]. These computational platforms provide substantial power, software and storage space that succors limited IoT resources, hence assisting in ubiquitous computing. In cloud processing, the data is usually stored on remote warehouse server and computation including processing are delivered as a service to the users, thus eliminating cumbersome management functions from its client users [105, 144]. Integration of two varied technologies, i.e., IoT and Cloud, will dispense structured computation and energy management, and for designing intelligent clinical services [31, 49]. The Cloud platform can handle delay sensitivity as well as provide service as per request to applications in a secure and agile setup. There are several reasons that favor adaptation of Cloud infrastructure for IoT in healthcare perspective. These include being cost effective, definitive and performance, agile and flexible, scalability, and state-of-the-art security [39, 144].

Adaptation of Cloud in clinical health dispenses a vital part in minimizing medical investment costs, augmenting people's ambient life and enhances services that push for new technology-based insights [42]. The Cloud system allows healthcare data to be pervasive and as such can be retrieved given any location with no time constraints [136]. The cloud also grants seamless authentication to healthcare workers and practitioners to a vast database of medical information collected from disparate data origins that include medical records, laboratory test reports, test results, prescription of doctors, and health insurance data [51, 121]. This data could be utilized across systems for flawless policy making, precise diagnosis and cure, fixing appointment with doctors, etc. [53]. The cloud provides innovative data analytics that will assist healthcare workers and medical professionals to monitor patients from a remote location precisely and accurately [30]. A number of Information Technology giants such as "Microsoft", "Google", and "Amazon" are offering innovative solutions in healthcare domain and provide service platforms that integrate with relevant stakeholders to design economical medical solutions [116]. For instance, Microsoft-powered Health-Vault is a web-based personalized EHR developed by Microsoft to store and manage healthcare and patient information. Similarly, Google Fit developed by Google is a health-tracking platform that stores biological data of its end-user in the cloud. The cloud platform provides four unique characteristics that segregate it from conventional computing methods [3]. First, it furnishes an "on-request working model" that permits a user to access drive space and computation on server according to his flexibility. Second, it dispenses a "large network access" by granting access to variety of devices such as smart phones, hand-held tablets, laptops, and also workstations. Third, it "aggregates diverse data sources" and integrates them to develop a huge repository of resources that are available on demand to users. Fourth, it advocates "agility" of computing infrastructure that allows a server to calibrate to user service as per request and demand.

As depicted in Figure 11.4, the Cloud interface provides interface to the users at three different hierarchies: "Infrastructure Level (IaaS)", "Software Level (SaaS)", and "Platform Level (PaaS)".

The IaaS offers a web platform to its users such as computing infrastructure that involve server computer, storage, and internetworking devices that are provided on demand. The leased infrastructure is extensible which is determined by user requirements and demand. The SaaS platform provides flawless entry to cloud interface and data-warehouse on lease. The implanting, augmentation, and amendments to software are handled by the SaaS interface. The "PaaS" dispenses a consistent software architecture and control interface to the client user.

As shown in Figure 11.5, the Cloud also offers different deployment platforms, i.e., public, private, and community cloud which provide abstraction of services at three different levels.

The cloud framework warrants that end user application performance is maintained in the platform [111]. For instance, when number of client requests that want to access the cloud platform increase, the cloud must automatically elevate and expand its processing capabilities to satisfy each and every request. Again when number of client requests decreases, the cloud must autonomously fine-tune its capacity to adjust the change.

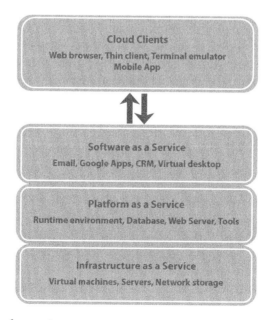

Figure 11.4 Interface services.

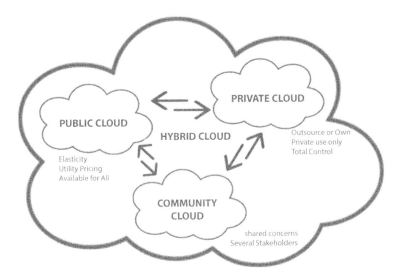

Figure 11.5 Deployment services.

Thus, implementation and adoption of CloudIoT seems to offer a coherent solution that is pliable, secure, less complex, and economical [81, 90].

However, with countless agile services offered by CloudIoT platform, the integration of two heterogeneous technologies is a challenging task [35]. The amalgamation process should take into consideration, problems that pertain to economy and cost viewpoint of internet service providers [25]. Also, CloudIoT platform must ensure reliable and secure communication and storage of data [39, 69]. The CloudIoT transacts private and sensitive medical data over its platform, as such is vulnerable to security threats from malicious users [79]. The problem becomes more complex in the scenario involving hybrid clouds. The main focal point on safety measures should be on ensuring that integrity, authentication, access, and isolation of data are maintained [94, 141].

11.2.1   Security Comparison Between Traditional and IoT Networks

It is evident from research that challenges and security issues of IoT and traditional networks vary in various aspects [63, 120]. The IoT involves RFID-based objects and nodes having constrained resources such as minimal CPU speeds and, often, objects are battery powered while as traditional networks such as internet is composed of high-end PCs, servers, smart phones, and tablet computers having abundant resources. Thus, traditional internet can support complex combination of security algorithms irrespective of resource usage and consumption [38, 115]. While as in case of IoT, lightweight algorithms having minimal resource usage that balance between security and computational power need to be implemented. The conventional cryptographic encryption algorithms demand swift computations, so it is not feasible to directly port them to IoT devices [79].

The IoT nodes communicate through slower and insecure wireless medium which is susceptible to data theft, privacy violation and node compromise. In comparison to this, traditional internet involves communication through faster wired medium such as optical fiber which is more secure and reliable. Even in case of wireless communication, the setup is built on top of complex and secure protocols which are not usually feasible with resource constrained IoT nodes. Additionally, IoT devices employ minimal data-rate radio technology for communication across the network. Thus, conventional security policies do not apply to IoT-enabled devices directly due to low-throughput transmission media implications [25].

Although internet consists of heterogeneous devices, but with the abstraction support provided by the operating system, the devices are able to share a common data format across multiple platforms. In case of IoT nodes, no such operating system or common data format exists. The nodes have embedded programs that vary with different chip hardware resulting in heterogeneous data contents and formats.

Table 11.1 shows typical feature difference between IoT and conventional networks.

Table 11.1 Feature contrast between IoT and conventional networks.

Characteristic	IoT	Conventional network
Power	Constrained power	Unbounded
Setup	Mobile and flexible	Static
Framework	Self-organized (*ad hoc*)	Established standard, hierarchical
Communication range	Short distance transmission	Long-distance transmission
Routing	Random and dynamically build	End-to-end connection
Packet delivery mode	Cooperative, DTN type, and need incentive mechanism to stimulate	Optimized packet delivery

11.3   Secure Protocols and Enabling Technologies for CloudIoT Healthcare Applications

The development of smart and interconnected objects entail for standard and robust secure communication protocols [38]. The IP engineered by Internet Engineering Task Force (IETF) is the standard delivery mechanism of Internet and is also used as a standard for interoperability of smart objects. As IPv4 addresses have exhausted completely, thus next-generation protocol, i.e., IPv6, seems to be a potential solution for enabling smart device communication [18, 115]. The protocol stack which CloudIoT will implement will be identical to the already deployed traditional internet in order to ensure interoperability and heterogeneous communications between devices. Thus, for seamless integration, security protocols that are developed for standard internet can be reused (or augmented in some cases) for smart device communication in a heterogeneous environment [63, 65].

11.3.1   Security Protocols

Internet Protocol Security (IPsec): At IoT's network layer, a device can exchange data securely by implementing IPsec in its communications. IPsec forms an integral component in IPv6 as a part of extension header while as in IPv4; it was added as an additional feature in order to augment its security and encryption. The principal objectives accomplished by employing IPsec in smart object communication over an unsecure network are the data integrity, confidentiality, authentication, and protection against replay attacks. The IPsec offers two protocols for achieving security. These are Authentication Header (AH) and Encapsulating Security Protocol (ESP). Both of these standards are implemented as a part of extension headers in IPv6.

Transport Layer Security (TLS): To protect data exchange at transport layer, the TLS protocol is employed. TLS dispenses secure communication via object-based authentication and key interchange. TLS is commonly used for data encryption at the IoT application layer between the IoT applications and the backend server. The encryption can also be extended to other services such as short message communication and VoIP.

Secure Socket Layer (SSL): SSL protocol uses certificates that ensure security, integrity and protect identity of IoT devices. Although there are different varieties of SSL certificates but all use asymmetric encryption to protect the data communication between two sensor objects.

11.3.2   Enabling Technologies

RFID: RFID is the short form for "Radio-Frequency Identification". In this communication technology, digital data which are concealed in RFID tags are detected by RFID reader using radio signal. RFID technology is analogous to bar-coding in which tag data is detected by a node and is then archived in data warehouse. In fact, RFID provides several merits over other devices that implement bar-code tracking software. The most significant advantage being that RFID tag data identification does not entail for line-of-sight communication. Using Automatic Identification and Data Capture (AIDC) methods, RFID automatically identifies objects, captures information, and stores that data directly into database without any human intervention. The base architecture of an RFID system consists of three main integral elements which include an RFID label, reader, and a communication media. The tags or smart labels consist of a microchip and an antenna to communicate data to the RFID reader. The reader transforms radio signals into readable data format which is then sent through a communication medium to an end computer system where data is archived in a database. In contrast with other available techniques, RFID offers optimized scanning, reliability, reuse, huge storage, non–line-of-sight communication, security, etc. Thus, RFID is an optimal choice to be used at IoT perception layer in order to identify, track and exchange data between objects in real time.

"Constrained Application Protocol (CoAP)": CoAP is a messaging standard hinged on REST (Representational State Transfer) architecture designed for low power and computationally constrained devices in order to operate in an IoT environment [19, 29]. CoAP is developed by IETF core working team and is enumerated as RFC 7252. CoAP was designed to enable M2M communication between constrained devices and networks having low bandwidth and availability. As most IoT nodes are resource constrained, HTTP cannot be operated in such an environment owing to its complexity. To vanquish the challenge, CoAP has evolved as an alternative to HTTP operations in an IoT network. The CoAP protocol underpins features such as group communication including push notifications, communication with HTTP, resource identification, and security [145].

Wireless Sensor Network (WSN): A WSN form an integral part of an IoT network. A WSN is a network of sensor devices that can transmit the monitored information through wireless links. The data gets transferred using multiple nodes which are further connected to other sensor networks via gateway. The sensor network typically consists of a single base station and a set of wireless nodes which are used to scan and monitor the status of devices and transmit this status data to the base station or sink nodes. The WSN connects the line between virtual world and physical world and dispenses features such as scalability, robust reconfiguration, minimized cost, and minimal energy consumption. Both RFID and WSN are employed for data collection in IoT; however, the RFID is mainly operated for object tracking, while as WSN is mainly used for the sensing of real-world physical parameters inherent in the neighboring environment.

IEEE 802.15.4: The IEEE 802.15.4 is a protocol designed by IEEE 802.15 working scientists which expounds the working of low-rate wireless personal area networks (LR-WPANs). The protocol identifies the physical and the Media Access Control (MAC) layer for wireless personal area networks (WPANs). This standard underpins protocols such as Zigbee, 6LoWPAN, MiWi, and Wireless-HART, each of which further define the upper layers of the standard. The IEEE 802.15.4 standard aims to dispense minimal rate connections in personal area networks with minimal cost and power consumption. IEEE 802.15.4 protocol stack is analogous to the layers of OSI model wherein each layer implements a predefined function and lower layers pass the data and control information to the upper layers.

6LoWPAN: 6LoWPAN standard aims to carry IPv6 datagram's with IEEE 802.15.4–based communication networks. The protocol dispenses E2E IPv6 connectivity, thereby providing direct communication with varied networks including internet. 6LoWPAN employs header compression technique for IPv6 datagram's that are motivated by constrained space offered by 802.15.4 frames to encapsulate IPv6 data packets. The encoding formats for compression are defined by 6LoWPAN itself due to the fact that certain fields are implicitly available to all network nodes or can be implied from MAC layer. 6LoWPAN offers number of advantages such as minimal packet size, low power, and optimized bandwidth utilization.

Zigbee: Zigbee is a wireless protocol hinged on open standards designed to bridge requirements of low-cost and optimized energy IoT networks. This protocol works on IEEE 802.15.4 physical radio guidelines and using unlicensed bands such as 2.4 GHz, 900 MHz and 868 MHz. The Zigbee technology focuses on short-term communication utilizing low power and energy and dispensing high reliability and security. Similar to TCP/IP model, Zigbee operates using five layers which are physical layer, the MAC layer, the data transmission layer, the networking layer, and the user interface/application layer. For network configuration, Zigbee supports topologies such as Star and Mesh.

Z-Wave: Z-wave is wireless communication technology commonly used in designing smart home networks thereby permitting the smart devices to communicate and interact with each other and also interchange control messages and data. With duplex communication and data acknowledgement system, the Z-Wave protocol standard eases out power consumption issues and delivers low-cost wireless networking. Thus, offering a low-power and long-range alternate solution to Wi-Fi and Bluetooth. One important thing to note in Z-wave network is that only 232 nodes (slaves), all having routing capacity can be connected at a time which are managed by a controller node. The controller is also responsible for updating routing table which is stored in the memory of each slave. Although both Zigbee and Z-wave provide short range wireless data communication, however they differ in the frequency band in which they operate. The Zigbee operates at 2.4-Ghz frequency band in the physical layer while as Z wave frequency band is less than 1 Ghz.

MQTT: Based on publish/subscribe method, MQTT is a short message standard which is employed for acquiring sensed data on deployed sensors and further transmission of this data to the server. MQTT is primarily designed for networks suffering from low bandwidth and latency. MQTT finds implementation at various platform levels and thus plays a substantial role in connecting IoT with the global internet.

Extensible Messaging and Presence Protocol (XMPP): Hinged on XML streaming protocols, XMPP is an instant messaging protocol. Due to inherited features from XML, XMPP dispenses greater extensibility, addressing and security features. The protocol can also be employed for applications such as multi user chatting and voice including video streaming. XMPP protocol supports three main functional components: client, server, and gateway and also inter communication between them. With XMPP integrated in IoT, object to object communication is possible based on XML supported text messages.

Data Distribution Service (DDS): The DDS protocol is a publish/subscribe-based standard underpinning highly effective device-to-device communication and suitable for constrained IoT communication. Designed by

Table 11.2 Characteristics of various enabling protocols and technologies.

Protocol	Spectrum	Transmission rate	Range
RFID	LF (126–135 kHz) HF (13.58 MHz) UHF (432, 860–960 MHz)	Upto 424 kbps	>10 cm
NFC	13.58 Mhz	Upto 424 kbps	<20 cm
Bluetooth	2.4–2.5 GHz	Upto 2.1 Mbps	~10 m
BLE	2.4–2.5 GHz	Upto 1 Mbps	~10 m
Zigbee	915 MHz/2.4 GHz	20 kbps–256 kbps	~10 m
UWB	3.1 GHz–10.6 GHz	> 100 Mbps	~80 m
Wi-Fi	2.4 GHz–6 GHz	Upto 2.4 Gbps	~100 m
Wi-Max	2 GHz–11 GHz	100 Mbps	~100 m
CDMA/ EDGE	896 MHz	Upto 2 Mbps	~100 m
6LoWPAN	816/915 MHz–2.4 GHz	250 kbps	~100 m

Object-Manage-Group (OMG), the protocol is highly data dependent and supports multicasting to achieve perceivable quality of service and reliability.

Table 11.2 lists the characteristics of various enabling protocols and technologies.

11.4   CloudIoT Health System Framework

CloudIoT-driven healthcare services can be designed by amalgamation and blending together of varied tools that employ wireless medium for communication and implement sensor network for perceiving and sensing data from the environment [49, 102]. This data undergoes analysis and is archived for storage on cloud [39]. To demonstrate smart healthcare process, the idea can be implemented by a conceptual architecture framework also referred to as CloudIoT Health architecture [31, 133]. The architectural framework as depicted in Figure 11.6 supports three layers that implements various services that involve data perception or acquisition, data communication or transmission, and Cloud-assisted archival or storage. The perception or

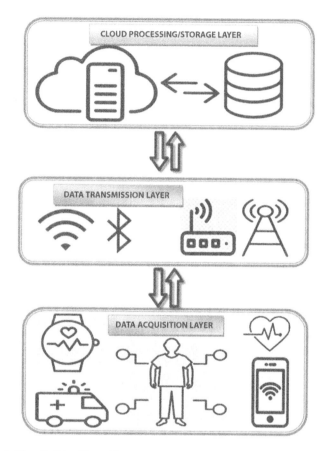

Figure 11.6 CloudIoT health architecture.

acquisition layers aggregates information which include various physiological and biological measure of people and communicates this information remotely to cloud platform for archival processing and storage.

11.4.1 Data Perception/Acquisition

This layer composes of deployed sensor network which include perception or wearable data acquisition things which perceive, measure, and store healthcare information of patients. These wearable devices track and sense critical patient parameters including temperature, blood pressure, and heart rate and record this data remotely in a backend database [96]. This recorded data is heterogeneous in nature and varies across diverse patient groups and cases. For instance, in heart disease patients, measuring ECG data, saturation of O_2, and pulse rate points to one of the basic components in the diagnosis of any heart related disease symptoms [44]. Similarly, for diabetic patients, measuring blood sugar levels periodically is very important. For applications that support the idea of ambient-based living or AAL in old people, monitoring and tracking their activities repeatedly is required [36]. Many application programs underpinning AAL are equipped with accelerometers and gyroscopic sensors that aid in medical data collection and tracking [121]. These sensors are usually classified into two categories: invasive and non-invasive sensors. Invasive sensors are permanently installed inside the patient's body and usually have better performance than non-invasive sensors due to the fact that they are in close proximity with the patient's body. However, these are not usually preferred by the elderly patients due to discomfort unless the issue is complex and severe in nature [5, 56]. In comparison, non-invasive sensors are usually preferred and are wearable on hand, forearm or any other body part of the patient. Some sensor-based application use actuators for generation of alerts if they sense or record any change with respect to physiological parameters of the patient [131]. The research community has been actively engaged in the design and development of intelligent body sensors which broaden the application area of CloudIoT-driven healthcare framework [101]. These body sensors generate massive volumes of data that require substantial amount of storage. One of the key considerations for the design of data acquisition layer is the cost implication, energy utilization and data transmission capacity of the network. The body sensor network design needs to be *ad hoc*, light, agile, and flexible in nature for accommodating any change [10, 103].

11.4.2   Data Transmission/Communication

The data communication level facilitates transmission of medical data to remote databases for archival storage [66]. The layer also provides seamless access to the vast collected data available in the cloud repositories [151]. This layer is assigned the task of communication of collected medical data of patient confidentially to an end healthcare data server. The data transmission occurs at the local as well as the global level. For local communication and for activities that involve monitoring and scanning the environment, wireless communication protocols such as Bluetooth and Zigbee are implemented. These protocols facilitate transmission between the data perception level and concentrator [12, 53, 125]. The wireless protocol such as Bluetooth is used for short range transmission having an working frequency as 2.4 GHz and offers a lost cost solution with economical energy consumption [125]. A similar communication standard like Zigbee protocol which is although not so popular as Bluetooth offers decent and reliable transmission of data. The alternate transmission standards employed at this level include RFID-based communication, "Near Field communication" (NFC), and "Ultra-Wide Bandwidth" (UWB) communication. RFID supports duplex mode of data transmission involving RFID tag and reader. In long-distance transmission, the information available in the concentrator is forwarded using the Wi-Fi or mobile data internet to the Cloud or Healthcare Organization (HCO) for long-term storage [23, 88]. The mobile data protocols such as 4G and LTE are utilized in varied health surveillance and communication devices. The data communication layer also underpins low-power hardware devices which include Arduino and Rasberry Pi that underpin IoT service deployment environment. These applications involve varied data crunching tasks that run on devices such as mobile phones, tablet computers, and microcontroller-based devices [49].

11.4.3   Cloud Storage and Warehouse

The CloudIoT-driven healthcare devices link heterogeneous things that transact considerable volume of bio-medical data and thus entail for efficient storage space and mechanism [148]. The Cloud processing layer involves three basic functionalities which include archival data storage, processing, or computation on stored data and finally analysis or mining data for information [85]. The Cloud service providers including "Google Cloud", "OpenIoT", "Amazon", "Thing-Wrox", and "GENI" provide an excellent interface for long-term storage of patient's biomedical information and provides an interface to healthcare professionals to access this data pervasively for mining and data analytics. The data analytics helps the medical practitioners in better disease diagnosis and prediction and thus helps realize the concept of smart e-healthcare including generating alerts and notifications [31]. In addition, this layer also provides various data visualization tools which enable physicians to present and conceptualize data in a given format.

11.4.4   Data Flow in Healthcare Architecture - A Conceptual Framework

Connecting technology with healthcare is an important challenging area of research and development [27]. Though this area has seen technological surge in recent years, however, planning and decision making process of medicos still counts on manual and traditional record system [13, 102]. To achieve an optimal, reliable, and secure healthcare framework is a daunting and challenging task [14]. The transaction of medical data is restricted between the health department and its subsidiaries. The other entities in the system such as clinical doctors, patients, HCO, and laboratories have no provision for sharing or access to this data. The CloudIoT health provides an underlying platform for guiding healthcare system to focus their resources on augmenting patient care by efficacious disease monitoring, timely diagnosis and cost effective treatment [150]. The CloudIoT improves traditional healthcare system by employing bio-sensors and RFID-enabled devices [40]. These devices and sensors enable real-time patient tracking, identification, diagnosis, and treatment and also in some cases, dispensing of medical supplies and drug management [133]. The CloudIoT-driven healthcare effectively connects patients, sensor objects, and network and checks for optimal medical waste management [30]. Recent advances in low-power devices have enabled the design of pervasive health framework [43, 62]. In healthcare, sensor networks have been replaced by a novel idea known as Wireless Body Area Networks (WBAN) that realizes the concept of e-health [24]. A WBAN integrates number of sensor devices for health surveillance which measure health parameters and report medical status of patient. The CloudIoT-driven health supports diverse services such as e-prescription system, "Electronic Health Records" (EHC), "Personal Health Records" (PHC), data analytics and decision systems, and drug recommendation system. These applications cater to varied stake holders which include patients, medical teams such as doctors, testing laboratories, and chemists across diverse interfaces offering a range of services [116].

To understand the working of a typical CloudIoT-driven healthcare system, let us consider a use case scenario as shown in Figure 11.7.

The figure depicts various entities and identifies actors involved in the healthcare system and illustrates the data transaction among the processes. For instance, the patient can wear a body sensor that monitors and collects biomedical data. These bio-medical sensors are deployed either as invasive or non-invasive implants on a human body. These sensors can also be placed as an ornament or also placed inside patient's clothing including footwear. These sensors work autonomously and are proficient enough to sense, monitor and record physiological parameters and transmit them over a wireless medium to backend database or cloud. The biomedical sensors are also equipped with GPS facility which enables them to track patients location and precisely determine their physiological and activity state, i.e., whether a patient is walking, sitting, running, or doing some other physical

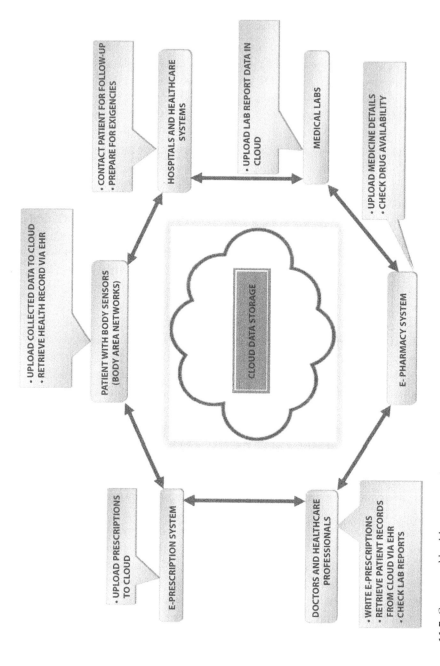

Figure 11.7 Conceptual healthcare scenario.

work. This collected data is then uploaded for archival storage in the cloud and can be accessed via an Electronic Health Record system (EHR). The EHR is maintained separately for each patient, which can be accessed ubiquitously and pervasively from any given location. This EHR is further shared among the medical team and clinical experts seeking their opinion as well as analysis. The medical team such as surgeons, doctors, and lab technicians access EHR and dispense prompt and timely patient treatment. The lab professionals would store MRI scans, X-Rays, and serum reports in cloud database or EHR after proper consent and permission from the patient. This EHR could be shared via cloud platform with other medical experts across the globe for their expert opinion and diagnosis, and hence, the patient could benefit with their prompt suggestions with shorter turn-around time period. Further, the clinical professionals can suggest certain drugs and emergency medicines which should be readily stocked at the pharmacy warehouses. The pharmacist can beforehand make those drugs available so that any shortage in future could be avoided. Additionally, the pharmacist can study the medical profile of a patient available to him via EHR for any allergic reactions, before he recommends or issues any drug to the patient. In the same way, the hospitals and nursing care institutions dealing with an exigency case such as accident can check patient's blood group, medical history and other pre-conditions before operating with any medical treatment. All this sensitive information would be available pervasively via EHR stored on the cloud and can be accessed from anywhere across geographical boundaries. Using CloudIoT healthcare system, e-health record of patient which includes medical history, serum sample reports, body scans, and information regarding allergic reactions can be available in digital format and can be accessed in a ubiquitous manner under secure authentication policies, thus implementing the idea of smart health management system.

11.4.5   Design Considerations

The wearable things that monitor and archive patient's bio-medical data consist of low-power sensors, small microcontroller chip, and a data transmission [26]. However, putting on bio-medical sensors by patients pose quite limitations on the overall design of bio-medical sensors [41, 122]. As an example, the sensors need to be light, minimal in dimension, and should not pose any hindrance to physical mobility of patient. The patient's should feel comfortable while wearing these devices and should not affect their daily work routine. One of the critical design considerations is regarding the energy efficiency of the sensor. These sensors are usually battery powered and thus have limited operational working capacity [30]. Though sensor batteries are recharged or replaced, however the prototype should guarantee that no information is deleted during idle transition periods. The sensor design must ensure that they are able to work for extended time periods without any downtime or idleness [126].

Nowadays, research has focused on designing low-power sensors that can augment the working lifespan of the wearable sensor devices [101]. One of the feasible steps toward achieving this would be to harness other sources of power such as solar energy [103].

A similar feasible approach involves designing programmed intelligent sleep procedures for sensing nodes [31]. The programmed routines would force the sensor device to go into inactive stage when no perception task occurs during particular time period. If an external event occurs in the environment, the sensor would be triggered automatically to work again. Additionally, the sensor devices can be turned on/off based on relative importance of a task, its usage and patient's current health status. As an example, in particular cases, when power usage is severely limited and health status of person requires working of only one particular bio-sensor, the other sensor devices attached with the patient could be turned off or put into sleep mode to conserve energy and increase working lifespan [127].

As data transmission consumes considerable energy, the limited battery power in sensors also entails for the design and usage of low energy consumption protocols. One of the efficient protocols for low-power communication is Zigbee using IEEE 802.15.4 which is usually utilized in "Low Rate Wide Personal Area Networks (LR-WPANs)". This protocol supports communication between sensors that operate in the radius of 10 mts (10m). The Zigbee standard underpins reliable fully connected networking with optimal power usage.

Bluetooth Low Energy (BLE) is another wireless communication standard protocol that operates with minimal power and enables short range sensor communication [125]. BLE works in the similar fashion as traditional Bluetooth standard (IEEE 802.15.1), however augments the overall communication efficiency by enforcing programmed sleep routines to optimize power usage. BLE achieves reasonable accuracy with precision.

To further optimize communication, "IPv6 over Low Power Wireless Personal Area Networks" or 6LoWPAN is currently employed to achieve seamless data transmission in energy constrained devices [31]. 6LoWPAN breaks down IPv6 datagram's in smaller fragments which are put as a payload in restricted IEEE 802.15.4 frame in order to achieve network connectivity.

The limited battery life also proves to be a bottleneck in determining data quality aggregated by a particular sensing node. The sensors need minimal power threshold to operate, however, if the system fails to maintain the minimal power threshold, then the sensor device may malfunction.

The sensor devices are capable of recording data efficiently and accurately when proximity with the patient's body is close [127, 141]. Most of the sensors available today are non-invasive sensors that with greater accuracy and precision [15, 32, 80].

One of the essential considerations for designing an efficient healthcare system is to offload and migrate complex computations and processing from sensor nodes to the cloud platform [136]. Cloud platform provides substantial computational processing and humongous warehouse capacity that increments the limited sensor resources, thus dispensing optimal interface for ubiquitous communication [3]. The processing capabilities of Cloud can further be augmented by implementing the concept of Fog computing. The Fog layer offers a feasible interface for low latency in real-time and sensitive services like healthcare. The Fog also acts as an intermediate component for performing complex operations before actually moving the data to the cloud.

An essential and sensitive design consideration for healthcare framework is the ability to maintain confidentiality of patient and ensure safe and reliable information storage in Cloud [94, 112]. When sensitive medical data is transacted in the CloudIoT environment, robust security and efficient privacy procedures need to be operated so that no information is openly susceptible to abuse by malicious users. The data needs to be protected from unauthorized and illegitimate access. This implies applying feasible authentication and authorization policies and firewall rules that secure access to the data [39]. To encrypt data, light weight and low-power consumption cryptographic algorithms like Elliptic curve cryptography (ECC) should be applied.

11.5   Security Challenges and Vulnerabilities

Amalgamation of Cloud and IoT underpins framework of interconnected objects supporting varied range of services which include efficient healthcare systems, tracking patient remotely, concept of smart metropolis and homes, self-regulating traffic systems, industrial waste management, environment surveillance, as well as how these objects transact information with each other [59, 119, 120]. Some of these application areas of CloudIoT

Table 11.3 CloudIoT application areas.

Application area	Common examples
Smart Home	Intrusion detection systems, smart alarm system, motion detection
Smart Healthcare	Remote patient monitoring, drug regimen alerts
Smart Ecosystem	Pollution alerts, tree fire detection, UV radiation monitoring
Smart Agriculture	Meteorological updates, remote farmer assistance, greenhouse emissions monitoring
Smart City	Traffic updates, smart lighting, automated parking systems
Smart Industry	Energy management, assembly line monitoring, quality checking, and packaging

are listed in Table 11.3. The Cloud offers an excellent service and backup platform for IoT objects and sustains seamless access to shared resources which include processing, data storage, application interoperability, data analytics, and knowledge extraction features [54, 105]. Although adoption of CloudIoT framework in healthcare sector seems to be instrumental, however there has been minimal consideration with respect to its security implications [72, 124]. If data breach and security loopholes are there, then the healthcare framework would be rendered ineffective and sensitive patient data could be abused by malicious users [102]. Integrating Cloud and IoT will make the issue more compounded and will expose hidden security flaws making billions of interconnected sensor objects vulnerable. As such, the security drawbacks will negate the benefits of CloudIoT [113]. Given the widespread deployment of infrastructure and cost implications, it is also not optimal that sensor devices should be re-organized and changed periodically. The rudimentary security framework needs to be profound and sustainable from the core to work for an extended time period.

11.5.1 Security Characteristics and Objectives

The CloudIoT enables information communication between interconnected sensor objects and remote systems to attain certain predefined objectives. For a secure communication in hostile scenarios, it is quite evident that security principles such as confidentiality, authenticity, privacy need to be protected [113, 115]. However, with limited security infrastructure and constrained resources, the models demand restructuring of existing security tools and algorithms to achieve perceptible security goals [22, 124]. The security framework should be imposed in CloudIoT throughout its developmental and working lifecycle [62]. Some of the secure principles that need to be practiced include the following:

- All installed software on CloudIoT platform should be authentic and robust.
- The initialization of IoT devices should be authenticated with the network servers before the device starts data perception and transmission.
- There should be periodic security updates on CloudIoT devices in order to plug security loopholes; however the process should not consume additional network bandwidth.

The following security parameters as depicted in Figure 11.8 need to be safeguarded for secure transmission between IoT and Cloud platform.

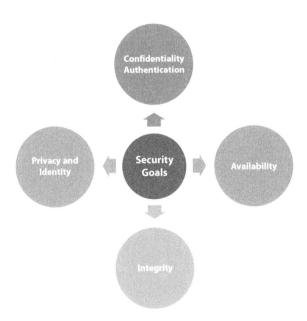

Figure 11.8 CloudIoT security goals.

11.5.1.1   Confidentiality

The confidentiality feature corroborates that data is accessible only to authenticated users and cannot be sniffed or eavesdropped. The collected data from the environment using sensor devices should not leak confidential information to the neighboring nodes and safeguard it from any illegal access. To enforce confidentiality, use of cryptographic techniques and secure key exchange mechanisms is highly recommended [62]. The confidentiality principle should also ensure how the data is managed in a hostile environment.

11.5.1.2   Integrity

The integrity principle warrants that data is tamper resistant and can withstand interference from malicious users during the transmission. The integrity features guarantees that accurate data which is also reliable is obtained by the intended destination. To ensure data integrity, robust security algorithms and cryptographic procedures should be operated in data communication and transmission.

11.5.1.3   Availability

This principle guarantees data of sensor devices is read only by authentic users whenever it is demanded. The sensor devices in internetwork involve real-time information transmission with minute delays. Non-availability of data would result is undesirable delays which will impact the performance of the sensor network. The most common threat to data availability is the denial-of-service attack that aims to render computational processing and resources inaccessible to its legitimate clients. To avert such issues, enhanced techniques such as secured and intelligent routing protocols need be employed into the network.

11.5.1.4   Identification and Authentication

The identification principle warrants that unauthorized objects or services should not get access to the network. The authentication, in turn, ensures that valid and legitimate data is transacted in the CloudIoT network. Due to diverse nature of Cloud and IoT, verifying and validating each and every object is quite cumbersome process [118]. The process should however be optimal, mutual and feasible so that only legitimate device transacts information in the network.

11.5.1.5   Privacy

The privacy principle warrants restricted information access and control to legitimate users. Contrary to confidentiality that utilizes encryption and cryptographic standards to avoid tampering of information, the privacy principle ensures limited authorization and limited operations over data. The privacy is one of the dominant components in data communication due to the fact that considerable number of devices and users transact sensitive information over an unsecured sensor network.

11.5.1.6   Light Weight Solutions

This feature is required due to underlying computational and processing power limitation imposed by CloudIoT platform. As sensor devices have constrained resources, the algorithms that run on these devices should be optimal without involving complex cryptographic procedures. The algorithms should be in tune with processing capabilities of the sensor nodes.

11.5.1.7   Heterogeneity

The objects in CloudIoT framework are intrinsically heterogeneous in nature with varying potential and complexities. These objects use diverse platforms and operating frequencies to support M2M and H2M communications. CloudIoT framework acts as a bridge between different heterogeneous components and networks. Thus, the protocols and algorithms must be developed keeping the dynamic nature of the technology in mind.

11.5.1.8   Policies

The standard policies must be in place to ascertain that data is organized, secured, and communicated in an optimal fashion. The current strategies applied for computer and network security may not suffice for CloudIoT framework due to its dynamic and heterogeneous characteristic nature.

11.5.2   Security Vulnerabilities

Security loopholes inherent in CloudIoT model involve problems in IoT sensor network including those immanent in the Cloud platform [12]. This section first highlights security vulnerabilities ingrained at each level of IoT model and thereafter draws attention toward vulnerabilities inherent in Cloud architecture. Figure 11.9 depicts list of CloudIoT vulnerabilities.

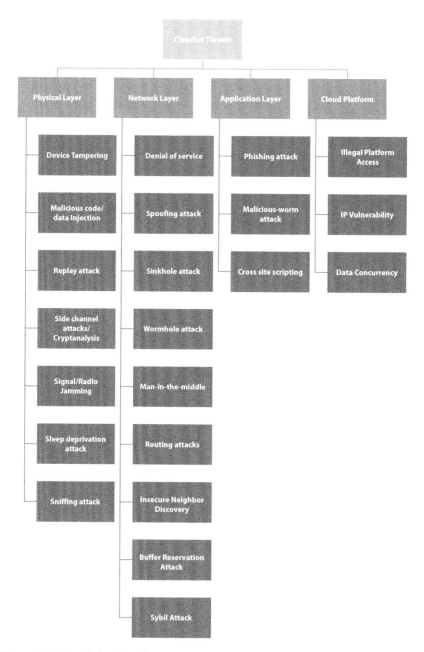

Figure 11.9 List of CloudIoT threats.

11.5.2.1   IoT Threats and Vulnerabilities

The IoT layered architecture is susceptible to disparate set of vulnerabilities from abusive users [12, 97]. These attacks are primarily classified as active or passive attacks depending on their source of origin which can be external or from inside the network. An active attack directly disrupts the normal operation of the service and is more minacious in nature. The passive attack works in stealth mode and monitors the network operations covertly [8, 62]. With large adoption rate of IoT, smart objects are vulnerable to security risks. Each layer of IoT should be secured in a way such that no data gets lost or modified in the network [22]. The IoT level wise elaborate security analysis is presented below.

11.5.2.1.1   Perception Level Threats

The principal function of this layer is to sense the physical environment, as such most of the attacks in this layer are directed toward altering or fiddling the captured data by malicious users. Some of the common attacks and threats in this layer are as follows:

"Node Hijacking Attack": The layer mostly comprises of sensors and RFID's which remains the prime focus for attackers whose aim is to cause physical damage to the hardware [155]. If a malicious user is successful in compromising the security of the physical deployed sensor object, then the sensitive information such as encryption and authentication keys becomes vulnerable to abuse. Also, to forge authentication with IoT network, the sensor object can copy vital information parameters from a compromised node. The attackers can also tamper software routines of sensor nodes by injecting malicious scripts and thus alter and downgrade its normal working operations.

"Replay Attacks": The attackers can manipulate trust via replay attacks and redirect critical data to inappropriate and malicious user systems [93].

"Eavesdropping": Eavesdropping is one of the common attacks leveraged by attackers in a wireless environment such as internet. In this attack vector, the malicious user transmits push notification to users using a compromised sensor node which enables it to collect sensitive private data.

"Sniffing Attacks": The attackers can sniff the network by placing malicious sensor objects in the vicinity of legitimate IoT devices in order to capture sensitive information. This leads to user identification, tracking, and profiling covertly by malicious nodes.

"Data Noise": The data transmission over unsecured wireless networks may contain noise and the data might be corrupted. Such incomplete information could be fatal especially in such scenarios where the working of IoT devices is hinged on reliability of available data.

"Sleep Deprivation attacks": These attacks are aimed at draining the limited battery resources of sensor nodes. The sensor batteries need to work in optimal way in order to operate for longer time periods. As such, the nodes may go into sleep mode in case of no sensing activity at a given point in time. The sleep deprivation attack tampers programmed sleep routines so that sensors work continuously resulting in energy drainage and sensor anomaly [23].

"Jamming Signals": The attackers deliberatively relay jamming or blocking signals that interfere with otherwise normal wireless signals [59]. These jamming or interference signals induce noise and deliberately disrupt normal communication between sensor nodes and backend data center.

11.5.2.1.2   Network Level Threats

This layer is heavily vulnerable to security leak as all the data aggregated with sensors gets communicated through this layer. This layer supports combination of traditional internet-based protocols and those that are unique to IoT. Therefore, this layer is open to both traditional TCP/IP network layer threats as well as threats that are unique to IoT architecture. Most of the security countermeasures aim at providing accessibility to the network infrastructure [88]. The security framework considers maintaining node integrity and privacy and ensures that authentic and reliable data is transmitted over the internetwork. A summary of common threats is listed below.

"Denial-of-Service (DoS) Attack": The main aim of this vulnerability is to make computational infrastructure unavailable to the legitimate user. In this attack, the sensor objects or devices are flooded with illegitimate data traffic which they cannot process or handle simultaneously. This leads to device shutdown and disrupts network operation. There are various types of DoS attacks which include bandwidth wastage, overloading processors with massive computations, encumber memory and storage. Common countermeasures employed for mitigating such attacks include applying strong firewall strategies and gateway rules.

"Gateway Attacks": The main focus of these attacks is to break down communication between sensor nodes and internet infrastructure. These are

different class of DoS or routing attacks that redirect erroneous information from internet toward deployed sensors. Thus, impeding the normal working operation of these nodes.

"*Storage Attacks*": A large volume of sensitive user data needs to be stored on Cloud data center which is vulnerable to abuse unless protected by strong cryptographic encryption algorithms. The attackers can replicate the data and cause data redundancy leading to wastage of storage space.

"*IP Spoofing*": This class of attacks is segregated in two classes: Address concealing and RFID tag tampering. In both classes, the attack destination is the backend control of IoT system. The attacks specifically aim to transfer malicious code across the network [88].

"*Black Hole Vulnerability*": In this vulnerability, network traffic gets altered and performance downgrades because malicious node drops some data packets. This results in information loss because the collected data does not reach the intended base station. Additionally, other attacks that attract traffic toward the victim node are "Illegal node access attack", "Sybil Attack", "Sink Hole attack", and "Worm Hole attack".

"*Routing Attacks*": In this attack, the main aim of the adversary is to tamper the routing policy including routing protocols and generate routing loop. This leads to network congestion and increased packet loss rate [23].

11.5.2.1.3   Application Level Threats

This is the topmost layer in the IoT network. This layer provides a platform for running client applications; therefore, most of the threats in this layer are directed toward shutting down applications. The main of the attacker is to inject software bugs in the program code that sets off the application to malfunction. There is no standard security protocol designed yet for IoT; therefore, these security vulnerabilities demand robust and substantial solutions. As disparate applications access application layer platform, therefore homogeneity of security architecture would be an arduous task. The common application level security threats are as follows:

"*Malicious code attack*": Also known as code injection attack, the vulnerability aims to breach security of the system and inject malicious code in the application program code. For example, a malicious worm could spread over the internet and attach itself to the embedded operating system of IoT node, thereby compromising its operation.

"Node Application Tampering": The attackers exploit vulnerability in sensor nodes and install malicious code. Failing to secure the sensor node would result in sensor malfunction and incorrect data collection. For example, malfunctioned temperature sensor would always display fixed temperature reading. Also, a compromised smart camera will record and display outdated pictures. Similar to this, in a scenario such as smart meter which transmits data utilization to the backend for real-time billing must be protected. The sensor devices should thus be robust and tamper resistant

"Failure to update security software": Although not a security threat, the inability to update security software on sensor devices can lead to catastrophic situations. For example, in case of real-time systems such as nuclear reactors, the failure to update security algorithms leaves the system vulnerable to disaster like situations.

11.5.2.2   Cloud-Based Threats

The vulnerabilities inherent in conventional cloud-based devices are also present in the CloudIoT platform; in fact the amalgamation of two disparate platforms will induce more complex security vulnerabilities that entail for robust solutions [58]. Most of the IoT devices demand computation and require storage space on the cloud platform. This necessitates ensuring that privacy and confidentiality of data is maintained. The cloud must also block unauthorized access to the data and strong encryption should be in place to ensure data abstraction [132]. As cloud platform is pervasive, the IoT objects access this platform via different networking protocols which are susceptible to various attack vectors like "Man-in-the-Middle attack", Eavesdropping, and "Denial-of-Service" attack [23].

Additionally to above, the Cloud suffers vulnerabilities owing its characteristic features.

According to NIST [92], the Cloud platform offers five unique characteristics. These include on-demand service, pervasive access to devices, pooling of resources, agility, and metered service. However, these characteristics invite vulnerabilities which are listed below:

Illegal platform access: As cloud supports on-demand service feature, it offers its management platform to varied number of users. As such, the probability that malicious users could access the platform is higher than the traditional systems which are monitored by only few administrators.

IP vulnerability: The ubiquitous nature of Cloud allows access to its platform using standard internet protocols. However, most of these network

Table 11.4 Summary of CloudIoT threats and vulnerabilities.

	Vulnerability	Description	Mitigation	References
"Perception layer"	"Device Tampering"	Control the working sensor device by physical damage or tampering its software code.	Physically checking the damaged site and monitoring malevolent code.	[12, 17, 39]
	"Malicious code/ data Insertion"	Inserting vulnerable code into software program of sensor device to alter its normal behavior.	Practicing secure code writing including code testing procedures need to be designed and developed.	[46]
	"Replay vulnerability"	Forging authentication keys to obtain trust of sensor node.	Ensuring robust timestamp methods in digital authentication of keys	[17]
	"Side channel abuse/ cryptanalysis"	Using normal-text/coded text, read cryptographic keys illegally.	Efficient and safe key development and encryption protocols need to be enforced.	[20, 70]
	"Radio jamming"	Mixing unwanted signal or radio waves to tamper and fiddle with wireless communication.	Intelligent noise reduction procedures and regenerating original needs to be designed.	[78, 88]

(Continued)

Table 11.4 Summary of CloudIoT threats and vulnerabilities. (*Continued*)

Vulnerability	Description	Mitigation	References
"Sleep mode tampering"	Imposing sensor node shutdown by fiddling with their normal sleep procedures so that they up and continuously running all the time even when not required.	Exploit alternate sources of energy like wind, solar. Practicing secure code writing including code testing procedures need to be designed and developed.	[23, 22]
"Sniffing attack"	The attackers sniff RFID-based wireless communication and extracts sensitive data like password thereby making the system open to exploit.	Ensure encrypted communication in the network. Use of asymmetric key cryptography is recommended.	[17, 22, 39]
"Network layer" "Denial of service"	Redirecting large volume of traffic on target system to make it work erratically and abnormally.	Developing secure firewall structure and packet inspection protocols in network devices.	[17, 39]
"Spoofing abuse"	Conceals identification (IP or RFID spoofing) of genuine nodes to obtain unauthorized authentication.	Developing efficient and advanced access control standards and authentication algorithms.	[25, 70]

(Continued)

Table 11.4 Summary of CloudIoT threats and vulnerabilities. (*Continued*)

Vulnerability	Description	Mitigation	References
"Sinkhole abuse"	To take over routing of information, the target node announces abnormal or unusual power/computation capacity.	Developing encrypted routing protocols and limited access to data forwarding nodes.	[57, 88, 109]
"Wormhole attack"	Targets a routing protocol in which a packet or individual bits of a packet are captured at one location, transferred to another location and then replayed at some different location.	Developing encrypted routing protocols and limited access to data forwarding nodes.	[57, 88]
"Man-in-the-middle"	The abusive node substitutes itself between two target nodes or systems. Spoofs their identity and obtains illegal access to data covertly.	Developing efficient and advanced access control standards and authentication algorithms. Practicing secure code writing including code testing procedures need to be designed and developed.	[70, 78]
"Routing attacks"	Idea of this vulnerability is to create routing loops that causes massive network congestion.	Developing encrypted routing protocols and limited access to data forwarding nodes.	[57, 63]

(*Continued*)

Table 11.4 Summary of CloudIoT threats and vulnerabilities. (*Continued*)

Vulnerability	Description	Mitigation	References
"Insecure neighbor discovery"	IP Address Spoofing	Employ light weight cryptographic procedures for authentication	[23, 63]
"Buffer reservation attack"	Blockage of Re-assembly Buffer	Split buffer approach requiring complete transmission of fragments	[70, 78]
"Sybil attack"	Attack results in privacy violation, spamming and unreliable broadcast from fake spoofed nodes	Analyze user behavior and keep record of trusted/un-trusted nodes.	[70, 78]
"Application layer" "Web phishing"	Aim is to extract authentication information that includes passwords/usernames by spamming network with mails and fake pages.	Practicing secure code writing including code testing procedures need to be designed and developed. Creating awareness within web developer community.	[23, 120]

(*Continued*)

Table 11.4 Summary of CloudIoT threats and vulnerabilities. (*Continued*)

	Vulnerability	Description	Mitigation	References
	"Worm attack"	Spam's the IoT network with Worms, Viruses and self-replicating Trojans etc. Maliciously deletes sensitive data.	Developing secure firewall structure and packet inspection protocols in network devices.	[57, 62]
	"XSS attacks"	To gain access to authentication information including cryptographic passwords by inserting applications with malicious code.	Practicing secure code writing including code testing procedures need to be designed and developed.	[62, 70]
Cloud platform	Illegal platform access	Attackers access the cloud platform illegally and perform malicious operation.	Ensure strong authorization and authentication measures.	[47, 49]
	IP vulnerability	Vulnerabilities persistent with standard IP model also exist within the Cloud.	Employing stripped and lighter versions of security protocols such as IPsec, SSL, and Https.	[23, 30]
	Data concurrency	Attacker leverages simultaneously operations on the interface.	Ensure Concurrency control measures.	[42, 58]

protocols have inherent vulnerabilities like man-in-the-middle attacks, session hijacking vulnerabilities, leaving the communication infrastructure as un-trusted and unsecure.

Data recovery issues: The Cloud platform allows resource pooling and rapid agility that allows computational resources to be assigned to multiple users at different intervals of time. However, it might happen that data written by the current user might be recovered by a different user accessing the same platform. This results in data privacy leakage and theft.

Tampering data usage: Every service rendered by the Cloud platform such as storage, processing or platform access is measured with metering capability with active user accounts. Based on the data usage, bills are generated and processed including payment. However, malicious user could play with the interface and cause data manipulation as well as billing evasion.

Table 11.4 lists the summary of various CloudIoT threats and vulnerabilities.

11.6   Security Countermeasures and Considerations

11.6.1   Security Countermeasures

For seamless integration of two disparate technologies, i.e., Cloud and IoT, the security framework should cover both these platforms. However, this security framework should ensure that principles of authentication, integrity and confidentiality are not violated. In this section, we discuss research highlighting security vulnerability awareness and various security counter measures that handle varied security threats.

11.6.1.1   Security Awareness and Survey

Authors in [156] address the security issues inherent at each IoT layer with some given security countermeasures. However, the security solution includes encryption only at the perception layer. Also, the authors do not reference to any specific evaluation framework that will evaluate the specified security measures.

Researchers in [128] present a generalized overview of IoT and Cloud with special reference to security issues inherent in both the technologies. Their work integrates the two technologies in order to study their common features and examine the benefits. The paper also presents the challenges associated with the amalgamation of Cloud with IoT and concludes that for seamless integration, the security issues must be resolved and reduced to minimum. The paper presents two cryptographic algorithms, AES and RSA, which authors claim can aid in the integration of IoT and Cloud; however, there is no mention of other lightweight cryptographic algorithms such as ECC, TEA, DESL, and LEA. These lightweight algorithms perform optimally well in constrained IoT environment.

In [118], authors provide short summary of security and privacy challenges and conclude that privacy and data integrity are fundamental security principles with respect of IoT and Cloud. The authors also argue that ensuring and warranting confidentiality comes under the prime reasons responsible for flawless CloudIoT operation. Similar work has been showcased in [132], where the authors highlight IoT implementation, security challenges and open issues.

In [70], the authors present a survey of IoT security framework and analyzed its various security aspects. The work presents a systematic summary of IoT security requirements as well as issues. The authors also highlight attack platforms, issues and temporal measures that must be taken into account while securing IoT network. The paper also elaborates discussion on various research issues including directions for future work.

11.6.1.2   Security Architecture and Framework

Diverse solutions with regard to IoT security architecture and applications are available in the literature. We summarize some of them briefly here [57, 61].

Authors in [72] present security architecture of IoT and discusses security vulnerabilities at each IoT layer along with potential solutions. The paper also contemplates discussion on key enabling technologies at each layer of IoT and presents their comparative analysis. The paper also presents a typical security comparison between IoT and Traditional networks and concludes that IoT system security needs to be augmented as they work with constrained and limited security resources. The paper however does not mention any technique to evaluate the proposed security architecture. Also, paper fails to provide any future directions for their research.

In [34], authors present an IoT security framework that highlight security loopholes in conventional IoT networks. The architecture includes black software defined networks (SDNs) including a Key Management System which ensures confidentiality, privacy, integrity, and optimal key distribution. However, presented architecture fails to sustain a full SDN implementation owing to limited power in IoT environment. This leaves IoT nodes susceptible to serious security threats such as node capturing, eavesdropping, and tampering. The framework also suffers from decreased network performance and complex data forwarding.

In [16], authors recommend a SDN as a potential remedy to tackle the vulnerability issues in IoT. SDN concept elevates the network performance and lowers hardware usage and also dispenses a robust security and privacy in comparison with traditional networks. The paper also outlines the architectural design of SDN and its suitability for IoT and *ad hoc* networks. The paper however does not evaluate the performance empirically and the concept is only a theoretical one.

Authors in [140] introduce SDN architecture for designing IoT applications that remove non-agile security setup of traditional networks. The motivation for the adoption of SDN was development of network OS that will assist administrators in containing various IoT threats and take control of the system. However, scalability and reliability are some limitations of SDNs. The SDNs also suffer from poor packet handling performance that leads to delays and DoS attacks. Similar work has been reported in [15].

In [52], researchers propose a new SDN architecture also called SDN domain using border controllers. The researchers explain the role of SDN in interconnecting heterogeneous IoT devices, augmentation of domain security and distribution of security rules. However, researchers fail in addressing the issue of securing legitimate as well as illegitimate traffic including enterprise security.

In [67], authors present a lightweight validation and authorization security model for low-power devices. However, the model has not been combined into limited IoT setup for authenticity including authorization and for determining different techniques that evaluate its accuracy.

11.6.1.3   Key Management

In [4], authors propose a lightweight and E2E key exchange standard. This standard is hinged on integration of various IoT security elements to develop a secure transmission path for low-power objects. The protocol ensures data confidentiality and authentication during the transmission process. However, the protocol delegates complex cryptographic procedures to third party applications. The protocol also fails to highlight tradeoff between communication cost and tally of third party applications.

Authors in [99] present a security toolbox for designing control architecture for IoT objects. The toolbox provides a fundamental base for development of various IoT engineering tools and components that address security and privacy requirements of IoT. The control framework also supports and augments inter network security management and interoperability.

The imitation of their technique is that authors fail to present a roadmap on deploying security and privacy vision for objects working in dynamic environments. The other limitation is that data integrity is not warranted.

In [87], authors propose PKI-based system that entails route encryption between the source and destination and employing key value for security and decryption of data. However, the concept is only theoretical with no formal evaluation and performance analysis.

11.6.1.4   Authentication

A varied range of algorithms have been proposed overtime for enforcing authentication on IoT devices in a CloudIoT environment.

For example, in [147], the researchers proposed an augmented authentication system for IoT devices. Their work is an improvement of the work done by researchers in [114]. The approach includes three principal components: addition of backup devices for control operation against each terminal device, addition of monitor devices for tracking and monitoring terminal devices, and addition of push alarm system for generating notification and alerts for unsuccessful authentications. However, this authentication system has not been tested empirically as no significant results have been presented.

To supplement authentication in IoT, researchers in [155] designed a novel IoT authentication technique for mutual identity. Their work proposes "Asymmetric Mutual Authentication Solution" that works across platforms and sink node hinged on "Secure Hash Algorithm", feature selection, and "Elliptic Curve Cryptography". Though researchers assert enhanced security having minimal computational and transmission cost, the conception is only hypothetical with no experimental backing and evaluation.

The work in [107] proposes two phase certificate-based authentication protocol that permits IoT devices as well as control stations to authenticate with each other. The system allows a secure connection to be established so that data is transmitted securely via a certificate authority. The protocol takes into consideration resource constraints of sensor nodes as well as scalability, reliability and heterogeneity factor of the network. The technique dispenses complete security and authentication mechanism at application level. However, the protocol fails to provide security against node capture attacks. The authors claim that protocol should use beacon message technique to avert damage due to node capture attack.

In [91], authors present "Identity Authentication and Capability based Access Control" (IACAC) model for IoT. The model presents a combined method of authenticating and authorization for IoT sensor objects and guarantees security against network layer attacks such as DoS. The security protocol verification tool is used for evaluation. The evaluation summary is mostly encouraging. However, this model does not altogether avert DoS attacks but reduces their frequency of happening substantially by permitting one ID periodically.

Authors in [143] propose one time cipher technique for ID authentication which is based on request-reply technique. In this cipher, the two end systems who have to undergo communication agree to a pre shared matrix. A user generates key from this matrix and sends encrypted message along with key and timestamp value. The communication between two parties is validated by this time stamp value. However, application of this method is very complex in a diverse IoT environment.

In [149], authors introduce a novel authentication and access control method. The technique achieves mutual authentication connecting the sensor objects and user by establishing a session key hinged on ECC. To realize agile access control to resources of legitimate users, the technique uses Attribute-based Access Control (ABAC). However, this technique solves resource limitation of only perception layer of IoT. Also, the authors further declare that ABAC policy requires further research and studies.

The work in [89] proposes authentication as well as access control in IoT devices in order to fix flaws related to security and integrity. In their proposed work, the user requires to seek permission from the Registration Authority (RA) for accessing a device which is granted after proper authentication. The technique is however flawed because if the RA is itself compromised, the whole network gets insecure.

11.6.1.5   Trust

In [146], authors focused their attention on item-layer access control for inter-node security and proposed an architecture for mutual trust in data transaction between varied computer system in IoT. The framework maintains trust using two methods: key creation and token. The proposed framework enables devices in IoT to verify the right owner and take a decision on whether a requesting node is allowed to perform certain actions to its system. The proposed framework is however theoretical and no experimental evaluation has been done by the authors.

For securing IoT communication, authors in [134] designed an augmented ant colony protocol for deciding trust level of devices in IoT. Trust is an important factor in determining reliability, security, and privacy of data that gets communicated over the network. The prominence of a node is used for deciding the trust level of a node and is calculated depending upon advance interaction of the node with rest of devices.

11.6.1.6   Cryptography

In [142], authors carry an in-depth performance evaluation of Attribute-Based Encryption (ABE), i.e., a public key encryption technique used for preserving privacy and enables access control including key management. The authors quantify two prime categories of ABE's, i.e., Key-Policy Attribute-Based Encryption (KP-ABE) and Ciphertext-Policy Attribute-Based Encryption (CP-ABE) on various mobile devices and laptops. The results highlight various practical issues of ABE such as requirement of computing resources in heterogeneous environment, cost benefits of ABE, and best case scenario for implementation of ABE in IoT. However, implementation of ABE on devices with limited computing power needs further investigation.

In [73], a secure mutual authentication protocol has been proposed for IoT and Cloud. The proposed protocol provides mutual authentication in addition to security. The technique employs ECC-based encryption which offers robust security in addition to being light weight with smaller key size. The protocol has been formally verified using AVISPA tool and the results are promising.

11.6.1.7   Device Security

In [11], authors propose a security approach that protects devices instead of data. The technique ensures security of devices which use RFID for communication with one another. However, this technique cannot be generalized for other wireless protocols such as Bluetooth, Zigbee which are also used in sensor communication. Also, the technique has not been evaluated empirically.

The main sensing devices at the IoT perception layer are RFID's and tiny sensors. As already discussed, these objects have limited computational power and as such use of traditional encryption algorithms is neither feasible nor recommended.

To tackle this issue, authors in [83] present a distinct validation approach for "RFID" tags. The approach employs XOR-based cryptography instead of heavy cryptographic algorithms. The technique is not complex and warrants mutual authentication in traditional RFID system. The technique is however limited to RFID communication only.

11.6.1.8   Identity Management

In [68], the Identity Framework Management technique has been presented that attempts to resolve the problem related with data authentication and processes between the cloud platform and underlying communication devices. The system proposes having an identity manager that performs the role of authentication and forwarding of data to the service manager that guides and affirms the implementation of the service. The framework however does not mention the required protocols that will implement the proposed architecture.

11.6.1.9   Risk-Based Security/Risk Assessment

Another adaptive security approach for smart IoT proposed by authors in [7] is based on Game Theory which involves employing simulated strategies by computers to build decisions for detection and avoidance of attacks. The approach takes into consideration the reliability and risk factors associated with the attacks. The framework however needs further studies and research for development of prototype models for predicting and estimating risks.

11.6.1.10   Block Chain–Based Security

In [78], authors highlight block chain technology for dispensing security in IoT. The block chain stands for a distributed, decentralized and immutable database registry that essentially controls and secures IoT objects. The underlying technology for block chain are cryptographic encryption algorithms, digital signatures and one way has functions that guarantee data integrity and access control. The authors have highlighted various block chain characteristics which are empirical for IoT protection and security.

11.6.1.11   Automata-Based Security

In [55], the authors suggest an automata-driven intrusion alert technique for diverse IoT environment. The technique uses labeled transition extension and can thwart three types of attacks which include jamming attack, replay attack, and spoofing attacks. The intrusion detection system offers a robust mechanism for ensuring IoT network security as all the traffic originating from or leaving the network is monitored.

Table 11.5 Overview of proposed security counter measures.

Security countermeasure	Suggested work	Advantage	Limitations	Reference
Authentication	Enhanced mutual authentication model of IoT	Includes three principal components: addition of backup devices for control operation against each terminal device, addition of monitor devices for tracking and monitor terminal devices, and addition of push alarm system for generating notification and alerts for unsuccessful authentications.	This authentication system has not been tested empirically as no significant results have been presented.	[147]
	Mutual identity authentication technique	Includes feature extraction involving hash functions. Avoids Collision attacks. Lightweight Improved Security using ECC.	Concept is only hypothetical and theoretical with no experimental backing and evaluation.	[155]

(Continued)

Table 11.5 Overview of proposed security counter measures. (*Continued*)

Security countermeasure	Suggested work	Advantage	Limitations	Reference
	Two-phase certificate-based authentication protocol	Permits authentication between IoT devices and control. Allows data transmission securely via a certificate authority. Takes into account resource constraints as well as scalability, reliability and heterogeneity factor of the network.	This protocol fails to avert node capture attacks.	[107]
	Identity Authentication and Capability-based Access Control	Uses public key technique for authentication. Congruent with lightweight communication such as 4G, 3G, and Bluetooth. Averts man-in-the-middle vulnerability by employing timestamp.	The model fails averting DoS attacks completely but reduces their frequency of happening substantially by permitting one ID periodically.	[91]
	One-time one cipher method-based on request-reply mechanism for ID authentication	Dynamic variable cipher operated with the help of pre-shared matrix. Two devices transact by certifying key and Timestamp value.	Application of this method is very complex in a diverse IoT environment.	[143]

(*Continued*)

Table 11.5 Overview of proposed security counter measures. (*Continued*)

Security countermeasure	Suggested work	Advantage	Limitations	Reference
	Efficient authentication and access control scheme for perception layer of internet of things	The technique achieves mutual authentication between the user and sensor objects by establishing a session key hinged on ECC. Uses Attribute-based Access Control (ABAC) to realize agile access control to resources of legitimate users.	The Attribute-based Access Control policy requires further research and studies. Solves resource limitation of only perception layer of IoT.	[149]
	Authentication and access control in the internet of things	Claims to solve security and Integrity issues in IoT via a central registration authority.	Technique is flawed because if the registration authority is itself compromised, the whole network gets insecure.	[89]

(*Continued*)

Table 11.5 Overview of proposed security counter measures. (*Continued*)

Security countermeasure	Suggested work	Advantage	Limitations	Reference
Architecture and Framework	Security of the Internet of Things: perspectives and challenges	Presents security architecture for IoT. Discusses security vulnerabilities for IoT layers along with potential solutions. Highlights key enabling technologies at each layer of IoT	Fails to mention any technique for evaluating the proposed security architecture.	[72]
	Secure IoT architecture for Smart Cities	Presents a secure IoT architecture that includes black software defined networks (SDNs) including a Key Management System. Claims to ensure confidentiality, privacy, integrity and optimal key distribution.	Architecture fails to sustain a full SDN implementation owing to limited power in IoT environment. Architecture also suffers from decreased network efficiency and complex routing.	[34]

(*Continued*)

Table 11.5 Overview of proposed security counter measures. (*Continued*)

Security countermeasure	Suggested work	Advantage	Limitations	Reference
	Software defined network	Present software defined network (SDN) as a potential solution to tackle the security issues in IoT. Outlines the architectural design of SDN and its suitability *ad hoc* networks like IoT.	Does not evaluate the performance empirically and the concept is only a theoretical one.	[16]
	Software defined network	Present SDN architecture for designing IoT applications that remove non-agile security setup of traditional networks. Assists administrators in containing various IoT threats and take control of the system.	Suffers from scalability and reliability. SDNs also have poor packet handling performance that leads to delays and DoS attacks.	[140]
	SDN-based security architecture	Propose a novel SDN architecture called SDN domain using border controllers. Interconnects heterogeneous IoT devices, augmentation of domain security and distribution of security rules.	Fails in addressing the issue of securing legitimate as well as illegitimate traffic including enterprise security.	[52]

(*Continued*)

Table 11.5 Overview of proposed security counter measures. (*Continued*)

Security countermeasure	Suggested work	Advantage	Limitations	Reference
	Secure access framework	A Lightweight validation and authorization security model for low-power devices.	The model has not been integrated into constrained IoT setup for authenticity and authorization and for determining different techniques that evaluate its accuracy.	[67]
Key management	End-to-End secure key management protocol	Presents a lightweight and end-to-end key management standard. Ensures data confidentiality and authentication during the transmission process.	Delegates complex cryptographic procedures to third party applications. Fails to highlight tradeoff between communication cost and count of third party applications.	[4]

(*Continued*)

Table 11.5 Overview of proposed security counter measures. (*Continued*)

Security countermeasure	Suggested work	Advantage	Limitations	Reference
	SecKit: a model-based security toolkit	Presents a security toolkit for designing a control framework for the IoT objects. Provides a fundamental base for development of various IoT engineering tools and components that address security and privacy requirements of IoT. Supports and augments inter domain security management and interoperability.	Fails to provide a roadmap on deploying security and privacy solutions for objects working in dynamic environments. Also data integrity is not warranted.	[99]
	PKI-based Protocol	Proposes PKI-based system that entails route encryption between the source and destination and employing key value for security and decryption of data.	The concept is only theoretical with no formal evaluation and performance analysis.	[87]

(Continued)

Table 11.5 Overview of proposed security counter measures. (*Continued*)

Security countermeasure	Suggested work	Advantage	Limitations	Reference
Trust	Item-level access control framework for inter-system security	For inter-system security, it offers item-level access control. Proposes a framework for mutual trust in data transaction among varied information system in IoT.	The proposed framework is however theoretical and no experimental evaluation has been done by the authors.	[146]
	Trust-based privacy	An augmented ant colony procedure for deciding trust values of devices in IoT. Determines reliability, security and privacy of data that gets communicated over the network. Uses previous reputation of node		[134]

(*Continued*)

Table 11.5 Overview of proposed security counter measures. (*Continued*)

Security countermeasure	Suggested work	Advantage	Limitations	Reference
Cryptography	Performance evaluation of attribute-based encryption	Evaluates performance of Attribute-Based Encryption (ABE) for preserving privacy and enables access control including key management. Highlights practical issues of ABE such as requirement of computing resources in heterogeneous environment, cost benefits of ABE and best case scenario for implementation of ABE in IoT.	Implementation of ABE on devices with limited computing power needs further investigation	[142]
	Secure authentication scheme	Proposes a secure mutual authentication protocol for IoT and Cloud. Employs ECC-based encryption.		[73]

(*Continued*)

Table 11.5 Overview of proposed security counter measures. (*Continued*)

Security countermeasure	Suggested work	Advantage	Limitations	Reference
Device security	Security in the Context of Internet of Things	Proposes a security approach that protects devices instead of data. Ensures security of devices which use RFID for communication.	Technique cannot be generalized for other wireless protocols such as Bluetooth, Zigbee. Technique is not evaluated empirically.	[11]
	Lightweight authentication protocol for internet of things	Present a distinct validation technique for "RFID" tags that employs XOR-based encryption instead of heavy cryptographic algorithms. Guarantees mutual authentication in a traditional RFID system without harboring any complexity.	Technique is however limited to RFID communication only.	[83]
Identity management	Identity management framework for cloud-based internet of things	Presents Identity Framework Management technique. Claims to resolve data authentication problem and processes between the cloud platform and underlying communication devices.	Framework does not mention the required protocols that will implement the proposed framework.	[68]

(Continued)

Table 11.5 Overview of proposed security counter measures. (*Continued*)

Security countermeasure	Suggested work	Advantage	Limitations	Reference
Risk-Based Security/Risk Assessment	Risk-based adaptive security for smart IoT	Security approach for smart is based on Game Theory. Takes into consideration the reliability and risk factors associated with the attacks.	The framework needs further studies and research for development of prototype models for predicting and estimating risks.	[7]
Block chain–based Security	Block Chain Review	Highlights block chain technology for dispensing security in IoT. Highlights various block chain features that are empirical for IoT security.	Block chain systems are susceptible to Security threats. Hashing power of miner can be compromised.	[78]
Automata-based Security	Automata-based intrusion detection method for IoT	Presents automata-driven intrusion detection for IoT. Uses labeled transition extension and can thwart three types of attacks which include jamming attack, replay attack and spoofing attacks.	Needs Standardization of protocol. Needs further empirical research.	[55]

(*Continued*)

Table 11.5 Overview of proposed security counter measures. (*Continued*)

Security countermeasure	Suggested work	Advantage	Limitations	Reference
Security Awareness & Survey	IoT Survey	Addresses the security challenges inherent at every IoT level having some given security countermeasures.	Includes encryption only at the perception layer. No reference to any specific evaluation framework that will evaluate the specified security measures.	[156]
	Secure integration of IoT and cloud computing	Present an overview of IoT and Cloud with special reference to inherent security issues. Work integrates the two technologies in order to study their common features and examine the benefits. Presents challenges associated with the amalgamation of IoT and Cloud.	No mention of other optimal lightweight cryptographic algorithms such as ECC, TEA, DESL, and LEA.	[128]

(Continued)

Table 11.5 Overview of proposed security counter measures. (*Continued*)

Security countermeasure	Suggested work	Advantage	Limitations	Reference
	Security and Privacy in Distributed IoT	Provide brief summary of security and privacy challenges with respect to IoT and Cloud.		[118]
	Security Analysis of IoT	Highlights a survey of IoT security framework and analyzes its various security aspects.		[70]

A number of solutions that focus on CloudIoT security are available in existing research; however, most of them emphasize on preserving confidentiality, integrity, privacy, and enforcing authentication. The demand for providing robust security architecture is one of the open issues in research today. Table 11.5 lists the summary of various security counter measures.

11.6.2   Security Considerations

Given the fact that collaboration of IoT and Cloud, i.e., two varied technological platforms will outpour security issues considerably, thus impregnable defense policies are required for averting threats [22, 23].

While designing the security for CloudIoT platform, the security of entire whole system should be taken into consideration [109]. The security setup however cannot be built by simply deploying solutions at each layer of the architecture together. Different CloudIoT applications such as smart home, traffic management, and intelligent healthcare entail for diverse heterogeneous security solutions [25, 65]. For example, for intelligent traffic management and smart healthcare, data privacy is of utmost importance [66]. However, for applications such as smart city and smart environment monitoring, data authenticity needs to be ensured [24]. This implies that every applications demands different level of security to be enforced. Applying security at only one level will not cater to the security requirements at other levels. For example, if a system has weak security applied at the application level, no matter how much strong security we implement at the lower levels (such as perception level); the system would still be insecure. Thus, we need to design a system that provides cross layer security and helps integrate the system as one entity [111]. The security systems should be designed keeping cross layer heterogeneous integration in mind [69, 121].

The security framework should also take into consideration security challenges in IoT as well as those inherent in Cloud platform [22, 97]. As an example, in order to avoid illegal access to a sensor node, strong authentication measures should be put into place. Also, strong cryptographic encryption should be practiced to guarantee data confidentiality. To ensure this, advanced encryption algorithms such as ECC should be practiced. This should be coupled with efficient key exchange policies [124]. As IoT sensor nodes are driven by batteries, thus to maximize their working time period, efficient power utilization mechanism like programmed sleep procedures should be executed so that nodes do not drain the limited battery power. Additionally, other renewable sources of power generation for IoT such as solar energy should be harnessed. Table 11.6 lists the various

Table 11.6 Node energy drainage factors and solutions.

Energy drainage factor	Description	Potential solutions
Idle Listening	Node listening to an idle channel in order to receive possible traffic (data)	Nodes should implement energy saving procedures and programmed sleep routines.
Packet collision	Node receives more than one packet at the same time lead to packet discarding or retransmission	Packet Firewall and Filtering mechanism should be implemented. Node Input should be throttled.
Overhearing	Node receives packets that are destined to other nodes	Efficient packet addressing needs to be done. Packet encryption for ensuring privacy of data.
Control packet overhead	A minimal number of control packets should be used to make a data transmission	Periodic transmission of data packets. Longer time interval between packet transmissions.
Over-emitting	A message is transmitted when the destination node is not ready	Handshaking and acknowledge mechanism between nodes should be implemented. Use of Sync packets before transmission is recommended

energy drainage factors of sensor nodes along with their potential solutions. To check for physical damage to sensor objects, it is recommended that periodic watch and monitoring needs to be implemented at remote deployed site. To prevent network-based attacks like DoS and DDoS, the optimal policy could be firewall implementation and access methods. The security at the network layer can be viewed from two perspectives:

wireless and wired security. To ensure security via both communication mediums, development of authentication protocols and key management is one of the essential components. Protocols such as SSL/TLS need to be employed to encrypt the communication link. Additionally, for IP security, IPsec-enabled communication needs to be practiced. This will ensure that data authenticity, confidentiality and integrity are maintained at each layer. Before establishing a new network, guest access and default passwords should be disabled and cleared immediately in routers and gateways. Ensuring periodic password changes, applying strong passwords with alphanumeric characters and numbers should be practiced. For mitigating replay attacks, synchronized timestamp techniques should be practiced. In general, it is recommended that cryptographic algorithms that dispense E2E security need to be implemented. It would ensure that data authenticity, integrity and genuineness is maintained [124]. To protect security threats at the Application layer, the mitigation policy would be writing secure programming algorithm and implement malicious script identification procedures. For sanitizing vulnerable scripts, code rewrite techniques should be implemented.

To secure data at the cloud platform, client access should be authenticated and authorized with no room for illegitimate access. The fundamental step toward this is to ascertain that only legitimate users get access to critical information perceived by sensor objects. The entails demand for defining the required physical identity and platform access policies. Any client nodes trying to access cloud should first identity and authenticate itself with the platform. Once authenticated, access may be given; however, the access may be restricted depending upon the user and mode of operation desired. Since cloud offers pervasive access to the users, the security professionals need to implement concurrency control measures so that data is not corrupted and redundancy operations could be avoided. Also, to ensure data security, approaches like multimedia compression, image stenography and compression, water marking, cryptography, and session timers should be practiced [123].

To track cybercrimes aimed at CloudIoT platform, the efficient solution would be to log every action on the cloud platform. This logged record can be checked in future to detect for any anomaly. Logging also enables the cyber forensic investigators to check and ascertain which operation went wrong so that it can be rectified. The Cloud as well as IoT are two completely different heterogeneous interfaces, and thus, to dispense optimal level of security is a daunting job for security researchers.

11.7 Open Research Issues and Security Challenges

It is an established fact that CloudIoT dispenses convenience and user comfort in our everyday life; however, majority of CloudIoT working components such as low-cost sensor and communication chips are designed without considering security [72, 97]. If successful malicious attack is executed successfully, then the CloudIoT system would lie insecure with loss of private sensitive information and critical damage to the infrastructure. The problem becomes more convoluted with the integration of IoT and Cloud platforms [63].

The CloudIoT security involves security of the entire system rather than the security of single individual layer or cloud. The CloudIoT treats entire system as an integrated framework for a cross platform security solution. To secure CloudIoT systems, heterogeneous security architectures need to be designed to allow blending of varied data generated from disparate sources [62, 63].

The CloudIoT platform has witnessed exponential surge nowadays in the areas such as healthcare monitoring, telemedicine, environment surveillance, and pollution control. Some researchers are also of the opinion that connected things will surge near to 26 billion by the year 2020 [84]. However, its security challenges and issues must be addressed to facilitate its unbounded growth. Listed below are some of the open areas for research that aim to make the platform robust and secure.

11.7.1 Security Architecture

The CloudIoT integrates varied objects, platforms and standards to realize certain goals. However, to fuse smaller micro frameworks for designing a larger framework entails for following well defined standards. The CloudIoT security framework demands data models and standard security protocols that underpin diverse range of devices, platforms and operating systems [76].

As CloudIoT security threats vary from application to application, so are their specific solutions. Different applications demand diverse solutions and security requirements. Thus, single security framework cannot provide solution to all application contexts [78]. However, what is required is to design an abstract security architecture that features similarities among the applications till a concrete security model comes up. This model hides the differences between different applications and offers an interface that highlights similarities.

11.7.2   Resource Constraints

The constrained power of sensor devices are the major bottlenecks in designing a vibrant and powerful security system for CloudIoT [109]. In contrast to traditional security systems, the cryptographic and encryption systems need to scale down and work with minimal features for working under these limitations. In addition to this, resource limitation also causes minimal broadcast or multicast of keys and certificates, access control and authentication as well as intelligent communication and storage of data that consumes less power.

However, this demands revamping of existing protocols and employing light weight cryptographic encryption algorithms such as ECC. The focus should also be on exploring and harvesting alternate energy sources such as solar power [74]. The applications computational and security requirements can also be broken down into several levels. Each level runs a different set of algorithms which have different energy requirements. In this way, some levels would consume less power while some need to be optimized.

11.7.3   Heterogeneous Data and Devices

The CloudIoT systems generate humongous volumes of data also known as big data. Research should focus on developing ways and techniques for efficiently handling this massive data volume [45]. Also, secure protocols and algorithms need to be developed that can effectively protect this data and comprehensive security solution is put into place. Also, multilayer and cross platform security framework needs to be employed for heterogeneous devices ranging from low-power sensors to high-end server systems. The security framework should be dynamic and should adapt itself to the existing resources.

11.7.4   Protocol Interoperability

To develop a global standard security framework for CloudIoT, the protocols functioning at various layers of IoT as well as Cloud need to interoperate and communicate with each other [115]. This entails designing conversion routines and dialog controllers. However, the interoperability design should take into consideration the architectural limitations and constraints. With heterogeneous networks such as CloudIoT, the security framework becomes vulnerable to a single point of failure [12]. Most of the data in the network gets transacted through a central controller node. If that node is compromised, then the security of entire network is at stake. It is thus required to introduce some amount of redundancy in the network while maintaining and balancing reliability and cost.

11.7.5 Trust Management and Governance

The level of compatibility in the network and flexible expansion capacity of a sensor device helps it to decide other trustworthy nodes in the network. This decision can be quite challenging because it is arduous to distinguish between a genuine and a rogue node in a pervasive and wireless environment such as CloudIoT. The IoT device must also not reveal identity to adversary that could prove fatal to the system. What is required is a robust and pliable authorization mechanism that performs identity management and grants access to the legitimate devices in the network. However, the identity management should be properly encrypted because the process is susceptible to interception by malicious users which can leverage man-in-the-middle attack and imperil entire CloudIoT architecture [9].

The actual security and control of the CloudIoT network is determined by the degree of governance. The security of the network and level of governance are directly proportional. If more control and monitoring mechanisms can be employed, then the network would become more secure. This implies that if every data transaction in the network is monitored, then any malicious activity would get easily detected and tracked. However, the amount of monitoring and surveillance should be balanced as it should not amount to the level of nuisance and uneasiness for user's privacy.

11.7.6 Fault Tolerance

The CloudIoT systems and objects should possess a certain degree of fault tolerance and self-repairing ability. These defense mechanisms should allow the device to recover from any possible damage on its own if the threat is not so severe. Different options are available for a device; for example, one way would be to report in case of intrusion to the central controller node or backend server. Another approach could be to lock sensitive operations and shutdown the entire system. However, there has to be a balance so that normal working of the node is not hampered. The decision depends upon the conditions and level of severity of the threat. In some other scenarios, complex approaches may be required.

11.7.7   Next-Generation 5G Protocol

For fully exploiting the potential of CloudIoT platform, Ipv4 will shortfall and lack behind in assigning IP address to each and every connected device. This is the prime reason for the genesis of Ipv6 which has 3.4×10^{38} addresses; enough to cater every connected device on earth. However, such a large address space and connected devices will generate large volumes of data that can draw network congestion and delay. Also, substantial bandwidth is required to support seamless access to internet for connected devices. The new generation communication protocol, i.e., 5G is expected to provide speeds of up to 800 Gbps. When compared with 4G which offers speed up to 1,000 Mbps, 5G is expected to efficiently manage traffic generated by connected devices in CloudIoT network. The 5G network is also expected to facilitate Ipv4 to Ipv6 migration by implementing inherent framework translation. The 5G security and implementation is one of the hot areas of research today and must be extensively studied [109]. The adoption of 5G network will completely realize the concept of CloudIoT.

11.8   Discussion and Analysis

Amalgamation of two diverse technology frameworks demands interconnectivity and transaction of data among heterogeneous networks. These heterogeneous networks need to be flexible and unrestricted and should support divergent data and services [39].

The security architecture of CloudIoT framework may be augmented by "privacy by design" method in which holistic view of security and privacy concerns of the entire system is addressed at the design and implementation time. To design security framework, enhanced security protocols, cryptographic methods, and algorithms should be employed which take into consideration constrained computing resources of connected devices [21].

The security architecture should also provide solution to the issue of fault tolerance and hardware failure which is quite common in these devices [109]. The CloudIoT security framework should feature detection of spurious and compromised data including protection of data identity [3].

The devices in CloudIoT network produce exponential data that need to be managed, processed and transmitted [12]. In an optimal system, the management of data is primarily handled by the Cloud platform. Thus, the security of this generated data depends upon the security framework implemented in the Cloud platform by the service providers. The security of data on the Cloud platform depends upon the secure allocation/re-allocation of resources from one virtual machine to another and safeguarding the virtualization process. The security of data on Cloud platform is often compromised by malevolent traffic exchanged between the virtual machines. This is usually avoided by monitoring the traffic and installing firewall systems between the virtual machines. Another approach is to separate and isolate varied virtual machine classes from one another. In addition to these, the attacks on CloudIoT platform may be launched by hostile users who upload malicious data with the intension of performing illegal operations. These threats are usually averted by anomaly detection systems that can distinguish between normal and abnormal behavior.

Thus, enforcing security and privacy on the platform is of supreme importance. This requires implementing cryptographic encryptions that abstract and authenticate communication data. Also, unauthorized access to the platform must be restricted. Ensuring robust security and reliability will be a major success factor in adopting and deployment of this technology.

The efficient solution could also be a tangible and robust security system that will encapsulate and abstract user information and safeguard confidentiality [94]. Such systems in particular, for delay-sensitive services like healthcare also entail for designing minimal energy gobbling efficient devices. Though number of power-saving architecture have been designed over a period of time, majority of them handle operation of IoT and Cloud asynchronously. Designing power efficient and reliable CloudIoT architecture can ameliorate sensor operational time which, in turn, can improve functionality of operational devices. To vanquish delay sensitivity and power utilization, operation of Fog computing technology significantly minimizes the data flow on cloud and additionally offers localized storage for IoT [3, 95]. As privacy issues are involved in healthcare data, the regional bindings and guidelines do not allow these to be transacted beyond the framework of healthcare application portals. Thus, Fog-based computation proves to be a flawless solution as it drives the complexity and processing nearer to the healthcare service providers [3, 97]. This leads to minimal latency, lower power consumption, data security, and privacy as well as ideal bandwidth consumption.

The CloudIoT involves amalgamation of disparate heterogeneous networks which raise certain compatibility issues. However, it is expected that by efficient key management and implementing routing protocols, the incompatibilities will be negated.

11.9   Conclusion

The evolutionary growth of CloudIoT platform has become the intrinsic factor for developing robust and organized healthcare applications that influence our daily life. The adoption of CloudIoT in healthcare is influenced by demand for robust processing architectures, humongous data storage, high performance networks, and resource availability. The Cloud platform also seems to be a panacea for several limitations such as resource constraints immanent within the IoT network. A wide majority of healthcare research literature has discussed the role of Cloud and IoT separately, highlighting their architecture and applications; however, shortfall from comprehensive and elaborate security issue examination. To bridge this gap, this chapter reviews CloudIoT literature and presents an overall insight on CloudIoT-driven healthcare services. In this chapter, we presented a brief background highlighting composition of CloudIoT platform and its enabling technologies. We also introduced a conceptual architecture for healthcare monitoring system which included a use case scenario depicting the actual data flow in a smart healthcare system. The chapter also tried to highlight various security vulnerabilities affecting IoT and cloud platform. These vulnerabilities demand efficient security architectures so that user data privacy is maintained. We also made an attempt to underline some open research issues and security challenges that can further motivate our research in this domain.

References

1. Aazam, M. and Huh, E.N., Fog computing and smart gateway based communication for cloud of things, in: *2014 International Conference on Future Internet of Things and Cloud*, 2014, August, IEEE, pp. 464–470.

2. Aazam, M. and Huh, E.N., Fog computing: The cloud-iot\/ioe middleware paradigm. *IEEE Potentials*, *35*, 3, 40–44, 2016.

3. Aazam, M., Huh, E.N., St-Hilaire, M., Lung, C.H., Lambadaris, I., Cloud of things: integration of IoT with cloud computing, in: *Robots and Sensor Clouds*, pp. 77–94, Springer, Cham, 2016.

4. Abdmeziem, M.R. and Tandjaoui, D., An end-to-end secure key management protocol for e-health applications. *Comput. Electr. Eng.*, 44, 184–197, 2015.

5. AbdulGhaffar, A., Mostafa, S.M., Alsaleh, A., Sheltami, T., Shakshuki, E.M., Internet of things based multiple disease monitoring and health improvement system. *J. Ambient Intell. Hum. Comput.*, 11, 3, 1021–1029, 2020.

6. Abduvaliyev, A., Pathan, A.S.K., Zhou, J., Roman, R., Wong, W.C., On the vital areas of intrusion detection systems in wireless sensor networks. *IEEE Commun. Surv. Tutorials*, 15, 3, 1223–1237, 2013.

7. Abie, H. and Balasingham, I., Risk-based adaptive security for smart IoT in eHealth, in: *Proceedings of the 7th International Conference on Body Area Networks*, pp. 269–275, 2012, February.

8. Abomhara, M. and Køien, G.M., Security and privacy in the Internet of Things: Current status and open issues, in: *2014 international conference on privacy and security in mobile systems (PRISMS)*, IEEE, pp. 1–8, 2014 May.

9. Aceto, G., Persico, V., Pescapé, A., Industry 4.0 and Health: Internet of Things, Big Data, and Cloud Computing for Healthcare 4.0. *J. Ind. Inf. Integr.*, 18, 100129, 2020.

10. Adhikary, T., Jana, A.D., Chakrabarty, A., Jana, S.K., The Internet of Things (IoT) Augmentation in Healthcare: An Application Analytics, in: *International Conference on Intelligent Computing and Communication Technologies*, Springer, Singapore, pp. 576–583, 2019, January.

11. Aggarwal, R. and Das, M.L., RFID Security in the Context of" Internet of Things, in: *Proceedings of the First International Conference on Security of Internet of Things*, pp. 51–56, 2012, August.

12. Ahemd, M.M., Shah, M.A., Wahid, A., IoT security: A layered approach for attacks & defenses, in: *2017 International Conference on Communication Technologies (ComTech)*, IEEE, pp. 104–110, 2017, April.

13. Ahmed, M.U., Banaee, H., Rafael-Palou, X., Loutfi, A., Intelligent healthcare services to support health monitoring of elderly, in: *International Internet of Things Summit*, Springer, Cham, pp. 178–186, 2014, October.

14. Ahmed, M.U., Björkman, M., Čaušević, A., Fotouhi, H., Lindén, M., An overview on the internet of things for health monitoring systems, in: *International Internet of Things Summit*, Springer, Cham, pp. 429–436, 2015, October.

15. Akhunzada, A., Gani, A., Anuar, N.B., Abdelaziz, A., Khan, M.K., Hayat, A., Khan, S.U., Secure and dependable software defined networks. *J. Netw. Comput. Appl.*, 61, 199–221, 2016.

16. Al Shuhaimi, F., Jose, M., Singh, A.V., Software defined network as solution to overcome security challenges in IoT, in: *2016 5th International Conference on Reliability, Infocom Technologies and Optimization (Trends and Future Directions)(ICRITO)*, IEEE, pp. 491–496, 2016, September.

17. Alaba, F.A., Othman, M., Hashem, I.A.T., Alotaibi, F., Internet of Things security: A survey. *J. Netw. Comput. Appl.*, 88, 10–28, 2017.

18. Alampalayam, S. and Kumar, A., An adaptive and predictive security model for mobile ad hoc networks. *Wirel. Pers. Commun.*, 29, 3–4, 263–281, 2004.

19. Al-Fuqaha, A., Guizani, M., Mohammadi, M., Aledhari, M., Ayyash, M., Internet of things: A survey on enabling technologies, protocols, and applications. *IEEE Commun. Surv. Tutorials*, 17, 4, 2347–2376, 2015.

20. Al-Hayajneh, A., Bhuiyan, Z.A., McAndrew, I., Improving Internet of Things (IoT) Security with Software-Defined Networking (SDN). *Computers*, 9, 1, 8, 2020.

21. Alohali, B.A., Vassilakis, V.G., Moscholios, I.D., Logothetis, M.D., A secure scheme for group communication of wireless IoT devices, in: *2018 11th*

International Symposium on Communication Systems, Networks & Digital Signal Processing (CSNDSP), IEEE, pp. 1–6 2018, July,.

22. Alsaidi, A. and Kausar, F., Security attacks and countermeasures on cloud assisted IoT applications, in: *2018 IEEE International Conference on Smart Cloud (SmartCloud)*, IEEE, pp. 213–217, 2018, September.

23. Andrea, I., Chrysostomou, C., Hadjichristofi, G., Internet of Things: Security vulnerabilities and challenges, in: *2015 IEEE Symposium on Computers and Communication (ISCC)*, IEEE, pp. 180–187, 2015, July.

24. Ansari, S., Aslam, T., Poncela, J., Otero, P., Ansari, A., Internet of Things-Based Healthcare Applications, in: *IoT Architectures, Models, and Platforms for Smart City Applications*, USA, pp. 1–28, IGI Global, 2020.

25. Atlam, H.F., Hemdan, E.E.D., Alenezi, A., Alassafi, M.O., Wills, G.B., Internet of Things Forensics: A Review. *Internet Things*, 11, 100220, 2020.

26. Azimi, I., Rahmani, A.M., Liljeberg, P., Tenhunen, H., Internet of things for remote elderly monitoring: a study from user-centered perspective. *J. Ambient Intell. Hum. Comput.*, 8, 2, 273–289, 2017.

27. Basanta, H., Huang, Y.P., Lee, T.T., Intuitive IoT-based H2U healthcare system for elderly people, in: *2016 IEEE 13th International Conference on Networking, Sensing, and Control (ICNSC)*, IEEE, pp. 1–6, 2016, April.

28. Bonomi, F., Milito, R., Zhu, J., Addepalli, S., Fog computing and its role in the internet of things, in: *Proceedings of the first edition of the MCC workshop on Mobile cloud computing*, ACM, pp. 13–16, 2012, August.

29. Bormann, C., Castellani, A.P., Shelby, Z., Coap: An application protocol for billions of tiny internet nodes. *IEEE Internet Comput.*, 16, 2, 62–67, 2012.

30. Botta, A., De Donato, W., Persico, V., Pescapé, A., Integration of cloud computing and internet of things: a survey. *Future Gener. Comput. Syst.*, 56, 684–700, 2016.

31. Bui, N. and Zorzi, M., Healthcare applications: a solution based on the internet of things, in: *Proceedings of the 4th international symposium on applied sciences in biomedical and communication technologies*, ACM, p. 131, 2011, October.

32. Capkun, S., Buttyán, L., Hubaux, J.P., Self-organized public-key management for mobile ad hoc networks. *IEEE Trans. Mob. Comput.*, 1, 52–64, 2003.

33. Catarinucci, L., De Donno, D., Mainetti, L., Palano, L., Patrono, L., Stefanizzi, M.L., Tarricone, L., An IoT-aware architecture for smart healthcare systems. *IEEE Internet Things J.*, 2, 6, 515–526, 2015.

34. Chakrabarty, S. and Engels, D.W., A secure IoT architecture for Smart Cities, in: *2016 13th IEEE annual consumer communications & networking conference (CCNC)*, IEEE, pp. 812–813, 2016, January.

35. Chen, S., Xu, H., Liu, D., Hu, B., Wang, H., A vision of IoT: Applications, challenges, and opportunities with china perspective. *IEEE Internet Things J.*, 1, 4, 349–359, 2014.

36. Cheng, Y., Jiang, C., Shi, J., A Fall detection system based on SensorTag and Windows 10 IoT core, in: *2015 International Conference on Mechanical Science and Engineering*, Atlantis Press, 2016, March.

37. Cirani, S., Ferrari, G., Veltri, L., Enforcing security mechanisms in the IP-based internet of things: An algorithmic overview. *Algorithms*, 6, 2, 197–226, 2013.

38. Čolaković, A. and Hadžialić, M., Internet of Things (IoT): A review of enabling technologies, challenges, and open research issues. *Comput. Networks*, 144, 17–39, 2018.

39. Cook, A., Robinson, M., Ferrag, M.A., Maglaras, L.A., He, Y., Jones, K., Janicke, H., Internet of cloud: Security and privacy issues, in: *Cloud Computing for Optimization: Foundations, Applications, and Challenges*, pp. 271–301, Springer, Cham, 2018.

40. Dang, L.M., Piran, M., Han, D., Min, K., Moon, H., A survey on internet of things and cloud computing for healthcare. *Electronics*, 8, 7, 768, 2019.

41. Darshan, K.R. and Anandakumar, K.R., A comprehensive review on usage of Internet of Things (IoT) in healthcare system, in: *2015 International Conference on Emerging Research in Electronics, Computer Science and Technology (ICERECT)*, IEEE, pp. 132–136, 2015, December.

42. Darwish, A., Hassanien, A.E., Elhoseny, M., Sangaiah, A.K., Muhammad, K., The impact of the hybrid platform of internet of things and cloud computing on healthcare systems: Opportunities, challenges, and open problems. *J. Ambient Intell. Hum. Comput.*, 10, 1–16, 2017.

43. Datta, S.K., Bonnet, C., Gyrard, A., Da Costa, R.P.F., Boudaoud, K., Applying Internet of Things for personalized healthcare in smart homes, in: *2015 24th Wireless and Optical Communication Conference (WOCC)*, IEEE, pp. 164–169, 2015, October.

44. De Capua, C., Meduri, A., Morello, R., A smart ECG measurement system based on web-service-oriented architecture for telemedicine applications. *IEEE Trans. Instrum. Meas.*, 59, 10, 2530–2538, 2010.

45. Dhanvijay, M.M. and Patil, S.C., *Internet of Things: A survey of enabling technologies in healthcare and its applications*, Computer Networks, Amsterdam, The Netherlands, 2019.

46. Dhillon, P.K. and Kalra, S., Multi-factor user authentication scheme for IoT-based healthcare services. *J. Reliab. Intell. Environ.*, 4, 3, 141–160, 2018.

47. Díaz, M., Martín, C., Rubio, B., State-of-the-art, challenges, and open issues in the integration of Internet of things and cloud computing. *J. Netw. Comput. Appl.*, 67, 99–117, 2016.

48. Dierckx, R., Pellicori, P., Cleland, J.G.F., Clark, A.L., Telemonitoring in heart failure: Big Brother watching over you. *Heart Fail. Rev.*, 20, 1, 107–116, 2015.

49. Din, I.U., Almogren, A., Guizani, M., Zuair, M., A decade of Internet of Things: Analysis in the light of healthcare applications. *IEEE Access*, 7, 89967–89979, 2019.

50. Distefano, S., Merlino, G., Puliafito, A., Enabling the cloud of things, in: *2012 Sixth International Conference on Innovative Mobile and Internet Services in Ubiquitous Computing*, IEEE, pp. 858–863, 2012, July.

51. Fanucci, L., Saponara, S., Bacchillone, T., Donati, M., Barba, P., Sánchez-Tato, I., Carmona, C., Sensing devices and sensor signal processing for remote monitoring of vital signs in CHF patients. *IEEE Trans. Instrum. Meas.*, 62, 3, 553–569, 2012.

52. Flauzac, O., Gonzalez Santamaría, C.J., Nolot, F., New security architecture for IoT network, Procedia Computer Science, Elsevier, 52, 1028–1033, 2015.

53. Fortino, G., Parisi, D., Pirrone, V., Di Fatta, G., BodyCloud: A SaaS approach for community body sensor networks. *Future Gener. Comput. Syst.*, 35, 62–79, 2014.

54. Fox, A., Griffith, R., Joseph, A., Katz, R., Konwinski, A., Lee, G., Stoica, I., Above the clouds: A berkeley view of cloud computing. Dept. Electrical Eng. and Comput. Sciences, University of California, Berkeley, Rep. UCB/EECS, 28(13), Technical Report No is UCB/EECS-2009-28. 2017, 1–13, February 10, 2009.

55. Fu, Y., Yan, Z., Cao, J., Koné, O., Cao, X., An automata based intrusion detection method for internet of things. *Mob. Inf. Syst.*, 2017, pp. 1–13, 2017.

56. Gasparrini, S., Cippitelli, E., Spinsante, S., Gambi, E., A depth-based fall detection system using a Kinect® sensor. *Sensors*, 14, 2, 2756–2775, 2014.

57. Granjal, J., Monteiro, E., Silva, J.S., Security for the internet of things: a survey of existing protocols and open research issues. *IEEE Commun. Surv. Tutorials*, 17, 3, 1294–1312, 2015.

58. Grobauer, B., Walloschek, T., Stocker, E., Understanding cloud computing vulnerabilities. *IEEE Secur. Privacy*, 9, 2, 50–57, 2010.

59. Gubbi, J., Buyya, R., Marusic, S., Palaniswami, M., Internet of Things (IoT): A vision, architectural elements, and future directions. *Future Gener. Comput. Syst.*, 29, 7, 1645–1660, 2013.

60. Gund, A., Ekman, I., Lindecrantz, K., Sjoqvist, B.A., Staaf, E.L., Thorneskold, N., Design evaluation of a home-based telecare system for chronic heart failure patients, in: *2008 30th Annual International Conference of the IEEE Engineering in Medicine and Biology Society*, IEEE, pp. 5851–5854, 2008, August.

61. Guo, J., Chen, R., Tsai, J.J., A survey of trust computation models for service management in internet of things systems. *Comput. Commun.*, 97, 1–14, 2017.

62. Gupta, P., Agrawal, D., Chhabra, J., Dhir, P.K., IoT based smart healthcare kit, in: *2016 International Conference on Computational Techniques in Information and Communication Technologies (ICCTICT)*, IEEE, pp. 237–242, 2016, March.

63. Hamad, S.A., Sheng, Q.Z., Zhang, W.E., Nepal, S., Realizing an Internet of Secure Things: A Survey on Issues and Enabling Technologies. *IEEE Commun. Surv. Tutorials*, 22, 2, 1372–1391, 2020.

64. Harper, S., Ageing Societies: Myths, in: *Challenges and Opportunities*, p. 116, 2006.

65. Hassan, Q.F. (Ed.), *Internet of Things A to Z: technologies and applications*, John Wiley & Sons, New Jersey, USA, 2018.

66. He, D., Ye, R., Chan, S., Guizani, M., Xu, Y., Privacy in the Internet of Things for smart healthcare. *IEEE Commun. Mag.*, 56, 4, 38–44, 2018.

67. Hernández-Ramos, J.L., Moreno, M.V., Bernabé, J.B., Carrillo, D.G., Skarmeta, A.F., SAFIR: Secure access framework for IoT-enabled services on smart buildings. *J. Comput. Syst. Sci.*, 81, 8, 1452–1463, 2015.

68. Horrow, S. and Sardana, A., Identity management framework for cloud based internet of things, in: *Proceedings of the First International Conference on Security of Internet of Things*, pp. 200–203, 2012, August.

69. Hosenkhan, M.R. and Pattanayak, B.K., Security Issues in Internet of Things (IoT): A Comprehensive Review, in: *New Paradigm in Decision Science and Management*, pp. 359–369, Springer, Singapore, 2020.

70. Hossain, M.M., Fotouhi, M., Hasan, R., Towards an analysis of security issues, challenges, and open problems in the internet of things, in: *2015 IEEE World Congress on Services*, IEEE, pp. 21–28, 2015, June.

71. Jimenez, F. and Torres, R., Building an IoT-aware healthcare monitoring system, in: *2015 34th International Conference of the Chilean Computer Science Society (SCCC)*, IEEE, pp. 1–4, 2015, November.

72. Jing, Q., Vasilakos, A.V., Wan, J., Lu, J., Qiu, D., Security of the Internet of Things: perspectives and challenges. *Wirel. Netw.*, 20, 8, 2481–2501, 2014.

73. Kalra, S. and Sood, S.K., Secure authentication scheme for IoT and cloud servers. *Pervasive Mob. Comput.*, 24, 210–223, 2015.

74. Kamalinejad, P., Mahapatra, C., Sheng, Z., Mirabbasi, S., Leung, V.C., Guan, Y.L., Wireless energy harvesting for the Internet of Things. *IEEE Commun. Mag.*, 53, 6, 102–108, 2015.

75. Kanuparthi, A., Karri, R., Addepalli, S., Hardware and embedded security in the context of internet of things, in: *Proceedings of the 2013 ACM workshop on Security, privacy & dependability for cyber vehicles*, pp. 61–64, 2013, November.

76. Karmakar, K.K., Varadharajan, V., Nepal, S., Tupakula, U., SDN Enabled Secure IoT Architecture, in: *2019 IFIP/IEEE Symposium on Integrated Network and Service Management (IM)*, IEEE, pp. 581–585, 2019, April.

77. Karthikeyan, S., Devi, K.V., Valarmathi, K., Internet of Things: Hospice appliances monitoring and control system, in: *2015 Online International Conference on Green Engineering and Technologies (IC-GET)*, IEEE, pp. 1–6, 2015, November).

78. Khan, M.A. and Salah, K., IoT security: Review, blockchain solutions, and open challenges. *Future Gener. Comput. Syst.*, 82, 395–411, 2018.

79. Khursheed, F., Sami-Ud-Din, M., Sumra, I.A., Safder, M., A Review of Security Machanism in internet of Things (IoT), in: *2020 3rd International*

Conference on Advancements in Computational Sciences (ICACS), IEEE, pp. 1–9, 2020, February.

80. Kim, D.H., Ghaffari, R., Lu, N., Rogers, J.A., Flexible and stretchable electronics for biointegrated devices. *Annu. Rev. Biomed. Eng.*, 14, 113–128, 2012.

81. Kovatsch, M., Mayer, S., Ostermaier, B., Moving application logic from the firmware to the cloud: Towards the thin server architecture for the internet of things, in: *2012 Sixth International Conference on Innovative Mobile and Internet Services in Ubiquitous Computing*, IEEE, pp. 751–756, 2012, July.

82. Krishnan, D. and Mallya, A., A Survey on Security Attacks in Internet of Things and Challenges in Existing Countermeasures, in: *Proceedings of International Conference on Wireless Communication*, Springer, Singapore, pp. 463–469, 2020.

83. Lee, J.Y., Lin, W.C., Huang, Y.H., A lightweight authentication protocol for internet of things, in: *2014 International Symposium on Next-Generation Electronics (ISNE)*, IEEE, pp. 1–2, 2014, May.

84. Leo, M., Battisti, F., Carli, M., Neri, A., A federated architecture approach for Internet of Things security, in: *2014 Euro Med Telco Conference (EMTC)*, IEEE, pp. 1–5, 2014, November.

85. Li, N. and Mahalik, N.P., A big data and cloud computing specification, standards and architecture: agricultural and food informatics. *Int. J. Inf. Commun. Technol.*, 14, 2, 159–174, 2019.

86. Li, S., Da Xu, L., Zhao, S., The internet of things: a survey. *Inform. Syst. Front.*, 17, 2, 243–259, 2015.

87. Li, Z., Yin, X., Geng, Z., Zhang, H., Li, P., Sun, Y., Li, L., Research on PKI-like Protocol for the Internet of Things, in: *2013 Fifth International Conference on Measuring Technology and Mechatronics Automation*, IEEE, pp. 915–918, 2013, January.

88. Lin, J., Yu, W., Zhang, N., Yang, X., Zhang, H., Zhao, W., A survey on internet of things: Architecture, enabling technologies, security and privacy, and applications. *IEEE Internet Things J.*, 4, 5, 1125–1142, 2017.

89. Liu, J., Xiao, Y., Chen, C.P., Authentication and access control in the internet of things, in: *2012 32nd International Conference on Distributed Computing Systems Workshops*, IEEE, pp. 588–592, 2012, June.

90. Liu, W., Zhao, X., Xiao, J., Wu, Y., Automatic vehicle classification instrument based on multiple sensor information fusion, in: *Third International Conference on Information Technology and Applications (ICITA'05)*, vol. 1, IEEE, pp. 379–382, 2005, July.

91. Mahalle, P.N., Anggorojati, B., Prasad, N.R., Prasad, R., Identity authentication and capability based access control (iacac) for the internet of things. *J. Cyber Secur. Mobil.*, 1, 4, 309–348, 2013.

92. Mell, P. and Grance, T., *The NIST definition of cloud computing*, Computer Security Division, Information Technology Laboratory, National Institute of Standards and Technology, Gaithersburg, USA, 2011.

93. Mo, Y. and Sinopoli, B., Secure control against replay attacks, in: *2009 47th annual Allerton conference on communication, control, and computing (Allerton)*, IEEE, pp. 911–918, 2009, September.

94. Moosavi, S.R., Gia, T.N., Nigussie, E., Rahmani, A.M., Virtanen, S., Tenhunen, H., Isoaho, J., End-to-end security scheme for mobility enabled healthcare Internet of Things. *Future Gener. Comput. Syst.*, 64, 108–124, 2016.

95. Mutlag, A.A., Ghani, M.K.A., Arunkumar, N.A., Mohamed, M.A., Mohd, O., Enabling technologies for fog computing in healthcare IoT systems. *Future Gener. Comput. Syst.*, 90, 62–78, 2019.

96. Namahoot, C.S., Brückner, M., Nuntawong, C., Mobile Diagnosis System with Emergency Telecare in Thailand (MOD-SET). *Proc. Comput. Sci.*, 69, 86–95, 2015.

97. Nawir, M., Amir, A., Yaakob, N., Lynn, O.B., Internet of Things (IoT): Taxonomy of security attacks, in: *2016 3rd International Conference on Electronic Design (ICED)*, IEEE, pp. 321–326, 2016, August.

98. Neagu, G., Preda, Ş., Stanciu, A., Florian, V., A Cloud-IoT based sensing service for health monitoring, in: *2017 E-Health and Bioengineering Conference (EHB)*, IEEE, pp. 53–56, 2017, June.

99. Neisse, R., Steri, G., Fovino, I.N., Baldini, G., SecKit: a model-based security toolkit for the internet of things. *Comput. Secur.*, 54, 60–76, 2015.

100. Oleshchuk, V., Internet of things and privacy preserving technologies, in: *2009 1st International Conference on Wireless Communication, Vehicular Technology, Information Theory and Aerospace & Electronic Systems Technology*, IEEE, pp. 336–340, 2009, May.

101. Olorode, O. and Nourani, M., Reducing leakage power in wearable medical devices using memory nap controller, in: *2014 IEEE Dallas Circuits and Systems Conference (DCAS)*, IEEE, pp. 1–4, 2014, October.

102. Panchatcharam, P. and Vivekanandan, S., Internet of things (IoT) in healthcare–smart health and surveillance, architectures, security analysis and data transfer: a review. *Int. J. Software Innov. (IJSI)*, 7, 2, 21–40, 2019.

103. Park, C., Chou, P.H., Bai, Y., Matthews, R., Hibbs, A., An ultra-wearable, wireless, low power ECG monitoring system, in: *2006 IEEE biomedical circuits and systems conference*, IEEE, pp. 241–244, 2006, November.

104. Parwekar, P., From internet of things towards cloud of things, in: *2011 2nd International Conference on Computer and Communication Technology (ICCCT-2011)*, IEEE, pp. 329–333, 2011, September.

105. Patel, C. and Doshi, N., Internet of Things: A Review on Major Challenges and Applications, in: *Reliability and Risk Assessment in Engineering*, pp. 427–437, Springer, Singapore, 2020.

106. Pollonini, L., Rajan, N.O., Xu, S., Madala, S., Dacso, C.C., A novel handheld device for use in remote patient monitoring of heart failure patients—Design and preliminary validation on healthy subjects. *J. Med. Syst.*, 36, 2, 653–659, 2012.

107. Porambage, P., Schmitt, C., Kumar, P., Gurtov, A., Ylianttila, M., Two-phase authentication protocol for wireless sensor networks in distributed IoT applications, in: *2014 IEEE Wireless Communications and Networking Conference (WCNC)*, Ieee, pp. 2728–2733, 2014, April.

108. Qadri, Y.A., Nauman, A., Zikria, Y.B., Vasilakos, A.V., Kim, S.W., The Future of Healthcare Internet of Things: A Survey of Emerging Technologies. *IEEE Commun. Surv. Tutorials*, 22, 2, 1121–1167 2020.

109. Rahimi, H., Zibaeenejad, A., Rajabzadeh, P., Safavi, A.A., on the Security of the 5G-IoT Architecture, in: *Proceedings of the international conference on smart cities and internet of things*, pp. 1–8, 2018, September.

110. Rao, B.P., Saluia, P., Sharma, N., Mittal, A., Sharma, S.V., Cloud computing for Internet of Things & sensing based applications, in: *2012 Sixth International Conference on Sensing Technology (ICST)*, IEEE, pp. 374–380, 2012, December.

111. Rath, M., Resource provision and QoS support with added security for client side applications in cloud computing. *Int. J. Inf. Technol.*, 11, 2, 357–364, 2019.

112. Rathore, S., Kwon, B.W., Park, J.H., BlockSecIoTNet: Blockchain-based decentralized security architecture for IoT network. *J. Netw. Comput. Appl.*, 143, 167–177, 2019.

113. Ray, P.P., Dash, D., Kumar, N., Sensors for internet of medical things: State-of-the-art, security and privacy issues, challenges and future directions. *Comput. Commun.*, 160, 111–131, 2020.

114. Rhee, K., Kwak, J., Kim, S., Won, D., Challenge-response based RFID authentication protocol for distributed database environment, in: *International Conference on Security in Pervasive Computing*, Springer, Berlin, Heidelberg, pp. 70–84, 2005, April.

115. Rodrigues, J.J., Segundo, D.B.D.R., Junqueira, H.A., Sabino, M.H., Prince, R.M., Al-Muhtadi, J., De Albuquerque, V.H.C., Enabling technologies for the internet of health things. *IEEE Access*, 6, 13129–13141, 2018.

116. Rohatgi, D., Srivastava, S., Choudhary, S., Khatri, A., Kalra, V., Smart Healthcare Based on Internet of Things, in: *International Conference on Application of Computing and Communication Technologies*, 2018, March, Springer, Singapore, pp. 300–309.

117. Roman, R., Najera, P., Lopez, J., Securing the internet of things. *Computer*, 44, 9, 51–58, 2011.

118. Roman, R., Zhou, J., Lopez, J., On the features and challenges of security and privacy in distributed internet of things. *Comput. Networks*, 57, 10, 2266–2279, 2013.

119. Samarati, P., di Vimercati, S.D.C., Murugesan, S., Bojanova, I., Cloud security: Issues and concerns, in: *Encyclopedia on cloud computing*, pp. 1–14, 2016.

120. Sengupta, J., Ruj, S., Bit, S.D., A Comprehensive survey on attacks, security issues and blockchain solutions for IoT and IIoT. *J. Netw. Comput. Appl.*, 149, 102481, 2020.

121. Shah, S.T.U., Yar, H., Khan, I., Ikram, M., Khan, H., Internet of Things-Based Healthcare: Recent Advances and Challenges, in: *Applications of Intelligent Technologies in Healthcare*, pp. 153–162, Springer, Cham, 2019.

122. Sharma, A. and Sharma, R., A Review of Applications, Approaches, and Challenges in Internet of Things (IoT), in: *Proceedings of ICRIC 2019*, Springer, Cham, pp. 257–269, 2020.

123. Sharma, R., Nah, F.F.H., Sharma, K., Katta, T.S.S.S., Pang, N., Yong, A., Smart living for elderly: design and human-computer interaction considerations, in: *International Conference on Human Aspects of IT for the Aged Population*, 2016, July, Springer, Cham, pp. 112–122.

124. Sicari, S., Rizzardi, A., Grieco, L.A., Coen-Porisini, A., Security, privacy and trust in Internet of Things: The road ahead. *Comput. Networks*, 76, 146–164, 2015.

125. Siekkinen, M., Hiienkari, M., Nurminen, J.K., Nieminen, J., How low energy is bluetooth low energy? comparative measurements with zigbee/802.15. 4, in: *2012 IEEE wireless communications and networking conference workshops (WCNCW)*, 2012, April, IEEE, pp. 232–237.

126. Soliman, M., Abiodun, T., Hamouda, T., Zhou, J., Lung, C.H., Smart home: Integrating internet of things with web services and cloud computing, in: *2013 IEEE 5th international conference on cloud computing technology and science*, 2013, December, vol. 2, IEEE, pp. 317–320).

127. Son, D., Lee, J., Qiao, S., Ghaffari, R., Kim, J., Lee, J.E., Yang, S., Multifunctional wearable devices for diagnosis and therapy of movement disorders. *Nat. Nanotechnol.*, 9, 5, 397, 2014.

128. Stergiou, C., Psannis, K.E., Kim, B.G., Gupta, B., Secure integration of IoT and cloud computing. *Future Gener. Comput. Syst.*, 78, 964–975, 2018.

129. Suciu, G., Vulpe, A., Halunga, S., Fratu, O., Todoran, G., Suciu, V., Smart cities built on resilient cloud computing and secure internet of things, in: *2013 19th International Conference on Control Systems and Computer Science*, 2013, May, IEEE, pp. 513–518.

130. Suh, M.K., Chen, C.A., Woodbridge, J., Tu, M.K., Kim, J.I., Nahapetian, A., Sarrafzadeh, M., A remote patient monitoring system for congestive heart failure. *J. Med. Syst.*, 35, 5, 1165–1179, 2011.

131. Suh, M.K., Evangelista, L.S., Chen, V., Hong, W.S., Macbeth, J., Nahapetian, A., Sarrafzadeh, M., WANDA B.: Weight and activity with blood pressure monitoring system for heart failure patients, in: *2010 IEEE International Symposium on" A World of Wireless, Mobile and Multimedia Networks"(WoWMoM)*, IEEE, pp. 1–6, 2010, June.

132. Suo, H., Wan, J., Zou, C., Liu, J., Security in the internet of things: a review, in: *2012 international conference on computer science and electronics engineering*, vol. 3, IEEE, pp. 648–651, 2012, March.

133. Suresh, A., Udendhran, R., Balamurgan, M., Varatharajan, R., A novel internet of things framework integrated with real time monitoring for intelligent healthcare environment. *J. Med. Syst.*, 43, 6, 165, 2019.

134. Suryani, V., Sulistyo, S., Widyawan, W., Trust-based privacy for Internet of Things. *Int. J. Electr. Comput. Eng.*, 6, 5, 2396, 2016.

135. Tewari, A. and Gupta, B.B., Security, privacy and trust of different layers in Internet-of-Things (IoTs) framework. *Future Gener. Comput. Syst.*, 108, 909–920, 2020.

136. Tyagi, S., Agarwal, A., Maheshwari, P., A conceptual framework for IoT-based healthcare system using cloud computing, in: *2016 6th International Conference-Cloud System and Big Data Engineering (Confluence)*, IEEE, pp. 503–507, 2016, January.

137. Ullah, K., Shah, M.A., Zhang, S., Effective ways to use Internet of Things in the field of medical and smart healthcare, in: *2016 International Conference on Intelligent Systems Engineering (ICISE)*, IEEE, pp. 372–379, 2016, January.

138. Upadhyay, S., Kumar, S., Dutta, S., Srivastava, A.K., Mondal, A.K., Kaundal, V., A Comprehensive Review on the Issues Related to the Data Security of Internet of Things (IoT) Devices, in: *Intelligent Communication, Control and Devices*, pp. 727–734, Springer, Singapore, 2020.

139. Usak, M., Kubiatko, M., Shabbir, M.S., Viktorovna Dudnik, O., Jermsittiparsert, K., Rajabion, L., Healthcare service delivery based on the Internet of things: A systematic and comprehensive study. *Int. J. Commun. Syst.*, 33, 2, e4179, 2020.

140. Valdivieso Caraguay, Á. L., Benito Peral, A., Barona Lopez, L.I., García Villalba, L.J., SDN: Evolution and opportunities in the development IoT applications. *Int. J. Distrib. Sens. Netw.*, 10, 5, 735142, 2014.

141. Velte, A.T., Velte, T.J., Elsenpeter, R.C., Elsenpeter, R.C., *Cloud computing: a practical approach*, p. 44, McGraw-Hill, New York, 2010.

142. Wang, X., Zhang, J., Schooler, E.M., Ion, M., Performance evaluation of attribute-based encryption: Toward data privacy in the IoT, in: *2014 IEEE International Conference on Communications (ICC)*, IEEE, pp. 725–730, 2014, June.

143. Wen, Q., Dong, X., Zhang, R., Application of dynamic variable cipher security certificate in internet of things, in: *2012 IEEE 2nd International Conference on Cloud Computing and Intelligence Systems*, vol. 3, IEEE, pp. 1062–1066, 2012, October.

144. Wu, M., Lu, T.J., Ling, F.Y., Sun, J., Du, H.Y., Research on the architecture of Internet of Things, in: *2010 3rd International Conference on Advanced Computer Theory and Engineering (ICACTE)*, vol. 5, IEEE, pp. V5–484, 2010, August.

145. Xiaohui, X., Study on security problems and key technologies of the internet of things, in: *2013 International conference on computational and information sciences*, IEEE, pp. 407–410, 2013, June.

146. Xie, Y. and Wang, D., An item-level access control framework for inter-system security in the internet of things, in: *Applied mechanics and materials*, Trans Tech Publications Ltd, Baech, Switzerland, vol. 548, pp. 1430–1432, 2014.

147. Yang, J.C., Hao, P.A.N.G., Zhang, X., Enhanced mutual authentication model of IoT. *J. China Univ. Posts Telecommun.*, 20, 69–74, 2013.

148. Yassine, A., Singh, S., Hossain, M.S., Muhammad, G., IoT big data analytics for smart homes with fog and cloud computing. *Future Gener. Comput. Syst.*, 91, 563–573, 2019.

149. Ye, N., Zhu, Y., Wang, R.C., Malekian, R., Lin, Q.M., An efficient authentication and access control scheme for perception layer of internet of things, Applied Mathematics and Information Sciences, 8, 1617–1624. 2014.

150. Yeole, A.S. and Kalbande, D.R., Use of internet of things (iot) in healthcare: A survey, in: *Proceedings of the ACM Symposium on Women in Research 2016*, ACM, pp. 71–76, 2016, March.

151. Yuriyama, M. and Kushida, T., Sensor-Cloud Infrastructure-Physical Sensor Management with Virtualized Sensors on Cloud Computing. *NBiS*, 10, 1–8, 2010.

152. Zarpelão, B.B., Miani, R.S., Kawakani, C.T., de Alvarenga, S.C., A survey of intrusion detection in Internet of Things. *J. Netw. Comput. Appl.*, 84, 25–37, 2017.

153. Zaslavsky, A., Perera, C., Georgakopoulos, D., Sensing as a service and big data. *arXiv preprint arXiv:1301.0159*, Proceedings of the International Conference on Advances in Cloud Computing (ACC), Bangalore, India, July, 2012, 2013.

154. Zhang, Z.K., Cho, M.C.Y., Wang, C.W., Hsu, C.W., Chen, C.K., Shieh, S., IoT security: ongoing challenges and research opportunities, in: *2014 IEEE 7th international conference on service-oriented computing and applications*, IEEE, pp. 230–234, 2014, November.

155. Zhao, G., Si, X., Wang, J., Long, X., Hu, T., A novel mutual authentication scheme for Internet of Things, in: *Proceedings of 2011 International Conference on Modelling, Identification and Control*, IEEE, pp. 563–566, 2011, June.

156. Zhao, K. and Ge, L., A survey on the internet of things security, in: *2013 Ninth international conference on computational intelligence and security*, IEEE, pp. 663–667, 2013, December.

157. Zhou, J., Cao, Z., Dong, X., Vasilakos, A.V., Security and privacy for cloud-based IoT: Challenges. *IEEE Commun. Mag.*, 55, 1, 26–33, 2017.

12

A Novel Usage of Artificial Intelligence and Internet of Things in Remote-Based Healthcare Applications

V. Arulkumar[1,2]*, D. Mansoor Hussain[1,2], S. Sridhar[1,3] and P. Vivekanandan[4]

[1]Department of Computer Science and Business Systems, Coimbatore, India
[2]Sri Krishna College of Engineering and Technology, Coimbatore, India
[3]Department of CSE, Saveetha School of Engineering, Saveetha Institute of Medical and Technical Sciences, Chennai, India
[4]Park College of Engineering and Technology, Coimbatore, India

Abstract

A whole host of apps now use IoT (Internet of Things). Smart car parks, smart homes, intelligent cities, smart environments, manufacturing areas, agricultural fields, and health management processes are all implementations of the IoT. In healthcare, such an application makes medical instruments more successful by allowing patient health tracking in real time to capture patient data and minimize human error. In this manner, patient health surveillance is tracked over the IoT. Health IoT is the solution for integrated real-time surveillance of people with psychiatric disabilities at low costs and traffic between the results of patients and the diagnosis of diseases. We have seen the health tracking system that gathers simple parameters including heart rate, temperature, blood pressure, and growth parameters up to now. We address in this study the control of the brain waves of the patient and the real-time detection of patient condition. We use mobile headset that deals with EEG technology to gather data from brain signals. The performance effect indicates the pattern of the waveform. The key objective is to provide optimized benefit to patients with mental disabilities in this proposed project by collecting data from brain signals with 24 channels.

*Corresponding author: arulkumaran.ckpc@gmail.com

Rohit Tanwar, S. Balamurugan, R. K. Saini, Vishal Bharti and Premkumar Chithaluru (eds.) Advanced Healthcare Systems: Empowering Physicians with IoT-Enabled Technologies, (255–274) © 2022 Scrivener Publishing LLC

Keywords: Artificial intelligence (AI), machine learning (ML), medical imaging, electronic health record (EHR), precision medicine, EEG technology, personalized healthcare, advanced healthcare

12.1 Introduction Machine Learning

Machine learning has been, in the past 20 years, a fundamental, though sometimes unseen part of our lives, one of the core cornerstones of data science. With information expertise increasingly available, there is a strong reason to think that critical data collection will even become a very thorough part of technical growth. The aim is to have insights into the vast range of applications that have a machine learning disadvantage and to give the zoological garden a certain degree of order. Some are basic statistical and applied mathematical methods. When they are entering, the vocabulary should be phrased to make several problems related to machine learning compatible. Finally, several reasonably easy but selective algorithms uncover a key drawback, especially those in the classification [1]. As for computers, we infer very generally that when a machine modifies its configuration, programmed, or knowledge, it learns to maximize its expected performance (based on its inputs or as a reaction to external information). Many of these changes are profound in various areas across the province and seem not to be fundamental, like recording an information base that is better interpreted as knowledge. But as an example, as soon as a speech recognition system increases its accuracy, we start to feel that the machine learns in this situation, even though we hear a lot of samples from a person's talk. Machine learning also refers to improvements in computer science–related programs (AI). These activities include acknowledgment, diagnosis, scheduling, management mechanisms, and predictions.

12.2 Importance of Machine Learning

Tasks can only be described by example; in other words, input/output pairs could be specified, but not a concisely related input/output relationship with the desired output (Figure 12.1). To generate the right output for a large number of sample inputs, we hope machinery will adapt their inner structures, thus properly restricting its input/output function to approximate the relationship implied in the examples [2].

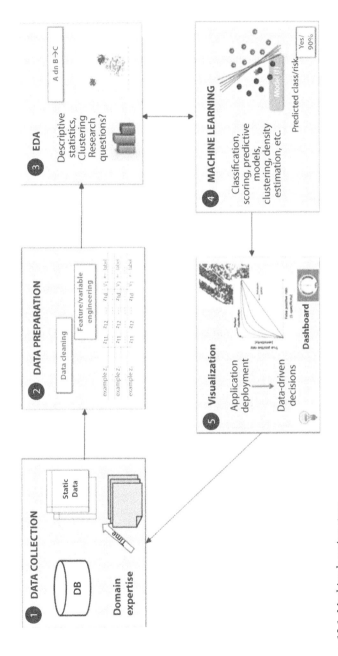

Figure 12.1 Machine learning steps.

12.2.1   ML vs. Classical Algorithms

- ML algorithms do not rely on human-specific guidelines. Rather, they use raw type material, such as text, emails, records, social media posts, pictures, voice, and video.
- A cc scheme is simply a system of study where a task is not scheduled so it is scheduled to execute the task.
- ML is also prediction-oriented, while the Modeling of Applied Mathematics is more interpretative. Not a difficult and swift distinction, particularly when the disciplines overlap but most historical differences between the two faculties of thought fell apart from that distinction in my expertise.
- Statistics emphasize p-value more and a robust yet intelligible paradigm in classical algorithms.
- Uninterruptible units of most cc models, and often for these purposes, are inadequate when connections or maybe partnerships are known. The only thing that works best is that you want forecasts everywhere (Figure 12.2) [2].
- Traditional methodologies such as model-building coaching and evaluation of the subsequent model against incoming knowledge are not practical, because the environment changes very steadily. Compared to the conventional method, older cc approaches, in many ways, are too expensive to cope with dynamically dynamic infrastructure conditions at intervals of internet and the outcomes in these areas are too stagnant.
- In the classical opposition solution, the defraying heaps of process control are not effective when studying a very sophisticated model of a very complex network atmosphere.
- The "statistical modeling", Pekka Kohonen, a professor of the Karolinska Institute distinguished, will gradually shift to "statistical learning" using sensitive components relating to and build tools for, the decoding in the model within the process [2].
- One of the key variations is that classical approaches have a lot of rigorous mathematical approach, whereas machine learning algorithms' area unit has a lot of data-intensive (Figure 12.3).

Many machine learning engineers and computer geeks mostly are using supervised and unattended strengthened learning to apply for questions that are very efficient and dynamic.

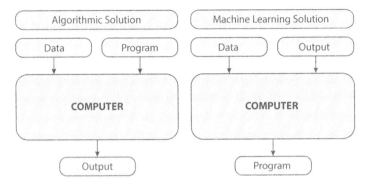

Figure 12.2 Difference between algorithmic and machine learning solution.

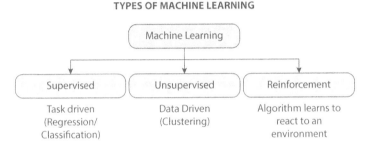

Figure 12.3 Algorithms for machine study types.

12.2.2   Learning Supervised

In general, supervised learning is functional machine learning. Regulated learning is where you have input (x) variables and output (Y), and the mapping function can be learned using an algorithm from the input to the output [3].

$$And = f(X)$$

The aim is to approximate the mapping function so well that you can predict the output variables (Y) for the data when new input data (x) is provided. The method of learning from a training dataset may be considered an instructor who supervises the learning process. This is known as supervised learning. We know the right answers, the algorithm predicts the training data iteratively and is corrected by the trainer. Learning ends

SUPERVISED LEARNING

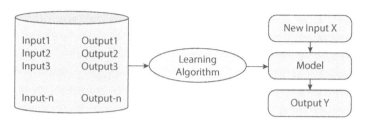

Figure 12.4 Supervised learning method.

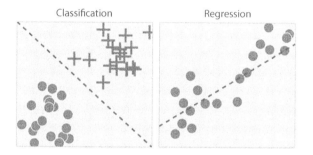

Figure 12.5 Classification separates the data; regression fits the data.

until a reasonable degree of success is achieved in the algorithm (Figures 12.4 & 12.5).

Training data

The training data includes both *Inputs* and *Labels* (*Targets*).

What are Inputs and Labels (Targets)? For example, addition of two numbers a = 5 and b = 6 result = 11, *Inputs* are 5 and 6 and *Target* is 11.

Classification

This is a category of problem in which the categorical answer value can be determined where data can be divided into specific "groups" (for example, we predict one of the values in a set of values).

Any examples are as follows:

- this mail is spam or not
- would it rain today or not?

The main thing called binary grouping is questions of type "Yes/No". Some examples are as follows:

- email or promotional mail.
- A cat or dog or tiger is this photo.
- This type is defined as the grouping of multiple groups.
- The last picture is here.

12.2.3   Unsupervised Learning

☐ Uncontrolled learning is where only data entry (X) and no appropriate output variables are available.

☐ To learn more about the data, unattended learning aims to model the underlying structure or distribution of data.

☐ These are considered unattended lessons, since there are no correct responses and no coach, unlike supervised learning above. Algorithms are left to explore and present the data's fascinating structure (Figure 12.6).

☐ Uncontrolled problem learning can be further divided into problems of clustering and association.

- **Clustering:** A issue with clustering is that you try to explore data groups such as consumer groupings through buying behavior.

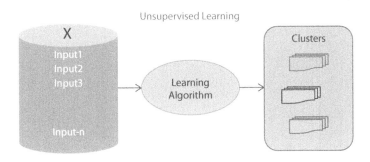

Figure 12.6 Unsupervised model.

- **Association:** A issue with learning by association rules is where you try to find rules defining vast sections of your results, for instance, people buying X who also buy y.

A few popular examples of unattended study algorithms are as follows:

- k-means for problems of clustering.
- association law learning challenges the *apriori* algorithm [4].

The training data do not provide objectives here, because the machine does not have to learn itself from the information we provide. The training data do not include targets (Figures 12.7 & 12.8).

Here, training data is not structured (contains noisy data, unknown data, etc.). For example, a random articles from different pages.

There are also various forms for uncontrolled study such as clustering and identification of anomalies (clustering is pretty famous).

Clustering: This is a problem in which we put together identical objects. We may not send the labels here. The framework knows the data itself and groups data. The bit is close to multi-class grouping.

Such examples are as follows:

- news items, cluster into various news categories
- several tweets, cluster dependent on message material
- cluster, a collection of photographs into various objects

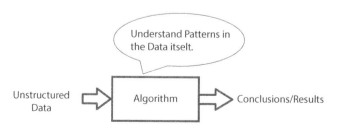

Figure 12.7 Unsupervised process.

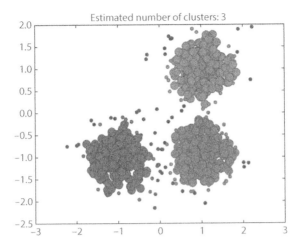

Figure 12.8 Clustering with three clusters.

Uncontrolled instruction is not so commonly used and impossible to execute.

12.2.4   Network for Neuralism

12.2.4.1   Definition of the Neural Network

Neural networks constitute a series of algorithms, closely modeled following the human brain. Sensory data is interpreted by some form of computer view, labeling, or classification of raw inputs. The patterns they know are numeric and include vectors, which have to be converted from all actual data, including pictures, voice, text, or time series.

Neural networks' cluster and mark: You can also view them as a grouping and classification sheet above the data stored and maintained. They help to group unlabeled data based on correlations between examples of inputs and identify data while a classified data set is used. Neural networks can also derive characteristics that are used to cluster and classify other algorithms; thus, deep neural networks can be seen as components of broader machine learning systems with algorithms for enhanced learning, classification, and regression [5].

12.2.4.2   Neural Network Elements

The term for the "stacked neural networks", which means networks made up of several layers, is profound learning.

The layers have nodes. A node is simply a site where measurements are focused approximately on a neuron that fires when there are adequate stimuli. A node blends the input with several weights and coefficients that amplify and dampen the input, thereby illustrating what the inputs in the algorithm are. (For example, error-free data classification is the best input?) These inputs are summarized to determine when and to what extent this signal passes through the network to produce the final result.

Here's a diagram (Figures 12.9 & 12.10) of what one node might look like.

A node layer is a series of neuronal switches which are activated by the net when the input is supplied. The output of a layer is simultaneous to the input of the corresponding layer from an initial layer that receives your information [5].

Pairing adjustable weights with input functions is how we attach importance to these characteristics about the classification and the input of clusters.

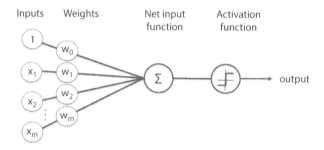

Figure 12.9 General block diagram of NN.

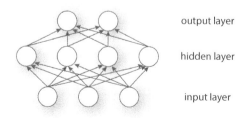

Figure 12.10 Internal layers of neural network.

12.3   Procedure

12.3.1   Dataset and Seizure Identification

The first series of data revealed an example of a serious seizure (probably a tonic-clonic one) and a second one was an example of a complicated partial seizure in one region of the brain that was followed several minutes later by a generalized seizure. The sample of both data sets is 500 Hz. The third and fourth data sets included interictal EEG data as the "baseline" for several minutes and were accompanied by episodes of ictal operation. The sampling date of these two data sets was 250 Hz [6].

Seizure types: SP, Simple Partial; CP, Partial Complex; GTC, Generalized Seizure Tonic-Clonic.

This study proposes a method that could predict the ongoing epileptic seizure by using several channel EEG signals in real time. A select number of EEG channels is given as input and the epileptic seizure state is reported every second. In this scheme, classifications are carried out as a simulation of complex real-time predictions and based on previous predictions. Therefore, exposure must be monitored to prevent seizures more frequently than they do. The system can be functionally reduced to the block diagram, as seen in Figure 12.11.

12.3.2   System

The overall system is filled with a 3-second multi-canal EEG stream, and several features are extracted and sampled each time. Any second these samples are taken so that the next window overlaps. As a consequence, the obtained samples display a progressive transition from one epileptic seizure to another. For each 3-second slice, a rectangular window is applied,

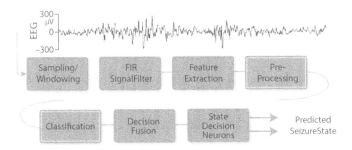

Figure 12.11 Block diagram of the EEG classification.

so that the frequency response has limited distortion (due to Gibb's phenomenon some distortion is present). The incoming EEG stream is broken down into their respective brain waves using an FIR signal buffer. Features are taken from the incoming data sources from the start to the end of the EEG so that a real-time situation can be simulated. If a sample is extracted, then it is discarded and skipped that produces mathematical errors that occur in sample values. In addition, 80% of the training data used by each classification is a new random permutation of the whole training set and the evaluation data are the samples that have been removed from the existing window. Once each classifier is predicted, a decision fusion algorithm uses a series of rules to produce an initial forecast [7–9].

12.4   Feature Extraction

One of the key steps in constructing a signal classification scheme is to generate mathematical representations and input data reductions that enable an adequate differentiation of the input signal into its respective groups. These mathematical representations of the signal in a way are mapping in a space of fewer dimensions in a multi-dimensional space (the input signals). This size reduction is called the extraction of features. Finally, only the key information from the original signal can be retained by the derived function package.

12.5   Experimental Methods

The methods discussed in this section have been developed to investigate the issue of seizure starting prediction and improve the classification of EEG signals. First, there is a feature set algorithm used to do a feature set analysis to discover the mathematical transformations most effective in forecasting predictability. Afterward, the seizure on a preventive method mentioned in this work has been part of a series of algorithms.

12.5.1   Stepwise Feature Optimization

An algorithm has been applied to estimate human functional power for any other function to find the features of maximum potential. The power of a feature was determined by the precise nature of the preictal state as an average of many classifications. This algorithm re-divides the features, performs classification, considers the best feature sets to remove, and then changes the feature area to include features that increase the consistency of the feature set (similar to cross-validation by elimination; as discussed in Section 12.5.2) [12].

Let $\{f_1, f_2, ..., f_K\}$ be the feature sets where K denotes these t numbers located in the first column of Table 12.1.

Algorithm 12.1 Stepwise feature optimization.

1. Determine the grouping accuracy of all K sets of characteristics.
2. Drop one of the features set at one time, divide the feature space into K, K − 1 and save each sub-setting position precision with the resulting accuracy of Kinvector os.
3. Denote the index Á with the maximum precision as Á and delete from the final function space all Á to K features specified in Á.

The resulting set of features is identical to the exactness of position Á in PO. Training and over-training also need to be taken into account as this will affect predictive performance.

Table 12.1 Defined epileptic states in transient EEG signals.

State #	Epileptic state
2	Interictal
3	Preictal
4	Ictal
1	Postictal

12.5.2   Post-Classification Validation

Both approaches have been carried out in this section to supplement the classification algorithms and increase their classification ability for noisy and time-changing dynamical systems. To classify samples by measuring the excess of correlations (determined by the precision of classifications), the first process, known as cross-validation by elimination, is used to exclude groups that are the less correlated classification to increase the consistency of the classifications. Each class isolates and contrasts the outcomes of the forecast and then decides based on independent predictions [10].

This method puts testing samples that were weakly classified that make accuracy.

The second, state determination neurons, is used to automatically decide when to move to the next specified state. If used in combination with a series of classifiers, then this algorithm allows the machine to decide on a closed-loop system based on predictions previously made. If in a noisy system three or four states can be distinguished, then state judgment neurons help to determine the necessary transition moments to another state.

12.5.3   Fusion of Classification Methods

In this thesis, the epileptic seizure onset prediction scheme employs several different classifiers to forecast the epileptic syndrome at some moment. A method to integrate the predictions is needed to make a final classification by using multiples classifiers. Four classifications are given for each study, namely, LDA, KNN, SVM, and CVE. A primary voting scheme and a decision tree for a projection of the present state are the tools used.

As there are four classifiers, voting by a plurality cannot cause a vote to be reached by all the classifiers. The classification module starts with the scheme suggested in this using the LDA and KNN algorithms, since they are the least computer-costly.

Where both LDA and KNN have different predictions than current or next to most likely, so CVE would have an additional forecast to achieve a majority vote. When no plurality is still present, SVM is employed to decide whether the current state or state with the largest vote (of the other classifiers) is most likely.

An initial projection is based on the State with a majority vote and the voting matrix contains the votes of each of the classifiers used in each of the single countries. The original forecast is then altered by a decision book so that it is dependent both on the actual and the initial predictions of the most probable condition. It was important to identify the progression of countries in this seizure prediction simulator in sequential and increasingly. Given this, the only additional conditions are to specify a reset if:

1) seizures will not occur or 2) they will occur and the system will become postictal. Since states may only transition sequentially, if State 4 holds two or more votes in State 2, the initial forecast from this stage is State 3. This modifies the state neuron 2 to make a transition to state 3 more likely, which allows for an earlier transition to state 4. Thus, a series of rules stated that there was a sequentially increase in the progression of state transitions [11].

12.6   Experiments

To describe the reaction characteristics of ictal EEG data to several mathematical technologies, a series of experiments were conducted. Finally, a multi-chain EEG stream simulator was developed which could indicate the state of a return seizure. The first experiment was to develop and evaluate a mechanism to move between several countries based on multiple classification algorithm predictions. This first test was carried out using the EEG data from the Toronto, Canada Krembil Neuroscience Center. The results from the Freiburg Seizure Estimation in Germany were used for all subsequent studies. This was achieved because the accuracy of the device for multiple seizures from the same patient was easier to test.

The second experiment has been planned to identify a potential preictal phase, better-showing EEG properties leading to the ictal state. The third test was to find an ideal horizon for all of these patients (SPH). After the alarm, the right estimation that no seizure would start should be seen as a period. This experiment is planned and studied independently but all of them are gathered from the same patient and different seizure events. Both the second and third experiments provide the best possible function sets to boost predictive precision. These tests show the relative strength of each algorithm and the behavior of state shift.

12.7   Framework for EEG Signal Classification

A structure was developed and tested in this experiment to predict the occurrence of seizures. As an analysis of the approaches proposed, the Krembil Neuroscience Center of Toronto performed the first trial using the tonic-clonic

Table 12.2 Initially defined epileptic states.

State	Epileptic state
5	Normal, Calm EEG
4	Seizure Onset Period
3	Preictal
2	Ictal
1	Ictal (full seizure state)

seizure scenario. Tonic-clonic seizure disorder is usually physically easy to see in an EEG, with signal amplitudes starting to peak and various frequencies predominate. The operation of the crisis prediction method was a simple predictor. Since the gold standard number of specific states cannot be distinguished between the identification of ictal pattern, an initial device of seven countries has been established This assumption was rendered by the most unique optical determination of portions of the EEG signal. The preparation and testing details employed in the same seizure case were taken from 80% of cases used for training and 20% used for testing to keep any confusing variables continuous (random new permutations for every classification). Table 12.2 shows the states originally described. In determining whether there was a steady change between the predictable and ictal seized states, the distinction between the seizure onset period and the preictal period was made.

The findings of this experiment demonstrated the usefulness and the decision fusion used to enhance the classification of the state decision-making neurons. Also, a multi-channel EEG signal segmentation module was developed, and a window function was applied and transmitted to the device at the required intervals. This allowed a more plausible scenario to be emulated.

12.8   Detection of the Preictal State

A condition that can only be seen by fundamental means is the preictal state. This experiment attempts to establish a feasible length of the preictal state by which this state and the interictal state are sufficiently different. In this experiment, the step-by-step feature optimization algorithm is used to evaluate feature sets that provide the highest predictability. The following question was taken into account in this experiment: Where is epilepsy mathematically evident within 100 seconds before the seizure occurs? This was a timetable to locate the predictory condition in an unreasonably limited or long area of time, only sufficient to effectively perform seizure intervention methods.

For this and all subsequent experiments, the data provided by the Freiburg Seizure Prediction Project in Germany is used for testing. In this experiment, the training and testing data were partitioned from the same dataset; 80% was used as training data and 20% was used as testing data. The states were redefined as seen in all subsequent experiments. For all EEG streams (especially States 1, 2, and 4), the epileptic state concepts were specified by the corresponding researchers who supplied data for the study. Initially, State 3 was described to be one second before State 4. State 3 was predicted. The length of the preictal state in this experiment was increased iterative to 100 seconds and several classifications were carried out for each brain wave at each point. The collection of features was optimized in every step by using the Step-Way Feature Optimization Algorithm described in Section 12.10. This showed that for each patient, and each form of epilepsy, it would be possible to forecast the prediction (one that could be predicted).

12.9   Determination of the Seizure Prediction Horizon

The Horizon Seizure Prevention is a significant parameter since it measures the period remaining before an ictal transition. Essentially, it enables the patient to know how much time is left to take the proper action before the seizure begins. This experiment aims to find the seizure horizon for any patient using the decision tree discussed in the section based solely on the individual classifiers [13].

The researchers who collected the data in Freiburg, Germany gave the description of the states over the EEG signals for the data used as the training collection. Similar to the previous experiment, the preictal state was first described as one second and increased with each brain wave iteratively to 100 seconds. Any stage was classified and the results were tabulated to determine the optimum seizure horizon. It was also harder because the training package was independent of the test set. The classifiers were not provided with data on the tester package.

New state meanings (classes) were defined for each seizure event, based on the results of this experiment, and the estimated weight matrices were determined for the state judgment neurons. As already said, the weight of a state neuron is a given transformation threshold. The weight of $w23$ has been calculated to represent the accuracy of State 3 with the preictal state specified for each case at the optimum seizure horizon determined in this experiment. As before also, the Stepwise Function Optimization Algorithm was conducted at each step and the best functionality was saved at each iteration to decide function sets that helped isolate precursor EEG results [14].

12.10   Dynamic Classification Over Time

Using the experimental information obtained from previous studies, a predictive model capable of detecting status is combined with all algorithms, functions, and other parameters. This new experiment in its fundamental nature is an emulation of what will happen in a real situation and built practically to ensure the viability of constructing such a device with this algorithm would be preserved. Also, the seizure prediction horizon was empirically defined as 65 seconds to safely provide enough preictal data for all of the seizure cases. This seizure prediction horizon was dynamically defined as each of the training sets was constructed for each case that was tested. For each testing case, the training data consisted of all other seizure cases from the same patient. This simulator can be reduced to the modules in Figure 12.12. A module that supplies the simulator with the last 3 seconds of multi-channel EEG data per second will mimic an incoming signal. Sampled at 250 Hz, this section is implemented with a rectangular window feature. An FIR filter is used to decompose input signals in the respective brain waves of the incoming EEG fluke. However, only the initial signal is checked with the device due to time limitations (unfiltered). Although each channel is comparable with the other, data segments from both channels are provided for each 3-second segment in the emulator on

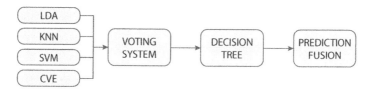

Figure 12.12 Decision fusion block diagram.

a single basis. This results in a PCA reduction of the current training data permutation where the application of the training data is a mixture of all epilepsy events by the same patient except the case used as research. PCA is often implemented with the same parameters in the test sample to correctly scale the test results with the training data.

12.11   Conclusion

The classifying systems LDA and KNN are then performed with the corresponding training and test set, and the decision fusion module is given its forecasts. To obtain majority votes on the epileptic condition, the Decisional Fusion Module determines whether or not a CVE or an SVM classifier is required. These projections are tabled and the decision tree is given an initial estimate. Several heuristic regulations ensure a transformation in a more linear order by the decision tree to correct the original forecast. This fusion of the prediction methods is then used to assess the final prediction of the current epileptic state by state decision neurons using the past three-two predictions (for this system neuron populations containing three two neurons) and to decide when state changes are to be made based on the specified weight matrix. Each test case assumes that each other has already existed in the same patient and the test case uses the overall ideal weight for each case. This emulator was given 140 seconds before ictus and was checked to ascertain the exactness of each status until 21 seconds after the ictal condition.

References

1. Sullivan, H.T. and Sahasrabudhe, S., Envisioning inclusive futures: technology-based assistive sensory and action substitution. *Future J.*, 87, 140–148, 2017.
2. Yin, Y., Zeng, Y., Chen, X., Fan, Y., The Internet of Things in healthcare: an overview. *J. Ind. Inf. Integr.*, 1, 3–13, 2016.
3. Saha, H.N., Auddy, S., Pal., S., Health Monitoring using Internet of Things (IoT). *IEEE J., 2017 8th Annual Industrial Automation and Electromechanical Engineering Conference (IEMECON)* paper, 69–73, 2017.
4. Khan, S.F., Healthcare Monitoring System in Internet of Things (IoT) by Using RFID. *IEEE International Conference on Industrial Technology and Management*, pp. 198–204, 2017.
5. Hassanalieragh, M., Page, A., Soyata, T., Sharma, G., Health Monitoring and Management Using Internet-of-Things (IoT) Sensing with Cloud-Based

Processing: Opportunities and Challenges, *2015 IEEE International Conference on Services Computing*, 27 June-2 July 2015.

6. Gupta, M.S.D., Patchava, V., Menezes, V., Healthcare based on iot using raspberry pi, in: *2015 International Conference on Green Computing and Internet of Things (ICGCIoT)*, pp. 796–799, Oct 2015.

7. Gupta, P., Agrawal, D., Chhabra, J., Dhir, P.K., Iot based smart healthcare kit, in: *2016 International Conference on Computational Techniques in Information and Communication Technologies (ICCTICT)*, pp. 237–242, March 2016.

8. Lopes, N.V., Pinto, F., Furtado, P., Silva, J., Iot architecture proposal for disabled people, in: *2014 IEEE 10th International Conference on Wireless and Mobile Computing, Networking and Communications (WiMob)*, pp. 152–158, Oct 2014.

9. Nagavelli, R. and Guru Rao, C.V., Degree of disease possibility (ddp): A mining based statistical measuring approach for disease prediction in healthcare data mining, in: *International Conference on Recent Advances and Innovations in Engineering (ICRAIE-2014)*, pp. 1–6, May 2014.

10. Sahoo, P.K., Mohapatra, S.K., Wu, S.L., Analyzing healthcare big data with prediction for future health condition. *IEEE Access*, 4, 9786–9799, 2016.

11. Krishnan, B., Sai, S.S., Mohanthy, S.B., Real time internet application with distributed flow environment for medical IoT, in: *International Conference on Green Computing and Internet of Things*, Noida, pp. 832–837, 2015.

12. Arulkumar, V., Latha, C.P., Jr Dasig, D., Concept of Implementing Big Data in Smart City: Applications, Services, Data Security in Accordance with Internet of Things and AI. *Int. J. Recent Technol. Eng.*, 8, 3.

13. Azariadi, D., Tsoutsouras, V., Xydis, S., Soudris, D., ECG signal analysis and arrhythmia detection on IoT wearable medical devices, in: *5th International Conference on Modern Circuits and Systems Technologies*, pp. 1–4, Thessaloniki, 2016.

14. Mohan, A., Cyber security for personal medical devices Internet of Things, in: *IEEE International Conference on Distributed Computing in Sensor Systems*, Marina Del Rey, pp. 372–374, CA, 2014.

13

Use of Machine Learning in Healthcare

V. Lakshman Narayana[1]*, R. S. M. Lakshmi Patibandla[2], B. Tarakeswara Rao[3] and Arepalli Peda Gopi[4]

[1]Department of IT, Vignan's Nirula Institute of Technology & Science for Women, Andhra, Pradesh, India, Guntur, AP, India
[2]Department of IT, Vignan's Foundation for Science, Technology, and Research, Vadlamudi, AP, India
[3]Department of CSE, Kallam Haranadha Reddy Institute of Technology, Guntur, AP, India
[4]Department of CSE, Vignan's Nirula Institute of Technology & Science for Women, AP, India

Abstract

At an early point, the health fragment expanded and gained fundamentally from new innovations. Late, AI (a sub-set of person-focused thinking) is playing a key role in various areas related to well-being, including the ability to take advantage of recent clinical methods, treat patient information and records, and thus treat continuous diseases. In an ongoing post, the New Yorker Sebastian Thrum told the researcher A.I. vs. M.D. that computers, like machines that make human muscles more than once grounded, can make the human mind more and stronger. Unlimited applications within the healthcare sector are part of computer preparation. Today, AI supports clinical authority, guides, and treats irresistible diseases and customizes clinical drugs with smoothing out authoritative procedures. With the assistance of AI, Quotient Health has developed a programme designed to "diminish the value of promoting EMR structures" by strengthening and standardising the structuring of these frames. The ultimate aim is to increase the cost of consideration. This paper discusses healthcare IA, various implementations of AI, certifiable healthcare benefits, morals of AI computations, and opportunities to improve quality of healthcare skills.

Keywords: Healthcare, machine learning, diseases, medical

*Corresponding author: lakshmanv58@vignannirula.org

Rohit Tanwar, S. Balamurugan, R. K. Saini, Vishal Bharti and Premkumar Chithaluru (eds.) Advanced Healthcare Systems: Empowering Physicians with IoT-Enabled Technologies, (275–294) © 2022 Scrivener Publishing LLC

13.1   Introduction

Medicinal services are a pivotal industry that gives cost-basically-based consideration to a large number of people, even as at the equivalent time transforming into zenith income workers for some countries. Nowadays, the human services venture alone procures an income of $1.668 trillion. America furthermore spends extra on social insurance per capita when contrasted with most other created or developing universal areas. Pleasant, cost, and result are three trendy expressions that consistently go with human services and guarantee a ton, and nowadays, social insurance experts and partners the world over are looking out creative strategies to flexibly on this guarantee. Time-empowered shrewd human services are not, at this point, a trip of extravagant, as web-associated clinical contraptions are saving the wellness device as we know about it all in all from falling aside underneath the populace trouble.

From playing a significant situation in influenced individual consideration, charging, and logical insights, these days' age is permitting human services experts to expand exchange staffing designs, IP capitalization, presents brilliant healthcare, and bringing down managerial and conveyance charges [1]. Machine picking up information on human services is one such territory that is seeing slow acknowledgment inside the social insurance industry. Google of late built up an AI set of rules to find harmful tumors in mammograms, and analysts in Stanford School are the utilization of profound figuring out how to get mindful of skin malignant growth. AI information on ML is as of now helping out in different circumstances in healthcare. ML in human services empowers to investigate several distinct records, focuses and underwrites impacts, gives all-around planned peril rankings and exceptional guide assignment, and has numerous different bundles. In this content, we can talk about some of the apex uses of contraption becoming acquainted with human services and how they remain to substitute the way we imagine the social insurance undertaking in 2018 and past.

13.2   Uses of Machine Learning in Pharma and Medicine

The increasingly creating scope of uses of device acing in social insurance grants us to look at a fate in which measurements, assessment, and advancement work connected at the hip to help boundless patients without them regularly getting it. Rapidly, it will be very regular to find ML-based bundles inserted with genuine-time influenced individual measurements to be had from one of a kind human services structures in a few worldwide areas, in this way expanding the viability of most recent cure options which had been inaccessible sooner than [2].

13.2.1 Distinguish Illnesses and Examination

The detection and evaluation of illnesses and conditions that are in any case deemed to be serious analysis is one of the groundbreaking applications of social insurance. This will involve something from tumors that are difficult to catch in different genetic diseases in the span of initial stages. IBM Genomics Watson offers a prime example of ways in which intellectual processing can be coordinated with genome-based tumor sequencing. Berr, the biopharmaceutical beast, uses AI in fields like oncology to create effective cures. P1vital's prediction (projected response to desperation) aims to establish a financingly acceptable way of analyzing and treating standard diseases.

13.2.2 Drug Discovery and Manufacturing

In the area of medical science, one of the most important uses of system mastering methods in drug development is system mastering. Technologies that will be applied to this field included changes to the next-generation sequencing and precision medicine which can aid in discovering new ways to treat ever-wider instances of illness. Approaches including greedy progressive neural networks (GPNNs) and adversarial nets (ANNs) are currently the key methodologies of machine learning that are not supervised, so that they are

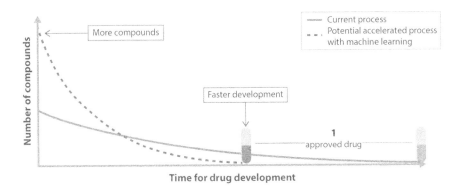

Figure 13.1 Drug development in ML.

just able to identify patterns in data without being able to predict stuff. The drug development in ML time levels are indictaed in Figure 13.1. In order to make production of ML-primarily-based technologies for more than a one projects, such as the AI-based totally era for most cancers care and the personalising drug aggregate for AML, Microsoft is using ML technologies across all its applications as well as its products (acute myeloid leukemia).

13.2.3　Scientific Imaging Analysis

Framework becoming more acquainted with and profound picking up information on are each at risk for the advancement time known as PC vision. This has decided appeal inside the inner eye activity progressed with the guide of Microsoft which matches on picture symptomatic apparatus for picture examination. As machines becoming acquainted with will turn out to be progressively reachable and as they create of their illustrative potential, expect to see more data assets from various clinical symbolisms develop to be a piece of this AI-pushed indicative technique.

13.2.4　Twisted Therapy

Tweaked medicines cannot most straightforward be extra successful utilizing blending man or lady well-being with prescient examination but, on the other hand, are ready for correspondingly studies and better affliction appraisal. Directly, doctors are constrained to choosing from a specific arrangement of findings or gauge the danger to the influenced individual dependent on his indicative records and to be had hereditary insights. Anyway, gadgets becoming more acquainted with in medication are making top-notch strides, and IBM Watson oncology is at the vanguard of this development by methods for leveraging persistent clinical history to help produce more than one cure choices. In the coming years, we can see more gadgets and biosensors with refined wellness measurement capacities hit the market, permitting more realities to turn out to be serenely accessible for such contemporary ML-based medicinal services advances [4].

13.2.5　AI to Know-Based Social Change

Conduct alteration is an urgent a piece of a preventive drug, and ever because the multiplication of device acing in healthcare, limitless startups in USA are springing up inside the fields of most malignancies' avoidance and characterization, understanding the cure, and numerous others. Somatix is a B2B2C-based measurement investigation association that has propelled an ML-based application to catch motions that we make in our everyday lives, permitting us to perceive our oblivious conduct and make fundamental alterations.

13.2.6 Perception Wellness Realisms

Holding refreshed well-being records is a comprehensive procedure, and even as time has played out its part in facilitating the records section framework, the reality is that even now, a dominant part of the strategies sets aside a significant number effort to wrap up. The guideline capacity of framework acing in social insurance is to ease systems to keep time, exer-tion, and money [5]. Recording the class methodologies, the utilization of vector machines, and ML-based OCR notoriety systems are gradually assembling steam, comprising of Google's cloud vision programming interface and MATLAB's contraption acing–based penmanship acknowledgment time. MIT is nowadays on the lessening edge of developing the ensuing age of wise, clever well-being insights, as an approach to contain ML-based costs starting from the earliest stage to help with analysis, clinical cure tips, etc.

13.2.7 Logical Preliminary and Exploration

AI has a few limited programs in the field of logical preliminaries and exploration. As everyone inside the pharma business could advise you, clinical preliminaries cost a ton of time and cash and may take a very long time to finish by and large. Applying ML-basically-based prescient examination to distinguish capacity logical preliminary candidates can assist scientists withdrawing a pool from a colossal sort of measurement focuses, comprising of going before clinical specialist visits, web-based life, and numerous others [6]. Gadget acing has additionally found utilization in guaranteeing genuine-time checking and measurements get admission to of the preliminary people, finding the palatable example size to be analyzed, and utilizing the vitality of electronic information to diminish data fundamentally-based blunders.

13.2.8 Publicly Supported Perceptions Collection

Publicly supporting is extremely popular inside the clinical subject these days, allowing specialists and professionals to get the right of section to a huge amount of realities transferred by utilizing individuals, depending on their own assent. This stay well-being reality includes fabulous consequences inside how medicine will be seen not far off. Apple's research kit allows clients to get to intelligent applications that watch ML-based facial notoriety to attempt to treat Asperger's and Parkinson's malady [7]. IBM presently banded together with Medtronic to interpret, assemble, and make to be had diabetes and insulin insights in real time fundamentally based at the publicly supported data. With the enhancements being made in IoT, the social insurance endeavor remains to find new methodologies in which to apply these records and address hard-to-analyze occurrences and help inside the normal improvement of analysis and restorative medication.

13.2.9   Better Radiotherapy

One of the greatest looked for after bundles of machine concentrating in medicinal services is inside the field of radiology. Clinical picture analysis has numerous discrete factors that can get up at any exact second of time. There are numerous injuries, most tumors foci, and so on, which can be no "ifs" and/or "buts" modeled the utilization of entangled conditions. Because ML-based calculations gain from a large number of various examples accessible close by, it transforms into less complex to analyze and find the factors. One of the most popular employments of gadget concentrating in clinical picture examination is the characterization of articles along with injuries into classes that incorporate normal or weird, lesion or noninjury, etc. Google's profound psyche wellness is effectively helping analysts in UCLH widen calculations that could recognize the contrast among healthy and destructive tissue and improve radiation solution for the equivalent.

13.2.10   Incidence Forecast

Man-made intelligence principally–based innovation and device acing are nowadays likewise being set to apply in checking and anticipating pestilences around the segment. Presently a day, researchers have got the right of section to a major amount of data collected from satellites, constant online life refreshes, Internet webpage realities, etc. Manufactured neural systems help to examine these records and are anticipating that the total from intestinal sickness flare-ups should extreme interminable irresistible ailments. Anticipating these episodes is especially helpful in 1/3-worldwide universal areas as they need an imperative clinical framework and instructive frameworks [8]. The main occurrence of this is the ProMED-mail, a web-based announcing stage in which video show units developing ailments and rising ones and gives episode reports progressively.

13.3   The Ongoing Preferences of ML in Human Services

It is safe to state there are such a large number of manual methodologies in medicine. While in tutoring, we handle composed lab esteems, analyze, and other diagram notes on paper. We generally knew this become a spot wherein age might need to help improve my work process and trusted it may likewise improve tolerant consideration. Because of the way that at that point, headways in electronically clinical realities have been amazing, yet the records they give are not parts higher than the old bar charts they supplanted. If innovation is to improve later, at that point, then the computerized data given to doctor will be increasingly appropriate through the intensity of examination and contraption becoming acquainted with.

Utilizing such a progressed examination, we can give higher realities to clinical specialists at the factor of patient consideration. Having smooth access to the blood strain and other basic signs once I see my patient is repeating and foreseen. Envision how parts extra helpful it would be, on the off chance that I was likewise demonstrated my patient's possibility for stroke, coronary corridor issue, and kidney disappointment dependent on the last 50 blood strain readings, lab investigate results, race, sexual orientation, hover of family members history, financial notoriety, and the present logical preliminary data [9].

We need to create more data to the clinician, because one knows one's own capacity for affecting others' analyses and treatment decisions and to truly decide what the fair outcomes and cost would be for all. On framework learning with Social Insurance like New Jersey's program, it teaches doctors that it is fine to utilize a massive amount of records incrementally. The results of those tests that are used to grant treatment are simpler since there is less information being lost. The expense of care is kept down, and there is value for additional care while there is no more depression, pain, and suffering. Patients are both happier and better physically by using this new efficient therapy.

Practical devices that are completed while being a part of social security and using knowledge from medicine have lately become a genuinely newsworthy thing. A recent advancement in Google News has been an algorithm, or software which picks out the information that comprises a news storey. It restricts the news it gets to those that are in alignment with a set of rules in order to make sure that harmful cancer cell codes are not absorbed into the process. Stanford University used a deep and logical thought approach in

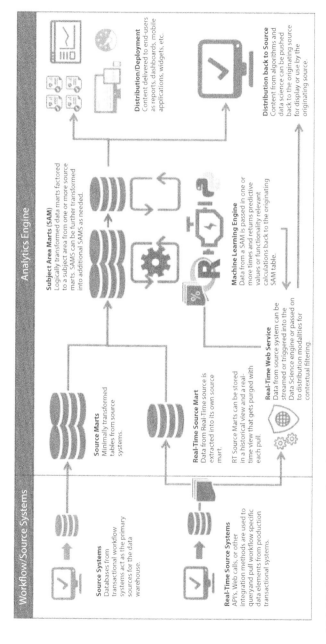

Figure 13.2 Machine learning in medicinal services.

conjuring a body of progress and information concerning skin disease [10]. An article published in the Journal of the American Medical Association expressed the implications of a profound system acquiring more acquainted with a collection of decides that triggered to be well prepared in the capacity to analyzing diabetic retinopathy in book images. The machine learning in medical services and its process is represented in Figure 13.2. Since the machine is so fine, it is a very good thing that this is the norm for clinical decision-making. Regardless, the gadget learning often blends into a few techniques, but not others. After applying data extracted from calculations, we are able to create a fast favorable location that is repeatable or normalized. For those who have big data sets, which are like radiology, cardiology, and pathology, they are the most outstanding candidates. ML experts should be prepared to display previews, identify bits of significance, and point to real places that need to be thought about so that the accuracy of these kinds of processes can be enhanced. Long term, artificial intelligence would allow the hover of family member's internist and expert at the bedside. Machine learning can provide an empirical supposition to minimize shortcomings in efficiency, utility, and reliability.

In the wellness imperative (we need to initiate the correct), we leverage restrictive programming research data, which we then circle back to doctors to assist in clinical dynamic. The use of ML algorithms in healthcare analysis and the complete process is represented in Figure 13.3. Much like prior to an

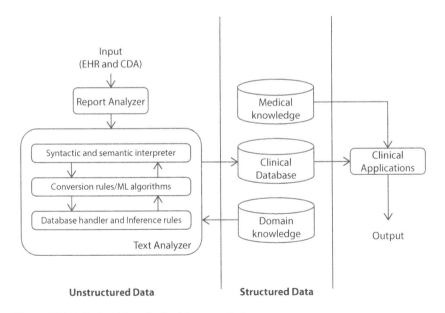

Figure 13.3 ML algorithms for healthcare analytics.

operator enters a patient's symptoms, indications, and manifestations into the EMR, devices in the vicinity that track the patient's well-being are learning as they look at the complete of that person. The well-being specialist is wearing a competent, informative, and revealing state of health for recommending, demanding a search, and clarifying a preventable disease. The markers will start to venture into all parts of drugs as they get increasingly useful and more integrated in the experiments. We will have the option to fuse more big units of records that will be able to be examined and in analysis in real an ideal opportunity to give all sorts of insights to the supplier and else person.

13.4 The Morals of the Use of Calculations in Medicinal Services

It has been expressed before that the incredible contraption picking up information on the device in human services is the specialist's brain. May need to there be a bowed for doctors to see framework learning as an unfortunate second sentiment? At a certain point, autoworkers expected that mechanical autonomy would push off their employments. Additionally, there might be doctors who stress that gadget becoming acquainted with is the start of a way that may render them out of date. Anyway, it is the specialty of drug that could not the slightest bit be changed. Victims will continually need the human touch and the being concerned and caring relationship with the people that flexibly care. Neither one of the gadgets acing, nor some other predetermination advances in the cure, will push off this, yet transforms into gear that clinicians use to improve continuous consideration [12].

The spotlight must be en route to utilize gadget picking up information on to upgrade influenced individual consideration. As an occasion, on the off chance that I am evaluating an influenced individual for malignancy, at that point, I need the most noteworthy top-notch biopsy impacts I can almost certainly get. A system gaining information on set of decisions that can appraise the pathology slides and help the pathologist with an investigation is cherished. On the off chance that I can get the impacts in a small amount of the time with an indistinguishable certificate of precision, at that point, over the long haul, that is going to improve influenced individual consideration and fulfilment. Social insurance wishes to move from considering gadget becoming more acquainted with as an advanced plan to considering it to be a real worldwide instrument that can be sent today. If a device picking up information on is to have a situation in social insurance, at that point, we should adopt an incremental strategy. We have to find explicit use cases wherein gadget picking up information on abilities bears an incentive from a chose innovative utility (e.g., Google and Stanford). This can be a bit by bit pathway to joining extra examination, framework learning, and prescient calculations into regular clinical practice.

To begin with, our fantasies need to accommodate our abilities. Training a contraption becoming more acquainted with a set of rules to see skin most malignancies from a major arrangement of pores and skin most diseases is something that most of the individuals caught. If we had been to break down that radiologists are being changed by methods for calculations, at that point, people could be justifiably reluctant. This ought to be crossed over as the years progressed. Radiologists would not ever develop as old, anyway, radiologists of things to come will administer and assess readings that have been at first perused a machine. They will employ gadget learning like a shared buddy that distinguishes explicit areas of mindfulness, enlightens commotion, and encourages acknowledgment on over the top open door districts of concern.

How would we arrive at the edge expected to consider gadget learning? Restorative medication has a strategy for examining and demonstrating that cures are sheltered and viable. It is an all-inclusive arrangement of experimentation—and putting together decisions concerning confirmation. We need those equivalent strategies in the area as we investigate framework picking up information on to guarantee its security and adequacy. We have to secure the morals stressed in turning in part of what we never really machine.

An "imagine a scenario in which" circumstance on the limit of gadget learning, a few months prior, I gave an introduction around the predetermination of investigation and its expected impact on logical consideration. In my slides, I demonstrated speculative EMR strolling prescient calculations even as a specialist was inspecting his influenced individual. A spring up field showed the constant finding, pathology results, and treatment choices, notwithstanding every elective's ability viability and expense for this influenced individual.

While the influenced individual in this circumstance can likewise have been theoretical, it was displayed after my dad who outperformed away several years before, from prostate malignant growth. We picked this circumstance to show impacts that could be conceivable and machine becoming acquainted with what to be had at that point.

With my long stretches of tutoring and ability, we might need to winnow the writing and propose the fantastic choices for my clinical specialist. In various words, I was the human arrangement of rules, the doctor's cerebrum, who had the technique and, most essentially, the inspiration and time to compositions in live execution with my PCP's well-being professional to extend the first arrangement, which, quite a while ago, run delayed his reality 9 years.

With an investigation stage and gadget becoming more acquainted with taking strolls inside the history, the human arrangement of rules—the additional layer of a once more up clinical specialist—would not be significant. The investigation motor could have unendingly more data than any individual man or lady ought to ever way. It may have a library of patients like my primary care physician, alongside his investigation and tissue kind. It may have treatment alternatives to be had with forecasts of ways long they could be powerful, mortality charges, aspect effects, and cost. Regardless of the entirety of the exertion by the method of a human parental figure, an investigation stage ought to introduce vastly more work behind the stage and flexibly conclusive insights to the specialist in genuine time.

Be that as it may, contraption learning wants a definite measure of information to produce an amazing arrangement of rules. Bunches of device acing will most importantly originate from offices with enormous datasets. Well-being impetus is developing aggregate examination for greatness (café™), a product based on a nationwide de-analyzed archive of human services data from business realities distribution centers (EDWS) and 0.33-birthday festivity data sources. It is miles empowering near viability and research and is producing interesting and powerful contraption contemplating calculations. Bistro presents joint effort among our healthcare contraption accomplices, gigantic, and little.

Some other opportunities for littler substances can be their ability to combine their measurements with enormous frameworks. Sooner or later, we may moreover observe neighborhood records' center points with datasets tweaked for topographical, ecological, and financial components, which convey social insurance frameworks of all sizes get right of passage to more records.

When broader databases are incorporated into AI, we will precisely enhance treatment in particular ways for each geographic area. What is more, thinking about exceptional afflictions with uninformed volumes, it should be suitable to consolidate provincial information into national sets to scale the degree required for gadget contemplating.

The e-cigarette will never be a product that is ready for immediate use across the population. But we are seeing early signs of e-cigarettes being discarded across the population and finding their niche in the environment. It is fascinating to think about the thinking until it leaves one's head. At later period, it is not abnormal to reason about where ever with a gadget that investigations before that, yet not exclusively what is unusual with those victims, yet additionally what is occurring with tantamount patients in various human services frameworks, what relevant logical preliminaries are nearly becoming in progress, and the vitality and price of on-going cure choices. It sounds like a new medical technology that will be advantageous to treatment; however, it is still just in its development phase at the time of this writing.

The great investigators are fit as a fiddle. Inside the diabetes vault occasion, we should rapid walk around how those specialized abilities shaped the structure of the partner.

1. Data inquiry, or square, transformed into used to take a crack at number one forecast to experiences just as patient sorts for the initial three guidelines. Separate inquiries have been produced for every reality flexibly, claims, and the EMR. Data inquiry got used to coax out suppositions about wherein lab requests and results lived inside the EMR.

2. Data development, or ETL as it is for the most part known, utilized the questions to drag just the needed records for guidelines. The resultant measurement units were arranged inside given systematic condition. By methods for following ETL top-notch rehearses, inquiries from the logical group around records trustworthiness and information genealogy were effectively tended to.

3. Data demonstrating rode at the impact points of realities question and realities development by a method of building up a touchdown zone for influenced individual standard capabilities, comprehensive of patients who qualified for more than one principle or the equivalent guideline two or three occasions. Each occurrence became caught and by so doing, turned out to be then accessible for investigation. Record demonstrating assumes a significant job in catching what the business endeavor thinks about and reporting that in a database, prepared for assessment.

4. Data investigation came after records question, records movement, and reality demonstrating. With a profound comprehension of the masses wellness business drivers and the issues to be comprehended, the examiner should do what he does five stars: dissect the records inside the information form considering the business undertaking drivers.

5. At last, data perception. In this diabetes vault developed, up hitherto, we had been best keen on what abilities have been

needed to build the accomplice for incorporation/avoidance. The examiner utilized exceeds expectations bar diagrams to feature the tallies of rule capability. This gets adequate to get purchase in for the guidelines of consideration.

Later a gadget like Qlik or scene benefited from the accompanying records models and featured the heat in an investigation; be that as it may, this was not significant for the incorporation measures. These are the five specialized capacities essentially crucial for experts to hold onto the great prospects inside social insurance structures. To be a successful healthcare investigator will require specialized inclination, the data capabilities referenced above, combined with know-how of medicinal services realities and tasks. The additional examiners perceive the issues them.

13.5 Opportunities in Healthcare Quality Improvement

The initial step is the open door in improving quality and procedure is figuring out where an industry misses the mark concerning its hypothetical potential. Human services miss the mark in the accompanying manners that are monstrous variety in clinical works on (causing it incomprehensible that all patients to get great consideration). High paces of wrong consideration (where the danger of damage inalienable in the treatment exceeds possible advantage).

A more critical glance at the five open door regions above reveals insight into the estimation of value as centre business systems seem to be as follows.

13.5.1 Variation in Care

The principal opened door region, above, has been a typical issue within our social life insurance that it is truly outlandish for all individuals, perhaps those who have complete or best route access to the best consideration, to get the best consideration. With respect to changing the drug, variety alone can drive down expenses by around 30% while improving clinical results.

13.5.2   Inappropriate Care

The social insurance industry does not ask the benefit/risks conundrum, but rather, it would like to imagine that a wrong consideration has occurred. In short, the social insurance industry thinks about care that is too focused on patient benefit.

No matter how diligent the physician is in diagnosing a patient with tuberculosis, this incorrect diagnosis will push the wrong kind of treatment for some patients. A new study suggests that a traditionalist master gauge puts wrong consideration at 20% to 25% of all consideration conveyed comprehensively, not simply in the U.S. It is not simply the expenses of the consideration that speak to squander, and it is the outcome of improper consideration—much of the time, medical services experts should convey more consideration to find out whether to recover the underlying damage or not.

13.5.3   Prevents Care–Associated Injurious and Death for Carefrontation

The National Academy of Medicine (IOM), which once upon a time had been known as the Institute of Medicine, and its Committee on Quality of Healthcare in America have recently committee concluded that all doctors make mistakes. When one-third of 1% of the U.S. population is hospitalized from a routine event and between 46000 and 9800 die from neglectful consequences of treatment, the Health Affairs report has spurred an idea to adjust treatment for reevaluation amidst emergency rooms and outpatient settings. The examination that occurred after the 1999 assessments was moderate, and it exhibited in the genuine cost that at least 210,000 passings should have been prevented.

Even though U.S. medical results are overall very good, including the fact that the average of 3.5 to 7 years of time may be gained back by the patient, the business can definitely be improved.

13.5.4   The Fact That People Are Unable to do What They Know Works

While understanding damage (above) is a physical issue of commission (because the consideration effectively hurts the patient), human services should likewise take a gander at its wounds of oversight, where clinicians neglect to execute on mediations they know work for specific conditions (i.e., profoundly dependable consideration). Despite having enough sensible medical treatment, American adults (on average) are over 40% accurate at critical thinking, 60% of the time.

In regard to human services, the framework supposes that it might be able to get to supernatural occurrences (e.g., including long periods of future) executing accurately generally a half the time, meaning issues every so often it should work—or near-constantly. Note that it is not quite supernatural occurrences executed precisely as forecast, rather things that include long periods of future executed well. From a point of view, the patient's family members have the power and ability to change their way of interacting with the patient. They also have the ability to encourage the patient to make a good choice in the future.

13.5.5   A Waste

The best, perhaps, patients following any of these territories with a theoretical potential to benefit on the option of the provider's services are clinical treatments. The waste to the environment is colossal. At any rate, 30% to 50% of all medicines expenses are incurred in creating waste by making second rate items from unusable materials, and more importantly, frivolously pouring down the drain medicines which could be utilized for the right things which are needing treating effectively.

In 2019, the U.S. will spend over $3.7 trillion on human services and will not be able to generate acceptable social insurance conveyance. The recovery of two trillion of that might be recoverable waste. For the well-being as a factor of concern frameworks, waste in current concern conveyance activities is by, a wide margin, the biggest open eco-friendly door of opportunity which will come by in the lives of those who are holding these frameworks.

13.6   A Team-Based Care Approach Reduces Waste

Following accounts in a collective, objective situated group-based consideration approach shows that when a consideration group's essential objective is improving the nature of care, the enhancements decrease a framework's waste and spare a great many dollars. Figure 13.4 shows investment funds with group-based consideration at a third-age tolerant focused clinical final. Figure 13.5 shows the financial impact of clinical quality improvement levels.

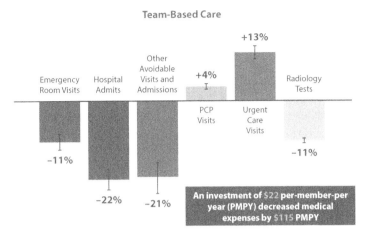

Figure 13.4 Team-based consideration effect and ROI.

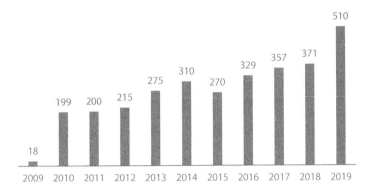

Figure 13.5 Financial impact of clinical quality improvement.

13.7   Conclusion

Those are a couple of likely regions wherein device acing can help the social insurance endeavor out of numerous circumstances. We see, with contraption becoming acquainted with applications, social insurance and cure section can form into a pristine domain and completely rebuild the medicinal services activities. An inside and out involvement with introducing diagnostics, assessment, and imaging, wearable and telemedicine answer for social insurance associations. In the fate, we have also outfitted cell empowered answers for clinical devices and clinical Software program, coordinating them safely with the cloud framework for distant and simple entry.

References

1. Lakshmi Patibandla, R.S.M., Tarakeswara Rao, B., Sandhya Krishna, P., Maddumala, V.R., Medical Data Clustering Using Particle Swarm Optimization Method. *J. Crit. Rev.*, 2020.
2. Sandhya Krishna, P., Ummadi Janardhan Reddy, R.S.M., Patibandla, L., Reshmi Khadherbhi, Sk., Identification of Lung Cancer Stages Using Efficient Machine Learning Framework. *J. Crit. Rev.*, 385–390, 2020.
3. Mounika, B., Reshmi Khadherbhi, Sk., Maddumala, V.R., Lakshmi Patibandla, R.S.M., Data Distribution Method with Text Extraction from Big Data. *J. Crit. Rev.*, 7, 6, 376–380, 2020.
4. Anveshini, D., Divakara Rao, D.V., Lakshmi Patibandla, R.S.M., Reshmi Khadherbhi, Sk., Digital Certificate Validation for Improving Security in Ad Hoc Networks. *Test Eng. Manag.*, 83, 11026–11034, 2020.
5. Naresh, A., Lakshmi Patibandla, R.S.M., Vidhya Lakshmi, G., Meghana Chowdary., M., Unsupervised Text Classification for Heart Disease Using Machine Learning Methods. *Test Eng. Manag.*, 83, 11005–11016, 2020.
6. Balayesu, N., Vidya Lakshmi, G., Maddumala, V., Lakshmi Patibandla., R.S.M., Channel Allocation in Wireless Sensor Networks Avoiding Node Collisions. *Int. J. Adv. Sci. Technol.*, 29, 5, 12705–12714, 2020.
7. Patibandla, R.S.M.L., Kurra, S.S., Mundukur, N.B., A Study on Scalability of Services and Privacy Issues in Cloud Computing, in: *Distributed Computing and Internet Technology. ICDCIT 2012.* Lecture Notes in Computer Science, vol. 7154, R. Ramanujam and S. Ramaswamy (Eds.), Springer, Berlin, Heidelberg, 2012.
8. Patibandla, R.S.M.L. and Veeranjaneyulu, N., Survey on Clustering Algorithms for Unstructured Data, in: *Intelligent Engineering Informatics.* Advances in Intelligent Systems and Computing, vol. 695, V. Bhateja, C. Coello Coello, S. Satapathy, P. Pattnaik (Eds.), Springer, Singapore, 2018.
9. Patibandla, R.S.M.L. and Veeranjaneyulu, N., Performance Analysis of Partition and Evolutionary Clustering Methods on Various Cluster Validation Criteria. *Arab J. Sci. Eng.*, 43, 4379–4390, 2018.
10. Lakshmi Patibandla, R.S.M., Kurra, S.S., Kim, H.-J., Electronic resource management using cloud computing for libraries. *Int. J. Appl. Eng. Res.*, 9, 18141–18147, 2014.

11. Lakshmi Patibandla, R.S.M. and Veeranjaneyulu, N., A SimRank based Ensemble Method for Resolving Challenges of Partition Clustering Methods. *J. Sci. Ind. Res.*, 79, 323–327, 2020.

12. Tarakeswara Rao, B., Patibandla, R.S.M.L., Murty, M.R., A Comparative Study on Effective Approaches for Unsupervised Statistical Machine Translation, in: *Embedded Systems and Artificial Intelligence*. Advances in Intelligent Systems and Computing, vol. 1076, V. Bhateja, S. Satapathy, H. Satori (Eds.), Springer, Singapore, 2020.

14

Methods of MRI Brain Tumor Segmentation

Amit Verma

School of Computer Science, UPES, Dehradun, Uttarakhand, India

Abstract

Till today, doctors manually see the MR images of the tumor to predict the presence of a tumor or not based on their experience. Automatic detection of the presence of a tumor and identifying various other properties of brain tumors is still a challenge. Identifying a tumor automatically requires the segmentation of the tumor in MRIs. Researchers have developed various state-of-the-art methods to carry out the process of segmenting the brain tumor in MRI, and almost every method of segmentation can be broadly classified in two ways that are generative and descriptive models. In this chapter, the requirement and the importance of brain tumor segmentation in MRIs and the basic methods of doing brain tumor segmentation are discussed. Further, region-based and generative models with weighted aggregation methods for performing brain tumor segmentation using MR images are also discussed.

Keywords: MRI, brain, tumor, segmentation, generative, automatic

14.1 Introduction

Magnetic Resonance Image (MRI) is an imaging technique used for medical purposes for generating pictures of various organs and tissues of the body based on strong magnetic fields and radio waves. MRI has proven as a great advantage for the doctors to diagnose the patient and to separate the healthy and the infected tissues. MRI is the most useful way to diagnose a brain tumor; for diagnosis, the MRI of the patient is manually analyzed by

Email: amit.uptu2006@gmail.com

Rohit Tanwar, S. Balamurugan, R. K. Saini, Vishal Bharti and Premkumar Chithaluru (eds.) *Advanced Healthcare Systems: Empowering Physicians with IoT-Enabled Technologies,* (295–304) © 2022 Scrivener Publishing LLC the doctor to detect the presence of the infected area in the brain. Since the development of the MRI technique, much research has been done to date to automate or semi-automate the process of detecting the tumor in the brain with much higher accuracy. For automating the process of detecting the tumor in the brain, segmentation of MRI images plays a vital role.

Basically, image segmentation is the process of partitioning or segmenting the image into various segments so the analysis of the image becomes simpler. Further, the segmentation makes it simpler to analyze the area of interest in the image and leave the rest. The process of image segmentation is used in the detection of brain tumor by analyzing the MRI images of the brain, and this process is named as Brain Tumor Segmentation. It is the process of segmenting the MRI image based on region, pixel, etc., to separate the tumor from the part of healthy tissues in the brain and to automate the process of tumor detection with higher accuracy. Based on segmentation the affected region, shape, location, texture, size, and many other features of the tumor can be detected with less or no intervention of the human being. Till now, many researchers are working on the segmentation process of brain tumors to automate the way of tumor detection with much high accuracy. BTS can be done on various features of the tumor-like the temperature of the infected tissues remains higher as compared to the healthy tissues. Still, it is a much challenging area of research to automate the process of analyzing MRI for tumor detection. Therefore, various states of arts have been done for proving the method of segmenting the MRI image for brain tumor detection. Various popularly known methods are discussed further in this chapter.

14.2   Generative and Descriptive Models

Broadly, the methods of brain tumor segmentation can be divided into two categories specifically generative and discriminative [1]. Majorly, both the techniques are based on conditional probability. Generative methods use probabilistic models for segmenting the tumor based on size and shape. Generative models do not require any manually labeled training data for detecting the brain tumor; basically, it is used for unsupervised training data. Let us consider the various features of brain tissues and compare them with the prior knowledge, its group, or label various brain tissues according to these features. More specifically, each pixel of the MRI is compared with some features of the healthy or infected tissue to categories the pixel accordingly. Progressively the pixels of the image are grouped accordingly in some shaped boundaries (regions). If the discriminative model is used, then the pre-labeled data set is required for making a hypothesis model. Considering the MRI image of a brain tumor, each pixel of the image would be already labeled. On the basis of the pre-labeled training data set, it is broadly classified into some regions such that mean squared error with respect to the training data set would remain minimum [2–5]. Now, we will discuss the generative and descriptive models in a more general way.

Basically, the generative model is used for unsupervised or non-labeled training data sets for making a model or to train a machine. Based on some feature(s), data is divided into the region(s). In this way, the training data set is used to train the machine for making a hypothesis model predict the new data according to the region the new data would belong to. Taking an example for mathematical understanding about the generative model, let us consider a training data set in which each data (tuple) could be either in category A or B. That means it is still not known which data belong to which category more specifically data is unsupervised data (non-labeled). In this case, each data is checked on the basis of some feature X whether the data belong to category A or B. According to Equation (14.1) based on Bayes Theorem, $P(X|Y = A)$ will be calculated for any data, say, D1. Here, data D1 is checked for feature X that how strong is the probability for data D1 to be in category A.

$$P(X|Y = A) = P(Y = A|X).P(X)/P(Y)$$ (14.1)

Similarly, $P(X|Y = B)$ will also be calculated for data D1, and if $P(X|Y = A) > P(X|Y = B)$, then the data D1 will be labeled as it belongs to category A. Progressively, all the data in the training data set are categorized as A or B and boundary accordingly as shown in Figure 14.1 specifying two regions named A and B.

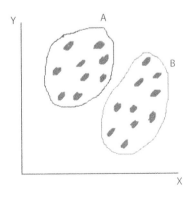

Figure 14.1 Training data set is categorized in A or B based on some feature X.

Now, these specified regions are used for making a hypothesis of any new data say D2 as shown in Figure 14.2 with a green colored dot. Please note that green color is not specified as a property or feature of data, it is just for making difference with other given data. The new data D2 is unknown and the hypothesis is to be made on the basis already learned machine. As the data, D2 is falling in the red colored boundary region so the data D2 is more likely to be in category B.

The discriminative model basically requires pre-labeled data set to train the machine according to the training data set for making a hypothesis model [6–9]. For example, we are having a training data set in which each data is already labeled with A or B as shown in Figure 14.3. For ease, red colored dots are representing data with label A and blue colored dots are representing data with label B.

Now, a decision boundary is drawn to broadly separate the data in such a way that the mean squared error would be minimum as shown in Figure 14.4. By the term error, we mean the decision boundary should divide the training data in such a way that the probability of data labeled A to be in a region belonging to data labeled B should be minimum. According to the data, linear or logistic regression with gradient descent can be used for making a decision boundary with a minimized error.

Now, as the hypothesis model is built according to the training data set using the discriminative model, it can be used for making a hypothesis on new data arrival. Let us say new data D2 (which is not pre-labeled) is shown with the green colored dot in Figure 14.5.

According to the hypothesis model prepared according to training the data set, data D2 is lying in a region belonging to category B. So, it would be labeled as B.

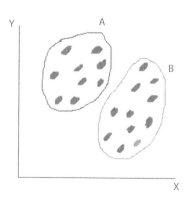

Figure 14.2 Showing arrival of new data (green colored dot) for making hypothesis.

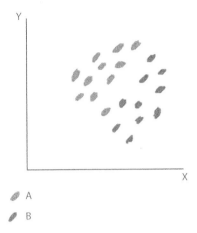

Figure 14.3 Pre-labeled data of training data set.

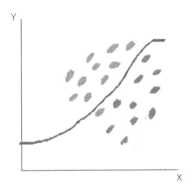

Figure 14.4 Decision boundary separating data.

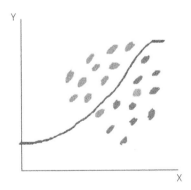

Figure 14.5 New data D2 is shown with green colored dot.

Based on the generative and discriminative approach, multiple states of arts were proposed for segmenting the brain tumor (abnormality) in MR images. Many researchers contributed to this field for automating the process of brain tumor detection in the MRIs. The most popular ways for doing segmentation of the MRI are as follows.

14.2.1   Region-Based Segmentation

In this approach, pixels of MRIs are group together based on some characteristics. These groups of similar pixels are considered as regions [10–14]. This approach can be used for partitioning the brain lesion structure into separate regions according to the characteristics of the pixels in MRIs. Kim *et al.* [15] used seeded region growing–based approach for segmentation in which the seed pixel(s) are chosen randomly. The surrounding pixels are compared with the seed pixels and categorize on the basis of homogeneity with the seed pixels. In the proposed work, region-based segmentation has been done, seeds are automatically selected, and the spatial domain is divided into small clusters on the basis of thresholding. The clusters are recursively divided into smaller regions to minimize the error and increase a better hypothesis for predicting the brain tumor in the MRIs.

14.2.2   Generative Model With Weighted Aggregation

Corso *et al.* [16] used multilevel segmentation for segmenting edema (swelling due to fluid leakage) and the tumor. The work has been done specifically on glioblastoma tumor of the brain. Glioblastoma initiates from

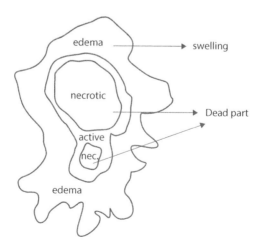

Figure 14.6 The different parts of brain tumor on the basis of T1 and T2 MRIs [16].

glial cells, which are responsible for maintaining the good health of the brain. It is a fast-growing tumor. The tumor is majorly comprised of a dead part which is known as the necrotic and active part. Adema is also the part of the brain which is basically the swelling caused by the leakage of the plasma. Figure 14.6 shows the region of various parts of growing glioblastoma tumor on the basis of MRI (T1 and T2 weighted).

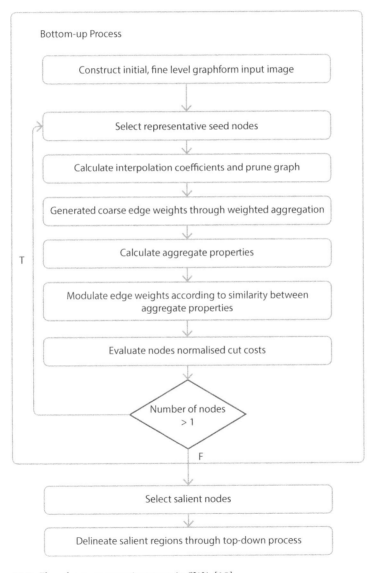

Figure 14.7 Flowchart representing steps in SWA [19].

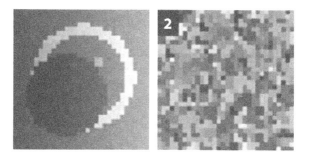

Figure 14.8 Coarsening of the pixel representation of the portion of MR image.

T1 and T2 are the types of MR images which differ on the basis of contrast and brightness to ease the manual prediction of brain tumor by the doctor. Glioblastoma is one of the common brain tumors which is nearly 40% [17] of all brain tumors patients of almost all ages and having a very short postoperative time of survival nearly 8 months [18]. Basically, in this method, the MR image is considered as a graph of pixels (vertex).

Each voxel in the MR image is considered as a node in a graph G connected with six neighbors. Now, the segmentation according to the weighted aggregation algorithm is used to coarsening the graph recursively until some portion of interest is encountered as shown in Figure 14.7. The flowchart of the process of segmentation on the basis of weight aggregation is shown in Figure 14.8.

The process of SWA (Segmentation by Weight Aggregation) is divided into two broad processes that are bottom-up in which the construction of graph pyramids is done. Followed by top-down, in which with the help of pyramids region of salient (interested) nodes are identified and defined in the boundary.

As we can see, image is just a grayscale representation of the portion of the MR image, and then in image 2, gray pixels are represented with colors. Then, iterative coarsening is done for getting the interesting region.

14.3   Conclusion

In this chapter, we discuss the importance of automatic analysis of MRIs for the detection of a brain tumor which could be achieved with the process of brain tumor segmentation. Many researchers have proposed various methods of segmentation, and almost every method of brain tumor segmentation can be categorized into two broad categories that are generative and discriminative models. These are the two basic approaches which are used in various state-of-the art methods for segmenting the brain tumor on MR images to automate the process of detecting tumor for the doctors. The generative model basically works on the data which are not pre-labeled, whereas discriminative model requires the pre-labeled data for the hypothesis.

References

1. Menze, B.H., Jakab, A., Bauer, S., Kalpathy-Cramer, J., Farahani, K., Kirby, J., Burren, Y., Porz, N., Slotboom, J., Wiest, R. *et al.*, The multimodal brain tumor image segmentation benchmark (brats). *IEEE Trans. Med. Imaging*, 34, 10, 1993–2024, 2015.

2. Agn, M., Puonti, O., Law, I., af Rosenschöld, P., van Leemput, K., Brain tumor segmentation by a generative model with a prior on tumor shape, in: *Proceeding of the multimodal brain tumor image segmentation challenge*, pp. 1–4, 2015.

3. Corso, J.J., Sharon, E., Dube, S., El-Saden, S., Sinha, U., Yuille, A., Efficient multilevel brain tumor segmentation with integrated bayesian model classification. *IEEE Trans. Med. Imaging*, 27, 5, 629–640, 2008.

4. Menze, B.H., Van Leemput, K., Lashkari, D., Weber, M.A., Ayache, N., Golland, P., A generative model for brain tumor segmentation in multimodal images, in: *International conference on medical image computing and computer-assisted intervention*, Springer, pp. 151–159, 2010.

5. Prastawa, M., Bullitt, E., Ho, S., Gerig, G., A brain tumor segmentation framework based on outlier detection. *Med. Image Anal.*, 8, 3, 275–283, 2004.

6. Bauer, S., Nolte, L.P., Reyes, M., Fully automatic segmentation of brain tumor images using support vector machine classification in combination with hierarchical conditional random field regularization, in: *International conference on medical image computing and computer-assisted intervention*, Springer, pp. 354–361, 2011.

7. Hamamci, A., Kucuk, N., Karaman, K., Engin, K., Unal, G., Tumor-cut: segmentation of brain tumors on contrast enhanced mr images for radiosurgery applications. *IEEE Trans. Med. Imaging*, 31, 3, 790–804, 2012.

8. Lun, T. and Hsu, W., Brain tumor segmentation using deep convolutional neural network, in: *Proceedings of BRATS-MICCAI*, 2016.

9. Pratondo, A., Chui, C.K., Ong, S.H., Integrating machine learning with region-based active contourmodels in medical image segmentation. *J. Vis. Commun. Image Represent.*, 43, 1–9, 2017.

10. Chang, Y.-L. and Li, X., Adaptive Image Region-Growing. *IEEE Trans. Image Process.*, 3, 6, 302, 1994.

11. Rays, S.P. and Udupa, J.K., Shape-based interpolation of multidimensional objects. *IEEE Trans. Med. Imaging*, 9, 1, 32–42, 1990.

12. Gong, I., Kulikowski, C., Mezrich, R., Valley-enhanced histogram computation for MR image segmentation. Presented at the *Ann. Meeting of the American Society of Neuroradiology*, Mar. 1991.

13. Adams, R. and Bischof, L., Seeded region growing. *IEEE Trans. PAMI*, 16, 6, 641–647, June 1994.

14. Reutter, B.W., Klein, G.J., Huesman, R.H., Automated 3-D Segmentation of Respiratory-Gated PET Transmission Images. *IEEE Trans. Nucl. Sci.*, 44, 302, 6, 1997.

15. Kim, J., Feng, D.D., Cai, T.W., Eberl, S., Automatic 3d temporal kinetics segmentation of dynamic emission tomography image using adaptive region growing cluster analysis, in: *Nuclear science symposium conference record*, vol. 3, IEEE, pp. 1580–1583, 2002.

16. Corso, J.J., Sharon, E., Dube, S., El-Saden, S., Sinha, U., Yuille, A., "Efficient multilevel brain tumor segmentation with integrated bayesian model classification". *IEEE Trans. Med. Imaging*, 27, 5, 629–640, 2008.

17. Smirniotopoulos, J.G., The newWHO classification of brain tumors. *Neuroimaging Clin. N. Am.*, 9, 4, 595–613, Nov. 1999.

18. Patel, M.R. and Tse, V., Diagnosis and staging of brain tumors. *Semin. Roentgenol.*, 39, 3, 347–360, 2004.

19. Neilson, R. and B.N.M., Image segmentation by weighted aggregation with gradient orientation histograms, in: *Southern African Telecommunication Networks and Applications Conference, SATNAC*, 2007.

15

Early Detection of Type 2 Diabetes Mellitus Using Deep Neural Network–Based Model

Varun Sapra[1] and Luxmi Sapra[2*]

[1]*Department of Systemics, University of Petroleum and Energy Studies, Dehradun, India*
[2]*Dev Bhoomi Institute of Technology, Dehradun, India*

Abstract

According to International Diabetes Federation, 463 million people are diabetic worldwide. Due to change in lifestyle, the disease has effected many people drastically affecting the quality of life and now considered as a global threat. Diabetes is aggravated over time if not treated properly. People with diabetes are more vulnerable to the severe effects of the COVID-19. It can lead to more disease such as kidney disease, stroke, heart disease, and many more. It is essential to identify the disease in its early stage so that preventive steps can be taken. Early detection can recommend the lifestyle changes and medication, hence delay its progression and further complication. Due to digital revolution, health sector produces enormous amount of data in the form of patient history, pathological reports, images, prescription and health insurance claims, etc. Extracting knowledge from these kinds of data is still a challenge. Advancement in computation methods enables researches to uncover the hidden, interesting, and complex pattern from data. One of such computational method is machine learning. Different intelligent computational methods have been explored by researchers in last one decade. This chapter focuses on implementing deep neural network for early identification of diabetes mellitus. For this purpose, benchmark datasets available on UCI machine repository and Kaggle are explored. In this chapter, a deep neural network–based framework is suggested for early detection of disease. This framework can be an adjunct tool in clinical practices.

Keywords: Machine learning, diabetes, artificial intelligence, computational intelligence, UCI machine repository

Corresponding author: luxmi.sapra@gmail.com

Rohit Tanwar, S. Balamurugan, R. K. Saini, Vishal Bharti and Premkumar Chithaluru (eds.) Advanced Healthcare Systems: Empowering Physicians with IoT-Enabled Technologies, (305–318) © 2022 Scrivener Publishing LLC

15.1   Introduction

Diabetes is one of the most common diseases that is escalating at an alarming rate. As per one of the reports of the World Health Organization, it is one of the foremost causes of mortality and morbidity in the world and about 422 million people worldwide are suffering from diabetes and around 1.6 million people died in 2016 [1]. Diabetes is classified as type 1 and type 2 diabetes, where 5% to 10% of all diabetes cases that belong to type 1 and type 2 account for more than 90% of all cases with higher risks for people over age of 45 and overweight people [2]. Type 2 diabetes is considered as a chronic disease which arises due to the inability of the body to use insulin properly, which results in unusual blood sugar levels. In one of the reports published by India Today, almost 98 million people will suffer with type 2 diabetes by 2030 in India [3, 4], and according to the survey conducted by American Diabetes Foundation in 2015, diabetes mellitus (DM) was considered as one of the top 10 causes of death in the US [5].

There are no obvious clinical indications for the early identification of type 2 diabetes which is the main reason for ignorance and patients are not able to get medications at right times. Therefore, it is important to detect the disease early to prevent and treat type 2 DM. As per the medical experts, if the disease is discovered at an early stage, the chances of recovery will be greater and people can live happy and healthy life [6, 7]. Due to digital revolution and advancements in computation methods, various intelligent learning schemes have been used for early detection of disease.

Krishnan *et al.* [8] conducted a methodical review to predict the risk of DM after gestational DM (GDM). The authors used prognostic machine learning techniques and identified predisposing factors that can be considered as input variables to the applied methods to predict the risk of DM. Bayu *et al.* [9] in their research applied different machine learning methods like C4.5, naïve Bayes, IBk, and decision tree to obtain information from historical data. For experimental purpose, they have collected data from Mohammad Hoesin public hospital in Southern Sumatera. During their study, they identified few major attributes like smoker, gestational history, and plasma insulin that contribute significantly to the study. Dewangan and Pragati [10], in their study, implemented hybrid methods by combining two different techniques. They have implemented hybrid method with C4.5 and random forest and second method with multi-layer perceptron (MLP) and Bayes net classification model. They also emphasized on data partitioning for training and testing data, and how performance indicators changed a lot on the basis of the ratio of training and testing data size. In their study, they have used 85:15 ratio for training and testing. Their study revealed that the hybrid model with MLP and Bayes net classification performed better with accuracy of 81.89% than the other models used by them. Ban *et al.* in their study examined the importance of gene-gene interactions. The author investigated data from Korean cohort studies with 408 single-nucleotide polymorphisms (SNPs) in 87 genes. They used support vector machine (SVM) to evaluate the association between SNPs and type 2 diabetes with 10-fold cross-validation. With radial basis function (RBF) with 14 SNPs and 12 genes, they were able to achieve the prediction rate of 65.3%. Similarly, they achieved the prediction rate of 70.9% and 70.6% on subpopulation datasets of men and women with different SNP combinations [11]. Mohebbi *et al.* in their study proposed a novel algorithm based on simulated Continuous Glucose Monitoring (CGM) signals for the early detection of type 2 diabetes. They further implemented different machine learning techniques on the CGM signals. They implemented MLP, logistic regression, and convolutional neural network (CNN) and were able to achieve 77.5% accuracy with CNN [12]. Faruqui *et al.* in their work used deep learning–based model for the forecasting of next day glucose levels of the patients. They have used mobile tools for the collection of data from 10 obese type 2 diabetic patients over 6 months. Their proposed model was able to achieve a considerable accuracy of ±10% of the actual values [13]. Frimpong *et al.* suggested a feed forward network for the detection of type 2 diabetes. They have used Pima Indian diabetes dataset for the experimental purpose and their proposed model was able to achieve 97.27% and 96.09% accuracy for training and testing data, respectively [14].

15.2 Data Set

In this work, a deep neural network machine learning model has been suggested for early detection of DM. The data set used for experimental purpose is obtained from UCI machine repository [15].

There are a total of 520 number of instances and 17 features such as age, gender (Gen), polydipsia (POLYD), sudden weight loss (SWL), weakness (WK), polyphagia (POLYP), polyuria (PLOY), genital thrush (GT), itching (ITC), irritability (IRT), partial paresis (PR), muscle stiffness (MS), alopecia (AP), visual blurring (VB), delayed healing (DH), and obesity (OB), as shown in Table 15.1.

Table 15.1 Description of the dataset.

S. no.	Attribute	Description	Value
1.	AGE	Age of the subject in years	Min - 16, Max - 90
2.	GEN	Gender of the subject	Male (0), Female (1)
3.	PLOY	Polyuria : frequent urination	(yes), (no)
4.	POLYD	Polydipsia : excessive thirst	(yes), (no)
5.	AP	Alopecia	(yes), (no)
6.	SWL	Sudden weight loss	(yes), (no)
7.	POLYP	Polyphagia : extreme hunger	(yes), (no)
8.	GT	Genital thrush	(yes), (no)
9.	WK	Weakness	(yes), (no)
10.	VB	Visual blurring	(yes), (no)
11.	PR	Partial paresis	(yes), (no)
12.	IRT	Irritability	(yes), (no)
13.	DH	Delayed healing	(yes), (no)
14.	MS	Muscle stiffness	(yes), (no)
15.	ITC	Itching	(yes), (no)
16.	OB	Obesity	(yes), (no)
17.	Class		Positive - 1 Negative - 0

15.2.1   Data Insights

The dataset contains records of 520 patients, out of which 328 were males and 192 were females. Figure 15.1 shows the ratio of males and females having type 2 diabetes. It is evident from the data under consideration that females are more prone to diabetes than men.

Figure 15.2 shows the ratio of obese and non-obese males and females having type 2 diabetes. It is clear from the data that obesity does not play a significant role in type 2 diabetes.

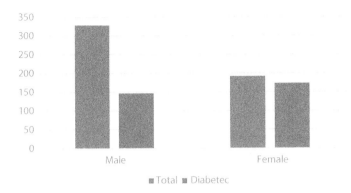

Figure 15.1 Ratio of number of males and females with type 2 diabetes.

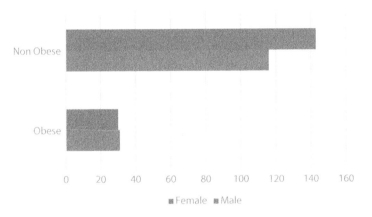

Figure 15.2 Number of obese and non-obese males and females with type 2 diabetes.

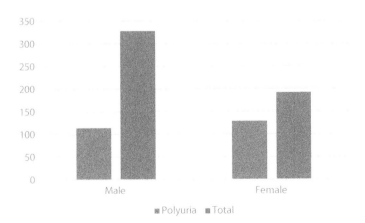

Figure 15.3 Ratio of males and females having polyuria and suffering from type 2 diabetes.

Polyuria is considered as one of the most evident factor for the type 2 diabetes. It is considered as one of the key attributes that contributes maximum for the occurrence of type 2 diabetes in patients [16, 17]. Figure 15.3 shows the ratio of males and females with polyuria and positive for type 2 diabetes.

15.3   Feature Engineering

In medical domain, all the features are not relevant to the analysis and may contain redundancy. Large feature space may increase the computation time and complexity. It may contain a false correlation that hinders the learning process of an algorithm. Hence, choosing relevant

Table 15.2 Weights of features with information gain measure.

S. no.	Weight	Features
1	0.362251	Polyuria
2	0.359056	Polydipsia
3	0.16342	Gender
4	0.148772	Sudden weight loss
5	0.144653	Partial paresis
6	0.087842	Polyphagia
7	0.072873	Irritability
8	0.051163	Alopecia
9	0.046606	Visual blurring
10	0.042666	Weakness
11	0.022394	Age
12	0.010973	Muscle stiffness
13	0.009046	Genital thrush
14	0.003851	Obesity
15	0.001595	Delayed healing
16	0.000129	Itching

features that contribute more to accurate prediction results in faster and accurate diagnosis of the disease [18]. Most of the researches used ranking methods because of its simplicity and their ability to rank features that has an influence on the target class. Information gain is widely used method for feature selection. It is a filter method that can be used for attribute selection [19]. It is based on evaluation of the gain of each feature with the perspective of the target class. It is defined as the amount of information provided by the attribute. In order to compute the information gain of the variable, entropy of the target variable is computed which requires frequency count of the target class. We implemented ranking by using information gain criteria. Table 15.2 presents the ranking of attributes obtained by information gain measure. Top 10 features are selected to construct the model. The features selected for modeling are polyuria, polydipsia, gender, sudden weight loss, partial paralysis, polyphagia, irritability, alopecia, visual blurring, and weakness.

The feature polyuria has the highest weightage and itching has the lowest weightage. As shown in Figure 15.4.

The correlation matrix displays the relationship between different attributes. The value in negative depicts negative correlation and in positive depicts positive correlation and zero depicts no correlation. We used Pearson's correlation coefficient formula to compute the correlation matrix. Figure 15.5 shows the correlation matrix [20, 21] of the features. Covariance matrix depicts covariance between each pair of features as well as the extent to which corresponding variables are moving in the same

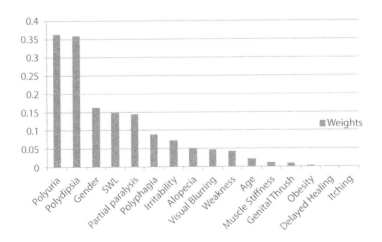

Figure 15.4 Ranking of attributes.

Attribut...	Gender	Polyuria	Polydip...	sudden ...	weakne...	Polypha...	visual bl...	Irritability	partial p...	Alopecia	class
Gender	1	0.269	0.312	0.282	0.124	0.220	0.208	0.014	0.332	-0.328	0.449
Polyuria	0.269	1	0.599	0.447	0.263	0.374	0.235	0.238	0.442	-0.144	0.666
Polydipsia	0.312	0.599	1	0.406	0.332	0.317	0.331	0.203	0.442	-0.311	0.649
sudden	0.282	0.447	0.406	1	0.283	0.244	0.069	0.140	0.264	-0.203	0.437
weakness	0.124	0.263	0.332	0.283	1	0.180	0.301	0.147	0.273	0.090	0.243
Polypha	0.220	0.374	0.317	0.244	0.180	1	0.294	0.239	0.374	-0.053	0.343
visual bl	0.208	0.235	0.331	0.069	0.301	0.294	1	0.077	0.364	0.015	0.251
Irritability	0.014	0.238	0.203	0.140	0.147	0.239	0.077	1	0.152	0.044	0.299
partial p	0.332	0.442	0.442	0.264	0.273	0.374	0.364	0.152	1	-0.222	0.432
Alopecia	-0.328	-0.144	-0.311	-0.203	0.090	-0.053	0.015	0.044	-0.222	1	-0.268
class	0.449	0.666	0.649	0.437	0.243	0.343	0.251	0.299	0.432	-0.268	1

Figure 15.5 Correlation matrix.

Attribut...	Gender	Polyuria	Polydip...	sudden ...	weakne...	Polypha...	visual bl...	Irritability	partial p...	Alopecia	class
Gender	0.233	-0.065	-0.075	-0.067	-0.030	-0.053	-0.050	-0.003	-0.080	0.075	-0.106
Polyuria	-0.065	0.250	0.149	0.110	0.065	0.093	0.059	0.051	0.110	-0.034	0.162
Polydipsia	-0.075	0.149	0.248	0.100	0.082	0.079	0.082	0.043	0.109	-0.074	0.157
sudden	-0.067	0.110	0.100	0.244	0.069	0.060	0.017	0.030	0.065	-0.048	0.105
weakness	-0.030	0.065	0.082	0.069	0.243	0.044	0.074	0.031	0.067	0.021	0.058
Polypha	-0.053	0.093	0.079	0.060	0.044	0.249	0.073	0.051	0.092	-0.013	0.083
visual bl	-0.050	0.059	0.082	0.017	0.074	0.073	0.248	0.016	0.090	0.003	0.061
Irritability	-0.003	0.051	0.043	0.030	0.031	0.051	0.016	0.184	0.032	0.009	0.063
partial p	-0.080	0.110	0.109	0.065	0.067	0.092	0.090	0.032	0.246	-0.052	0.104
Alopecia	0.075	-0.034	-0.074	-0.048	0.021	-0.013	0.003	0.009	-0.052	0.226	-0.062
class	-0.106	0.162	0.157	0.105	0.058	0.083	0.061	0.063	0.104	-0.062	0.237

Figure 15.6 Covariance matrix.

direction. Variance is defined as the degree of variability in data. Figure 15.6 shows the covariance matrix.

15.4 Framework for Early Detection of Disease

The framework is developed for early detection of the diabetes. The framework consists of different modules such as feature engineering modules where feature reduction is done with the help of filtering out the low ranking attributes with the help of information gain filter method. The neural network model is then trained using deep learning neural network. The performance measures such as accuracy, precision, recall, and F-score are

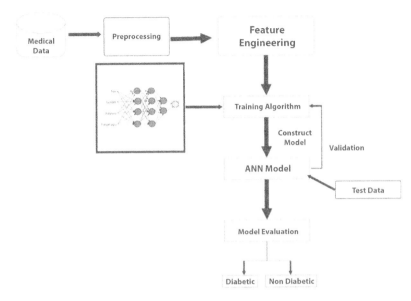

Figure 15.7 Machine learning framework for identification of diabetic.

used to evaluate the deep learning model. Figure 15.7 presents the proposed framework for early detection of the disease.

15.4.1   Deep Neural Network

It is an artificial neural network with one input, one output, and multiple inner layers or hidden layers for computation. The more the number of layers of computation, the deeper the network is considered. These networks are widely used for recognizing complex relationships between inputs and outputs and for the processing of information that contains a number of layered interconnected elements [22, 23]. Deep neural network has the ability to combine low-level features layer by layer to form high-level features, and hence, it has better feature expression and ability to find complex relationships between vast dataset [24, 25].

In the proposed model, deep learning model is trained by using 70% of data and tested using 30% data with 400 epochs. ReLU activation function is used with Adam optimizer. We trained the deep learning model with four layers.

15.5   Result

The model when implemented on complete dataset achieved the accuracy of 97% as shown in Figure 15.8 and when implemented on reduced dataset with 10 features achieved the accuracy of 98.9% as shown in Figure 15.9. Diabetes data set is used for analysis purpose. Reducing the dimensionality of the data set is proved efficient. Table 15.4 shows the 1.9% improvement of accuracy. Other performance parameters such as value of precision is also improved in case of non-diabetic subjects as well as diabetic subjects.

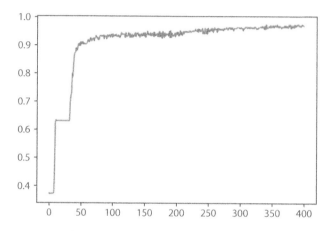

Figure 15.8 Accuracy of deep learning–based neural network without dimensionality reduction.

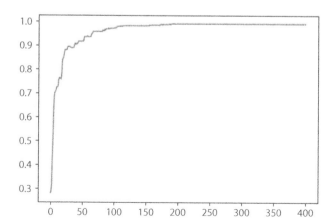

Figure 15.9 Accuracy of deep learning–based neural network with dimensionality reduction.

Table 15.3 Performance parameters of deep learning–based model without dimensionality reduction.

	Precision	Recall	F1 score	Accuracy
Non-diabetic	0.94	0.99	0.96	97%
Diabetic	0.99	0.97	0.98	

Table 15.4 Performance parameters of deep learning–based model with dimensionality reduction.

	Precision	Recall	F1 score	Accuracy
Non-diabetic	0.98	0.99	0.99	98.9%
Diabetic	1.00	0.99	0.99	

Tables 15.3 and 15.4 show the value of performance parameters. Recall and F1score for diabetic patients are improved by 2% and 1%, respectively.

15.6   Conclusion

Nowadays, researchers are using artificial neural network approaches to solve complex problems. Even in medical domain, artificial neural network–based methods are popular. Early diagnosis of disease is essential in order to take the proper course of action so that fatalities can be reduced. Machine learning–based framework is proposed for early detection of diabetes. The results show that deep learning–based approach leads to promising results by using routine clinical parameters. These parameters can be easily obtained from the hospitals. The proposed method uses feature engineering to reduce the feature space by filtering out the redundant and irrelevant variables. Feature engineering improves the computational time and accuracy of the algorithms. The framework can be considered an aid to medical practitioners for fast and accurate identification of disease.

References

1. Swapna, G., Vinayakumar, R., Soman, K.P., Diabetes detection using deep learning algorithms. *ICT Express*, 4, 4, 243–246, 2018.

2. Marshall, M.C., Diabetes in African Americans. *Postgrad. Med. J.*, 81, 962, 734–740, 2005.

3. Chang, X. and Lilly, J.H., Evolutionary design of a fuzzy classifier from data. *IEEE Trans. Syst. Man Cybern. Part B (Cybern.)*, 34, 4, 1894–1906, 2004.

4. Ampofo, A.G. and Boateng, E.B., Beyond 2020: Modelling obesity and diabetes prevalence. *Diabetes Res. Clin. Pract.*, 167, 108362, 2020.

5. Li, H.X., Wang, Y., Zhang, G., Probabilistic fuzzy classification for stochastic data. *IEEE Trans. Fuzzy Syst.*, 25, 6, 1391–1402, 2017.

6. Akula, R., Nguyen, N., Garibay, I., Supervised Machine Learning based Ensemble Model for Accurate Prediction of Type 2 Diabetes, in: *2019 SoutheastCon*, pp. 1–8, IEEE, 2019, April.

7. Carrier, M.A. and Beverly, E.A., Focus on the Positive: A Qualitative Study of Positive Experiences Living With Type 1 or Type 2 Diabetes. *Clin. Diabetes*, Vol 39, 2, 176–187, 2021.

8. Krishnan, D.R., Menakath, G.P., Radhakrishnan, A., Himavarshini, Y., Aparna, A., Mukundan, K., Maddipati, C., Evaluation of predisposing factors of diabetes mellitus post gestational diabetes mellitus using machine learning techniques, in: *2019 IEEE Student Conference on Research and Development (SCOReD)*, IEEE, pp. 81–85, 2019, October.

9. Tama, B.A., An early detection method of type-2 diabetes mellitus in public hospital. *Telkomnika*, 9, 2, 287–294, 2011.

10. Kumar Dewangan, A. and Agrawal, P., Classification of diabetes mellitus using machine learning techniques. *Int. J. Eng. Appl. Sci.*, 2, 5, 257905, 2015.

11. Ban, H.J., Heo, J.Y., Oh, K.S., Park, K.J., Identification of type 2 diabetes-associated combination of SNPs using support vector machine. *BMC Genet.*, 11, 1, 1–11, 2010.

12. Mohebbi, A., Aradóttir, T.B., Johansen, A.R., Bengtsson, H., Fraccaro, M., Mørup, M., A deep learning approach to adherence detection for type 2 diabetics, in: *2017 39th Annual International Conference of the IEEE Engineering in Medicine and Biology Society (EMBC)*, 2017, IEEE, pp. 2896–2899, 2017, July.

13. Faruqui, S.H.A., Du, Y., Meka, R., Alaeddini, A., Li, C., Shirinkam, S., Wang, J., Development of a deep learning model for dynamic forecasting of blood glucose level for type 2 diabetes mellitus: secondary analysis of a randomized controlled trial. *JMIR mHealth uHealth*, 7, 11, e14452, 2019.

14. Frimpong, E.A., Oluwasanmi, A., Baagyere, E.Y., Zhiguang, Q., A feedforward artificial neural network model for classification and detection of type 2 diabetes. *J. Phys.: Conf. Ser.*, 1734, 1, 012026, 2021, January, IOP Publishing.

15. https://archive.ics.uci.edu/ml/datasets/Early+stage+diabetes+risk+prediction+dataset.#

16. Pawar, S.D., Thakur, P., Radhe, B.K., Jadhav, H., Behere, V., Pagar, V., The accuracy of polyuria, polydipsia, polyphagia, and Indian Diabetes Risk Score in adults screened for diabetes mellitus type-II. *Med. J. Dr. DY Patil Univ.*, 10, 3, 263, 2017.

17. Nigro, N., Grossmann, M., Chiang, C., Inder, W.J., Polyuria-polydipsia syndrome: a diagnostic challenge. *Intern. Med. J.*, 48, 3, 244–253, 2018.

18. Nargesian, F., Samulowitz, H., Khurana, U., Khalil, E.B., Turaga, D.S., Learning Feature Engineering for Classification, in: *Ijcai*, pp. 2529–2535., 2017, August.

19. Azhagusundari, B. and Thanamani, A.S., Feature selection based on information gain. *Int. J. Innov. Technol. Exploring Eng. (IJITEE)*, 2, 2, 18–21, 2013.

20. Kijsipongse, E., Suriya, U., Ngamphiw, C., Tongsima, S., Efficient large pearson correlation matrix computing using hybrid mpi/cuda, in: *2011 Eighth International Joint Conference on Computer Science and Software Engineering (JCSSE)*, 2011, IEEE, pp. 237–241, 2011, May.

21. Langfelder, P. and Horvath, S., Fast R functions for robust correlations and hierarchical clustering. *J. Stat. Software*, 46, 11, pp. 1–17, 2012.

22. Samek, W., Binder, A., Montavon, G., Lapuschkin, S., Müller, K.R., Evaluating the visualization of what a deep neural network has learned. *IEEE Trans. Neural Networks Learn. Syst.*, 28, 11, 2660–2673, 2016.

23. Bau, D., Zhu, J.Y., Strobelt, H., Lapedriza, A., Zhou, B., Torralba, A., Understanding the role of individual units in a deep neural network. *Proc. Natl. Acad. Sci.*, 117, 48, 30071–30078, 2020.

24. Nadesh, R.K. and Arivuselvan, K., Type 2: Diabetes mellitus prediction using Deep Neural Networks classifier. *Int. J. Cognit. Comput. Eng.*, 1, 55–61, 2020.

25. Bengion, Y. and Delalleau, O., On the expressive power of deep architectures. *Proc. of the 14th International Conference on Discovery Science*, pp. 18–36, Springer-Verlag, Berlin, 2011.

16

A Comprehensive Analysis on Masked Face Detection Algorithms

Pranjali Singh[1]*, Amitesh Garg[2] and Amritpal Singh[1]

[1]Dept. of Computer Science & Engineering, Dr B.R. Ambedkar National Institute of Technology, Jalandhar, India
[2]Sabre Travel Technologies Pvt. Ltd., Bengaluru, Karnataka, India

Abstract

The COVID-19 is an ongoing crisis that has resulted in a large number of fatalities and safety concerns. People also carry masks to cover themselves to effectively prevent the transmission of this virus. In this situation, recognizing a face is very challenging. In certain cases, like facial attendance, face access control, and facial security, this makes traditional facial recognition technology ineffective, for that urgent requirement to improve this recognition performance and use the technology on the masked face. During the current pandemic, the main objective of researchers is to deal with these problems through quick and accurate approaches. Throughout this chapter, we suggest a clear way centered on removing masked area and deep learning–related techniques to resolve the issues of mask detection. Another way of finding the masked face is to go through TensorFlow, YOLOv5, SSDMNV2, SVM, OpenCV, and Keras. The first phase is discarding the area of the masked face. Next, to determine the best aspects from the areas collected for that, we use a pre-instruction of deep CNN (Convolutional Neural Network). We used labeled image data to train the CNN model. With a 98.7% accuracy, a face mask is identified by the proposed system. By using the SVM classifier, the dataset of RMFD had a testing accuracy of 99.64%. In SMFD, it achieved 99.49% testing accuracy, and in LFW, it achieved 100% testing accuracy. SSDMNV2 used in this paper yields a 92.64% accuracy score and a 93% F1 score.

*Corresponding author: pranjalis.cs.19@nitj.ac.in

Rohit Tanwar, S. Balamurugan, R. K. Saini, Vishal Bharti and Premkumar Chithaluru (eds.) *Advanced Healthcare Systems: Empowering Physicians with IoT-Enabled Technologies*, (319–334) © 2022 Scrivener Publishing LLC

Keywords: COVID-19 epidemic, face recognition, machine learning algorithms and frameworks

16.1   Introduction

The COVID-19 outbreak has been major healthcare and social problem in the world since November 2019. As per the WHO (World Health Organization), the pandemic is causing a global health emergency, making this the most recent human health virus outbreak throughout the last century so wearing a mask is required. Before this pandemic, people used to carry the mask only to protect themselves from air pollution. This pandemic is circulated through the respiratory system which is spreading very fast. Given the fact that many states mandate people to wear masks in public areas, a lot of people forget or fail to wear masks or wear masks incorrectly [1]. Such facts will increase the speed of disease and bring a greater burden on the public healthcare system. Despite the effectiveness of many vaccinations, wearing a mask is also one of the most successful and cost-effective ways to avoid 80 % of respiratory infections. As a result, many monitoring systems have been established to provide efficient supervision in airports, hospitals, public transit systems, sporting events, and retail locations to detect the mask. This pandemic affects many areas like the institute, Organization.

Medical masks are surgical or procedure masks that are flat or pleated (some appear like cups) that are attached to the head with belts. Wearing a surgical mask is among the ways of preventing the transmission of such respiratory infections, such as COVID-19, in afflicted regions. Masks, on the other hand, should be worn in compliance with good practice guidelines to be safe. Single-use options include FFP2 face masks, surgical face masks, and N95 face masks. Even so, wearing a mask alone would be inadequate and provide proper security, and additional, similarly important steps should be taken. To avoid the spread of COVID-19, masks should be used in conjunction with hand washing as well as other IPC interventions.

Presently, there is no single drug or vaccine available to prevent. Over five million cases across 188 countries have been infected with COVID-19 in less than 6 months and because of close contact. So, the only choice left is just to take the best care and keep away from the disease. For example, keep social distancing, wear a mask, and regularly wash hand. Many countries have regulations that require people to wear masks in public. This legislation has been started in many countries as an approach to the rapid rise in cases and deaths. Researchers have discovered that wearing masks will minimize the risk of COVID-19.

The method of screening requires the identification of someone who does not wear a face mask. Here, the dataset is a collection without mask and with mask images and is using real-time mask detection through a webcam. Mask detection by using the popular deep learning technique is useful for figuring out who wears the mask and who does not and that can be used on any common device.

Deep transfer learning was used to extract features, and it was paired with three traditional machine learning algorithms. The greatest thing regarding deep learning is that there is deep architecture in all the models. Deep architecture has many layers, becoming the biggest opponents of deep architecture that has a few hidden layers. The CNN is used to function extraction from images, and then, several hidden layers learn these features. Also, SSDMNV2 technology and SVM technology are used to detect the mask detection.

Here, a comparison among them to identify the most appropriate algorithm that reached the best accuracy while taking the least amount of time during the training and detection processes is performed.

16.2 Literature Review

Mostly, studies focused on deciding whether or not such a person wears a mask. For that, many algorithms are there to determine this like LLE-CNN, SVM, SSDMNV2, and K-NN classifier.

Z. Wang *et al.* [1] introduce an article and mentioned the challenges faced by the United States in this Epidemic, such as how the epidemic developed day by day due to respiratory droplets created by breathing, talking, coughing, and sneezing [3, 4]. To avoid this, mask is mandatory to keep safe from this epidemic, and also mask can reduce respiratory infection up to 80%, and for this, the mask detection system which can monitor and provide supervision for many places like hospitals, transport, venues, airports, and other location is made [1, 2]. In this article, the author proposed browser-based edge computing which can detect the face mask. This edge computing-based solution is serverless and can be handled on any devices like tablet, mobile, and desktops through internet connections with the help of the browser. Edge computing solution reduces the hardware costs and this is integrating with YOLO (deep learning model), NCNN, and virtual machine. It is design with minimal limitation and risk and has the low computation, low network bandwidth, and high speed for detection.

This solution assists in determining whether or not the individual is wearing a mask, as well as whether or not the mask is appropriate.

This pandemic is generating a health issue. M. Loey *et al.* [2] introduced the paper using the hybrid model like machine learning and deep learning to detect the mask. Here, models have two parts, the first part is having extraction of feature by ResNet50 and the other second part is for the process of classification for face mask by using SVM, decision tree, and another ensembled base algorithm. Here, the authors choose three datasets for determining the masked face. The datasets are the Simulated Masked Face Dataset (SMFD), the Real-World Masked Face Dataset (RMFD), and the Labeled Faces in the Wild (LFW). Herein, the result shows 99.64% accuracy in the dataset of RMFD by using SVM classifier, 99.49% accuracy in the SMFD dataset, and 100% accuracy in the LFW dataset.

Several techniques and algorithm are used in mask detection with various models. P. Nagrath *et al.* [3] introduced masked detection by using computer vision and image processing. Here, the approaches used in this paper to detect mask are deep learning, Keras, OpenCV, and Tensorflow, which can be helpful in the purpose of safety. The authors introduced one term that is SSDMNV2 approach which is the combination of MobileNetV2 and single-shot detector. These are the models which can be used for training and development of dataset and having very lightweight and can be used for mask detection using webcam in devices like Rasberry Pi and NVIDIA Jetson Nano. Dataset has been collected from different sources. Other researchers can be used this dataset for an advanced model like a facial landmark, part of face detection, and recognition of face process. By this technique and algorithm, the accuracy is 92.64% and the F1 score is 93%.

Almost every sector which belongs to development has collapsed because of COVID-19. Md. M. Rahman *et al.* [4] introduced a paper in which it talks about the healthcare system which gets affected in COVID-19 and one of the major precautionary measures is to use the mask [2]. The major part of this paper is to find out those people who are not carrying the mask in a smart city by using CCTV cameras which can reduce the growth of this pandemic. When an individual without a mask is identified, the city network notifies the appropriate authority. The main motive of this work is to find out who does not wear a mask. Dataset is collected from various sources which consist of with mask and without mask label and the architecture of deep learning is trained on these datasets. The dataset includes 1539 samples, with 80% of them being used for the training process and 20% for the testing. There are 1,231 and 308 images throughout the training and testing datasets, respectively. Here, by using this deep learning architecture, the accuracy is 98.7%.

To spread awareness about the mask in this epidemic, Y. Chen *et al.* [5] proposed a detection method based on the cell phone to fix the cause of the challenge in this epidemic. The gray level co-occurrence matrices (GLCMs) of the mask are first used to retrieve four elements and the K-Nearest Neighbor (KNN) algorithm is used to build a three-result detection technique. By using this technique, it shows an accuracy of 82.87%. The type I precision and type III recall is reached up to 92.00% and 92.59%, respectively. The authors also focused on future work to add more mask types to the detection objects. This research demonstrated that the developed mobile microscope device can be used as a helper while wearing a face mask.

Furthermore, many private and public service providers require customers to utilize the service only if they correctly wear masks. S. K. Dey *et al.* [6] proposed image processing and artificial intelligence to detect mask detection. This paper proposed a deep learning-based MobileNet Mask for multi-phase mask detection. Two datasets are trained and tested that have more than 5,200 images to detect the mask from the webcam and images. MobileNet Mask obtained an accuracy of 93% with 770 test data and nearly 100% with 276 test data. Finally, the proposed MobileNet Mask model can be implemented on light-weight computing technologies such as smartphones or embedded devices. Furthermore, this developed model incorporates cutting-edge technology to aid public and government health recommendations in the implementation of compulsory face mask legislation around the world.

Because of this pandemic, the academy faces lots of problems. S. V. Militante and N. V. Dionisio [7] proposed a certain situation that can affect the institute because still there is no vaccine available and preventive measures are only to keep safe. One of the preventive measures is to wear a face mask and use a 70% alcohol base sensitizer. Here, for detecting that a person is wearing a mask or not, deep learning is effective in detecting and classifying through the image process. The dataset comprises 25,000 images with a resolution of 224×224 pixels, and the model's accuracy after training is 96%. If the person being identified is not wearing a mask, the computer produces a Raspberry Pi–based real-time face mask recognition system that alerts and captures facial features. This paper provided a study on real-time mask detection with an alarm system using deep learning techniques and CNN. This can get more accurate and faster using this tool. By using the VGG-16 CNN model, the qualified model was able to complete its task with an output accuracy of 96%.

Detecting mask manually is a very difficult task in a crowded place. G. Jignesh Chowdary, Narinder Singh Punn *et al.* [8] used a transfer learning method to simplify the process of recognizing people who do not wear masks [3, 4]. The model is built by fine-tuning InceptionV3, a deep learning model that has already been trained. The proposed model is trained and tested using the SMFD. It achieved 99.9% accuracy during preparation and 100% accuracy during testing.

COVID-19 creates a major impact in every area like academic and organization, and manual checking of every person for the mask is a very difficult task. A. Nusrat Zereen *et al.* [9] used a technology that can automatically detect the face mask. So, two-stage mask detection is introduced. Clustering and extraction is the first phase and the second is to analyze nose reason. So, here, the total accuracy is 97.13%.

C. Li *et al.* stated in an article [10] that, to identify masked faces, the information can be completely extracted and transformed. Studies on observational and functional datasets demonstrate the feasibility of the proposed solution.

Hariri Walid introduced an article [11]. Here, author is concerned about the security during COVID-19 pandemic and gives some efficient solution based on deep learning [1]. In this paper, a method like CNN to get the best feature is applied and the MLP problem is used for convolution neural network [2].

Locally Linear Embedding-CNN (LLE-CNN) is also working for detecting face mask. LS. Ge *et al.* introduced an article [12] that used LLE-CNN to find the masked faces [2]. The first one is a large dataset of mask face that is absent and the other one is the absence of facial signals from the masked areas. To handle these issue authors introduced a dataset which is known as MAFA which has 35,806 masked faces and 30,811 images. Based on that, LLE-CNN comes into the picture and experimental findings on the MAFA dataset showed that the suggested technique substantially performs at least 15.6% of six state-of-the-art approaches.

A. Anwar and A. Raychowdhury introduced a paper [13]. This paper looks at how to improve existing facial datasets by using devices that enable masked faces to be identified with lower detection costs and higher overall classification without having to recreate the user dataset by taking new recognition photos. It is an open-source platform to effectively mask faces to create a massive dataset of masked faces [3]. The dataset developed with this tool is then used for the training of an efficient facial recognition system for masked faces with target accuracy. For the FaceNet scheme, an increase of about 38% in the positive result is reported. On a specific real-world MFR2 dataset, the performance of the retrained model is also improved and comparable accuracy is reported. In this article, the authors explored the problem of identifying masked faces with accurate accuracy across existing face detection.

16.3   Implementation Approach

A short description of the methods shown in this paper is given in this section of the paper. The approach developed here involves four major phases. The first phase is data collection, the second phase is model creation, the third phase is model training, and the final phase is evaluation of the model produced.

They have used the existing facial datasets by improving them with tools that allow the identification with a low false-positive rate of masked faces and higher overall accuracy despite allowing the user dataset to be reproduced for identification by introducing better photographs.

16.3.1   Feature Extraction

This section contains the convolutional layers which extract image features by the resize images, as well as the ReLU, which is connected after each convolution. By combining the maximum and average values, the size of the feature extraction is decreased. To produce those image characteristics, both convolutional and pooling layers work as purifiers.

16.3.2   Image Processing

During processing, the collected images that will be used in a preprocessing phase are improved explicitly for features of the image. Images are segmented during the segmentation process, which is then used to remove mask-covered regions from the background of a person's face.

16.3.3   Image Acquisition

The acquisition of images is the first step in a real-time mask detection method. Digital cameras, cellphone cameras, and scanners are used to capture high-quality photographs of a subject appearing with and without a face mask.

16.3.4   Classification

The final step is to distinguish images and train deep learning models on how to identify and classify images based on trained visual features using the labeled images. Python and OpenCV, as well as the VGG-16 CNN model, to deploy an open-source architecture through the TensorFlow module are used.

16.3.5   MobileNetV2

MobileNetV2 is a versatile architecture that can be applied to embedded systems with limited processing capabilities. Inception Net, AlexNet, LeNet, ResNet, MobileNet, and other pre-trained and well-architecture networks are examples of CNN variants. MobileNetV2 is a mobile-oriented model that is both lightweight and efficient.

16.3.6   Deep Learning Architecture

The deep learning architecture explores several important nonlinear features based on the collected data. The trained architecture is then used to forecast samples that have never been seen before. Images from various sources to train deep learning architecture are collected. CNN plays a significant role in the learning technique's architecture.

16.3.7   LeNet-5, AlexNet, and ResNet-50

LeNet-5 is a classic and basic neural network and has seven layers and seems to be computationally less demanding. Despite having the lowest scores among the chosen pre-trained models, it outperforms most models throughout the performance metric due to the simple architecture. AlexNet can do a lot of work and gets good results in our tests, but these results need a lot of model depth, which makes AlexNet computationally strong. The ResNet-50 is 50 layers in a deep residual network. Although this network has high accuracy and F1 score, it is difficult to implement in real-time due to its computational complexity.

16.3.8   Data Collection

Here, for facial recognition, two kinds of datasets, namely, with_mask and without_mask are taken. From with_mask datasets, persons who wear masks are identified, and from without_mask dataset, persons who do not wear masks are identified.

Here, this dataset is consists of 3,846 images with two classes: without mask have 1,930 images and with mask have 1,916 images as shown in Figures 16.1 and 16.2 [2].

   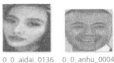

0_0_aidai_0014   0_0_aidai_0029   0_0_aidai_0043   0_0_aidai_0074   0_0_aidai_0084   0_0_aidai_0136   0_0_anhu_0004

Figure 16.1 Dataset of without mask [2].

0_0_≈◊¢   0_0_≈◊¢   0_0_≈◊¢   0_0_≈◊¢   0_0_≈◊¢   0_0_≈◊¢   0_0_≈◊¢
2020-02-23 2020-02-24 2020-02-24 2020-02-24 2020-02-24 2020-02-24 2020-02-24
132400   171804   172039   202509   205216   215234   215615

Figure 16.2 Dataset of with mask [2].

Here, the training dataset is taken, and a facial recognition system deep learning-based is designed. A high number of masked faces and unmasked faces are needed for this.

Here, it did not sustain the training images directly. For all of that, the images are eventually needed to be marked. It is among the significant processes related to the processing of data. The researcher has used a technique known as "Labeling" in this project. This tool allows developers to access labels for both the training process mostly on images and stores the details.

16.3.9 Development of Model

TensorFlow is created by the Google rank brain team and is widely used open-source library. It is among the best libraries for image processing. Throughout this project, this tool is being used to build the model. The algorithm makes the whole process easier and faster to incorporate into assignments.

The great reason for the choice of this method for data processing is the scalability of such a tool. The process of model development began with the python deployment of TensorFlow. API of TensorFlow python has already been used. Extra libraries are built into the system as well. The important aspects of TensorFlow are graphs of data flow. Here, the graphs reflect the data flow. That node in the graph contains an expression of mathematical functions. As a tensor, each edge is described. In general, the tensor is a dataset of multidimensional. All the tensor operations are conducted here. TensorFlow is being used in this project for the object detection phase.

16.3.10 Training of Model

The next move after configuring the model is to train. In deep learning, the process of training is a time-consuming resource process. Since the outcome of the process depends primarily on the efficiency of the learning process. In this phase, a training dataset that includes information, like who wears face masks correctly and who does not, has already created. All of the data is classified with the aid of another piece of software.

16.3.11 Model Testing

The final phase of the experience is checking the built model. The built model is tested to use the test dataset throughout this process. Similar to the training dataset, the device performs the set of data. After that, the procedure calculates the coefficient value and compares it to the training value.

16.4 Observation and Analysis

We got the result after studying papers by using different technologies like Tensorflow, YOLO, Keras, SSDMNV2, SVM, CNN model.

16.4.1 CNN Algorithm

Since the further result of training in overfitting on the training data, the built architecture is trained for 100 epochs. When an algorithm performs the undesirable patterns of the training samples, this is known as overfitting. As a result, training accuracy improves while test accuracy declines. Here, the trained model showed accuracy of 98.7% [4].

For about 100 epochs, the training and testing accuracy curve is shown and shows that the accuracy of both is the same. This indicates that the model is capable of generalizing to previously unknown data while avoiding overfitting.

As the number of epochs increases, the training loss decreases. The study loss is smaller than the training loss for about 30 epochs, but after that, it begins to increase, implying that now the prediction confidence begins to decline. The research loss varies within an appropriate range, reaching a peak around the 98th epoch.

The proposed framework's receiver operating characteristic (ROC) curve. The graph of ROC shows the classifier's ability to predict at various thresholds. The true positive rate and the false positive rate abbreviated as TPR and FPR, respectively, which are determined using (16.1) and (16.2), are shown on the ROC curve. For different threshold, TPR and FPR are calculated. For every possible threshold binary classifier's performance get measures in the ROC curve (AUC), here, the range of AUC is 0 to 1. When 100% correctly predicted by model, then AUC is 1, and for 100% wrong prediction, the value of AUC is 0. Here, AUC is 0.985, which means that it is a strong classifier [4].

$$\text{True Positive Rate} = \frac{True\ Positive}{True\ Positive + False\ Negative} \qquad (16.1)$$

$$\text{False Positive Rate} = \frac{False\ Positive}{True\ Negative + False\ Positve} \qquad (16.2)$$

Here, a deep learning mechanism is used to obtain the result, which has a 98% accuracy rate, as shown in Table 16.1.

By using CNN model, the accuracy achieved is 99%. The binary classification problem is solved using a deep learning model. Keras is a high-level artificial neural network API that can be used to construct a classification model.

Table 16.1 Classification report using CNN [4].

	Precision	Recall	F1 score	Support
With mask	0.99	1.00	0.99	384
Without mask	1.00	0.99	0.99	386
Accuracy			0.99	770
Macro avg	0.99	0.99	0.99	770
Weighted avg	0.99	0.99	0.99	770

16.4.2   SSDNETV2 Algorithm

The model attempted to extract feature for 60 epochs for accuracy. The training accuracy is 87.51% after 100 epochs, while when augmentation of data was used, the training accuracy is 92.64%.

After 100 epochs, the training accuracy found to be 92.64% [3]. The model's average accuracy for evaluating whether or not someone wears a mask is '93%' on a dataset [3]. The accuracy of the training dataset is almost equal to 99%. Shows a loss of less than 0.1 in the training dataset, while the loss of less than 0.1 in the validation datasets [3].

The model's roc overall accuracy is comparable to, but not equal to, the optimal roc curve. The ROC overall accuracy of 93% indicates that the model values were correctly predicted [3].

The classification report in Table 16.2 describes the SSDMNV2 model's level of recall, F1 score, precision, and accuracy.

Tables 16.3 and 16.4 display the precision, F1 score, and comparison of different models, respectively, and describe how the proposed work compares to other models.

Table 16.2 Classification report using SSDMNV2 [3].

	Precision	Recall	F1 score	Support
With mask	1.00	0.85	0.93	1104
Without mask	0.87	1.00	0.93	1105
Accuracy			0.93	2209
Macro average	0.94	0.93	0.93	2209
Weighted average	0.94	0.93	0.93	2209

Table 16.3 A comparison of various models' accuracy [3].

Architectures used	Year	Accuracy (%)	Percentage improvement
LeNet-5	1198	84.6	+9.37%
AlexNet	2012	89.2	+3.73%
SSDMNV2 (proposed method)	2020	92.64	+0%

Table 16.4 A comparison of the various models' F1 score [3].

Architectures used	Year	F1 Score	Percentage improvement
LeNet-5	1998	0.85	+9.41%
AlexNet	2012	0.88	+5.68%
VGG-16	2014	0.92	+1.09%
ResNet-50	2016	0.91	+2.2%
SSDMNV2 (proposed method)	2020	0.93	+0%

16.4.3   SVM

By using the SVM classifier on three different datasets, i.e., RMFD, SMFD, and LFW here, datasets split into three-part (testing phase, training phase, validation phase). The testing phase has 20%, the training phase has 70%, and the validation phase has 10% of data. Performance matrices will be studied in this research to test the performance of the various classifiers.

$$Accuracy = \frac{TP + TN}{TP + FP + TN + FN} \qquad (16.3)$$

$$Recall = \frac{TP}{TP + FN} \qquad (16.4)$$

$$Precision = \frac{TP}{TP + FP} \qquad (16.5)$$

$$F1\ score = 2 * \frac{Precision * Recall}{Precision + Recall} \qquad (16.6)$$

Table 16.5 Comparative analysis between different machine learning algorithms [2].

Datasets	Decision tree classifier	SVM classifier	Ensemble classifier
RMFD	~92% to 94%	98%	97%
SMFD	96%	100%	94%
Combination of RMFD and SMFD	98%	99%	100%

This accuracy, recall, precision and F1-score [2, 3] are commonly used. In the confusion matrix, true positive, true negative, false positive, and false negative sample count are all abbreviated as TP, TN, FP, and FN. The experimental findings will be summarised in three subsections, with the first describing the results of the decision trees classifier and the second presenting the results of the SVM classifier and the last shows the result of the ensemble classifier [2] (Table 16.5).

Higher accuracy achieved in the SVM classifier is 100% for the SMFD dataset, while the highest accuracy of the decision tree classifier achieved 98% and the ensemble classifier achieved 100%.

16.5   Conclusion

COVID-19 is causing havoc on the global health system. Governments around the world are fighting to keep this virus away. A hybrid model like SSDMNV2, SVM, deep learning, and machine learning for face mask detection is presented in this paper. To train the CNN model, labeled image data were used, with the images being facial images with masks and without masks. With a 98.7% accuracy, the proposed device detects a face mask.

The SSDMNV2 model was compared to other pre-existing models by training them on the same dataset. For this reason, LeNet-5, AlexNet, VGG-16, and ResNet-50 were chosen. The methodology used in this paper yields a 0.9264 accuracy score and a 0.93 F1 score. The MobilenetV2 image classifier was used to accurately identify images, which is one of the proposed approach's unique features. The SVM classifier was able to reach the highest level of accuracy while consuming the least amount of time during the training period. In RMFD, the SVM classifier had a testing accuracy of 99.64%. It achieved 99.49% testing accuracy in SMFD and 100% testing accuracy in LFW. With related works, a comparative result is obtained. In terms of research precision, the proposed model outperformed the related works.

References

1. Wang, Z., Wang, P., Louis, P.C., Wheless, L.E., Huo, Y., WearMask: Fast In-browser Face Mask Detection with Serverless Edge Computing for COVID-19. arXiv preprint arXiv:2101.00784, 2021.
2. Loey, M., Manogaran, G., Taha, M.H.N., Khalifa, N.E.M., A hybrid deep transfer learning model with machine learning methods for face mask detection in the era of the COVID-19 pandemic. *Measurement*, 167, 108288, 2021.
3. Nagrath, P., Jain, R., Madan, A., Arora, R., Kataria, P., Hemanth, J., SSDMNV2: A real-time DNN-based face mask detection system using a single shot multibox detector and MobileNetV2. *Sustain. Cities Soc.*, 66, 102692, 2021.
4. Rahman, M.M., Manik, M.M.H., Islam, M.M., Mahmud, S., Kim, J.-H., An Automated System to Limit COVID-19 Using Facial Mask Detection in Smart City Network. *2020 IEEE International IOT, Electronics and Mechatronics Conference (IEMTRONICS)*, pp. 1–5, Vancouver, BC, Canada, 2020.
5. Chen, Y. *et al.*, Face Mask Assistant: Detection of Face Mask Service Stage Based on Mobile Phone. *IEEE Sens. J.*, https://ieeexplore.ieee.org/document/9360639
6. Dey, S.K., Howlader, A., Deb, C., MobileNet Mask: A Multi-phase Face Mask Detection Model to Prevent Person-To-Person Transmission of SARS-CoV-2, in: *Proceedings of International Conference on Trends in Computational and Cognitive Engineering*, pp. 603–613, Springer, Singapore, 2021.
7. Militante, S.V. and Dionisio, N.V., Real-Time Facemask Recognition with Alarm System using Deep Learning. *2020 11th IEEE Control and System Graduate Research Colloquium (ICSGRC)*, pp. 106–110, Shah Alam, Malaysia, 2020.
8. Chowdary, G.J., Punn, N.S., Sonbhadra, S.K., Agarwal, S., Face mask detection using transfer learning of inceptionv3, in: *International Conference on Big Data Analytics*, 2020, pp. 81–90, Springer, Cham, 2020, December,.
9. Zereen, A.N., Corraya, S., Dailey, M.N., Ekpanyapong, M., Two-Stage Facial Mask Detection Model for Indoor Environments, in: *Proceedings of International Conference on Trends in Computational and Cognitive Engineering*, pp. 591–601, Springer, Singapore, 2021.
10. Li, C., Ge, S., Zhang, D., Li, J., Look Through Masks: Towards Masked Face Recognition with De-Occlusion Distillation, in: *Proceedings of the 28th*

ACM International Conference on Multimedia (MM '20), pp. 3016–3024, Association for Computing Machinery, New York, NY, USA, 2020.

11. Walid, H., *Efficient Masked Face Recognition Method during the COVID-19 Pandemic*, 2020, 10.21203/rs.3.rs-39289/v1.

12. Ge, S., Li, J., Ye, Q., Luo, Z., Detecting Masked Faces in the Wild with LLE-CNNs. *2017 IEEE Conference on Computer Vision and Pattern Recognition (CVPR)*, pp. 426–434, Honolulu, H.

13. Anwar, A. and Raychowdhury, A., Masked Face Recognition for Secure Authentication. arXiv preprint arXiv:2008.11104, 2020 Aug 25.

14. Sharma, V., Face Mask Detection using YOLOv5 for COVID-19, 2020.

17

IoT-Based Automated Healthcare System

Darpan Anand* and Aashish Kumar

Department of CSE, Chandigarh University, Punjab, India

Abstract

In the era of 20th century, the advancement in Internet of Things (IoT) technologies leads to revolutionary development in healthcare. Since there is tremendous growth in the IoT devices which therefore leads to the problem of load balancing, dynamic IP allocation, change in routing, bandwidth management end-to-end reachability, innovation, etc. SDN and NFV solve these problems. SDN decouples the control plane and data plane. But the command line interface and absence of doctors lead to the death of patients in many developing countries. Apart from them, various reports show that around 25% of errors are found in writing medical records. To overcome the various real-life problems as well as network problems SDN-based IoT devices came into the picture. In this paper, we have given an overview of SDN, NFV, and types of sensors used in IoT devices. Apart from it, the various researcher views are also given. We have given an SDN-based IoT device for healthcare architecture and also discuss the challenges.

Keywords: e-Healthcare system, Internet of Things, software defined network, information security

17.1 Introduction

In many countries, health is the primary concern that affects the quality of life. Shaik and Chitre [1] demonstrated that the non-presence of electronic medical services frameworks and over-reliance on paper-based frameworks in numerous essential medical care centers in rustic regions prompted patients to keep their clinical records without anyone else. In a few examples, this has prompted a patient's passing because of the inaccessibility of

---

*Corresponding author: darpan.anand.agra@gmail.com

Rohit Tanwar, S. Balamurugan, R. K. Saini, Vishal Bharti and Premkumar Chithaluru (eds.) *Advanced Healthcare Systems: Empowering Physicians with IoT-Enabled Technologies*, (335–350) © 2022 Scrivener Publishing LLC

a doctor. Additionally, medical attendants in clinics gather indispensable signs information, for example, circulatory strain, temperature, respiratory rate, and also beat rate to screen patient advancement and abnormalities [2]. The attendants commonly record these essential signs readings of patients physically, which is manageable to numerous blunders [3]. As per [4], the worldwide medical services savvy wearable medical care (SWH) gadgets, SDN_Based Secure Healthcare Monitoring System (SDN-SHMS) market, will increment at an accumulated yearly development rate of 5.6% and will arrive at 25 billion by 2020. Managing billions of devices is not easy. This leads to the problem of network complexity, network delay, vendor-specific components, etc. Software-Defined Network and Network Function Virtualization solved the issues. SDN-based Internet of Things (IoT) devices has a large number of advantages such as follows:

1) Network management is easy
2) Security and privacy is enhanced
3) Accessing information from anywhere
4) Efficient use of resource utilization
5) Energy management

These SDN IoT devices have a great effect on healthcare. SDN IoT architecture is divided into several parts, namely, the data plane layer, core backbone network, SDN controller, and data center network. Apart from benefits, there are a lot of challenges, and SDN IoT devices have to be faced in the healthcare system.

17.1.1   Software-Defined Network

In a traditional network, the network plane and control plane are tightly coupled; this led to the problem of dynamic IP assignment, change in steering, data transfer capacity, the executives start to finish reachability, etc. To solve the above problem, the SDN came into the picture. SDN [5] bifurcates the control plane and information plane. It is currently used in various data centers of big giant companies such as Amazon, Google, Facebook, and also in a 5G network [6]. The architecture is shown in Figure 17.1 [7–9].

Infrastructure Layer: These are the dumb switches and routers and route the packets according to the set of instructions defined in the forwarding table [10].

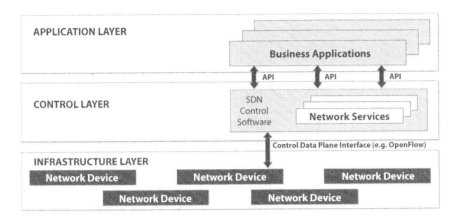

Figure 17.1 SDN architecture.

Control Layer: These are called "brain of the network". The controller has the global view of the network, so that management and securing the network become easy as compared to traditional network [11].

Management Plane: It is used to access and help in management of our network devices [12]. The correspondence between the foundation layer and control layer is performed by OpenFlow protocol [13]. It is the most normally utilized southward API in the SDN and created, normalized by the Open Flow Networking Foundation (ONF). SDN integrated with IoT devices [14] has many advantages, as discussed in the latter part of this section.

17.1.2   Network Function Virtualization

A conventional organization depends on the idea of "One Node One Service", which implies that an assistance is sent on explicit equipment. This conventional organization causes versatility, adaptability, speed decrease, delay, and other organization dormancy issues. These issues will be hurtful to the business and the association. Consequently, we need a stage to defeat the previously mentioned issues and it is reasonable to determine NFV issues with virtualization of organization assets. NFV utilizes three systems as virtualization [15], programming [16], and orchestration [17] for network virtualization, as shown in Figure 17.2. NFV is likewise helpful for supplanting costly, devoted, and explicit reason equipment with non-exclusive equipment.

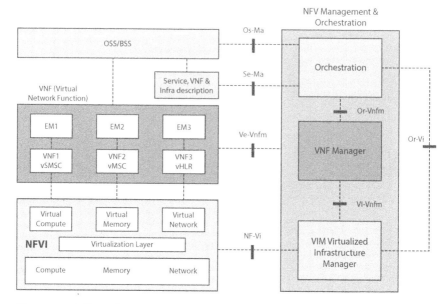

Figure 17.2 NFV architecture.

Now, we will discuss sensor used in IoT devices in details.

17.1.3   Sensor Used in IoT Devices

1) Ring sensor: It measures the human heart rate and oxygen concentration, and the other name of ring sensor is pulse oximetry sensor [18], as shown in Figure 17.3.
2) ECG sensor: It measures the electrical and macular function of the heart. It continuously measures the heart rate of the human body [19], as shown in Figure 17.4.
3) GSR sensor: GSR stands for Galvanic Skin response sensor. It can be used to detect the emotion and stress of human body [20], as shown in Figure 17.5.
4) Graphene vapor sensor: It can measure chemical evaporates through skin. It can also detect the diabetes, high blood pressure, anemia [21], as shown in Figure 17.6.
5) Health patch sensor: It can detect the chronic disease and fix with chest of the human body and measure the temperature, heart rate, and ECG of the human body [22], as shown in Figure 17.7.

Figure 17.3 Ring sensor.

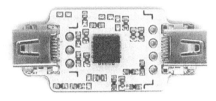

Figure 17.4 ECG sensor.

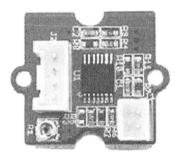

Figure 17.5 GSR sensor.

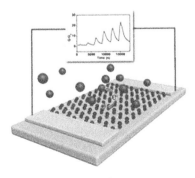

Figure 17.6 Graphene vapor sensor.

Figure 17.7 Health patch sensor.

Figure 17.8 Oximeter sensor.

6) Oximeter sensor: Oximeter sensor detects amount of oxygen present in the blood (hemoglobin) [23], as shown in Figure 17.8.

7) QTM sensor: This sensor detects emotion of the human by response of physiological behavior [24].

8) Airflow sensor: It is thin nasal sensor which detects the respiratory rate of the patients by using prongs. It detects the asthma, anxiety, pneumonia, and drug overdose [25].

9) Optical biosensor: It detects the continuous signs from the optical creation of biomolecules [26], as shown in Figure 17.9.

10) Respiration sensor: It measures the rate of thoracic breathing as well as normal breathing [27], as shown in Figure 17.10.

Till now, we have discussed overview of SDN, NFV, and sensors used in IoT devices. Section 17.2 discusses about SDN-based IoT framework.

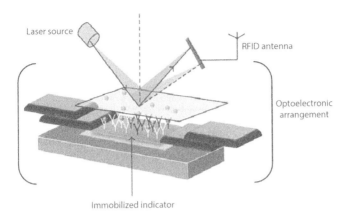

Figure 17.9 Optical biosensor.

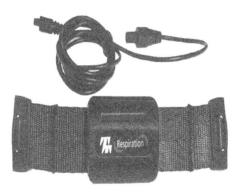

Figure 17.10 Respiration sensor.

17.2 SDN-Based IoT Framework

The following discusses the need of the of SDN-IoT framework [28].

1) **Network Management:** In this era, millions of devices are interconnected by the IoT technology; therefore, a large amount of information is generated and needs to be executed efficiently. To solve the above problem, a separate technology is introduced, i.e., SDN. As we have discussed, SDN has a global view of the network and solves the problem of network delay, bandwidth utilization, etc.

2) **Accessing Information From Anywhere:** Since the billions of equipment are joined through IoT technology. So that

the equipment can be accessed from anywhere around the world and functionality can be changed according to the user need. This can be achieved by SDN technology.

3) **Resource Utilization:** Overexploitation of resources or underutilization of resources degrades the network performance. To achieve high network performance, the overall view of the entire network should be available. SDN solves the problem.

4) **Energy Management:** IoT devices are battery-operated devices and therefore are power constraint devices. SDN utilizes the resources efficiently and reliably and led to the efficient utilization of power resources to take place.

Figure 17.11 shows software-defined IoT framework. The framework is divided into four parts.

1) **Data plane layer:** It has IoT devices such as ECG machines and pulse oximeter that are connected to SDN switches and routers through Wi-Fi or any other LTE technology. Router may be Juniper MX-Series, PC engines, Pronto 3220/3290, HP curve, etc. Their main aim is to collect the data from the patients.

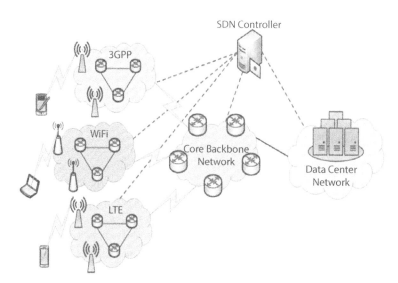

Figure 17.11 A schematic view of software-defined Internet of Things.

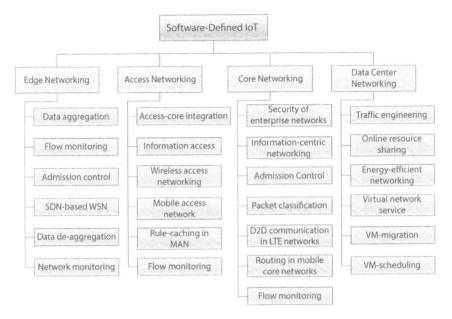

Figure 17.12 Overview of different aspects of SDN-based IoT networks.

2) **Core Backbone Network:** This is internet through which the information collected from sensing devices and transferred to the controller and data center network.

3) **SDN Controller:** It has the global view of the network; therefore, the network management and routing of data can be done efficiently. It can be located at various geographical areas.

4) **Data Center Network:** In this, actual processing of the sensed data takes place and be used for further use.

Figure 17.12 shows the SDN-based IoT networks.

17.3   Literature Survey

The authors in [29] have thought about the test of gathering and totalling and playing out the investigation on the organization information from different IoT gadgets. This crude information can huge information and can happen in any structure like sound, video, and text. For continuous transmission on the hugely huge measure of information, creators have proposed a unified and adaptable framework design that can give the security, protection, and other security fundamentals for different associated medical care applications.

Khayat *et. al* [30]explain the utilization, experience and benefits of IoT. The subtleties of the planning are furthermore and other segment necessity is additionally represented by them. Creators have proposed engineering on IoT-medical services along with the further different examination headings and difficulties.

In this paper [31], researchers have analyzed the troubles related to weak points and assurance of the standard medical administrations monitoring system (HMS). This plan can be utilized to regulate IoT devices based on clinical benefit checking structures. It guarantees the security and protection; however, the dependability of the different conveyed benefits too. These administrations and strategies are expected for old individuals and patients.

This paper depicts the situation with IoT with various measurements [32]. The nine examination headings specifically enormous scaling, designing and conditions, making data, force, responsiveness, security, assurance, protection, and human on top of it have been examined to give the expanding usage of sensors and actuators [38].

The paper proposed a blend of advancements specifically SDN and IoT [33]. New improvement in different areas like remote for example, remote and optical space along with provocations identified with the two advancements from security and, furthermore, adaptability points of view, are likewise featured to combine the innovation. SDN innovation is not just structure up a focus on industry and the scholarly world yet additionally is the best innovation in diminishing the network with a predefined convention in the innovative space.

SDN from different points of view tackles the issue of productivity, versatility, sensibility, and cost adequacy in IoT [34]. The various plans related to frameworks organization have furthermore been portrayed, which supports the association with SDN [34].

17.4   Architecture of SDN-IoT for Healthcare System

In Figure 17.13, architecture of SDN-IoT–based medical services is outlined. The network is incorporated further with different associations of different crisis facilities. These facilities are moreover connected with different works where data exchange from various IoT contraptions. It might be seen that the network is incorporated further with different associations of different crisis facilities. These facilities are moreover connected with the subnet works, in which data exchange from various IoT contraptions,

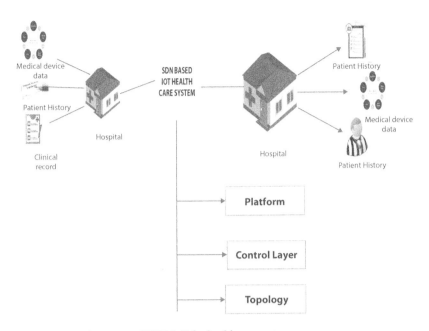

Figure 17.13 Architecture of SDN-IoT for healthcare system.

sufferer data, etc., is cultivated. The server farm at which all the connected information is put away is halfway positioned. The organization utilized at this server farm is additionally included a three-layered engineering. The principal layer is the system's administration layer in which the organization geographies like physical setup and organizing gadgets (switches and switch) are situated. The layer above the principal layer consists of SDN regulator. Conventional organizations included various system administration gadgets; these gadgets comprise of the insight and the hidden organization framework inside; however, SDN changes the entire thought. The differed organizing gadgets utilized at the foundation layer as referenced before are only the idiotic gadgets that are utilized to convey the traffic from one spot to another. The guidance to them is given by the SDN regulator as it were. The end layer is the client layer where applications such as firewall and intrusion detection are installed. Using these applications in a SDN-based association improves the challenges.

17.5 Challenges

There are difficulties in IoT in four areas due to hardware challenges, architecture challenges, technical challenges, and safety and security issues.

In coordination of alignment, information and understanding of different reference models are researched with the aim of improving compatibility and data in the gadget. In a clear examination, the problems identified with the openness of the mastermind, the long-distance relationships with trusted communities were investigated. Problems identified with the use of control and cost-common sense in gears are described. Means and focused blueprints on safety and security challenges control the issues of low laziness and issues of compatibility on the IoT foundation's standardized test discussions. Attempts to coordinate specific requirements with terms of use have been included in industry issues [35].

Authors in [36] introduced difficulties like normalization, framework design, interoperability and reconciliation, accessibility and unwavering quality, information stockpiling and handling, adaptability, the board and self-arrangement, execution and QoS, ID and interesting personality, force and energy utilization, security and protection, and natural issues. Every one of these difficulties has been faced alongside the issues identified with specific difficulties with the writing, which has been shrouded in a specific test.

Authors in [37] depicted the challenges as enlisting, correspondence and ID, innovations, appropriated understanding, security, and coursed structures development as an undertaking to arrange these troubles in these spaces. The selecting stage covers the mix of standard articles with the sensors having irrelevant effort and low power utilization. The possibility of inactivity has moreover been inspected. The association among computation and correspondence to diminish the use of IoT contraptions is moreover explained.

Zarca *et. al* [38] explained the vital difficulties in IoT and SDN are naming the character of the board, interoperability and normalization, data protection, objects thriving and security, affiliation security, information request and encryption, range, and greening of IoT, which have been depicted in [39]. The creators have zeroed in on the superb character of sensors and interoperability; moreover, normalization of sensor contraptions and prosperity attempts from unapproved access clients have been founded on with game plan and the confirmation of the utilization of IoT gadgets at a low speed is portrayed the inconveniences.

Security is one of the applications of CSE [40], while authentication is the one of major security services required for any application [41–44]. The same techniques are very useful and advantageous for society and organizations [45–47]. Some of the major applications of computer science, communications, and distributed computing give better results with high-speed network as of 5G-enabled network [48–54].

17.6 Conclusion

This chapter explains the concept of the IoT for the Healthcare sector. It is very important for this sector due to migration to the Industry 4.0. There are various sensors available to measure the various health parameters such as Health Patch Sensor and Oximeter sensor to measure various important health parameters. The use of these technologies has been seen by all of us in case of COVID-19 pandemic too where the temperature, oxygen level, etc., are also be measured through these devices. Further, there are various devices and systems also be developed to identify the vulnerable patients. It is also good for the critical patients to monitor them on the basis of the real-time health parameters. Therefore, this chapter is very important to know about the IoT concepts used in the sector of healthcare to make it under the flagship of the Industry 4.0, i.e., Healthcare 4.0.

References

1. Shaikh, S. and Chitre, V., Healthcare monitoring system using IoT. *2017 International Conference on Trends in Electronics and Informatics (ICEI)*, pp. 74–377, 2017.
2. Evans, D., Hodgkinson, B., Berry, J., Vital signs in hospital patients: A systematic review. *Ijns*, 38, 6, 643–650, 2001.
3. Yang, Z., Kankanhalli, A., Ng, B.-Y., Lim, J.T.Y., Examining the pre-adoption stages of healthcare IT: A case study of vital signs monitoring systems. *Inf. Manage.*, 52, 4, 454–467, 2015.
4. Vikash, M., Gupta, M., Upadhayay, Kumar, S., A survey on wireless body area network: Security technology and its design methodologyissue. *2015 International Conference on Innovations in Information, Embedded and Communication Systems (ICIIECS)*, pp. 328–337, 2015.
5. Xia, W., Wen, Y., Foh, C.H., Niyato, D., Xie, H., A survey on software-defined networking. *IEEE Commun. Surv. Tutorials*, 17, 1, 27–51, 2014.
6. Gupta, A. and Jha, R.K., A survey of 5G network: Architecture and emerging technologies. *IEEE Access*, 3, 1206–1232, 2015.
7. Hu, Z., Wang, M., Yan, X., Yin, Y., Luo, Z., A comprehensive security architecture for SDN, in: *2015 18th International Conference on Intelligence in Next Generation Networks*, IEEE, pp. 30–37, 2015, February.
8. Hayes, M., Ng, B., Pekar, A., Seah, W.K., Scalable architecture for SDN traffic classification. *IEEE Syst. J.*, 12, 4, 3203–3214, 2017.
9. Sufiev, H. and Haddad, Y., A dynamic load balancing architecture for SDN, in: *2016 IEEE International Conference on the Science of Electrical Engineering (ICSEE)*, IEEE, pp. 1–3, 2016, November.

10. Dhamecha, K. and Trivedi, B., Sdn issues-a survey. *Int. J. Comput. Appl.*, 73, 18, pp. 30–35, 2013.

11. Jimenez, Y., Cervello-Pastor, C., Garcia, A.J., On the controller placement for designing a distributed SDN control layer, in: *2014 IFIP Networking Conference*, IEEE, pp. 1–9, 2014, June.

12. Wang, Y. and Matta, I., Sdn management layer: Design requirements and future direction, in: *2014 IEEE 22nd International Conference on Network Protocols*, IEEE, pp. 555–562, 2014, October.

13. McKeown, N., Anderson, T., Balakrishnan, H., Parulkar, G., Peterson, L., Rexford, J., Turner, J., OpenFlow: enabling innovation in campus networks. *ACM SIGCOMM Comput. Commun. Rev.*, 38, 2, 69–74, 2008.

14. Huh, S., Cho, S., Kim, S., Managing IoT devices using blockchain platform, in: *2017 19th international conference on advanced communication technology (ICACT)*, IEEE, pp. 464–467, 2017, February.

15. Chiueh, S.N.T.C. and Brook, S., A survey on virtualization technologies. School of Computing as Rpe report, https://arxiv.org/abs/1701.08971, 142, 2005.

16. Salahuddin, M.A., Al-Fuqaha, A., Guizani, M., Shuaib, K., Sallabi, F., Softwarization of internet of things infrastructure for secure and smart healthcare. arXiv preprint arXiv:1805.11011, https://arxiv.org/abs/1701.08971. 2018.

17. Adler, S. and Hesterman, P., *The study of orchestration*, vol. 2, WW Norton, New York, NY, 1989.

18. Rhee, S., Yang, B.H., Chang, K., Asada, H.H., The ring sensor: a new ambulatory wearable sensor for twenty-four hour patient monitoring, in: *Proceedings of the 20th annual International Conference of the IEEE Engineering in Medicine and Biology Society*, 20, 4, 1906–1909, 1998, October.

19. Nemati, E., Deen, M.J., Mondal, T., A wireless wearable ECG sensor for long-term applications. *IEEE Commun. Mag.*, 50, 1, 36–f4, 2012.

20. Bakker, J., Pechenizkiy, M., Sidorova, N., What's your current stress level? Detection of stress patterns from GSR sensor data, in: *2011 IEEE 11th international conference on data mining workshops*, 2011, December, IEEE, pp. 573–580.

21. Bogue, R., Graphene sensors: a review of recent developments. *Sens. Rev.*, Vol. 34 No. 3, pp. 233–238, https://doi.org/10.1108/SR-03-2014-631, 2014.

22. Wu, T., Wu, F., Qiu, C., Redouté, J.M., Yuce, M.R., A Rigid-Flex Wearable Health Monitoring Sensor Patch for IoT-Connected Healthcare Applications. *IEEE Internet Things J.*, 7, 8, 6932–6945, 2020.

23. Fernandez, M., Burns, K., Calhoun, B., George, S., Martin, B., Weaver, C., Evaluation of a new pulse oximeter sensor. *Am. J. Crit. Care*, 16, 2, 146–152, 2007.

24. Zareie, S., Khosravi, H., Nasiri, A., Dastorani, M., Using Landsat Thematic Mapper (TM) sensor to detect change in land surface temperature in relation to land use change in Yazd, Iran. *Solid Earth*, 7, 6, 1551–1564, 2016.

25. Zhao, Y., Wang, P., Lv, R., Liu, X., Highly sensitive airflow sensor based on Fabry–Perot interferometer and Vernier effect. *J. Lightwave Technol.*, 34, 23, 5351–5356, 2016.

26. Cross, G.H., Reeves, A.A., Brand, S., Popplewell, J.F., Peel, L.L., Swann, M.J., Freeman, N.J., A new quantitative optical biosensor for protein characterisation. *Biosens. Bioelectron.*, 19, 4, 383–390, 2003.

27. Güder, F., Ainla, A., Redston, J., Mosadegh, B., Glavan, A., Martin, T.J., Whitesides, G.M., Paper-based electrical respiration sensor. *Angew. Chem. Int. Ed.*, 55, 19, 5727–5732, 2016.

28. Salahuddin, M.A., Al-Fuqaha, A., Guizani, M., Shuaib, K., Sallabi, F., Softwarization of internet of things infrastructure for secure and smart healthcare. arXiv preprint arXiv:1805.11011, 2018.

29. Hu, L., Qiu, M., Song, J., Hossain, M.S., Ghoneim, A., Software defined healthcare networks. *IEEE Wireless Commun.*, 22, 6, 67–75, 2015.

30. Khayat, M., Barka, E., Sallabi, F., SDN_Based SecureHealthcare Monitoring System (SDN-SHMS), in: *2019 28th International Conference on Computer Communication and Networks (ICCCN)*, IEEE, pp. 1–7, 2019, July.

31. Stankovic, J.A., Research directions for the internet of things. *IEEE Internet Things J.*, 1, 1, 3–9, 2014.

32. Sood, K., Yu, S., Xiang, Y., Software-defined wireless networking opportunities and challenges for Internet-of-Things: A review. *IEEE Internet Things J.*, 3, 4, 453–463, 2015.

33. Badotra, S. and Panda, S.N., A Review On Software-DefinedNetworking Enabled Iot Cloud Computing. *IIUM Eng. J. Commun. Systems (ICIIECS)*, 20, 2, 105–126, 328–337, 2019.

34. Li, J., Altman, E., Touati, C., A general SDN-based IoT framework with NVF implementation. *ZTE Commun.*, 13, 3, 42–45, 2015.

35. Kim, H. and Feamster, N., Improving network management with software defined networking. *IEEE Commun. Mag.*, 51, 2, 114–119, 2013.

36. Hamed, M., II, ElHalawany, B.M., Fouda, M.M., Eldien, A.S.T., A novel approach for resource utilization and management in SDN, in: *2017 13th International Computer Engineering Conference (ICENCO)*, IEEE, pp. 337–342, 2017, December.

37. Aujla, G.S. and Kumar, N., SDN-based energy management scheme for sustainability of data centers: An analysis on renewable energy sources and electric vehicles participation. *J. Parallel Distrib. Comput.*, 117, 228–245, 2018.

38. Zarca, A.M., Bernabe, J.B., Trapero, R., Rivera, D., Villalobos, J., Skarmeta, A., Gouvas, P., Security management architecture for NFV/SDN-aware IoT systems. *IEEE Internet Things J.*, 6, 5, 8005–8020, 2019.

39. Chen, S., Xu, H., Liu, D., Hu, B., Wang, H., A vision of IoT: Applications, challenges, and opportunities with chinaperspective. *IEEE Internet Things J.*, 1, 4, 349–359, 2014.

40. Anand, D., Khemchandani, V., Sharma, R.K., Identity-based cryptography techniques and applications (a review), in: *2013 5th International Conference*

and *Computational Intelligence and Communication Networks*, IEEE, pp. 343–348, 2013.

41. Anand, D., Singh, M.P., Gupta, M., Application of rule based fuzzy inference system in predicting the quality and quantity of potato crop yield in agra, in: *Proceedings of the Third International Conference on Soft Computing for Problem Solving*, Springer, pp. 211–223, 2014.

42. Anand, D. and Khemchandani, V., An analytical method to audit Indian e-governance system. *Int. J. Electron. Gov. Res. (IJEGR)*, 13, 3, 18–37, 2017.

43. Anand, D. and Khemchandani, V., Identity and access management systems, in: *Security and Privacy of Electronic Healthcare Records: Concepts, paradigms and solutions*, p. 61, 2019.

44. Anand, D. and Khemchandani, V., Study of e-governance in india: a survey. *Int. J. Electron. Secur. Digit. Forensics*, 11, 2, 119–144, 2019.

45. Anand, D. and Khemchandani, V., Unified and integrated authentication and key agreement scheme for e-governance system without verification table. *Sādhanā*, 44, 9, 192, 2019.

46. Anand, D. and Khemchandani, V., Data security and privacy functions in fog computing for healthcare 4.0, in: *Fog Data Analytics for IoT Applications*, pp. 387–420, Springer, Singapore, 2020.

47. Darpan Anand, V., The challenges for authentication in Indian e-governance system (a survey on Indian administrative staff). *Int. J. Control Theor. Appl.*, 2016.

48. Dubey, S., Anand, D., Sharma, J., Lfsr based block cipher technique for text. *Int. J. Comput. Sci. Eng.*, 6, 2, 53–60, 2018.

49. Gaharana, S. and Anand, D., Dynamic id based remote user authentication in multi server environment using smart cards: a review, in: *2015 International Conference on Computational Intelligence and Communication Networks (CICN)*, IEEE, pp. 1081–1084, 2015.

50. Gaharana, S. and Anand, D., A new approach for remote user authentication in a multi-server environment based on dynamic-id using smart-card. *Int. J. Comput. Netw. Inf. Secur.*, 8, 10, 45, 2016.

51. Gupta, M., Anand, D., Parmar, G., Gupta, R., A new approach for information security using asymmetric encryption and watermarking technique. *Int. J. Comput. Appl.*, 57, 14, 2012.

52. Heer, S. and Anand, D., An improved hand gesture recognition system based on optimized msvm and sift feature extraction algorithm, tech. rep., EasyChair, 2020.

53. Kabta, N., Karhana, A., Thakur, N., Anand, D. *et al.*, Information security in software-defined network, in: *Mobile Radio Communications and 5G Networks*, pp. 305–319, Springer, Singapore, 2021.

54. Saxena, S. and Anand, D., A novel digital signature algorithm based on biometric hash. *Int. J. Comput. Netw. Inf. Secur.*, 9, 1, 2017.

Index

Printed and bound by CPI Group (UK) Ltd, Croydon, CR0 4YY